—Thomas More

LIVES

OF

THE LORD CHANCELLORS

AND

KEEPERS OF THE GREAT SEAL

OF

ENGLAND,

FROM THE EARLIEST TIMES TILL THE REIGN OF QUEEN VICTORIA.

BY

LORD CAMPBELL.

SEVENTH EDITION.

ILLUSTRATED.

VOL. II.

WILDSIDE PRESS

CONTENTS

OF

THE SECOND VOLUME.

CHAP.	PAGE
XXX.—Life of Sir Thomas More, Lord Chancellor of England, from his birth till the end of the reign of Henry VII.	1
XXXI.—Life of Sir Thomas More from the accession of Henry VIII. till his appointment as Lord Chancellor	12
XXXII.—Life of Sir Thomas More from his appointment as Lord Chancellor till his resignation	28
XXXIII.—Life of Sir Thomas More from his resignation of the Great Seal till his death	49
XXXIV.—Life of Lord Chancellor Audley	85
XXXV.—Life of Lord Chancellor Wriothesley from his birth till the death of Henry VIII.	123
XXXVI.—Conclusion of the Life of Lord Chancellor Wriothesley	138
XXXVII.—Life of Sir William Paulet, Lord Paulet of St. John Basing Earl of Wiltshire, and Marquess of Winchester, Lord Keeper of the Great Seal	146
XXXVIII.—Life of Lord Chancellor Rich	153
XXXIX.—Life of Lord Chancellor Goodrich	171
XL.—Life of Stephen Gardyner, Lord Chancellor of England, from his birth to the end of the reign of Henry VIII.	181
XLI.—Life of Lord Chancellor Gardyner, from the accession of Queen Mary	196
XLII.—Life of Lord Chancellor Heath	212
XLIII.—Life of Lord Keeper Sir Nicholas Bacon	225
XLIV.—Life of Sir Thomas Bromley, Lord Chancellor of England	251
XLV.—Life of Sir Christopher Hatton, Lord Chancellor of England	272

CONTENTS.

CHAP.	PAGE
XLVI.—Life of Sir John Puckering, Lord Keeper of the Great Seal	316
XLVII.—Life of Lord Ellesmere from his birth till the execution of the Earl of Essex	328
XLVIII.—Continuation of the Life of Lord Ellesmere till the end of the reign of Elizabeth	355
XLIX.—Continuation of the Life of Lord Ellesmere from the accession of James I.	368
L.—Conclusion of the Life of Lord Ellesmere	382
LI.—Life of Lord Bacon from his birth till he became a member of the House of Commons	412
LII.—Continuation of the Life of Lord Bacon till the fall of the Earl of Essex	425

LIVES

OF THE

LORD CHANCELLORS OF ENGLAND.

CHAPTER XXX.

LIFE OF SIR THOMAS MORE, LORD CHANCELLOR OF ENGLAND, FROM HIS BIRTH TILL THE END OF THE REIGN OF HENRY VII.

THE Great Seal having been surrendered, as we have seen, by Cardinal Wolsey, into the hands of the Dukes of Norfolk and Suffolk, they delivered it to Taylor, the Master of the Rolls, to carry to the King; who, having himself sealed certain letters patent with it, enclosed it in a bag under his own signet and under the seals of the Master of the Rolls and Stephen Gardyner, afterwards the famous Bishop of Winchester.[1]

Considerable difficulty arose about the appointment of a new Chancellor. Some were for restoring the Great Seal to Ex-Chancellor Archbishop Warham; and Erasmus states that he refused it; but there is reason to think that a positive resolution had been before taken by Henry and his present advisers, that it should not be again intrusted to any churchman.[2]

There was an individual designated to the office by the public voice. To give credit to the new administration, there was a strong desire to appoint him, for he was celebrated as a scholar in every part of Europe; he had long practiced with applause as a lawyer; being called to Court, he had gained the highest credit there for his

---

[1] Rot. Cl. 21 Hen. 8, m. 19.   [2] Ep. p. 1347.
[3] On the 22nd October the Bishop of Bayonne writes to his court, "On ne sçait encore qui aura le sceau. Je croy bien que les prestres n'y toucheront plus, et que en ce parliament ils auront de terribles alarmes."

abilities and his manners; and he had been employed in several embassies abroad, which he had conducted with dexterity and success. The difficulty was that he had only the rank of a simple knight; and there had been no instance hitherto of conferring the Great Seal on a layman who was not of noble birth, or had not previously gained reputation by high judicial office. In consequence there was a struggle in favor of the selection of one of the chiefs of the Common Law Courts at Westminster. But the hope that the person first proposed was the best fitted to manage the still pending negotiation for the divorce, came powerfully in aid of his claims on the score of genius, learning, and virtue; and, on the 25th of October, in a Council held at Greenwich, the King delivered the Great Seal to Sir THOMAS MORE, and constituted him Lord Chancellor of England.[1]

This extraordinary man, so interesting in his life and in his death, was born in the year 1480, near the end of the reign of Edward IV. He was the son of Sir John More, a Judge of the Court of King's Bench, who lived to see him Lord Chancellor. The father's descent is not known, but he was of "an honorable though not distinguished family," and he was entitled to bear arms, a privilege which showed him to be of gentle blood, and of the class which in every other country except ours is considered noble. The old Judge was famous for a facetious turn, which he transmitted to his son. There is only one of his sayings handed down to us, and this, we must hope, was meant rather as a compliment to the good qualities of his own partner for life than as a satire on the fair sex. " He would compare the multitude of women which are to be chosen for wives unto a bag full of snakes, having among them a single eel: now, if a man should put his hand into this bag, he may chance light on the eel; but it is a hundred to one he shall be stung by a snake."[2] The future Chancellor sprung from that rank of life which is most favorable to mental cultivation, and which has produced the greatest number of eminent men in England; for, while we have instances of gifted individuals overcoming the disadvantages of high birth and affluence as well as of obscurity and poverty, our Cecils and Walpoles, our Bacons and Mores, have mostly had good

[1] Rot. Cl. 21 Hen. 8, m. 19.   [2] Camden's Remains, p. 251.

education and breeding under a father's care,—with habits of frugality, and the necessity for industry, energy, and perseverance to gain distinction in the world.

The lawyers in those days, both judges and barristers, lived in the City, and young More first saw the light in Milk Street, Cheapside, then a fashionable quarter of the metropolis. He received the early rudiments of his education at St. Anthony's school, in Threadneedle street, a seminary which gained great and well-deserved repute, having produced Archbishop Heath, Archbishop Whitgift, and many other eminent men. In his fifteenth year, according to the custom of which we have seen various examples, he became a page in the family of Cardinal Morton, Archbishop of Canterbury, and Lord Chancellor under Henry VII. Here, along with sons of the best families in England, he waited at table, and was instructed in all learning and exercises. His lively parts soon attracted the attention of his master, who, though turned of eighty, and filling such dignified offices, still encouraged amusement, and had the sagacity to discover the extraordinary merit, and to fortell the future celebrity of his page. "For the Cardinal often would make trial of his present wit, especially at Christmas merriments, when having plays for his recreation, this youth would suddenly step up among the players, and never studying before upon the matter, make often a part of his own invention, which was so witty and so full of jests, that he alone made more sport than all the players besides; for which his towardliness, the Cardinal much delighted in him, and would often say of him, unto divers of the nobility, who at sundry times dined with him, '*This child here, waiting at the table, whosoever shall live to see it, will prove a marvelous rare man.*'"[1] The youthful page was not behind in penetration of character, and duly appreciated the qualities of the wary courtier, who, the model for future Talleyrands, had continued to flourish amid all the vicissitudes of the state, and having united the Red and White Roses, still enjoyed without abatement the confidence of the founder of the House of Tudor. The historian of Richard III., drawing the character of Morton, says (no doubt from early recollections), "He was a man of great

[1] More's Life, 19. Roper, 4.

natural wit, very well learned, honorable in behavior, *lacking in no wise to win favor.*"[1]

But, by the kind advice of his patron, who had great care in his bringing up, and was afraid he might not profit in sound learning so much as might be desired amid the distractions of the archiepiscopal palace, he was removed to the University of Oxford. He lodged at New Hall, but studied at Canterbury College, afterwards Christ Church. He must now have led a very different life from what he had enjoyed at Lambeth; for, "in his allowance, his father kept him very short, suffering him scarcely to have so much money in his own custody as would pay for the mending of his apparel; and, for his expenses, he would expect of him a particular account."[2] Though much pinched, and somewhat dissatisfied at the time, he often spoke of this system with much praise when he came to riper years; affirming, that he was thereby curbed from all vice, and withdrawn from gaming and naughty company.[3]

Here More remained above two years, devoting himself to study with the utmost assiduity and enthusiasm. Erasmus, invited to England by Lord Mountjoy, who had been his pupil at Paris, was now residing at Oxford, and assisting in spreading a taste for Greek literature recently introduced there by Grocyn, Linacre, and Collet, who had studied it in Italy under Politian and Chalcondylas. More and Erasmus, resembling each other in their genius, in their taste, in their acute observation of character and manners, in their lively sense of the ridiculous, in their constant hilarity, and in their devotion to classical lore, soon formed a close friendship which lasted through life without interruption or abatement, and which was fostered during absence by an epistolary correspondence still extant, affording to us the most striking sketches of the history and customs of the times in which they lived.

[1] In his *Utopia* he praises him more liberally, but still with a touch of satire, as " of incomparable judgment, a memory more than credible, eloquent in speech, and, which is more to be wished in clergymen, of singular wisdom and virtue."

[2] More's Life of Sir T. More, 18.

[3] His great grandson, who wrote in the reign of Charles I., more than two centuries ago, in describing how his ancestor when at College escaped "play and riot," adds, "wherein most young men in these our lamentable days plunge themselves too timely, to the utter overthrow as well of learning as all future virtue."

At the University, while More "profited exceedingly in rhetoric, logic, and philosophy," he likewise distinguished himself very much by the composition of poems, both Latin and English. Some of these are to be found in collections of his works; and though inferior to similar efforts in the succeeding age, they will be found interesting, not only as proofs of his extraordinary precocity, but as the exercises by which he became the earliest distinguished orator, and the earliest elegant prose-writer using the English language.[1]

More had been destined by his father to wear the long robe; and, having completed his course at Oxford, he was transferred to London, that he might apply to the study of the law. According to the practice then generally followed, he began at New Inn, "an Inn of Chancery,"

---

[1] As a specimen I will give a few extracts from that which is considered the most successful of his poetical effusions in Latin. It proceeds on the idea, that, become an old man, he sees again a lady whom he had loved when they were both very young, and who is still charming in his eyes.

"*Gratulatur quod eam reperit incolumem quam olim ferme puer amaverat.*

"Vivis adhuc, primis o me mihi charior annis,
   Redderis atque oculis Elizabetha meis:
Quæ mala distinuit mihi te fortuna tot annos,
   Pene puer vidi, pene reviso senex.
Tempora quæ teneræ nunquam non invida formæ
   Te rapuere tibi, non rapuere mihi."

He afterwards refers in touching language to their first interview, and gives a description of her charms, after the fashion of the Song of Solomon:—

"Jam subit illa dies quæ ludentem obtulit olim
   Inter virgineos te mihi prima choros.
Lactea cum flavi decuerunt colla capilli,
   Cum gena par nivibus visa, labella rosis
Cum tua perstringunt oculos duo sydera nostros,
   Perque oculos intrant in mea corda meos."

Their flirtation was very marked:—

"Cum sociis risum exhibuit nostrisque tuisque
   Tam rudis et simplex et male tectus amor,"

Now comes the constancy of his attachment:—

"Ergo ita disjunctos diversaque fata secutos
   Tot nunc post hyemes reddidit ista dies.
Ista dies qua rara meo mihi lætior ævo,
   Contigit accursu sospitis alma tui.
Tu prædata meos olim sine crimine sensus,
   Nunc quoque non ullo crimine chara manes."

Let it be remembered that these verses were written in the middle of the reign of Henry VII., when the war of the Roses had almost extinguished in England the remembrance of Chaucer and no other poetical genius had yet arisen.

where was acquired the learning of writs and procedure; and he afterwards belonged to Lincoln's Inn, "an Inn of Court," where were taught the more profound and abstruse branches of the science. With us a sufficient knowledge of jurisprudence is supposed to be gained by eating a certain number of dinners in the hall of one of the Inns of Court, whereby men are often called to the bar wholly ignorant of their profession; and, being pushed on by favor or accident, or native vigor of mind, they are sometimes placed in high judicial situations, having no acquaintance with law beyond what they may have picked up as practitioners at the bar. Then the Inns of Court and Chancery presented the discipline of a well-constituted University; and, through Professors, under the name of "Readers," and exercises, under the name of "Mootings," law was systematically taught, and efficient tests of proficiency were applied, before the degree of barrister was conferred, entitling the aspirant to practice as an advocate.

More so much distinguished himself, that he was early appointed Reader to Furnival's Inn, an Inn of Chancery, under the superintendence of Lincoln's Inn; and there he delivered lectures, with great applause, for three years.

It rather puzzles us to understand the nature of his next appearance in public. "After this, to his great commendation, he read for a good space a public lecture of St. Augustine, *De Civitate Dei*, in the church of St. Lawrence, in the Old Jewry; whereunto there resorted Doctor Grocyn, an excellent cunning man, and all the chief learned of the city of London."[1] We cannot understand a parish church converted into a lecture-room; and a young lawyer mounting the pulpit, and discoursing to a large congregation on things sacred and secular. It is said, that he did not so much discuss points of divinity, as moral philosophy and history. He was run after by the great, the learned, and the fashionable; and Collet, his Oxford friend, now dean of St. Paul's, and the future founder of St. Paul's School, was wont to say at this time, that "there was but one wit in England, and that was young Thomas More."[2]

[1] Roper, 16.
[2] "Augustini libros de civitate Dei publice professus est adhuc pene adolescens auditorio frequenti; nec puduit nec pœnituit sacerdotes ac senes a juvene provano sacra discere."—Eras. Ep.

Though called to the degree of barrister, he had not begun to plead in Court; and he was now disposed for ever to renounce the pomp and vanity of the world, and to bury himself in a convent. His modern biographers very improperly shrink from this passage of his life; for if it were discreditable to him (which it really is not), still it ought to be known, that we may justly appreciate his character. He was so transported with the glory of St. Augustine, and so enraptured with the pleasures of piety, and so touched with the peace, regularity, and freedom from care of a monastic life, that he resolved to enter the order of St. Francis. But before taking the irrevocable vow of celibacy, shaving his crown, putting on the grey serge garment fastened by a twisted rope, and walking barefoot in quest of alms, he prudently made an experiment how strict monastic discipline would permanently suit him. "He began to wear a sharp shirt of hair next his skin. He added also to his austerity a whip every Friday and high fasting days, thinking that such cheer was the best alms that he could bestow upon himself. He used also much fasting and watching, lying often upon the bare ground or upon some bench, laying a log under his head, allotting himself but four or five hours in a night at the most for his sleep, imagining, with the holy saints of Christ's church, that his body was to be used as an ass, with strokes and hard fare, lest provender might pride it, and so bring his soul, like a headstrong jade, to the bottomless pit of hell."[1] With this view he took a lodging close by the Carthusian monastery, now the site of the Charterhouse School, and as a lay brother practiced all the austerities which prevail in this stern order. He found these after a time not edifying to his piety, and he, a rigid Roman Catholic, doubted the advantages supposed to be conferred on religion by the monastic orders, which a certain section of professing Protestants are now so eager to re-establish.[2]

[1] More, p. 25.
[2] Although Sir Thomas More thenceforth renounced most of these austerities, he appears to have worn a hair shirt next his skin for the rest of his life. A few days before his execution he gave one which he had been wearing to his daughter Margaret. She bequeathed it to her cousin, Margaret Clements, an Augustinian nun, at Louvain. There it remained till the French revolution, and it is now carefully preserved as a relic in a convent established at Spilsburg, near Blandford.

He then wished to become a priest; and, as such, he might, according to received notions, have enjoyed, with little restraints, all the pleasures of the world; but he was too conscientious to avail himself of licenses or dispensations, or to consider custom an excuse for violating the engagements of the clerical state if should enter into it. Finding that these would not permanently suit him, he resolved to marry, and having returned to his profession, to exert all his energies in it, that he might rise to distinction and be able creditably to maintain his family. "God had allotted him for another state,—not to live solitary—but that he might be a pattern to reverend married men how they should carefully bring up their children; how dearly they should love their wives; how they should employ their endeavors wholly for the good of their country, yet excellently perform the virtues of religious men as piety, humility, obedience, yea conjugal chastity."[1] Owing to the tenderness of his nature, the sweetness of his disposition, his equal flow of mirthful thoughts, as well as his habits of regularity and industry, he was singularly well adapted to domestic life; and no one ever more exquisitely enjoyed its blessings.

From his descendant we have the following curious account of his courtship. "Sir Thomas having determined, by the advice and direction of his ghostly father, to be a married man, there was at that time a pleasant conceited gentleman of an ancient family in Essex, one Mr. John Colt, of New Hall, that invited him unto his house, being much delighted in his company, proffering unto him the choice of any of his daughters, who were young gentlewomen of very good carriage, good complexions, and very religiously inclined; whose honest and sweet conversation and virtuous education enticed Sir Thomas not a little; and although his affection most served him to the second, for that he thought her the fairest and best favored, yet when he thought with himself that it would be a grief and some blemish to the elder to have the younger sister preferred before her, he, out of a kind of compassion, settled his fancy upon the eldest, and soon after married her with all her friends' good liking."[2]

Some have said that he selected a rustic girl whom he

[1] More, 26. "Maluit maritus esse castus quam sacerdos impurus."— Eras. Ep.   [2] More, 39.

might fashion according to his own notions of female propriety;[1] but the probability is, that he was exceedingly delighted to exchange the company of the Carthusian brethren for that of the "Mistress Colts," having been long a stranger to female society;—that he preferred the conversation and manners of Jane, the eldest, although the second was a more showy beauty; and that, although he had a good deal to teach his bride when he brought her to London, she was as well educated and accomplished as country squires' daughters generally were in the beginning of the sixteenth century.

There never was a happier union. He settled her in a house in Bucklersbury, where they lived in uninterrupted harmony and affection.

He now applied himself with unremitted assiduity to the business of his profession, being stimulated, and cheered, and comforted, and rewarded by the smiles of his bride. When he was Lord High Chancellor, he must have looked back with a sigh to this portion of his career. He rose very rapidly at the bar, and was particularly famous for his skill in international law.

It seems strange to us that he at the same time accepted and retained the office of under-sheriff of the City of London. This office was then judicial, and of considerable dignity. I conjecture that the under-sheriff, besides his other duties, sat in the Court of the Lord Mayor and of the Sheriffs, in which causes of importance were then determined, and the jurisdiction of which, by the process of foreign attachment, was very extensive. Erasmus, after stating that his Court was held every Thursday, observes that no judge of that Court ever went through more causes; none decided them more uprightly,—often remitting the fees to which he was entitled from the suitors. His deportment in this capacity endeared him extremely to his fellow-citizens.[2]

[1] This notion is an improvement upon Erasmus, who is silent on the sacrifice of inclination to compassion. "Virginem duxit admodum puellam, claro genere natam rudem adhuc utpote ruri inter parentes ac sorores semper habitam, quo magis illi liceret illam ad suos mores fingere. Hanc et literis instruendam curavit, et omni musices genere doctam reddidit."—Eras. Ep.

[2] Eras. Ep. Although Roper, himself a lawyer, distinctly narrates that his father-in-law was under-sheriff, some, from an affected regard for the dignity of the Chancellor, have tried to deny that he held an office which would now be declined by an eminent solicitor; but in his epitaph, prepared by himself, we find these words: "In urbe sua pro Shyrevo dixit;" and an entry has

But he was now to make a figure in a new line. After an intermission of parliaments for about seven years, one was called in the beginning of the year 1504, for the purpose of obtaining a subsidy on the marriage of Margaret, the King's eldest daughter, with James IV., King of Scots. More was returned to the House of Commons, " for many had now taken notice of his sufficiency ;" and he is recorded as the first member of that assembly who gained celebrity by public speaking, and who, as a successfu leader of opposition, incurred the enmity of the Court. Henry was entitled, according to the strictest feudal law, to a grant on this occasion ;[1] but he thought it a favorable opportunity for gratifying his avarice, and he required a much greater sum than he intended to bestow upon the Scottish Queen. " When the consent of the Lower House was demanded to these impositions, most of the rest holding their peace or not daring to gainsay them, though they seemed unwilling, Sir Thomas, making a grave speech, pronounced such urgent arguments why these exactions were not to be granted, that thereupon all the King's demands were crossed, and his request denied ; so that Mr. Tyler, one of the King's Privy Chamber, went presently from the House, and told his Majesty that a beardless boy had disappointed him of all his expectations."[2]

been found in the records of the Common Council, "that Thomas More, gent., *one of the under-sheriffs of London*, should occupy his office and chamber by a sufficient deputy during his absence as the King's ambassador in Flanders." Edward Dudley, Attorney-General to Henry VII., was one of the under-sheriffs, and Thomas Marrow, one of the greatest lawyers of his day, filled the office about the same time. More himself set the highest value on this office ; for he informs Erasmus, that, on his return from Flanders, he declined a handsome pension offered him by the King, which he could not hold without resigning his under-sheriffship, for in case of a controversy with the King about the privileges of the city, he might be deemed by his fellow-citizens to be disabled by dependence on the Crown from securely and manfully maintaining their rights.—Morus Erasmo, 1516. In the first edition of the *Utopia*, printed at Louvain by Theodore Martin in 1516, the work is stated to be " Per clarissimum et eruditissimum Virum D. Thomam Morum, Civem et *Vice-comitem* Londinensem,"—from which some have supposed that he had reached the dignity of High Sheriff ; but this designation must have proceeded from ignorance of the different degrees of *shrieval* dignity in England.

[1] The King, like every feudal lord, could claim an aid to knight his eldest son, to marry his eldest daughter, or to redeem himself from captivity.

[2] More. 45. To add to the marvel of this brilliant success in the House of Commons, More's biographers roundly assert that he was then only twenty-one years of age ; but it appears from the Statute Book and the Parliament Roll, that this parliament met on the 16th of January, 1504, so that he was

"Whereupon the King, conceiving great indignation towards him, could not be satisfied until he had some way revenged it."[1]

According to the Tudor practice established in subsequent reigns, More ought to have been sent to the Tower for his presumption ; but Henry had always a view to his Exchequer, "and forasmuch as he, nothing having, nothing could lose, his Grace devised a causeless quarrel against his father, keeping him in the Tower till he had made him pay to him a hundred pounds fine. Shortly hereupon it fortuned that Sir Thomas More coming in a suit to Dr. Fox, Bishop of Winchester, one of the King's Privy Counsel, the Bishop called him aside, and pretending great favor towards him, promised that if he would be ruled by him he would not fail into the King's favor again to restore him,—meaning, as it was afterwards conjectured, to cause him thereby to confess his offenses against the King, whereby his Highness might with the better color have occasion to revenge his displeasure against him ; but when he came from the Bishop he fell into communication with one Maister Whitforde, his familiar friend, then chaplain to that Bishop, and showed him what the Bishop had said, praying for his advice. Whitforde prayed him by the passion of God not to follow the counsel, for my Lord, to serve the King's turn, will not stick to agree to his own father's death. So Sir Thomas More returned to the Bishop no more."[2] To show that More acted wisely in not making confessions to the King in the hope of pardon, it is related that when Dudley was afterwards led to execution, along with Empson, meeting Sir Thomas More, he said to him,—"Oh, More, More! God was your good friend that you did not ask the King forgiveness, as manie would have had you do, for if you had done so, perhaps you should have been in the like case with us now."

Henry VII. continued to regard the young patriot with an evil eye, and watched for an opportunity of effectually wreaking his vengeance upon him, insomuch that "he was determined to have gone over sea, thinking that being in the King's indignation he could not live in England without great danger."[3] In the meanwhile he almost

full twenty-four, and as old as William Pitt when Prime Minister of Great Britain.   [1] Roper, 7.   [2] Ibid. 8.   [3] Ibid. 9.

entirely withdrew from his practice at the bar, and devoted himself to study, "perfecting himself in most of the liberal sciences, as music, arithmetic, geometry, and astronomy, and growing to be a perfect historian."[1] With a view to his foreign residence, "he studied the French tongue at home, sometimes recreating his tired spirits on the viol."[2]—But while he was meditating exile, the death of the tyrant preserved him to his country.

CHAPTER XXXI.

LIFE OF SIR THOMAS MORE FROM THE ACCESSION OF HENRY VIII. TILL HIS APPOINTMENT AS LORD CHANCELLOR.

MORE hailed the commencement of the new reign in a Latin poem, which contained lines not only praising the good qualities of the youthful sovereign, but reflecting with great bitterness on the oppression from which the nation had escaped:—

" Meta hæc servitii est, hæe libertatis origo,
   Tristitiæ finis, lætitiæque caput,
Nam juvenem secli decus O memorabile nostri
   Ungit et in Regem præficit ista tuum.
Regem qui cunctis lachrymas detergat ocellis,
   Gaudia pro longo substituat gemitu.
Omnia discussis arrident pectora curis,
   Ut solet, excussa nube, nitere dies.—
Leges invalidæ prius, *imo nocere coactæ*,
   Nunc vires gaudent obtinuisse suas.
Non metus occultos insibilat aure susurros
   Nemo quod taceat, quodve susurret, habet."

Little did the poet foresee that this was to be the most tyrannical and bloody reign in the annals of England, and that he himself was to be doomed to a cruel death by him whose clemency he celebrates.[3]

Meanwhile, More resumed his profession, and rose in

---

[1] More, 47.   [2] Roper, 9.
[3] A poem on the union of the Red and White Roses, entitled "De utraque Rosa in unum Coalita," written by him soon after, he thus prophetically concludes (whether through accident or second sight, I know not):
" At qui tam ferus est, ut non amet, ille timebit.
Nempe etiam spinas flos habet iste suas."

Westminster Hall to still greater eminence than he had before attained. "There was at that time in none of the Prince's Courts of the laws of this realm, any matter of importance in controversy wherein he was not with the one party of counsel."[1] "He now gained, without grief, not so little as £400 by the year," an income which, considering the relative profits of the bar and the value of money, probably indicated as high a station as £10,000 a year at the present day.

He was ere long introduced to the young King and to Wolsey, now the prime favorite rising rapidly to greatness. They were both much pleased with him, and were desirous that he should give up the law for politics, and accept an office at Court,—the Cardinal thinking that, from his retired habits and modest nature, he never could be dangerous as a rival. More long resisted these solicitations, truly thinking his situation as an eminent barrister more independent as well as more profitable.

He was about this time engaged in a *cause célèbre*, of which a circumstantial account has come down to us. A ship belonging to the Pope having being seized at Southampton, as forfeited to the Crown for a breach of the law of nations, the Pope's Nuncio at the Court of London instituted proceedings to obtain restitution, and retained More, "at which time there could none of our law be found so meet to be of counsel."

The hearing was in the Star Chamber before the Chancellor, the Chief Justices, the Lord Treasurer, and other officers of state. To plead against the Crown before such a tribunal was rather an arduous task; but More displayed great firmness and zeal, and, availing himself not only of his own learning, but of the authorities and arguments furnished to him by his client (himself a great civilian), he made such an unanswerable speech for his Holiness that the judgment was in his favor, and restitution was decreed.

The King was present at the trial; and to his credit be it spoken, instead of being mortified by the loss of his prize, and offended with the counsel who had been pleading against him, he joined all the hearers in praising More for "upright and commendable demeanor therein; and

---

[1] Roper, 7. [2] Ibid. 11.

for no entreaty would henceforth be induced any longer to forbear his service."[1]

In the early part of his reign, Henry VIII. was one of the most popular Sovereigns that ever filled the throne of England, and deserved to be so; for, beyond his fine person, his manly accomplishments, his agreeable manners, and the contrast he presented to his predecessor, he showed a disposition to patronize merit wherever it could be found; and his Court was the resort of the learned and the witty, as well as the high born and chivalrous.

More still retained his office in the City, but was prevailed upon to give up his practice at the bar. He was made Master of the Requests, knighted, and sworn of the Privy Council.[2]

He was now removed from Bucklersbury, and took up his residence at Chelsea, in what might then be considered a country-house, which he built for himself, and where he amused himself, with an extensive garden and farm. To his inexpressible grief, he had lost his first wife after she had brought him four children; and he had entered into a second matrimonial union, not of sentiment but convenience, with Mrs. Alice Middleton, a widow lady, "of good years, and of no favor or complexion." She was seven years older than himself, and it is to be feared not always of the sweetest disposition. "This he did because she might have care of his children; and she proved a kind step-mother to them." Erasmus, who was often an inmate in the family, speaks of her as a keen and watchful manager, with whom More lived on terms of as much respect and kindness as if she had been fair and young. "No husband gained so much obedience from a wife by authority and severity, as More by gentleness and pleasantry. Though verging on old age, and not of a yielding temper, he prevailed on her to take lessons on the lute, the cithara, the viol, the monochord, and the flute, which she daily practiced to him.[3]

Yet from some of their conjugal dialogues, recorded by members of the family, we are made to doubt whether the sweetness of their intercourse was not occasionally flavored with a little acid. He would say of her, "that she was penny-wise and pound-foolish, saving a candle's end and spoiling a velvet gown." She rated him for not

---

[1] Roper, 11.   [2] Ibid, 13.   [3] Erasm. Ep.

being sufficiently ambitious; and because he had no mind to set himself forward in the world, saying to him, "Til lie vallie! Tillie vallie! Will you sit and make goslings in the ashes? My mother hath often said unto me, it is better to rule than to be ruled."—"Now, in truth," answered he, "that is truly said, good wife; for I never found you yet willing to be ruled."[1]

He had soon a very numerous household; for his daughters marrying, they and their husbands and their children all resided under his roof, and constituted one affectionate family; which he governed with such gentleness and discretion that it was without broils or jealousies.

The course of his domestic life is minutely described by eye-witnesses. "His custom was daily (besides his private prayers with his children) to say the seven psalms, the litany, and the suffrages following; so was his guise with his wife and children, and household, nightly, before he went to bed; to go to his chapel, and there on his knees ordinarily to say certain psalms and collects with them."[2] Says Erasmus, "You might imagine yourself in the academy of Plato. But I should do injustice to his house by comparing it to the academy of Plato, where numbers and geographical figures, and sometimes moral virtues, were the subjects of discussion; it would be more just to call it a school and exercise of the Christian re-

---

[1] Rop. More. In the metrical inscription which he wrote for his own monument, there is a labored commendation of Alice, which in tenderness is outweighed by one word applied to Jane, the beloved companion of his youth:

"Chara Thomæ jacet hic Joanna *uxorcula* Mori."

On the other hand the following epigram, which he composed after his second marriage, shows a bitter feeling towards Alice as a *shrew:*

"Some man hath good,
But children hath he none;
Some man hath both,
But he can get none health:
Some hath all three,
But up to honor's throne
Can he not creep by no manner of stealth.
To some she sendeth children,
Riches, wealth,
Honor, worship, and reverence, all his life,
*But yet she pincheth him
With a shrewd wife.*
    Be content
With such reward as fortune hath you sent."
        Sir Thomas More.

[2] Roper.

ligion. All its inhabitants, male or female, applied their leisure to liberal studies and profitable reading, although piety was their first care. No wrangling, no angry word was heard in it; no one was idle; every one did his duty with alacrity, and with a temperate cheerfulness.[1]

But the most charming picture of More as a private man is carelessly sketched by himself in a hurried Latin letter to Peter Giles, his friend at Antwerp, lamenting the little time he could devote to literary composition:—

"For while in pleading, in hearing, in deciding causes, or composing disputes as an arbitrator, in waiting on some men about business, and on others out of respect, the greatest part of the day is spent on other men's affairs, the remainder of it must be given to my family at home; so that I can reserve no part to myself, that is, to study. I must gossip with my wife and chat with my children, and find something to say to my servants;[2] for all these things I reckon a part of my business, unless I were to become a stranger in my own house; for with whomsoever either nature or choice or chance has engaged a man in any relation of life, he must endeavor to make himself as acceptable to them as he possibly can. In such occupations as these, days, months, and years slip away. Indeed all the time which I can gain to myself is that which I steal from my sleep and my meals, and because that is not much I have made but a slow progress."[3]

His time was now more than ever broke in upon by visits from distinguished foreigners, who were eager to see him from his great reputation abroad, and whose opinion of him he still farther exalted by the charms of his manner and conversation.

To his great grief he was often obliged to lodge in the palace, and his favor with the King and the Court threatened utterly to interfere with all his domestic enjoyments, and to ruin his literary projects. "The King's custom was, upon holydays, when he had done his own devotions, to send for Sir Thomas into his traverse, and there, sometimes in matters of astronomy, geometry, and divinity, and such other faculties, to sit and confer with

---

[1] Eras. Ep.
[2] He curiously adapted his conversation to the different members of his establishment. "Cum uxore fabulandum est, garriendum cum liberis, colloquendum cum ministris," &c.   [3] Morus Aegedio.

him; otherwhiles also, in the clear night, he would have him walk with him on the leads, there to discourse with him of the diversity of the courses, motions, and operations of the stars; and, because he was of a very pleasant disposition, it pleased his Majesty and the Queen, after the council had supped, commonly to call for him to hear his pleasant jests." There was no remedy but to be dull. " When Sir Thomas perceived his pleasant conceits so much to delight them that he could scarce once in a month get leave to go home to his wife and children, and that he could not be two days absent from the Court but he must be sent for again, he much misliking this restraint of his liberty, began therefore to dissemble his mirth, and so little by little to disuse himself, that he from thenceforth at such seasons was no more so ordinarily sent for."[1]

In spite of all these distractions he not only most creditably performed all his public duties, but wrote works which gained the highest degree of celebrity in his own time, and are now interesting and instructive.

Between the years 1514 and 1523 More was repeatedly emplyoyed on embassies to the Low Countries, chiefly to settle disputes about trade and to negotiate commercial treaties, an employment which he seems particularly to have disliked. On the first occasion he was consoled for a long detention at Bruges by the company of his colleague, Tunstal, then Master of the Rolls, and afterwards Bishop of Durham, whom he celebrates as one not only fraught with all learning, and sincere in his life and morals, but inferior to no man as a delightful companion. Subsequently he had no one associated with him; and although he was pleased to meet the friends of Erasmus, and was struck by the wealth and civilization he saw among the Flemings, he longed much for the repose of his retreat at Chelsea, and for the embraces of his children.

He was much annoyed by being stationed a long time at Calais, a place from which negotiations could be conveniently carried on with the Continental states. On this occasion Erasmus writes to Peter Giles, their common friend, " More is still at Calais, of which he is heartily tired. He lives at great expense, and is engaged in business most odious to him. Such are the rewards reserved by kings for their favorites."[2] Afterwards More himself

---

[1] More.
[2] Eras. Ep.

writes to Erasmus: "I approve your determination never to be engaged in the busy trifling of princes; from which, as you love me, you must wish that I were extricated. You cannot imagine how painfully I feel myself plunged in them, for nothing can be more odious to me than this legation. I am here banished to a petty seaport, of which the air and earth are equally disagreeable to me. Abhorrent as I am by nature from strife, even when it is profitable, as at home, you may judge how wearisome it is here, where it actually causes a loss to me." He must have been much relieved by the agreeable society of Wolsey, who crossed the Channel for a short time, to superintend the King's negotiations and his own.

In 1519 he was reluctantly obliged to resign his favorite office of under-sheriff, the City being tired of giving him leave of absence when he went upon the King's business; but in 1512 he was rewarded with the office of Treasurer of the Exchequer, which was of considerable profit as well as dignity.[1]

The next step in More's advancement was the chair of the House of Commons. The great, or rather the only, object of calling the Parliament which met in April, 1523, being to obtain money, some management was thought necessary to provide against the parsimonious turn always shown by the representatives of the people; for, though generally willing to comply with any other demand of the Crown,—when their pockets were touched, they were stern and resolute, granting only moderate and temporary supplies.[2] A good deal depended on the Speaker, who not only exercised influence over the assembly as president, but himself was in the habit of taking an active part in the discussions. Although the choice of Speaker was nominally with the Commons themselves, in reality

[1] This appointment gave great satisfaction to all More's friends. Erasmus, writing to Budæus, says, "Est quod Moro gratuleris, nam Rex illum nec ambientem nec flagitantem munere magnifico honestavit, addito salario nequaquam penitendo, est enim principi suo a thesauris." He adds, "Nec hoc contentas, equitis aurati dignitatem adjecit." But Roper, who could not be mistaken, states that he was knighted within a month after he was made Master of Requests.

[2] To this stinginess of the Commons we must ascribe the liberties of England; for large and permanent grants would have led to the disuse of national assemblies in this island, as well as on the Continent of Europe. Except the Customs, no permanent tax was imposed before the middle of the seventeenth century.

it was dictated by the Court; and on this occasion Sir Thomas More was selected from his great fame and popularity, and from his having hitherto co-operated with Wolsey, as yet not liable to much exception, and from the dread of his again acting the part of a popular leader. The Commons were much gratified by the recommendation, and joyfully presented their favorite as their Speaker to the King sitting on his throne in the House of Lords.

More disqualified himself, referring to the story of Phormio the philosopher, "who desired Hannibal to come to his lectures, which when he consented to and came, Phormio began to read *De Re Militari*—of chivalry; but as soon as Hannibal heard this, he called the philosopher an arrogant fool to presume to teach him who was already master of chivalry and all the arts of war." "So," says Sir Thomas, "if I should presume to speak before his Majesty of learning and the well ordering of the government, or such like matters, the King who is so deeply learned, such a master of prudence and experience, might say to me as Hannibal to Phormi." Wherefore he humbly besought his Majesty to order the Commons to choose another Speaker.

To this the Chancellor, by the King's command, replied that "His Majesty, by long experience of his service, was well acquainted with his wit, learning, and discretion, and that therefore he thought the Commons had chosen the fittest person of them all to be their Speaker."[1]

More then delivered a prepared speech, which was published by his son-in-law, as is supposed from the original MS., and which is curious as an authentic specimen of the state of the English language in the beginning of the 16th century, and of the taste in oratory which then prevailed;—

"Sith I perceive, most redoubted Sovereign, that it standeth not with your pleasure to reform this election, and caused it to be changed, but have, by the mouth of the most reverend father in God, the Legate, your Highness's Chancellor, thereunto given your most royal assent, and have of your benignity determined far above that I may bear for this office to repute me meet, rather than that you should seem to impute unto your Commons that they had unmeetly chosen, I am ready obediently to con-

[1] 1 Parl. Hist. 486.

form myself to the accomplishment of your Highness's pleasure and commandment."

Having begged a favorable construction on all his own words and actions, he apologises for the rusticity of the Commons, and prays privilege of speech. He says that great care had been taken to elect discreet men according to the exigency of the writs, and thus proceeds:—

"Whereby it is not to be doubted but that there is a substantial assembly of right wise, meet, and politique persons; yet, most precocious Prince, sith among so many wise men, neither is every man wise alike, nor among so many alike well witted, every man well spoken; and it often happeth that as much folly is uttered with pointed polish speech, so many boisterous and rude in language give right substantial counsel; and sith also in matters of great importance the mind so occupied in the matter that a man rather studieth what to say than how; by reason whereof the wisest man and best speaker in a whole country fortuneth, when his mind is fervent in the matter, somewhat to speak in such wise as he would afterwards wish to have been uttered otherwise, and yet no worse will had when he spake it, than he had when he would so gladly change it. Therefore, most generous Sovereign, considering that in your high court of parliament is nothing treated but matter of weight and importance concerning your realm and your own royal estate, it could not fail to put to silence from the giving of their advice and counsel many of your discreet Commons, to the great hindrance of your common affairs, unless every one of your Commons were utterly discharged of all doubt and fear how anything that it should happen them to speak should happen of your Highness to be taken. And in this point, though your well known and proved benignity putteth every man in good hope, yet such is the weight of the matter, such is the reverend dread that the timorous hearts of your natural subjects conceive towards your Highness our most redoubted King and undoubted Sovereign, that they cannot in this point find themselves satisfied, except your gracious bounty therein declared put away the scruple of their timorous minds, and put them out of doubt, It may, therefore like your most abundant Grace to give to all your Commons here assembled, your most gracious license and pardon freely, without doubt of your dreadful displeasure, every man to discharge his conscience, and boldly in everything incident among us to declare his advice ; and whatever happeneth any man to say, that it may like your noble Majesty, of your inestimable goodness, to take all in good part, interpreting every man's words, how uncunningly however they may be couched, to proceed yet of good zeal towards the profit of your realm and honor of your royal person ; and the prosperous estate and preservation whereof, most excellent Sovereign, is the thing which we all, your Majesty's humble, loving subjects, according to the most bounden duty of our natural allegiance, most highly desire and pray for."[1]

This address has been blamed for servility; but the epithets applied to the King are merely in conformity to the established usage of the times, and in pleading for the necessity of liberty of speech More shows considerable boldness, while he indulges in a few sarcasms on the country squires over whom he was to preside.

To please him still more, and to ensure his services in the subsidy, Judge More, his father, in spite of very advanced age, was named in the Lords one of the " Triers of Petitions for Gascogny," an office which is still filled up at the commencement of every parliament, and which, although become a sinecure, was then supposed to confer great dignity.

We have seen in the Life of Wolsey[2] the independent spirit which, in spite of these blandishments, in a few days after, More displayed ; and the noble stand he made for the privileges of the House of Commons. A reasonable supply, constitutionally asked, he was willing to have supported ; but the extortionate demand which Wolsey thought, by his personal appearance in the House, surrounded by all his pageantry, violently to enforce, was dexterously resisted, to the disgrace and ridicule of the chief actor in the scene. Well might the wish have been entertained, " that More had been at Rome when he was made Speaker."[3]

Wolsey, who, according to Erasmus, had " rather feared than loved More," after this time became seriously jealous of him as a rival ;[4] and meditating a refined vengeance,

---
[1] Roper, 13.   [2] Ante, vol. i. p. 440, 441.   [3] Roper, 20.
[4] More has been censured for having, while comparatively obscure, flattered

attempted to banish him to Spain under the title of ambassador, with strong professions of admiration for the learning and wisdom of the proposed diplomatist, and his peculiar fitness for a conciliatory adjustment of the difficult matters which were at issue between the King and his kinsman the Emperor. The overture being made to More, he immediately perceived the artifice of it; but resisted it on the allegation that the Spanish climate would be fatal to his constitution, beseeching Henry "not to send a faithful servant to his grave." It is believed that the King saw into Wolsey's motives, and wished to have near him a man whom he destined, at some future period, to become his chief minister. He kindly answered, therefore, "It is not our meaning, Mr. More, to do you any hurt, but to do you good we should be glad. We shall, therefore, employ you otherwise."[1]

He continued in great favor with the King; and, in the end of the year 1525, on the death of Sir R. Wingfield, he was appointed Chancellor of the Duchy of Lancaster, an office illustrated by distinguished lawyers and statesmen down to our own time,[2] and which More continued to hold till he received the Great Seal of England.

As he was reluctant to visit the Palace, and seemed not quite happy when he was there, "the King would, on a sudden, come over to his house at Chelsea, and be merry with him—even dining with him without previous invitation or notice." On such occasions, from a true sense of hospitality, More did his best to entertain his royal guest, and put forth all his powers of pleasing. Roper particularly celebrates one of these visits, when the King was so much delighted with his conversation that, after dinner, he walked with him in the garden by the space of an hour, holding his arm about his neck. As soon as his

---

the great man; but I think without reason, as he confined his commendation to Wolsey's love of learning and patronage of the learned. Thus

" Unice doctorum pater ac patrone virorum,
   Pieridum pendet cujus ab ore chorus."

[1] Roper, 21.
[2] Be it remembered that I wrote the text in the year 1843, before I held, and when I little expected ever to hold, this office.—*Note to Third Edition,* 1848. When Lord John Russell offered to make me Chancellor of the Duchy of Lancaster, I hesitated; but he overcame my scruples by saying, "Remember the office has been held by Sir Thomas More and by Dunning."—*Note to Fourth Edition,* 1856.

Majesty was gone, Roper congratulated his father-in-law on the distinguished honor that had been paid to him; saying, "how happy must he be with whom the King was so lovingly familiar, the like of which had never been seen before except once, when he walked arm in arm with Cardinal Wolsey." "I thank our Lord," quoth he, "I find his Grace my very good Lord indeed; and I believe he doth as singularly favor me as any subject within this realm. Howbeit, son Roper, I may tell thee I have no cause to be proud thereof; for if my head would win a castle in France, it should not fail to go."[1]

This authentic anecdote shows in a very striking manner how More had early penetrated the intense selfishness, levity, heartlessness, and insensibility to remorse which constituted the character of the King, while these bad qualities were yet disguised by a covering of affability, hilarity, and apparent good humor, and before they had shed the blood of a wife or a friend. The world could little anticipate that Henry would actually one day cut off More's head, even without any such substantial advantage as the winning of a castle. For the present his Majesty delighted to honor him.

On account of his facetiousness and his learning, he was generally obliged to attend the Court in the royal progresses, and at Oxford and Cambridge he was always the person appointed to answer the Latin addresses to the King by the University orators. Attending Henry to France, he was employed to make the speech of congratulation when the English and French monarchs embraced. So, when the Emperor landed in England, More welcomed him in the King's name with such eloquence and grace, as to call forth the admiration of Charles as well as of all his Flemish and Spanish attendants.

More's European reputation was now at its height. He had published his "Epigrams," his "Utopia," and his "Refutation of the Lutherans," all of which had been frequently reprinted in Germany and France. He carried on an epistolary correspondence with all the most celebrated foreign literati, and he had spread his fame in a way of which we can now have but an imperfect notion, by academical disputations. Visiting every university which he approached in his travels, "he would learnedly dispute

[1] Roper, 22.

among them to the great admiration of the auditory." On one occasion, when at Bruges, he gained no small applause by putting down an arrogant pedant, who published a universal challenge to dispute with any person "in omni scibili et de quolibet ente." The Englishman who studied at Lincoln's Inn, proposed the question,—"*An averia carucæ capta in vetito namio sint irreplegbilia?*" "This Thraso or braggadocio not so much as understanding those terms of our common law, knew not what to answer to it, and so he was made a laughing stock to the whole city for his presumptuous bragging."[1]

Now began the controversy about the King's divorce, which entirely changed the aspect of affairs, both civil and ecclesiastical, in England, and had a lasting effect upon the destinies of the nation. More lies under the suspicion of some dissimulation or culpable concealment of his sentiments upon this subject. When consulted by Henry respecting the legality of his marriage with his brother's widow, he said it was a question only fit for theologians, and referring him to the writings of St. Augustine and other luminaries of the Western Church, never would give any explicit opinion from himself. It is possible that, unconsciously to himself, More dissembled from prudence or ambition, and that he cherished a secret hope of farther advancement, which would have been extinguished by a blunt opposition to the royal inclination; but it is likewise possible that he sincerely doubted on a question which divided the learned world, and we are not hastily to draw inferences against him from his subsequent condemnation of the King's union with Anne Boleyn before his marriage with Catherine had been canonically dissolved according to the rule of the Romish Church, which he most potently believed to be binding on all Christians.[2]

While the suit for divorce was going on at Rome through negotiations with Clement, and before the

---

[1] 3 Black. Com. 148.
[2] In his gratulatory verses on the King's accession, he had pronounced this marriage to be most auspicious:

"Conjugio, superi quod decrevere benignl,
    Quo tibi, quoque tuis consuluere bene."

He then goes on to compare Catherine to Penelope, Cornelia, and the most meritorious matrons of antiquity, showing that she excelled them all.

Legatine Court opened its sittings after the arrival of Campeggio, More appears to have observed a strict neutrality, and he enjoyed the confidence of both parties. Queen Catherine said,—" The King had but one sound councillor in his kingdom, Sir Thomas More; and as for Cardinal Wolsey, then the greatest subject in the realm, for his own benefit or end he cared not what counsel he gave." On the other hand, the Duke of Norfolk, the uncle of Anne Boleyn, the Earl of Wiltshire, her father, and Anne herself, who now secretly directed the King's counsels, had great hopes of bringing More into their designs as an active partisan, and intended that he should be the successor to Wolsey, whom they doomed to destruction if the divorce was not speedily pronounced.

The Chancellor of the Duchy was still very submissive to the Lord High Chancellor; but we have an account of a scene at the council-board about this time, which proves that there was " no love lost between them," The Cardinal showed Sir Thomas the draft of a treaty with a foreign power, asking his opinion of it, and pressing him so heartily to say " whether there were anything therein to be misliked," that he believed there was a desire to hear the truth, and pointed out some great faults committed in it. Whereupon the Cardinal, starting up in a rage, exclaimed,—" By the Mass, thou art the veriest fool of all the Council!" at which Sir Thomas, smiling, said,— " God be thanked, the King our Master hath but one fool in his Council."

Nevertheless, being again associated with Tunstal, now Bishop of Durham, he was sent Ambassador to Cambray to treat of a general peace between England, France, and the extensive states ruled over by Charles V. In this his last foreign mission he was supposed to have displayed the highest diplomatic skill, and " he so worthily handled himself, that he procured far more benefits unto this realm than by the King or the Council had been thought possible to be compassed."[1] During his stay abroad he became very homesick, but wrote thus merrily to Erasmus:— " I do not like my office of an ambassador; it doth not suit a married man thus to leave his family: it is much

---

[1] Roper, 36.

fitter for you ecclesiastics, who have no wives and children at home, *or who find them wheresoever you go.*"[1]

Soon after his return he paid a visit to the King at Woodstock, where he heard of the great misfortune that the principal part of his house at Chelsea, and all his outhouses and barns filled with corn, had been consumed by a fire, raised by the negligence of a neighbor's servant. The letter he wrote to his old wife on this occasion excites our admiration of him more than all his learned works, his public despatches, or his speeches in parliament. I must likewise observe, that for style it is much better and much nearer the English of the present day than the elaborate compositions which he wrote for publication. But besides the delightful glance that it gives of the manners and customs of private life in a remote age, its great charm will be found in the unaffected piety, in the gaiety of heart, and in the kindness of disposition which it evinces :

"MISTRESS ALYCE,—In my most harty will, I recommend me to you. And whereas I am enfourmed by my son Heron of the loss of our barnes, and our neighbours also, w^t all the corne that was therein, albeit (saving God's pleasure) it is a gret pitie of so much good corne lost, yet sith it hath liked hym to send us such a chance, we must not only be content, but also be glad of his visitation. He sent us all that we have lost: and sith he hath by such a chance taken it away againe, his pleasure be fulfilled. Let us never grudge thereat, but take it in good worth, and hartely thank him, as well for adversitie, as for prosperitie. And par adventure we have more cause to thank him for our losse, than for our winning. For his wisdom better seeth what is good for us than we do ourselves. Therefore I pray you be of good cheere, and take all the howsold with you to church, and there thank God both for that he hath given us, and for that he hath left us, which if it please hym, he can increase when he will. And if it please hym to leave us yet lesse, at hys pleasure be it. I praye you to make some good ensearche what my poor neighbours have loste, and bidde them take no thought therefore, and if I shold not leave myself a spone, there shall no poore neighbour of mine bere no losse by

[1] "Qui primum uxores ac liberos aut domi non habetis *aut ubique reperitis.*"
—Ep. 227.

chance happened in my house. I pray you be with my children and household mery in God. And devise somewhat with your friends, what way wer best to take, for provision to be made for corne for our household, and for sede thys yere coming, if ye thinke it good that we keepe the ground still in our handes. And whether ye think it good ye we so shall do or not, yet I think it were not best sodenlye thus to leave it all up, and to put away our folk of our farme, till we have somewhat advised us thereon. Howbeit if we have more nowe than ye shall neede, and which can get the other maister's, ye may then discharge us of them. But I would not that any man wer sodenly sent away he wote nere wether. At my coming hither, I perceived none other, but that I shold tary still with the kinges grace. But now I shall (I think), because of this chance, get leave this next weke to come home and se you; and then shall we further devise together uppon all thinges, what order shall be best to take; and thus as hartely fare you well with all our children as you can wishe. At Woodstok the thirde daye of Septembre, by the hand of

"Your loving husband,
"THOMAS MORE, Knight."

The Court was now sojourning at Woodstock after its return from Grafton, where Henry had taken his final leave of Wolsey.[1] More having rendered an account of his embassy was allowed to visit his family at Chelsea, and Henry, with Lady Anne, first moved to Richmond, and then to Greenwich, where, as we have seen, Wolsey being deprived of the Great Seal and banished to Esher, the new arrangements were completed, and Sir THOMAS MORE was sworn in Lord Chancellor.[2]

[1] Ante, vol. i.   [2] Ante, p. 2.

CHAPTER XXXII.

LIFE OF SIR THOMAS MORE FROM HIS APPOINTMENT AS LORD CHANCELLOR TILL HIS RESIGNATION.

THE merit of the new Lord Chancellor was universally acknowledged, and Wolsey himself admitted "that he was the fittest man to be his successor;"[1] but there was a great apprehension lest, having no ecclesiastical dignity, no crosses to carry before him, no hereditary rank, and no judicial reputation beyond what he had acquired when under-sheriff of London,—from the prejudices of the vulgar, the office might be considered lowered in dignity after being held by a Cardinal-Archbishop, the Pope's Legate, and prime minister of the Crown.

To guard against this impression, a very splendid pageant was got up for More's installation. The procession was headed by the Duke of Norfolk, the first Peer in the realm, and the Duke of Suffolk, the King's brother-in-law,—all the nobility and courtiers in and near London, and all the judges and professors of the law following.

When they had reached Palace Yard, the new Chancellor, in his robes, was led between the Dukes of Norfolk and Suffolk up Westminster Hall to the Stone Chamber, at the south-west corner of it, where were the marble table and marble chair,—and there being placed in the high judgment seat of Chancellor, the Duke of Norfolk, by the command of the King, spoke thus unto the people there with great applause and joy gathered together:

"The King's Majesty (which I pray God may prove happy and fortunate to the whole realm of England) hath raised to the most high dignity of Chancellorship Sir

---

[1] Shakspeare has rather lowered the terms of the compliment, although he makes the Cardinal behave very gracefully when he hears of the new appointment.

"*Crom.* ——— Sir Thomas More is chosen Lord Chancellor in your place."
"*Wols.* That's somewhat sudden:
But *he's a learned man.* May he continue
Long in his Highness favor, and do justice
For truth's sake, and his conscience; that his bones,
When he has run his course, and sleeps in blessings,
May have a tomb of orphan's tears wept on 'em."
Henry VIII. act iii. scene 2.

Thomas More, a man for his extraordinary worth and sufficiency well known to himself and the whole realm, for no other cause or earthly respect, but for that he hath plainly perceived all the gifts of nature and grace to be heaped upon him, which either the people could desire, or himself wish for the discharge of so great an office. For the admirable wisdom, integrity, and innocency, joined with most pleasant facility of wit, that this man is endued withal, have been sufficiently known to all Englishmen from his youth, and for these many years also to the King's majesty himself. This hath the King abundantly found in many and weighty affairs, which he hath happily despatched both at home and abroad; in divers offices, which he hath borne in most honorable embassages, which he hath undergone, and in his daily counsel and advices upon all other occasions. He hath perceived no man in his realm to be more wise in deliberating, more sincere in opening to him what he thought, nor more eloquent to adorn the matter which he uttered. Wherefore because he saw in him such excellent endowments, and that of his especial care he hath a particular desire that his kingdom and people might be governed with all equity and justice, integrity and wisdom: he of his own most gracious disposition hath created this singular man Lord Chancellor; that by his laudable performance of this office, his people may enjoy peace and justice, and honor also and fame may redound to the whole kingdom. It may perhaps seem to many a strange and unusual matter, that this dignity should be bestowed upon a lay-man, none of the nobility, and one that hath wife and children; because heretofore none but singular learned prelates, or men of greatest nobility, have possessed this place; but what is wanting in these respects, the admirable virtues, the matchless gifts of wit and wisdom of this man doth most plentifully recompense the same. For the King's majesty hath not regarded how great, but what a man he was: he hath not cast his eyes upon the nobility of his blood, but upon the worth of his person; he hath respected his sufficiency, not his profession; finally he would show by this his choice, that he hath some rare subjects amongst the gentlemen and laymen, who deserve to manage the highest offices of the realm, which bishops and noblemen think they only can deserve: which the rarer it is, so much he thought it would be to you the more acceptable, and to the whole kingdom most grateful. Wherefore receive this your Chancellor with joyful acclamations, at whose hands you may expect all happiness and content."

"Sir Thomas More," says his great-grandson, "according to his wonted modesty, was somewhat abashed at this the Duke's speech, in that it sounded so much to his praise; but recollecting himself as that place and time would give him leave, he answered in this sort:—

"Although, most noble Duke, and you right honorable Lords, and worshipful gentlemen, I know all these things which the King's majesty, it seemeth, hath been pleased should be spoken of me at this time and place, and your Grace hath, with most eloquent words, thus amplified, are as far from me as I could wish with all my heart they were in me for the better performance of so great a charge: and although this your speech hath caused in me greater fear than I can well express in words, yet this incomparable favor of my dread Sovereign, by which he showeth how well, yea how highly he conceiveth of my weakness, having commanded that my meanness should be so greatly commended, cannot be but most acceptable unto me; and I cannot choose but give your most noble Grace exceeding thanks, that what his Majesty hath willed you briefly to utter, you of the abundance of your love unto me have, in a large and eloquent oration, dilated. As for myself, I can take it no otherwise but that his Majesty's incomparable favor towards me, the good will and incredible propension of his royal mind (wherewith he hath these many years favored me continually) hath alone, without any desert of mine at all, caused both this my new honor, and these your undeserved commendations of me; for who am I, or what is the house of my father, that the King's highness should heap upon me, by such a perpetual stream of affection, these so high honors? I am far less than any the meanest of his benefits bestowed on me; how can I then think myself worthy or fit for this so peerless dignity? I have been drawn by force, as the King's majesty often professeth, to his Highness's service, to be a courtier; but to take this dignity upon me, is most of all against my will; yet such is his Highness's benignity, such is his bounty, that he highly esteemeth the small dutifulness of his meanest subjects, and seeketh still magnificently to recompense his servants ; not only such as deserve well, but even such as have but a desire to deserve well at his hands. In which number I have always wished myself to be reckoned, because I cannot challenge myself to be one of the former; which being so, you may all perceive with me, how great a burden is laid upon my back, in that I must strive in some sort with my diligence and duty to correspond with his royal benevolence, and to be answerable to that great expectation which he and you seem to have of me ; wherefore those so high praises are by so much the more grievous unto me, by how much I know the greater charge I have to render myself worthy of, and the fewer means I have to make them good. This weight is hardly suitable to my weak shoulders ; this honor is not correspondent to my poor deserts ; it is a burthen, not glory; a care, not a dignity; the one therefore I must bear as manfully as I can, and discharge the other with as much dexterity as I shall be able. The earnest desire which I have always had, and do now acknowledge myself to have, to satisfy by all means I can possible the most ample benefits to his Highness, will greatly excite and aid me to the diligent performance of all; which I trust also I shall be more able to do, if I find all your good wills and wishes both favorable unto me, and conformable to his royal munificence ; because my serious endeavors to do well, joined with your favorable acceptance, will easily procure that whatsoever is performed by me, though it be in itself but small, yet will it seem great and praiseworthy, for those things are always achieved happily which are accepted willingly ; and those succeed fortunately which are received by others courteously. As you therefore do hope for great matters, and the best at my hands, so though I dare not promise any such, yet do I promise truly and affectionately to perform the best I shall be able."—When Sir Thomas had spoken these words, turning his face to the high judgment-seat of the Chancery, he proceeded in this manner: " But when I look upon this seat, when I think how great and what kind of personages have possessed this place before me, when I call to mind who he was that sat in it last of all ; a man of what singular wisdom, of what notable experience, what a prosperous and favorable fortune he had for a great space, *and how, at last dejected with a heavy downfall, he hath died inglorious;* I have cause enough, by my predecessor's example, to think honor but slippery, and this dignity not so grateful to me as it may seem to others; for both it is a hard matter to follow with like paces or praises a man of such admirable wit, prudence, authority, and splendor, to whom I may seem but as the lighting of a candle when the sun is down; and also the sudden and unexpected fall of so great a man as he was doth terribly put me in mind that this honor ought not to please me too much, nor the lustre of this glistering seat dazzle mine eyes. Wherefore I ascend this seat as a place full of labor and danger, void of all solid and true honor; the which by how much the higher it is, by so much greater fall I am to fear, as well in respect of the very nature of the thing itself, as because I am warned by this late fearful example. And truly I might even now at this very first entrance stumble, yea faint, but that his Majesty's most singular favor towards me, and all your good wills, which your joyful countenance doth testify in this most honorable assembly, doth somewhat recreate and refresh me; otherwise, this seat would be no more pleasing to me than that sword was to Damocles, which hung over his head, and tied only by a hair of a horse's tail, seated him in the chair of state of Denis, the tyrant of Sicily; this, therefore, shall be always fresh in my mind; this will I have still before mine eyes—that this seat will be honorable, famous, and full of glory unto me, if I shall with care and diligence, fidelity and wisdom, endeavor to do my duty, and shall persuade myself that the enjoying thereof may chance to be but short and uncertain; the one whereof my labor ought to perform, the other, my predecessor's example may easily teach me. All which being so, you may easily perceive what great pleasure I take in this high dignity, or in this noble Duke's praising of me."[1]

[1] These inaugural speeches, as here given, are taken from More's Life by his great-grandson, and are adopted without suspicion by his subsequent biographers,—among others by the acute Sir James Mackintosh;—but there is reason to question their genuineness. Unless the expression, "dejected with a heavy downfall, *he hath died inglorious*," means by way of figure, his *political death*, it betrays fabrication and a gross anachronism, for Wolsey was now alive (if not merry) at Esher, and he did not meet his natural death at

More's elevation was not only very popular in England, but was heard with great satisfaction by the learned in foreign countries. To prove this it will be enough to copy a single sentence addressed by Erasmus to John Fabius, Bishop of Vienna. "Concerning the new increase of honor experienced by Thomas More, I should easily make you believe it, were I to show you the letters of many famous men, rejoicing with much alacrity, and congratulating the King, the realm, himself, and also me, on his promotion to be Lord Chancellor of England."[1]

When the fleeting flutter of pleasurable excitement from the first entrance into high office had passed away, More himself must have looked back with regret to the period of his life when he was first making way in his profession as an advocate, or when he was quietly engaged in his literary pursuits; and as nothing happened while he was Chancellor which might not easily have been foreseen, we may rather feel surprised that, with a delicate conscience and a strong sense of duty, he should accept this dangerous office, and associate himself with such unscrupulous colleagues. He well knew the violent and reckless character of the King; he must have expected very painful work in the pending proceedings against his predecessor; he was sure that the divorce would be prosecuted; and other subjects of dispute were springing up with the See at Rome to cause a conflict between his

Leicester Abbey till late in the following year. The Chancellor's great-grandson is exceedingly inaccurate about dates, and ignorant of history. He really does suppose that Sir Thomas More was not made Chancellor till after Wolsey's death (edition 1828, by Hunter, p. 169), which may afford a fair inference that the speeches are of his manufacture. Roper gives a very brief sketch of the Duke of Norfolk's speech, being charged by the King to make declaration "how much all England was beholden to Sir Thomas More for his good service, and how worthy he was to have the highest room (office) in the realm, and how dearly his Grace loved and trusted him." In return, Sir Thomas "disabled himself to be unmeet for that room, wherein considering how wise and honorable a Prelate had lately before taken so great a fall, he had no cause thereof to rejoice." More, the great-grandson, had so much degenerated in historical lore as to assert that his ancestor was the first layman who ever held the Great Seal,—forgetting not only the Scropes and the Arundels, but the Parnynges and the Knyvets, celebrated by Lord Coke, his own contemporary.

[1] Erasm. Epist. More, 177. In a letter to another correspondent, written at the same time, Erasmus, after stating that on Wolsey's disgrace the office of Chancellor was declined by Warham, says, "Itaqae provincia delegata est Thomæ Moro magno omnium applausu, nec minore bonorum omnium lætitiâ subvectus, quam dejectus Cardinalis."—Ep. 1115.

interest and his duty. He probably hoped, either that the divorce would be finally sanctioned and decreed by the Pope, or that Henry, tired of Anne Boleyn, would abandon the project of making her his wife; and that all minor difficulties might disappear or be overcome.

During the two years and a half he held the Great Seal, be must have enjoyed solid satisfaction in the assiduous, honest, and admirable discharge of his duties as a Judge; but, except when sitting in the Court of Chancery, his mind must have been filled with doubts, scruples, apprehensions, and antagonist wishes—sometimes overborne by an inclination to support the plans of the King, and sometimes struck with the conviction that they were inconsistent with his allegiance to the Head of the Church; —sometimes thinking that he should add to the splendor of his reputation, by directing, in high office, the government of a great empire, and sometimes dreading lest the fame he had already acquired should be tarnished by his acquiescence in measures which would be condemned by posterity;—sometimes regarding only the good he did by the improved administration of justice, and sometimes shocked by the consideration that this might be greatly overbalanced by the sanction he might be supposed to give to tyrannical acts in other departments of the government over which he had no control;—sometimes carried away by the desire to advance his family and his friends, and at last seeing that he could only continue to have the means of serving them by sacrificing his country.

A few days after his installation he was called upon, as Chancellor, to open the parliament, which had been summoned for the impeachment of Wolsey. The King being on the throne, and the Commons attending at the bar, the new Chancellor spoke to this effect:[1]—

"That, like as a good shepherd, who not only tendeth and keepeth well his sheep, but also foreseeth and provideth against everything which either may be hurtful or noisome to his flock, or may preserve and defend the same against all chances to come; so the King, who was the shepherd, ruler, and governor of this realm, vigilantly foreseeing things to come, considered how divers laws, by long continuance of time and mutation of things, were

[1] 1 Parl. Hist. 491.

now grown insufficient and imperfect: and also that, by the frail condition of man, divers new enormities were sprung up amongst the people for the which no law was made to reform the same, he said, was the very cause why, at this time, the King had summoned his High Court of Parliament. He resembled the King to a shepherd or herdsman also for this cause: if a King is esteemed only for his riches, he is but a rich man; if for his honor, he is but an honorable man; but compare him to the multitude of his people and the number of his flock, then he is a ruler, a governor of might and power; so that his people maketh him a prince, as of the multitude of sheep cometh the name of a shepherd. And as you see that amongst a great flock of sheep some be rotten and faulty, which the good shepherd sendeth from the sound sheep, so the great WETHER which is late fallen, as you all know, juggled with the King so craftily, scabbedly, and untruly, that all men must think that he imagined the King had no sense to perceive his crafty doings, or presumed that he would not see or understand his fradulent juggling and attempts. But he was deceived; for his Grace's sight was so quick and penetrable, that he not only saw him but saw through him, both within and without; so that he was entirely open to him. According to his desert, he hath had a gentle correction; which small punishment the King would not should be an example to other offenders; but openly declareth that whosoever hereafter shall make the like attempt, or commit the like offenses, shall not escape with the like punishment."[1]

It must be confessed that he does not here mention his predecessor with the same generosity and good taste as in his inaugural discourse in the Court of Chancery, but he might feel obliged to consult the feelings of those whom he addressed, particularly the members of the Upper House, to whom the Ex-Chancellor's name was most odious, and who were impatient to see a severe sentence pronounced upon him.

Sir Thomas Audley, the future Lord Chancellor, being elected Speaker, the business of the session began by the appointment of a committee, of which Lord Chancellor More was chairman, to prepare articles of charge against

[1] 1 Parl. Hist. 490.

Wolsey. It is a curious fact, that the two Chief Justices, Fitzherbert and Fitzjames, were called in to serve on this committee, and signed the articles. These to the number of forty-four, were immediately agreed to by the House of Lords, and sent down to the Commons. I have already observed that, considering how many of these articles were frivolous or were unfounded in fact, and that Wolsey's violation of the law and constitution by raising taxes without the authority of parliament, and other excesses of the prerogative, were entirely passed over, the proceeding is not very credible to the memory of Sir Thomas More; and seeing the subsequent fate of the accusation in the other House, we cannot help suspecting that he was privy to a scheme for withdrawing Wolsey from the judgment of parliament, and leaving him entirely at the mercy of his arbitrary master.

We must give praise to the Chancellor, however, for having suggested several statutes, which were now passed, to put down extortion on the probate of wills,[1] and in the demands for mortuaries,[2] and to prevent clerical persons from engaging in trade.[3] Other ecclesiastical reforms were loudly called for, but he did not venture to countenance them; and, to his great relief, on the 17th of December the session was closed. Not being a member of the House, he did not openly take any part in the debates, but he was named on committees, and the proceedings of the Lords were entirely governed by him.

He had now leisure to attend to the business of Chancery. Notwithstanding the great abilities of Wolsey as a Judge, abuses had multiplied and strengthened during his administration, and a very loud cry arose for equity reform. To the intolerable vexation of the subject, writs of subpœna had been granted on the payment of the fees, without any examination as to whether there were any probable cause for involving innocent individuals in a Chancery suit; a heavy arrear of causes stood for adjudication, some of which were said to have been pending for twenty years; and the general saying went, that "no one could hope for a favorable judgement unless his fingers were tipt with gold;"—which probably arose, not from the bribes received directly by the Chancellor himself, but

---

[1] 21 Hen. 8, c. 5.   [2] Ibid. c. 6.   [3] Ibid. c. 13.

from the excessive fees and gratuities demanded by his officers and servants.

The new Chancellor began by an order that "no subpœna should issue till a bill had been filed, signed by the attorney; and, he himself having perused it, had granted a fiat for the commencement of the suit."

It is related that, acting under this order, he showed his characteristic love of justice and jesting. When he had perused a very foolish bill, signed "A. Tubbe," he wrote immediately above the signature the words, "A Tale of." The luckless attorney being told that the Lord Chancellor had approved his bill, carried it joyfully to his client, who, reading it, discovered the gibe.[1]

Having heard causes in the forenoon between eight and eleven,—after dinner he sat in an open hall, and received the petitions of all who chose to come before him; examining their cases and giving them redress where it was in his power, according to law and good conscience; and "the poorer and meaner the suppliant was, the more affably he would hearken to his cause, and with speedy trial despatch him."[2] This was looked upon as a great contrast to the demeanor of the haughty Cardinal.

The present Chancellor himself not only refused all corrupt offers that were made to him, but took effectual measures to prevent any one dependent on him, or connected with him, from interfering improperly with the even march of justice. This rigor called forth a remonstrance from his son-in-law, Dancey, who, on a time, merrily said unto him: "When Cardinal Wolsey was Lord Chancellor, not only divers of his Privy Chamber, but such also as were his doorkeepers, got great gains by him; and sith I have married one of your daughters, I might of reason look for some commodity; but you are so ready to do for every poor man, and keep no doors shut, that I can find no gains at all, which is to me a great discouragement; whereas else, some for friendship, some for profit, and some for kindred, would gladly use my furtherance to bring them to your presence; and now, if I should take any thing of them, I should do them great wrong, because they may daily do as much for themselves; which thing, though it is in you, sir, very commendable, yet to me I find it nothing profitable." The

---

[1] More, 182.   [2] Ibid. 178.

first part of the Chancellor's answer can only be accounted for by supposing that he wished not only to mollify, but to mystify his son-in-law; or, that such practices as would now be matter of severe censure or impeachment, were then considered praiseworthy by the most virtuous; he winds up in a manner to convince us that in no particular, however small, would he have swerved from what he considered right: "I do not mislike, son, that your conscience is so scrupulous;[1] but there be many other ways wherein I may both do yourself good, and pleasure your friends: for sometime, by my word, I may stand your friend instead; sometime I may help him greatly by my letter; if he hath a cause depending before me, I may hear it before another, at your entreaty; *if his cause be not all the best, I may move the parties to fall to some reasonable end by arbitrament.* But this one thing I assure thee, on my faith, that if the parties will at my hands call for justice and equity, then, although it were my father, whom I reverence dearly, that stood on the one side, and the devil, whom I hate extremely, were on the other side, his cause being just, the devil of me should have his right."[2]

Of this stern impartiality, he soon after gave a practical proof; for another son-in-law, *Heron*, having a suit depending before him, and refusing to agree to any reasonable accommodation, because the Judge was the most affectionate father to his children that ever was in the world, "then made he, in conclusion, a flat decree against him."[3]

He was cautious in granting injunctions, yet granted and maintained them with firmness, where he thought that justice required his interference with the judgments of the Courts of common law. Differing from Lord Bacon in the next age, he was of opinion that law and equity might be beneficially administered by the same tribunal, and he made an effort to induce the common-law Judges to relax the rigor of their rules, with a view to meet the justice of particular cases; but, not succeeding in this, he resolutely examined their proceedings, and stayed trials and executions wherever it seemed to him that wrong would be done from their refusal to remedy the effects of

---

[1] That is, not taking a bribe when he could do no service for it.
[2] More, 179.   [3] Ibid. 180.

accident, to enforce the performance of trusts, or to prevent secret frauds from being profitable to the parties concerned in them.

These injunctions issued, however cautiously, from the Court of Chancery, having on the other side of the Hall caused much grumbling, which reached the ears of the Chancellor, through Roper, his son-in-law and biographer, —" thereupon caused he one Master Crooke, chief of the Six Clerks, to make a docket, containing the whole number and causes of all such injunctions, as either in his time had already passed, or at that present depended, in any of the King's Courts at Westminster, before him. Which done, he invited all the Judges to dine with him in the Council Chamber at Westminster; where, after dinner, when he had broken with them what complaints he had heard of his injunctions, and moreover showed them both the number and causes of every one of them, in order so plainly, that upon full debating of those matters they were all enforced to confess that they, in like case, could have done no otherwise themselves."[1] At this same compotation, he again offered, " that if the Justices of every Court unto whom the reformation of the rigor of the law, by reason of their office, most especially appertained, would, upon reasonable considerations, by their own discretion (as they were as he thought in conscience bound), mitigate and reform the rigor of the law themselves, there should, from thenceforth, by him no more injunctions be granted." They still refusing, he said to them, " Forasmuch as yourselves, my Lords, drive me to that necessity for awarding out injunctions to relieve the people's injury, you cannot hereafter any more justly blame me."[2]

When these reverend sages had swallowed a proper allowance of Gascony wine and taken their departure, the Chancellor intimated to Roper his private opinion that they were not guided by principle, and merely wished to avoid trouble and responsibility. " I perceive, son, why they like not so to do. For they see that they may, by the verdict of the jury, cast off all quarrels from themselves, and therefore am I compelled to abide the adventure of all such reports."[3]

The commissions for hearing causes issued in Wolsey's

[1] Roper, 42.   [2] Ibid.   [3] Ibid. 43.

time were not renewed, and very little assistance was required from Taylor, the Master of the Rolls; yet the Chancellor himself, from his assiduity, quickness, and early experience as a judge, in the course of a few terms, completely subdued all the arrears, and during the rest of his Chancellorship every cause was decided as soon as it was ripe for hearing. Nor did he acquire a reputation for despatch by referring everything to the Master, but, on the contrary, " he used to examine all matters that came before him, like an arbitrator; and he patiently worked them out himself to a final decree, which he drew and signed."

One morning before the end of term, having got through his paper, he was told by the officers that there was not another cause or petition to be set down before him; whereupon, with a justifiable vanity he ordered the fact to be entered of record, as it had never happened before; —and a prophecy was then uttered which has been fully verified :

"When MORE some time had Chancellor been,
No *more* suits did remain ;
The same shall never *more* be seen
Till MORE be there again."

But there is no circumstance during his Chancellorship that affects our imagination so much, or gives us such a lively notion of the manners of the times, as his demeanor to his father. Sir John More, now nearly ninety years of age, was hale in body and sound in understanding, and continued vigorously to peform the duties of senior puisne Judge in the Court of King's Bench. Every day during term time, before the Chancellor began business in his own Court, he went into the Court of King's Bench, and, kneeling before his father, asked and received his blessing.[2] So if they met together at readings in Lincoln's Inn, notwithstanding his high office, he offered the preeminence in argument to his father, though, from a regard to judicial subordination, this offer was always refused.

In about a year after Sir Thomas's elevation, the old

[1] Roper, 44.
[2] I am old enough to remember that when the Chancellor left his Court, if the Court of King's Bench was sitting, a curtain was drawn, and bows were exchanged between him and the Judges, so that I can easily picture to myself the "blessing scene" between the father and son.

Judge was seized with a mortal illness—(as it was supposed) from a surfeit of grapes. " The Chancellor, for the better declaration of his natural affection towards his father, not only while he lay on his death-bed, according to his duty, ofttimes with kindly words came to visit him, but also at his departure out of the world, with tears taking him about the neck, most lovingly kissed and embraced him, commending his soul into the merciful hands of Almighty God."[1]

Instead of imitating Wolsey's crosses, pillars, and poll-axes, More was eager to retreat into privacy, and even in public to comport himself with all possible simplicity. On Sundays, while he was Lord Chancellor, instead of marching with great parade through the city of London to outrival the nobles at the Court at Greenwich, he walked with his family to the parish church at Chelsea, and there, putting on a surplice, sung with the choristers at matins and high mass.

It happened one day that the Duke of Norfolk, coming to Chelsea to dine with him, found him at church, with a surplice on his back, singing. As they walked homeward together arm in arm, after service, the Duke said, " God's body! God's body! My Lord Chancellor a parish clerk! a parish clerk! You dishonor the King and his office." " Nay," quoth he, smiling; "your Grace may not think that the King your master and mine, will with me, for serving his Master, be offended, or thereby account his office dishonored."[2]

In religious processions he would himself carry the cross; and in " Rogation Week," when they were very long, and he had to follow those who carried the rood round the parish, being counseled to use a horse for his dignity, he would answer, " It seemeth not the servant to follow his master prancing on cockhorse, his master going on foot."

After diligently searching the books, I find the report of only one judgment which he pronounced during his Chancellorship, and this I shall give in the words of the reporter:—

" It happened on a time that a beggar-woman's little dog, which she had lost, was presented for a jewel to Lady More, and she had kept it some se'nnight very carefully;

---

[1] More, 184.   [2] Roper, 49.

but at last the beggar had notice where the dog was, and presently she came to complain to Sir Thomas, as he was sitting in his hall, that his lady withheld her dog from her. Presently my lady was sent for, and the dog brought with her; which Sir Thomas taking in his hands, caused his wife because she was the worthiest person, to stand at the upper end of the hall, and the beggar at the lower end, and saying that he sat there to do every one justice, he bade each of them call the dog; which, when they did, the dog went presently to the beggar, forsaking my Lady. When he saw this, he bade my Lady be contented, for it was none of hers; yet she, repining at the sentence of my Lord Chancellor, agreed with the beggar, and gave her a piece of gold which would well have bought three dogs, and so all parties were agreed; every one smiling to see his manner of finding out the truth."[1]

It must be acknowledged that Solomon himself could not have heard and determined the case more wisely or equitably.[2]

But a grave charge has been brought against the conduct of More while Chancellor,—that he was a cruel and even a bloody persecutor of the Lutherans. This is chiefly founded on a story told by Fox, the Martyrologist—" that Burnham, a reformer, was carried out of the Middle Temple to the Chancellor's house at Chelsea, where he continued in free prison awhile, till the time that Sir Thomas More saw that he could not prevail in perverting of him to his sect. Then he cast him into prison in his own house, and whipped him at the tree in his garden called '*the tree of Troth*,' and after sent him to the Tower to be racked."[3] Burnet and other very zealous Protestants have likewise countenanced the supposition that More's house was really converted into a sort of prison of the Inquisition, he himself being the Grand Inquisitor; and that there was a tree in his garden called "*the tree of Troth*." But let us hear what is said on this subject by More himself—allowed on all hands (however erroneous his opinions on religion) to have been the most sincere, candid, and truthful of men :—

[1] More, 121.
[2] For some cases *in part materia*, vid. Rep. Barat. Tem. Sanch. Pan.
[3] Mart. vol. ii. Hist. Reform. vol. iii. "When More was raised to the chief in the ministry, he became a persecutor even to blood, and defiled those hands which were never polluted with bribes."

"Divers of them have said, that of such as were in my house when I was Chancellor, I used to examine them with torments, causing them to be bound to a tree in my garden and there piteously beaten. Except their sure keeping, I never else did cause any such thing to be done unto any of the heretics in all my life, except only twain; one was a child, and a servant of mine in mine own house, whom his father, ere he came to me, had nursed up in such matters, and set him to attend upon George Jay. This Jay did teach the child his ungracious heresy against the blessed sacrament of the altar; which heresy this child, in my house, began to teach another child. And upon that point I caused a servant of mine to strip him, like a child, before mine household, for amendment of himself and ensample of others. Another was one who, after he had fallen into these frantic heresies, soon fell into plain open frenzy; albeit that he had been in Bedlam, and afterwards, by beating and correction, gathered his remembrance. Being therefore set at liberty, his old frenzies fell again into his head. Being informed of his relapse, I caused him to be taken by the constables, and bounden to a tree in the street, before the whole town, and there striped him till he waxed weary. Verily, God be thanked, I hear no harm of him now. And of all who ever came in my hand for heresy, as help me God, else had never any of them any stripe or stroke given them, so much as a fillip in the forehead."[1]

We must come to the conclusion that persons accused of heresy were confined in his house, though not treated with cruelty, and that the supposed tortures consisted in flogging one naughty boy, and administering stripes to one maniac, according to the received notion of the times, as a cure for his malady.[2] The truth is, that More, though in his youth he had been a warm friend to religious toleration, and in his "Utopia" he had published opinions on this subject rather latitudinarian, at last, alarmed by the progress of the Reformation, and shocked by the excesses of some of its votaries in Germany,

---

[1] Apology, c. 36. English Works, 902.
[2] At the Common Law moderate chastisement of a servant might be justified,—and to an action of assault, battery, and false imprisonment, it was a good plea "that the plaintiff, being a lunatic, the defendant arrested him, confined him, *and whipped him.*"

became convinced of the expediency of uniformity of faith, or, at least, conformity in religious observances; but he never strained or rigorously enforced the laws against Lollardy. "It is," says Erasmus, "a sufficient proof of his clemency, that while he was Chancellor no man was put to death for these pestilent dogmas, while so many, at the same period, suffered for them in France, Germany, and the Netherlands."[1] That he was present at the examination of heretics before the Council, and concurred in subjecting them to confinement, cannot be denied; for such was the law, which he willingly obeyed;[2] but we ought rather to wonder at his moderation in an age when the leaders of each sect thought they were bound in duty to Heaven to persecute the votaries of every other. It was not till More had retired from office, and was succeeded by the pliant and inhuman Audley, that heresy was made high treason, and the scaffold flowed with innocent blood.

But More's great stumbling block—which he encountered on entering into office, and which caused his fall—was the divorce. The suit had been evoked before Clement VII. himself at Rome, and there it made no progress, the only object of his Holiness being delay, that he might not offend the Emperor on the one hand, nor, on the other, tempt Henry to set the Papal supremacy at defiance.

The first expedient resorted to, with More's concurrence, was to obtain the opinions of foreign Universities, as well as Oxford and Cambridge, against the legality of a marriage between a man and his brother's widow, the first marriage having been consummated;[3] and, under the title of fees or honoraries, large bribes were offered for a favorable answer. Bologna, Padua, Ferrara, and other Italian Universities responded to Henry's wishes; but he met with no success in Germany, where the influence of the Emperor was felt, and Luther had his revenge of "THE

[1] Erasm. Ep.
[2] He did not disguise his earnest wish to put down the new doctrines in religion. Thus in the epitaph which he wrote for his own tomb, he describes himself as "furibus, homicidis, *hæreticisque molestus*;" and afterwards, in writing to Erasmus, he justifies this expression: "Quod in epitaphio profiteor *hæreticis me molestum fuisse*, ambitiose feci."
[3] This fact was introduced by Henry into his case, but was strenuously denied by Catherine.

DEFENDER OF THE FAITH," by declaring "that it would be more lawful for the King to have two wives at the same time than to separate from Catherine for the purpose of marrying another woman."[1] From France the opinions were divided. Thus the hope of influencing Clement by the universal voice of the Christian world was abandoned.

The next experiment in which More joined, was a letter to the Pope, subscribed by the Lords spiritual and temporal, and certain distinguished Commoners, in the name of the whole nation, complaining in forcible terms of Clement's partiality and tergiversation. "The kingdom was threatened with the calamities of a disputed succession, which could be averted only by the King being enabled to contract a lawful marriage; yet the celebration of such a marriage was prevented by the effectual delays and undue bias of the Pontiff. Nothing remained but to apply the remedy without his interference. This was admitted to be an evil, but it would prove a less evil than the precarious and perilous situation in which England was now placed."[2]

Clement mildly and plausibly replied to this threat, that the danger of a disputed succession in England would be augmented by proceedings contrary to right and justice; that he was ready to proceed with the cause according to the rules of the Church; and that they must not require of him, through gratitude to him, to violate the immutable commandments of God.

Thomas Cromwell had effectually insinuated himself into Henry's confidence by his boldness, versatility, and unscrupulousness; and he strongly counseled an immediate rupture with Rome, which the King resolved upon, unless Clement should yield to his menaces.

With this view parliament was assembled. Cromwell had so well managed the elections, that he had a clear majority in the Lower House ready to second his purposes; and among the Peers, no one hazarded any show of resistance.

---

[1] Luther had a great leaning towards polygamy, and thought that it would be better that a priest should be allowed several wives than none at all, and that the practice of the Patriarchs and Jewish Kings might be safely followed. He gravely writes on this occasion, "Antequam tale repudium probarem, potius Regi permitterem alteram reginam quoque ducere, et exemplo Patrium et Regum duas simul uxores seu Reginas habere."—Luth. Epist. Halæ. [2] Herbert, 331.

The plan was to make it apparent to the world, that the King had both the courage and the power to throw off all dependence upon the see of Rome, if such a step should be necessary for the dissolution of the marriage; but at the same time, not to run the serious hazard to the stability of the throne and the public tranquillity, which might arise from shocking the religious feelings of the people and suddenly changing an ecclesiastical polity as old as the first introduction of Christanity in England.

Lord Chancellor More was now in a very difficult dilemma. The great offices to which he had been raised by the King, the personal favor hitherto constantly shown to him, and the natural tendency of his gentle and quiet disposition, combined to disincline him to resistance against the wishes of his friendly master. On the other hand, his growing dread and horror of heresy, with its train of disorders, and his belief that universal anarchy would be the inevitable result of religious dissensions, made him recoil from designs which were visibly tending towards disunion with the Roman Pontiff, the centre of Catholic union, and the supreme magistrate of the spiritual commonwealth. His opinions, relating to Papal authority, continued moderate and liberal; but he strongly thought that it ought to be respected and upheld as an ancient and venerable control on licentious opinions, and that the necessity for it was more and more evinced by the increasing distractions in the Continental states, where the Reformation was making progress. He resolved to temporise as long as possible—perhaps foreseeing that, if he retired from the King's councils, all restraint would be at an end, and the dreaded catastrophe would be precipitated.

He agreed to an Act, which was actually passed, for preventing appeals to the Court of Rome;[1] and other measures of the same tendency being postponed, he was prevailed upon by the King and Cromwell, at the close of a short session, to go down with twelve spiritual and temporal Peers to the House of Commons, and there to deliver the following address, meant to prepare the world for what might follow:

"You, of this worshipful House, I am sure you be not so ignorant, but you know well that the King, our Sove-

---
[1] 24 Hen. 8, c. 12.

reign Lord, hath married his brother's wife; for she was
both wedded and bedded by his brother Prince Arthur,
and therefore you may surely say that he hath married
his brother's wife if this marriage be good—as so many
clerks do doubt. Wherefore the King, like a virtuous
Prince, willing to be satisfied in his conscience, and also
for the surety of his realm, hath with great deliberation
consulted with great clerks, and hath sent my Lord of
London, here present, to the chief Universities of all
Christendom, to know their opinion and judgment in that
behalf. And although the Universities of Oxford and
Cambridge had been sufficient to discuss the cause, yet
they being in his realm, and to avoid all suspicion of partiality, he hath sent into the realms of France, Italy, the
Pope's dominions, and the Venetians, to know their judgment in that behalf, which have concluded, written, and
sealed their determinations, according as you shall hear
read."

A box was then opened, and many opinions were read
—all on one side, holding the marriage void. Whereupon the Chancellor said —"Now you of this Common
House may report in your countries what you have
seen and heard, and then all men shall perceive that
the King hath not attempted this matter of will or pleasure, as some strangers report, but only for the discharge
of his conscience, and the security of the succession of
his realm. This is the cause of our repair hither to you,
and now we will depart."[1] Whoever reads this address
must perceive the Chancellor's great embarrassment, and
his distressing anxiety to appear to have spoken on this
subject without saying any thing by which he might be
compromised either with the King or the Church.

His state of mind at this time may be gathered from a
dialogue between him and his son-in-law, who thus re-
lates it:—"Walking with me along the Thames' side
at Chelsea, he said unto me, 'Would to our Lord, son
Roper, on condition that three things were well-estab-
lished in Christendom, I were put into a sack, and were
presently cast into the Thames.' 'What great things be
those, sir,' quoth I, 'that should move you so to wish?'
'In faith, son, they be these,' said he. 'The first is, that
whereas the most part of Christian princes be at mortal

[1] 1 Parl. Hist. 515.

war, they were at universal peace. The second that where the Church of Christ is at present sore afflicted with many errors and heresies, it were well settled in perfect uniformity of religion. The third, that the matter of the King's marriage were, to the glory of God and quietness of all parties, brought to a good conclusion.'"[1]

He had great misgivings as to the progress of the reformers, and even anticipated the time when, in England, those who adhered to the old faith be denied religious liberty. "I pray God," he said, "as high as we sit upon the mountains, treading heretics under our feet like ants, live not the day that we gladly would wish to be at league and composition with them to let them have their churches, so that they would be contented to let us have ours quietly."

After the prorogation of parliament, he enjoyed a little respite from the divorce; but being again moved by the King to speed this great matter, he fell down on his knees, and, reminding Henry of his own words on delivering the Great Seal to him, "First look upon God, and after God upon me," added, that nothing had ever so pained him as that he was not able to serve his Grace in that matter without a breach of that original injunction which he had received on the acceptance of his office. The King affected to promise that he would accept his service otherwise, and would continue his favor;—never with that matter molesting his conscience afterwards.

But More soon perceived that there was no chance of the divorce being granted by the court of Rome; that the King's marriage with Anne Boleyn would nevertheless be celebrated; and that measures were resolved upon which he could not, by remaining in office, have the appearance of countenancing without an utter sacrifice of his character.

He therefore made suit, through his "singular good friend the Duke of Norfolk," that he might have leave to resign the Great Seal,—the plea of declining health being urged to soften the King's displeasure. After much hesitation the King consented, and on the 10th day of May, 1532, the ceremony took place at Whitehall, when "it pleased his Highness to say to him, that *for the good service which he before had done him, in any suit which he*

[1] Roper, 24.

should after have unto him, that should either concern his honor (for that word it pleased his Highness to use unto him), *or that should appertain unto his profit, he should not fail to find him a good and gracious Lord..*" "But," says his great-grandson, "how true these words proved let others be judges, when the King not only not bestowed upon him the value of one penny, but took from him and his posterity all that ever he had either given him by himself, or left him by his father, or purchased by himself."[1]

CHAPTER XXXIII.

LIFE OF SIR THOMAS MORE FROM HIS RESIGNATION OF THE GREAT SEAL TILL HIS DEATH.

IT is said that the two happiest days of a man's life are the day when he accepts a high office, and the day when he resigns it; and there can be no doubt that with Sir Thomas More the resignation day was by far the more delightful. He immediately recovered his hilarity and love of jest, and was "*himself again.*"

He had not consulted his wife or his family about resigning, and he concealed from them the step he had taken till next day. This was a holiday; and there being no Court Circular or Newspaper on the breakfast-table, they all went to church at Chelsea, as if nothing extraordinary had happened. "And whereas upon the holydays during his High Chancellorship one of his gentlemen, when the service at the church was done, ordinarily used to come to my Lady his wife's pew-door, and say unto her, '*Madam, my Lord is gone,*' he came into my Lady his wife's pew himself, and making a low courtesy, said unto her, '*Madam, my Lord is gone,*' which she, imagining to be but one of his jests, as he used many unto her, he sadly affirmed unto her, that it was true. This was the way he thought fittest to break the matter unto his wife, who was full of sorrow to hear it."[2]

[1] More, 200. It seems rather strange that the pious biographer should not have thought it worth while to introduce "the chopping off his ancestor's head on the most friviolous of pretexts," as an item in the bill of particulars to prove his Highness's ingratitude and breach of promise.
[2] Roper, 54.

He immediately set about providing for his officers and servants who were to leave him, and he succeeded in placing them with bishops and noblemen. His state barge, which carried him to Westminster Hall, he transferred, with his eight watermen, to his successor. His Fool, who must have been a great proficient in jesting, practicing under such a master, he made over to the Lord Mayor of London, with a stipulation that he should continue to serve the office of fool to the Lord Mayor for the time being."[1]

After this he called together all his children and grandchildren who had dwelt with him, and asked their advice how he might now, in the decay of his ability, bear out the whole charges of them all, as he gladly would have continued to do. When they were all silent—" Then will I (said he) show unto you my mind : I have been brought up at Oxford, at an Inn of Chancery, at Lincoln's Inn, and in the King's Court, from the lowest degree to the highest; and yet have I, in yearly revenues at this present, little left me above a hundred pounds by the year: so that now, if we wish to live together, you must be content to be contribituaries together. But my counsel is, that we fall not to the lowest fare first : we will not, therefore, descend to Oxford fare, nor to the fare of New Inn, but we will begin with the Lincoln's Inn diet, where many right worshipful men, of great account and good years,

[1] "This fool, whose name was Pattison, appears in Holbein's famous picture of the More family. One anecdote of him has been often related. When at a dinner at Guildhall, the subject of his old master having refused to take the oath of supremacy was discussed, the fool exclaimed, 'Why, what aileth him that he will not swear? Wherefore should he stick to swear? I have sworn the oath myself.'"

In the "Il Moro," an Italian account of Sir Thomas More, printed at Florence, and dedicated to Cardinal Pole, there is another anecdote of this jester, supposed to be related by the Chancellor himself, giving us not a very exalted notion of the merriment caused by these simpletons. "Yesterday, while we were dining, Pattison seeing a guest with a very large nose said 'there was one at table who had been trading to the PROMONTORY OF NOSES.' All eyes were turned to the great nose, though we discreetly preserved silence, that the good man might not be abashed. Pattison, perceiving the mistake he had made, tried to set himself right, and said, 'He lies who says the gentleman's nose is large, for on the faith of a true knight it is rather a small one.' At this all being inclined to laugh, I made signs for the fool to be turned out of the room. But Pattison, who boasted that he brought every affair that he commenced to a happy conclusion, resisted, and placing himself in my seat at the head of the table said aloud, with my tone and gesture, 'There is one thing I would have you to know. That gentleman there has not the least bit of nose on his face.'"

do live full well; which if we find ourselves the first year not able to maintain, then will in the next year come down to Oxford fare, where many great, learned, and ancient fathers and doctors are continually conversant; which, if our purses stretch not to maintain neither, then may we after, with bag and wallet, go a begging together, hoping that for pity some good folks will give us their charity, and at every man's door to sing a *Salva Regina*, whereby we shall still keep company, and be merry together."[1]

In those times there were no pensions of £5,000 a year for Ex-Chancellors, nor sinecures for their sons; and More might truly have said—

"Virtute me involvo, probamque
Pauperiem *sine dote* quæro."

He certainly never repented the step he had taken, although, after severe sufferings, it led him to the scaffold; and, but for the persecutions of the tyrant whom he refused to serve, there can be no doubt that he would have spent most happily the remainder of his days in the bosom of his family, ardently engaged in those literary and philosophical pursuits which professional avocations and official duties had so often interrupted. He had not treated the law as a mere trade; and when the first day of term afterwards came round, he had no inclination to join in the procession to Westminster Hall—not participating the feelings of the retired tallow-chandler, who could not keep away from his old shop on "*melting-days.*" He now experienced the delightful calm which he describes in his letter of congratulation on the resignation of Lord Chancellor Warham :—

"I have always esteemed your most reverned fatherhood happy in your courses, not only when you executed with great renown the office of Chancellorship, but also more happy now, when being rid of that great care, you have betaken yourself to a most wished quietness, the better to live to yourself, and to serve God more easily; such a quietness, I say, that is not only more pleasing than all these troublesome businesses, but also more honorable far, in my judgment, than all those honors which you there enjoyed. Wherefore many, and amongst them myself, do applaud and admire this your act, which pro-

[1] More, 203.

ceeded from a mind, I know not whether more modest in that you would willingly forsake so magnificent a place, or more heroical in that you would condemn it, or more innocent in that you feared not to depose yourself from it; but, surely, most excellent and prudent it was to do so; for which, your rare deed, I cannot utter unto you how I rejoice for your sake, and how much I congratulate you for it, seeing your fatherhood to enjoy so honorable a fame, and to have obtained so rare a glory, by sequestering yourself far from all worldly businesses, from all tumults of causes, and to bestow the rest of your days, with a peaceable conscience for all your life past, in a quiet calmness, giving yourself wholly to your book, and to true Christian philosophy."[1]

Writing now to Erasmus, he says that "he himself had obtained what, from a child, he had continually wished—that, being freed from business and public affairs, he might live for a time only to God and himself."

Accordingly, he passed the first year of his retirement in reviving his recollection of favorite authors, in bringing up his acquaintance with the advancing literature of the day, in retouching his own writings, and planning new works for the further increase of his fame and the good of his fellow-creatures. His happiness was only alloyed by witnessing the measures in progress under his successor and Cromwell, which he had the sagacity to foresee would soon lead to others more violent and more mischievous.

The threats to break off all intercourse with Rome having proved ineffectual, it was at last openly resolved to carry them into effect, and, without any divorce from Catherine by the Pope's authority, that the King should marry Anne Boleyn. In September, 1532, she was created Marchioness of Pembroke, and, notwithstanding the gallant defense of Burnet and other zealous Protestants, who think that the credit of the Reformation depends upon her purity, it seems probable that Queen Catherine having been banished from Court, and taken up her abode at Ampthill, Anne, in the prospect of the performance of the ceremony, had, after a resistance of nearly six years, consented to live with Henry as his wife.[2] On the 25th of

[1] More, 207.
[2] I must be allowed to say that I consider still more absurd the attempts of Romish zealots to make her out to have been a female of abandoned character from her early youth. See Lingard, vol. vi. ch. iii.

January, 1533, she being then in a state of pregnancy, they were privately married.'

The marriage was kept secret till Easter following, when she was declared Queen, and orders were given for her coronation.²

The troubles of the Ex-Chancellor now began. To give countenance to the ceremony, he was invited to be present by three Bishops as the King's messengers, who likewise offered him £20 to buy a dress suitable to the occasion. He declined the invitation, and thereby gave mortal offense to the new Queen, who ever afterwards urged violent proceedings against him. But instead of considering him disloyal or morose, we ought rather to condemn the base servility of the clergy and nobility who yielded to every caprice of the tyrant under whom they trembled, and now heedlessly acquiesced in a measure which might have been the cause of a civil war as bloody as that between the houses of York and Lancaster. There had as yet been no sentence of divorce, nor act of parliament, to dissolve Henry's first marriage; all lawyers, in all countries, agreed that it was valid till set aside by competent authority; and the best lawyers were then of the opinion, at which I believe those most competent to consider the question have since arrived, that even upon the supposition of the consummation of Catherine's marriage with Arthur (which she, a most sincere and pious lady, always solemnly denied, and which Henry, when she appealed to him,³ did not venture to assert), the marriage was absolutely valid,— as, according to the then existing law, the Pope's dispensation was sufficient to remove the objection of affinity; and there is no ground for saying that the Pope, in granting the dispensation, exceeded his powers by expressly violating any divine precept. Little weight is to be attributed to the divorce pronounced by Cranmer, holding his court at Dunstable, whether Catherine

---

[1] An attempt has been made to show a marriage on the 14th Nov. 1532, nine months before the birth of Queen Elizabeth, which happened on the 7th Sept. 1533; but this is disproved by the testimony of Cranmer himself. See 1 Hallam's Const. Hist. p. 84.

[2] It is curious that Shakspeare, living so near the time, places the marriage and coronation of Anne in the lifetime of Cardinal Wolsey, who died three years before; but the dramatist is not more inaccurate as to dates than most of our prose historians of that period. See *Hen. VIII.* act iv.

[3] "De integritate corporis usque ad secundas nuptias servatâ."

appeared in it or not; for there was another suit for the same cause, which had been regularly commenced in England before Wolsey and Campeggio, still pending at Rome. But all doubt as to the legitimacy of Elizabeth was removed, not only by a subsequent marriage between her parents after Cranmer's divorce, and a judgment by him that their marriage was valid, but by an act of the legislature,[1] which in our country has always been supreme, notwithstanding any opposition of bishops, popes, or councils.

The first attempt to wreak vengeance on More for his obstinacy, was by summoning him before the Privy Council to answer a charge of having been guilty of bribery while he was Lord Chancellor. One Parnell was induced to complain of a decree obtained against him by his adversary Vaughan, whose wife, it was alleged, had bribed the Chancellor with a gilt cup. The accused party surprised the Council at first by owning that "he had received the cup as a new year's gift." Lord Wiltshire, the King's father-in-law, indecently but prematurely exulted. "Lo! did I not tell you, my Lords, that you would find this matter true?" "But, my Lords," replied More, "hear the other part of my tale. After having drunk to her of wine, with which my butler had filled the cup, and when she had pledged me, I restored it to her, and would listen to no refusal."[2]

The only other cases of bribery brought forward against him were, his acceptance of a gilt cup from a suitor of the name of Gresham, after he had given Gresham a cup of greater value for it in exchange; and his acceptance from a Mrs. Croker, for whom he had made a decree against Lord Arundel, of a pair of gloves, in which were contained £40 in angels; but he had told her with a smile, that though it were ill manners to refuse a lady's present, and he should keep the gloves, he must return the gold, which he forced her to carry back.[3]

The next proceeding against him, equally without foundation, wore a more alarming aspect; and, at one time, seemed fraught with destruction to him. A bill was introduced into parliament to attaint of high treason Elizabeth Barton, a woman commonly called "the Holy Maid of Kent," and her associates, upon the suggestion,

[1] 25 Hen. 8 c. 22.   [2] More, 221.   [3] Ibid. 221.

that, under pretense of revelations and miracles, she had spoken disrespectfully of the King, and insisted that Catherine was still his lawful wife. She had obtained a great reputation for piety; and some sensible men of that age were inclined to think that supernatural gifts were conferred upon her by Heaven. Among these were Archbishop Warham, Fisher, Bishop of Rochester, and probably Sir Thomas More.[1] Being in the convent at Sion, More was prevailed upon to see and converse with her there; but he most studiously prevented her from saying a word to him about the King's divorce, the King's marriage, or the King's supremacy, or any such subject. However, this interview being reported at Court, More's name was introduced into the bill of attainder as an accomplice; not with the intention at first of making him a sacrifice, but in the expectation that, under the impending peril, his constancy would yield. He begged to be heard, to make his defense against the bill openly at the bar; but this proposal raised great alarm from his legal knowledge and his eloquence, and the influence of his name. It was resolved, therefore, that he should only be heard privately before a committee named by the King, consisting of Cranmer, the new Archbishop, Audley, the new Chancellor, the Duke of Norfolk, and Cromwell.

When he came before them, in respect of the high office he had filled, they received him courteously, requesting him to sit down with them; but this he would on no account consent to. Having got him among them, instead of discussing his guilt or innocence, on the charge of treason made against him by the bill of attainder, they tried to make a convert of him to the King's views. They began quietly—telling him how many ways the King's Majesty had showed his love and favor towards him—how gladly he would have had him continue in his office—how desirous he was to have heaped still more and more benefits upon him—and, finally, that he could ask no worldly honor or profit at his Highness's hands but that he should obtain it, so that he would add his consent to

---

[1] We need not wonder at the credulity of the most eminent men of that age, when in our own day a nobleman, distinguished by his talents and his eloquence, as well as by his illustrious birth, has published a pamphlet to support two contemporaneous miraculous maids, the "Estatica" and the "Adolorata."

that which the King, the Parliament, the Bishops, and many Universities had pronounced for reason and Scripture.

The Ex-Chancellor fully admitted the many obligations the King had laid upon him; but mildly observed that he hoped never to have heard of this matter any more, as his Highness, like a gracious Prince, knowing his mind therein, had promised no more to molest him therewith; since which time, he had seen no reason to change; and if he could, there was no one in the whole world would be more joyful.

Seeing that persuasion would not move him, " then began they more terribly to threaten him; saying, the King's Majesty had given them in command expressly, if they could by no gentle means win him, they should in his name with great indignation charge him, that never there was servant so villanous to his Sovereign, nor any subject so traitorous to his Prince, as he."—And what was this terrible accusation?—that More had provoked the King to set forth the book on the seven sacraments, and the maintenance of the Pope's authority,—whereby the title of " Defender of the Faith" had been gained, but in reality a sword had been put into the Pope's hand to fight against him, to his great dishonor in all parts of Christendom.

His answer lets us curiously into the secret history of Henry's refutation of Luther. " My Lords," answered he, " these terrors be frights for children, and not for me; but to answer that wherewith you chiefly burthen me, I believe the King's Highness, of his honor, will never lay that book to my charge; for there is none that can, in that point, say more for my clearance than himself, who right well knoweth that I never was procurer, promoter nor counselor of his Majesty thereunto: only after it was finished, by his Grace's appointment, and *the consent of the makers of the same.* I only sorted out and placed in order the principal matters therein; wherein when I had found the Pope's authority highly advanced, and with strange arguments mightily defended, I said thus to his Grace: 'I must put your Highness in mind of one thing —the Pope, as your Majesty well knoweth, is a prince, as you are, in league with all other Christian princes; it may hereafter fall out that your Grace and he may vary upon some points of the league, whereupon may grow breach of amity between you both; therefore I think it best that place be amended, and his authority more slenderly touched.' 'Nay,' said the King, 'that it shall not; we are so much bound to the See of Rome, that we cannot do too much honor unto it. Whatsoever impediment be to the contrary, we will set forth that authority to the uttermost; for we have received from the See our Crown imperial!' which till his Grace with his own mouth so told me, I never heard before. Which things well considered, I trust when his Majesty shall be truly informed thereof, and call to his gracious remembrance my sayings and doings in that behalf, his Highness will never speak more of it, but will clear me himself." Thereupon they, with great displeasure, dismissed him: and knowing whom, in the defense of his innocence, he taunted and defied, he well knew the price he was to pay for his boldness.[1]

Nevertheless, he was in high spirits, and taking boat for Chelsea, his son-in-law, Roper, who accompanied him, believed from his merriment by the way, that his name had been struck out of the bill. When they were landed, and walking in the garden, Roper said, "I trust, sir, all is well, you are so merry." "It is so indeed, son, thank God." "Are you, then, sir, put out of the bill?" "Wouldest thou know, son, why I am so joyful? *In good faith I rejoice that I have given the devil a foul fall; because I have with those Lords gone so far, that without great shame I can never go back.*" This heartfelt exultation at having, after a struggle to which he felt the weakness of human nature might have been unequal, gained the victory in his own mind, and though with the almost certain sacrifice of life, made it impossible to resile,—bestows a greatness on these simple and familiar words which belongs to few uninspired sayings in ancient or modern times.[2]

The result of the conference of the four councillors being reported by them to Henry, he flew into a transport of rage, swore that More should be included in the attainder, and said, when the bill was to be discussed, he himself should be personally present to ensure its passing. Then they all dropped down on their knees before him and implored him to forbear; for if, sitting on the throne,

[1] More, 225.

he should receive an overthrow, it would not only encourage his subjects ever after to contemn him, but also redound to his dishonor among foreign nations—adding, that "they doubted not they should find a more meet occasion to *serve his turn*, for that in this case of the Nun he was well known to be clearly innocent." Henry was obliged to yield, and once in his reign his thirst for blood was not immediately gratified.

Cromwell having next day informed Roper that his father-in-law was put out of the bill, this intelligence reached More himself by the lips of his favorite daughter, when he calmly said, "In faith, Meg, *quod differtur non aufertur*,—what is postponed is not abandoned."

A few days afterwards, the Duke of Norfolk made a last attempt upon him, saying, "By the mass, Master More, it is perilous striving with princes; therefore I could wish you, as a friend, to incline to the King's pleasure, for by God's body, Master More, *indignatio principis mors est*." "Is that all?" said Sir Thomas; "why then there is no more difference between your Grace and me, but that I shall die to-day, and you to-morrow." Norfolk, it is well known, was attainted, ordered for execution, and only saved by Henry's death.

But More's other prophecy of the same sort was literally fulfilled. Having asked his daughter Roper how the world went, and how Queen Anne did, "In faith, father," said she, "never better; there is nothing else in the Court but dancing and sporting." "Never better!" said he. "Alas! Meg, it pitieth me to remember unto what misery, poor soul, she will shortly come. These dances of hers will prove such dances that she will spurn our heads off like footballs; but it will not be long ere her head will dance the like dance."

The policy of Henry and his ministers now was to conform to the new *régime*, a course which More had anticipated with apprehension, when he was told by Roper of the King's marriage and final rupture with Rome, saying, "God give grace, son, that these matters within a while be not confirmed with *oaths*."

The Lord Chancellor, Cranmer, Cromwell, and the Abbot of Westminster were appointed commissioners to ad-

---

[1] More, 231.

minister the required oath, drawn up in a form which the law did not then authorize. Statutes had been passed to settle the succession to the crown on the issue of the King's present marriage, and to cut off intercourse with Rome by prohibiting the accustomed payment of first fruits, or Peter's pence, and forbidding appeals to the Pope or dispensations from him; but no statute had passed to constitute the King supreme head of the Church, or to annex any penalty to the denial of his supremacy.[1] Nevertheless an oath was framed " to bear faith and true obedience to the King, and the issue of his present marriage with Queen Anne, *to acknowledge him the Head of the Church of England, and to renounce all obedience to the Bishop of Rome, as having no more power than any other bishop.*"

The administration of this oath began a few days after the Holy Maid of Kent and her associates, under the act of attainder against them, had been hanged and beheaded at Tyburn; and it was taken very freely by the clergy. It had not yet been propounded to any layman, and the commissioners resolved to begin with Sir Thomas More, knowing that if he should submit, no farther resistance need be apprehended.

For a considerable while he had been expecting a summons before the inquisitors, and that his family might be alarmed as little as possible when it should really come, he hired a man dressed as a poursuivant, suddenly to come to his house, while they sat at dinner, and knocking loudly at his door, to warn him to appear next day before the commissioners. The were at first in great consternation; but he soon relieved them by explaining the jest.

In sad earnest early in the morning of the 13th of April, 1534, the real poursuivant entered the house, and summoned him to appear before the commissioners that day at Lambeth. According to his custom when he entered on any matter of importance (as when he was first chosen

---

[1] All the biographers of More, from Roper downwards, have fallen into a mistake upon this subject, although they have recorded More's own declaration that the warrant of his commitment was bad in point of law; but a reference to the Statute Book makes the matter clear beyond all question; for he was committed to the Tower in April 1534, and the session of parliament in which the act of supremacy was passed did not meet till the month of November following. 26 H. 8, c. 1.

of the Privy Council, sent Ambassador, chosen Speaker, made Lord Chancellor, or engaged in any weighty undertaking), he went to church "to be confessed, to hear Mass, and to be houseled;" but from a foreboding mind he could not trust himself to take leave of his family with his usual marks of affection: "whereas he evermore used before, at his departure from his wife and children, whom he tenderly loved, to have them bring him to his boat, and there to kiss them and bid them all farewell,—then would he suffer none of them forth of the gate to follow him, but pulled the wicket after him, and shut them all from him, and with a heavy heart took boat towards Lambeth." On his way he whispered into the ear of his son-in-law who accompanied him, "I thank our Lord the field is won,"[1]—indicating an entire confidence in his own constancy.

Being brought before the commissioners, and the oath being tendered to him, he referred to the statute and declared his readiness to swear that he would maintain and defend the order of succession to the crown, as established by parliament; he disclaimed all censure on those who had simply taken the oath; but it was impossible that he should swear to the whole contents of it without wounding his conscience. He was commanded to walk in the garden awhile, and the oath was administered to many others. When called in again, the list of those who had taken it was shown to him, and he was threatened with the King's special displeasure for his recusancy without any reason assigned. He answered that "his reasons might exasperate the King still more; but he would assign them on his Majesty's assurance that they should not offend him nor prove dangerous to himself." The commissioners observed, that such assurances could be no defense against a legal charge. He offered to trust himself to the King's honor; but they would listen to no qualification or explanation. Cranmer, with some subtlety, argued that his disclaiming all blame of those who had sworn, showed that he thought it only doubtful, whether the oath was unlawful; whereas the obligation to obey the King was absolutely certain. He might have replied, that an oath on matter of opinion might be lawfully taken by one man, and could not be taken without

---

[1] More, 70.

perjury by another; but he contented himself with repeating his offer to swear to the succession, and his refusal to go further. Thereupon he was given in ward to the Abbot of Westminster, in the hope that the King might relent. It is said that, a council being held, the qualified oath would would have been accepted had it not been that "Queen Anne, by her importunate clamors, did exasperate the King," and at the end of four days, the oath containing an acknowledgment of the King's supremacy, and an abjuration of the Bishop of Rome, being again tendered and refused, More was committed close prisoner to the Tower of London.

Having delivered his upper garment as *garnish* to the porter standing at the Traitor's Gate, by which he entered, he was conducted by "Master Lieutenant" to his lodging, where he swore John a Wood, his servant appointed to attend him, "that if he should see or hear him at any time write or speak any matter against the King or the state of the realm, he should open it to the Lieutenant, that it might incontinent be revealed to the Council.

The Lieutenant apologizing for the poor cheer the place furnished, his prisoner waggishly answered, "Assure yourself I do not mislike my cheer; but whenever I do, then spare not to thrust me out of your doors."

In about a month he was permitted to receive a visit from his dearly beloved daughter, whom he tried to comfort by saying, "I believe, Meg, they that have put me here ween they have done me a high displeasure; but, I assure thee on my faith, mine own good daughter, if it had not been for my wife, and ye that be my children, I would not have failed, long ere this, to have closed myself in as straight a room, and straighter too. But since I am come hither without mine own desert, I trust that God, by his goodness, will discharge me of my care, and, with his gracious help, supply my lack among you." Having pointed out to her the illegality of his imprisonment, there being then no statute to authorize the required oath, he could not refrain from expressing some indignation against the King's advisers. "And surely, daughter, it is a great pity that any Christian Prince should, by a flexible Council ready to follow his affections, and by a weak clergy, lacking grace constantly to stand to their learning, with flattery be so shamefully abused."

It unluckily chanced while she was with him on another occasion, that in their sight Reynolds, the Abbot of Sion, and three monks of the Charterhouse were marched out for execution on account of the supremacy. He exclaimed, "Lo! dost though not see, Meg, that these blessed fathers be now as cheerfully going to their deaths as bridegrooms to their marriage?" and he tenderly tried to strengthen her mind for the like destiny befalling himself. Having conceived, from some expression he used, that she wished him to yield, he wrote a letter, rebuking her supposed purpose with the utmost vehemence of affection, and concluding with an assurance, "that none of the terrible things that might happen to him touched him so near, or were so grievous to him, as that his dearly beloved child, whose judgment he so much valued, should labor to persuade him to do what would be contrary to his conscience." Margaret's reply was worthy of herself. "She submits reverently to his faithful and delectable letter, the faithful messenger of his vertuous mind," and almost rejoices in his victory over all earth-born cares. She subscribes herself, "Your own most loving, obedient daughter and bedeswoman, Margaret Roper, who desireth above all earthly things, to be in John Wood's stede, to do you some service."

He had a very different subject to deal with when he received a visit from his wife, who had leave to see him, in the hope that she might break his constancy. On her entrance, like a plain rude woman, and somewhat worldly, she thus saluted him: "What, the goodyear, Mr. More, I marvel that you, who have been hitherto always taken for a wise man, will now so play the fool as to lie here in this close, filthy prison, and be content to be shut up thus with mice and rats, when you might be abroad at your liberty, with the favor and good will both of the King and his Council, if you would but do as the Bishops and best learned of his realm have done; and, seeing you have at Chelsea a right fair house, your library, your books, your gallery, and all other necessaries so handsome about you, where you might, in company with me, your wife, your children and household, be merry, I muse what, a God's name, you mean, here thus fondly to tarry." Having heard her out,—preserving his good humor, he said to her, with a cheerful countenance, "I pray thee, good Mrs

Alice, tell me one thing." "What is it?" saith she. "Is not this house as near heaven as my own?" She could only come out with her favorite interjection, which she used, like Dame Quickly, to express impatience, "Tilly vally! Tilly vally!"[1] By pointing out the short time he could enjoy his house compared with the long and secure tenure of heaven, and various other arguments and illustrations, he, to no purpose, tried to convince her that it was better to remain in the Tower than to dishonor himself. He was little moved by her persuasions, thinking (but not saying) as Job, when tempted by his wife, "Quasi una ex stultis mulieribus locuta es."

We must render her the justice to recollect, however, that she continued actively to do what she could for his comfort; and in a subsequent part of his imprisonment, when all his property had been seized, she actually sold her wearing apparel to raise money to provide necessaries for him.[2]

The parliament, which had answered Henry's purposes so slavishly that it was kept on foot for six years, met again on the 4th of November, and proceeded to pass an act of attainder for misprision of treason against More, and Fisher, Bishop of Rochester, the only surviving minister of Henry VII., and the son's early tutor, councillor and friend,—on the ground that they had refused to take the oath of supremacy,—for which alleged offense, created by no law, they were to forfeit all their property, and to be subject to perpetual imprisonment.[3] But this was insufficient for the royal vengeance; and soon after, not only was an act passed to declare the King the Supreme Head of the Church,[4] but authority was given to require an oath acknowledging the supremacy,[5] and it was declared to be high treason by words or writing to deny it.[6]

---

[1] "*Hostess (addressing Falstaff). Tilly-fally!* Sir John. Never tell me your ancient swaggerer comes not in my doors."—*Hen. IV., Part II.*, act ii scene 4.

[2] See her letter to Cromwell, in which she says, "I pass weekly 15 shillings for the bord-wages of my poure husband and his servant, for the mayntaining whereof I have been compellyd of verey necessyte to sell part of myn apparel, for lack of other substance to make money of."—App. to Hunter's ed. of More.

[3] This is not in the statutes at large, but will be found in the Statutes of the Realm, vol. iv. 527, 528.   [4] 26 Hen 8, c. 1.   [5] 26 Hen. 8, c. 2.

[6] 25 Hen. 8, c. 3. The offense described in this last act applicable to the supremacy, is to "desire to deprive the King of his dignity, title, or name of

As More was now actually suffering punishment by imprisonment and forfeiture of his property for having refused to take the oath, it was impossible to make the enactment about oaths, the foundation of a new prosecution, and the plan adopted was to inveigle him into a verbal denial of the supremacy, and so to proceed against him for high treason.

With this view, the Lord Chancellor, the Dukes of Norfolk and Suffolk, Cromwell, and others of the Privy Council, several times came to him in the Tower, "to procure him by all means and policies they could, either to confess precisely the King's supremacy, or plainly to deny it." But he was constantly on his guard, and they could get nothing more from him than "that the statute was like a two-edged sword: if he should speak against it, he should procure the death of his body; and if he should consent unto it, he should procure the death of his soul."

The next contrivance was plotted and executed by one who has brought a greater stain upon the bar of England than any member of the profession to which I am proud to belong,—a profession generally distinguished, even in bad times, for integrity and independence, and never before or since so far degraded as to have its honors won by palpable fraud, chicanery, and perjury. Rich *(horresco referens)*,—afterwards Lord Chancellor,—had just been made Solicitor General, on an understanding that he was effectually to put in force the recent acts against all recusants, and most especially against the refractory ex-Chancellor. Accordingly, fortified by an order of the Council, he accompanied Sir Richard Southwell and a Mr. Palmer to the Tower for the avowed purpose of depriving More of the small library with which he had hitherto been permitted to soothe his solitude. While they were packing up the books, Rich, under pretense of ancient friendship, fell into conversation with him; and in a familiar and confidential tone, after a compliment to his wisdom and learning, put a case to him: "Admit that there were an act of parliament made, that all the realm should take me for King, would not you, Mr. More, take me for King?" "Yes, sir," said Sir Thomas, "that I would." Rich, much elated, said, "I put the case further,—that there

his royal estates;"—and "Supreme Head of the Church" coming within this description, to deny the supremacy was thus ingeniously made high treason.

were an act of parliament that all the realm should take me for Pope, would you not then take me for Pope?" "For answer," said Sir Thomas, "to your first case,— "the parliament may well meddle with the state of temporal princes; but to make answer to your other case,— Suppose that parliament should make a law that God should not be God, would you then, Mr. Rich, say so?" "No, sir," said Mr. Solicitor, "that I would not; for no parliament could make such a law." More, suspecting his drift, made no reply; the conversation took another turn; and, the books being carried off, they soon after parted.

Trusting rather to partial judges and a packed jury than the evidence which could be brought forward against him, a special commission was issued for bringing Sir Thomas More to a solemn trial,—the commissioners being the Lord Chancellor Audley, the Duke of Norfolk, Fitzjames and Fitzherbert, the Chief Justices, and several puisne Judges. They sat in the Court of King's Bench at Westminster Hall.[1] The arraignment took place on the 7th of May, but the trial was postponed till the 1st of July, in the hope of strengthening the case for the Crown.

On the morning of the trial, More was led on foot, in a coarse woolen gown, through the most frequented streets, from the Tower to Westminster Hall. The color of his hair, which had become gray since he last appeared in public, his face, which though still cheerful, was pale and emaciated, his bent posture and his feeble steps, which he was obliged to support with his staff, showed the rigor of his confinement, and excited the sympathy of the people, instead of impressing them, as was intended, with dread of the royal authority. When, sordidly dressed, he held up his hand as a criminal in that place, where, arrayed in his magisterial robes and surrounded by crowds who watched his smile, he had been accustomed on his knees to ask his father's blessing before mounting his own tribunal to determine, as sole judge, on the most important rights of the highest subjects in the realm,—a general feeling of horror and commiseration ran through the spectators;—and after the lapse of three centuries, during which statesmen, prelates, and kings, have been unjustly brought to trial under the same roof,—considering

[1] From this circumstance it has been erroneously stated that this was a trial at bar in the Court of King's Bench.

the splendor of his talents, the greatness of his acquirements, and the innocence of his life, we must still regard his murder as the blackest crime that has ever been perpetrated in England under the forms of law.

Sir Christopher Hale, the Attorney General, who conducted the prosecution, with some appearance of candor (strongly contrasted with the undisguised asperity of Mr. Solicitor Rich, who assisted him), began with reading the indictment, which was of enormous length, but contained four principal charges:—1st, The opinion the prisoner had given on the King's marriage. 2ndly, That he had written certain letters to Bishop Fisher encouraging him to resist. 3rdly, That he had refused to acknowledge the King's supremacy; and, 4thly, That he had positively denied it, and thereby attempted to deprive the King of his dignity and title. When the reading of the indictment was over, the Lord Chancellor made a last attempt to bend the resolution of the prisoner by saying, "You see how grievously you have offended his Majesty, yet he is so merciful, that if you will lay away your obstinacy and change your opinion, we hope you may obtain pardon." More calmly replied, "Most noble Lords, I have great cause to thank your Honors for this your courtesy; but I beseech Almighty God that I may continue in the mind I am in, through his grace, unto death."

The last was the only charge in the indictment which was at all sufficient in point of law to incur the pains of treason; and it was unsupported by evidence. The Counsel for the Crown at first contented themselves with putting in the prisoner's examinations, showing that he had declined answering the questions propounded to him by the Privy Councillors, with his answer, "that the statute was a two-edged sword." An excuse was made for not proving the supposed letters to Fisher, on the ground that they had been destroyed.

The Lord Chancellor, instead of at once directing an acquittal, called upon the prisoner for his defense. A deep silence now prevailed—all present held their breath —every eye was fixed upon the victim. More was begining with expressing his apprehension "lest, his memory and wit being decayed with his health of body through his long imprisonment, he should not be able properly to meet all the matters alleged against him," when he found that he was unable to support himself by his staff, and his judges evinced one touch of humanity by ordering him a chair. When he was seated, after a few preliminary observations, he considered the charges in their order. "As to the marriage," he said, "I confess that I always told the King my opinion thereon as my conscience dictated unto me, which I neither ever would, nor ought to have concealed; for which I am so far from thinking myself guilty of high treason, as that of the contrary, I being demanded my opinion by so great a Prince on a matter of such importance, whereupon the quietness of a kingdom dependeth, I should have basely flattered him if I had not uttered the truth: then I might have been accused as a wicked subject, and a perfidious traitor to God. If herein I have offended the King, it must be an offense to tell one's mind plainly when our Prince asketh our advice." 2. As to the letters to Fisher, he himself stated the contents of them, and showed that they were free from all blame. 3. On the charge that he had declined his opinion, when interrogated, respecting the supremacy, he triumphantly answered, "that he could not transgress any law, or incur any crime of treason, by holding his peace, God only being judge of our secret thoughts." Here he was interrupted by Mr. Attorney, who said, "Although we had not one word or deed to object against you, yet have we your silence, when asked whether you acknowledged the King to be Supreme Head of the Church, which is an evident sign of a malicious mind." But Mr. Attorney was put down (and notwithstanding the gravity of the occasion, there was probably a laugh against him) by More quietly reminding him of the maxim among civilians and canonists—"Qui tacet, consentire videtur." "He that holdeth his tongue is taken to consent." 4. On the last charge he argued, that the only proof was his saying that "the statute was a two-edged sword," which was meant as a reason for his declining to answer, and could not possibly be construed into a positive denial of the King's supremacy. He concluded with a solemn avowal, that "he never spake word against this law to any living man."

The jury, biassed as they were, seeing that if they credited all the evidence, there was not the shadow of a case against the prisoner, were about to acquit him; the

Judges were in dismay—the Attorney General stood aghast—when Mr. Solicitor, to his eternal disgrace, and to the eternal disgrace of the Court who permitted such an outrage on decency, left the bar, and presented himself as a witness for the Crown. Being sworn, he detailed the confidential conversation he had had with the prisoner in the Tower on the occasion of the removal of the books;—and falsely added, that upon his admitting that "no parliament could make a law that God should not be God," Sir Thomas declared, "No more could the parliament make the King Supreme Head of the Church."

The prisoner's withering reply must have made the mean and guilty wretch feel compunction and shame, for which his subsequent elevation must have been a miserable recompense; "If I were a man, my Lords, that did not regard an oath, I needed not at this time in this place, as is well known unto every one, to stand as an accused person. And if this oath, Mr. Rich, which you have taken be true, then I pray that I may never see God in the face; which I would not say were it otherwise to gain the whole world." Having truly related the whole conversation, he continued, "In good faith, Mr. Rich, I am more sorry for your perjury than for mine own peril. Know you that neither I, nor any man else to my knowledge, ever took you to be a man of such credit as either I or any other would vouchsafe to communicate with you in any matter of importance. As you well know, I have been acquainted with your manner of life and conversation a long space, even from your youth upwards; for we dwelt long together in one parish; where as yourself can well tell (I am sorry you compel me to speak it) you were always esteemed very light of your tongue, a great dicer and gamester, and not of any commendable fame either there or in the Temple, the Inn to which you have belonged. Can it therefore seem likely to your honorable Lordships, that, in so weighty a cause, I should so unadvisedly overshoot myself as to trust Mr. Rich, a man always reputed of me for one of so little truth and honesty, about my sovereign Lord the King, to whom I am so deeply indebted for his manifold favors, or any of his noble and grave counselors, that I should declare only to him the secrets of my conscience, touching the King's supremacy, the special point and only mark so long sought for at my hands, which I never did nor ever would reveal after the statute once made, either to the King's Highness himself, or to any of his noble counsellors, as it is well known to your Honors, who have been sent for no other purpose at sundry times from his Majesty's person to me in the Tower? I refer it to your judgments, my Lords, whether this can seem a thing credible unto any of you."

This address produced a deep effect upon the by-standers, and even on the packed jury; and Mr. Solicitor was so much alarmed, that, resuming his capacity of counsel for the Crown, he called and examined Sir Richard Southwell and Mr. Palmer, in the hope that they might be as regardless of truth as himself, and corroborate his testimony; but they both said they were so busy in trussing up the books in a sack, they gave no ear to the conversation.

The Chief Commissioner, however, gallantly restored the fortune of the day; and in an ingenious, animated, and sarcastic summing up, pointed out the enormity of the offense charged;—the danger to the King and the public tranquillity from the courses followed by the prisoner;—that the evidence of the Solicitor General, which he said was evidently given with reluctance and from a pure motive, stood uncontradicted, if not corroborated, as the denial of the prisoner could not be taken into account;—that as the speech related by the witness undoubtedly expressed the real sentiments of the prisoner, and was only drawing a necessary inference, there was every probability that it was spoken; and that, if the witness was believed, the case for the Crown was established.

The jury retired from the bar, and in about a quarter of an hour (to the horror, if not the surprise, of the audience) brought in a verdict of GUILTY; "for," says his descendant, "they knew what the King would have done in that case."[1] But it is possible that being all zealous Protestants, who looked with detestation on our intercourse with the Pope, and considering that the King's

---

[1] It is hardly possible to read without a smile the statement of the verdict by Erasmus in his "Epistola de Morte Thomæ Mori:" "Qui [duodecim viri] quum per horæ quartam partem secessissent, reversi sunt ad principes ac judices delegatos ac pronunciarunt KILLIM, hoc est, *dignus est morte.*"

supremacy could not be honestly doubted, they concluded that, by convicting a Papist, they should be doing good service to religion and the state,—and that, misled by the sophistry and eloquence of the presiding Judge, they believed that they returned an honest verdict.

Audley was so delighted, that, forgetting the established forms of proceeding on such an occasion, he eagerly began to pronounce judgment.

More interrupted him, and his pulse still beating as temperately as if sitting in his library at Chelsea talking to Erasmus, " My Lord," said he, " when I was towards the law, the manner in such cases was to ask the prisoner before sentence whether he could give any reason why judgment should not proceed against him." The Chancellor in some confusion owned his mistake, and put the question.

More was now driven to deny the power of parliament to pass the statute transferring the Headship of the Church from the Pope to the King, and he took some exceptions to the frame of the indictment. The Chancellor, being loth to have the whole burden of this condemnation to lie upon himself, asked openly the advice of my Lord Chief Justice of England, Sir John Fitzjames, "whether this indictment were sufficient, or no?"— *Fitzjames*, C. J. " My Lords all, by St. Gillian (ever his oath), I must needs confess, that if the act of parliament be not unlawful, then the indictment is not, in my conscience, insufficient."[1]

Lord Chancellor. " Lo! my Lords, lo! You hear what my Lord Chief Justice saith. *Quod adhuc desideramus testimonium? Reus est mortis.*" He then pronounced upon him the frightful sentence in cases of treason, concluding with ordering that his four quarters should be set over four gates of the city, and his head upon London Bridge.

The prisoner had hitherto refrained from expressing his

[1] Sharon Turner, actuated by his sense of the "mild and friendly temper" of Henry VIII. (taking a very different view of his character from Wolsey or More, when they were most familiar and in highest favor with him), is desirous of palliating this prosecution; and a full copy of the indictment not being forthcoming, supposes that there were other charges against More of which we know nothing; but the whole course of the proceeding, as well as all contemporary evidence, shows that he was tried under 26 H. 8, c, 13, for "imagining to deprive the King of his title and dignity,"—the denial of the supremacy being the overt act relied upon.—See *Turn. Hist. H. VIII.*

opinion on the question of the supremacy, lest he might appear to be wantonly courting his doom; but he now said, with temper and firmness, that, after seven years' study, he never could find that a layman could be the head of the church. Taking the position to mean, as we understand it,—that the Sovereign, representing the civil power of the state, is supreme,—it may easily be assented to;—but in Henry's own sense, that he was substituted for the Pope, and that all the powers claimed by the Pope in ecclesiastical affairs were transferred to him, and might be lawfully exercised by him,—it is contrary to reason, and is unfounded in Scripture, and would truly make any church *Erastian* in which it is recognized. I therefore cannot say, with Hume, that More wanted " a better cause, more free from weakness and superstition."

The Lord Chancellor asked him if he was wiser than all the learned men in Europe. He answered, that almost the whole of Christendom was of his way of thinking.

The Judges courteously offered to listen to him if he had any thing more to say. He thus answered:—"This farther only have I to say, my Lords, that like as the blessed apostle St. Paul was present and consenting to the death of the protomartyr St. Stephen, keeping their clothes that stoned him to death, and yet they be now twain holy saints in heaven, and there shall continue friends together for ever; so I verily trust, and shall therefore heartily pray, that, though your Lordships have been on earth my judges to condemnation, yet that we may hereafter meet in heaven merrily together to our everlasting salvation; and God preserve you all, especially my Sovereign Lord the King, and grant him faithful councillors."[1]

Having taken leave of the Court in this solemn manner, he was conducted from the bar,—an axe, with its edge now towards him, being carried before him. He was in the custody of his particular friend, Sir William Kingston, who, as Lieutenant of the Tower, witnessed the last moments both of Wolsey and More, and extended to both

---

[1] This speech, which seems to me to be so much in the true spirit of the Christian religion, is censured by Sharon Turner as showing that More presumptuously compared himself with St. Stephen.—*Turner's Hist.* vol. x. p. 302, *n.*

of them all the kindness consistent with obedience to the orders of his stern master.

They came back by water, and on their arrival at the Tower wharf a scene awaited the illustrious convict more painful to his feelings than any he had yet passed through. Margaret, his best-beloved child, knowing that he must land there, watched his approach, that she might receive his last blessing; "whom, as soon as she espied, she ran instantly unto him, and, without consideration or care of herself, passing through the midst of the throng and guard of men, who with bills and halberds compassed him round, there openly, in the sight of them all, embraced him, took him about the neck, and kissed him, not able to say any word but 'Oh, my father! Oh, my father!' He gave her his fatherly blessing, telling her that 'whatsoever he should suffer, though he were innocent, it was not without the will of God, and that she must therefore be patient for her loss.' After separation she, all ravished with the entire love of her dear father, suddenly turned back again, ran to him as before, took him about the neck, and divers times kissed him most lovingly; a sight which made even the guard to weep and mourn."[1] So tender was the heart of that admirable woman, who had had the fortitude to encourage her father in his resolution to prefer reputation to life![2]

After this farewell he felt that the bitterness of death was over, and he awaited the execution of his sentence with a cheerfulness that, with severe censors, has brought some reproach upon his memory. But it should be remembered that he had long foreseen the event, and with all humility, sincerity, and earnestness had submitted to all the observances which, according to his creed, were the fit preparations for the change he was to undergo.

From the notion that more would be gained by his recantation than his death, fresh attempts were made to

---

[1] More, 276.
[2] ROGERS has pathetically interwoven with his theme the story of this
—— "blushing maid,
Who through the streets as through a desert stray'd,
And when her dear, dear father pass'd along
Would not be held; but bursting thro' the throng,
Halberd and battle-axe, kiss'd him o'er and o'er,
Then turn'd and wept, then sought him as before,
Believing she should see his face no more."—*Human Life.*

bend his resolution; and, these failing, a warrant was issued for his execution, all parts of the frightful sentence, as to the manner of it, being remitted, except beheading, in respect of his having filled the high office of Lord Chancellor. On receiving this intelligence, he expressed a hope "that none of his friends might experience the like mercy from the King."

The day before he was to suffer, he wrote with a piece of coal, the only writing implement now left to him, a farewell letter to his dear Margaret, containing blessings to all his children by name, with a kind remembrance even to one of her maids. Adverting to their last interview, at which the ceremonial which then regulated domestic intercourse had been so little observed, he says,—" I never liked your manner towards me better than when you kissed me last, for I am most pleased when daughterly love and dear charity have no leisure to look to worldly courtesy."

Early the next day, being Tuesday the 6th of July, 1535,[1] came to him his "singular good friend," Sir Thomas Pope, with a message from the King and Council that he should die before nine o'clock of the same morning. More having returned thanks for these "good tidings," Pope added, "the King's pleasure farther is, that you use not many words at your execution." "I did purpose," answered More, "to have spoken somewhat, but I will conform myself to the King's commandment, and I beseech you to obtain from him that my daughter Margaret may be present at my burial." "The King is already content that your wife, children, and friends shall have liberty to be present thereat." Pope now taking leave, wept bitterly; but More said to him, "Quiet yourself, Mr. Pope, and be not discouraged, for I trust we shall yet see each other full merrily where we shall be sure to live and love together in eternal bliss." Then, to rally the spirits of his friend (in reference to a medical practice then in great vogue),—as if he had been a fashionable doctor giving an opinion upon the case of a patient, he took his urinal in his hand, and, casting his water, said in a tone of drollery,

---

[1] More's recent biographers, by erroneously fixing his trial on the 7th of May, make an interval of two months instead of six days between that and his execution: but it is quite certain that although he was arraigned on the 7th of May, he was not tried till the 1st of July.—1 St. Tr. 385.

" I see no danger but this man may live longer if it please the King."[1]

Being conducted by Sir William Kingston to the scaffold, it seemed weak, and he had some difficulty in mounting it. Whereupon he said merrily, " Master Lieutenant, I pray you see me safe up, and for my coming down let me shift for myself."

Having knelt and pronounced the "*Miserere*" with great devotion, he addressed the executioner, to whom he gave an angel of gold, saying, " Pluck up thy spirit, man, and be not afraid to do thy office ; my neck is very short; take heed, therefore, that thou strike not awry for saving thy honesty." When he had laid his head on the block he desired the executioner " to wait till he had removed his beard, for that he had never offended his Highness."[2] One blow put an end to his sufferings and his pleasantries.

What zealot shall venture to condemn these pleasantries after the noble reflections upon the subject by Addison, who was never suspected of being an infidel, a favorer of Romanism, or an enemy to the Protestant faith? " The innocent mirth which had been so conspicuous in his life did not forsake him to the last. His death was of a piece with his life; there was nothing in it new, forced, or affected. He did not look upon the severing of his head from his body as a circumstance which ought to produce any change in the disposition of his mind, and as he died in a fixed and settled hope of immortality, he thought any unusual degree of sorrow and concern improper."[3]

> "Lightly his bosom's Lord did sit
> Upon its throne, unsoften'd, undismay'd
> By aught that mingled with the magic scene
> Of pity and fear ; and his gay genius play'd
> With the inoffensive sword of native wit,
> Than the bare axe more luminous and keen."[4]

More's body was interred in the Chapel of the Tower of London, but to strike terror into the multitude, his head stuck on a pole was placed on London Bridge. The affectionate and courageous Margaret, however, procured it to be taken down, preserved it as a precious relic during

---

[1] This anecdote which so strikingly illustrates the character of More and the manners of the age, is omitted by his modern biographers as *indelicate!*
[2] More, 287.   [3] Spectator, No. 349.   [4] Wordsworth.

her life, and, at her death, ordered it to be laid with her in the same grave.¹

When the news of the execution was brought to Henry, who was at that time playing at tables with the Queen, turning his eyes upon her, he said, "Thou art the cause of this man's death;" and, rising immediately from his play, shut himself up in his chamber. But if he felt any remorse, recollecting the times when he put his arm round More's neck in the garden at Chelsea, or was instructed by him in the motion of the heavenly bodies from the house-top, or was amused by his jests at supper, —the feeling was transitory; for he not only placed the head where it must have been conspicuous to his own eye, in passing between Whitehall and Greenwich, but he immediately expelled Lady More from the House at Chelsea, seizing whatever property More left behind him; he even set aside assignments which, for the purpose of making some provision for the family, had been legally executed before the commission of the alleged offense, thereby giving fresh evidence of his "mild and friendly temper."²

The letters and narrative of Erasmus diffused the story of More's fate over Europe, and every where excited horror against the English name. Henry's ministers were regarded at every Court with averted eyes, as the agents of a monster. Charles V. sent for Sir T. Elliot, the English Ambassador, and said to him, "We understand that

---

[1] "As for his head, it was set upon a pole on London Bridge, where abiding about fourteen days, was then privily bought by the said Margaret, and by her for a time carefully preserved in a leaden box, but afterwards, with great devotion, 't was put into a vault (the burying-place of the Ropers), under a chapel joyning to St. Dunstan's Church, in Canterbury, where it doth yet remain, standing on the said box on the coffin of Margaret his daughter, buried there."—Wood's Ath. Ox. vol. i. p. 86. The Rev. J. Bowes Bunce, a clergyman at Canterbury, who had inspected the repairs of St. Dunstan's Church in 1835, has made me the following communication:—Wishing to ascertain whether Sir T. More's skull was really there, I went down into the vault, and found it still remaining in the place where it was seen many years ago, in a niche in the wall, in a leaden box, something of the shape of beehive, open in the front, and with an iron grating before it."—Sir Thomas had prepared a tomb for himself in his parish church at Chelsea, which is still preserved with great veneration, although an empty cenotaph.

[2] See Turn. Hist. Eng. vol. x. 333. We may be amused by a defense of Richard III., but we can feel only indignation and disgust at an apology for Henry VIII., whose atrocities are as well authenticated as those of Robespierre, and are less excusable. For trial and execution of More, see 1 St. Tr. 385-475.

the King, your master, has put to death his wise councillor, Sir Thomas More." Elliot, abashed, pretended ignorance of the event. "Well," said the Emperor, "it is true; and this we will say, that if he had been ours, we should have sooner lost the best city in our dominions than so worthy a councillor."

Holbein's portraits of More have made his features familiar to all Englishmen. According to his great-grandson, he was of " a middle stature, well proportioned, of a pale complexion; his hair of chestnut color, his eyes gray, his countenance mild and cheerful; his voice not very musical, but clear and distinct; his constitution, which was good originally, was never impaired by his way of living, otherwise than by too much study. His diet was simple and abstemious, never drinking any wine but when he pledged those who drank to him; and rather mortifying, than indulging, his appetite in what he ate."[1]

His character, both in public and in private life, comes as near to perfection as our nature will permit. Some of his admirers have too readily conceded that the splendor of his great qualities was obscured by intolerance and superstition, and that he voluntarily sought his death by violating a law which, with a safe conscience, he might have obeyed. We Protestants must lament that he was not a convert to the doctrines of the Reformation; but they had as yet been very imperfectly expounded in England, and they had produced effects in foreign countries which might well alarm a man of constant mind. If he adhered conscientiously to the faith in which he had been educated, he can in no instance be blamed for the course he pursued. No good Roman Catholic could declare that the King's first marriage had been absolutely void from the beginning; or that the King could be vested, by act of parliament, with the functions of the Pope, as Head of the Anglican Church. Can we censure him for submitting to loss of office, imprisonment, and death, rather than make such a declaration? He implicitly yielded to the law regulating the succession to the Crown; and he offered no active opposition to any other law;—only requiring that, on matters of opinion, he might be permitted to remain silent.

The English Reformation was a glorious event, for

[1] More, 294.

which we never can be sufficiently grateful to Divine Providence: but I own I feel little respect for those by whose instrumentality it was first brought about;—men generally swayed by their own worldly interests, and willing to sanction the worst passions of the tyrant to whom they looked for advancement. With all my Protestant zeal, I must feel a higher reverence for Sir Thomas More than for Thomas Cromwell or for Cranmer.[1]

I am not permitted to enter into a critical examination of his writings; but this sketch of his life would be very defective without some further notice of them. His first literary essay is supposed to have been the fragment which goes under his name as "the History of Edward V. and Richard III.," though some have ascribed it to Cardinal Morton, who probably furnished the materials for it to his precocious page, having been intimately mixed up with the transactions which it narrates. It has the merit of being the earliest historical composition in the English language; and, with all its defects, several ages elapsed before there was much improvement upon it, this being a department of literature in which England did not excel before the middle of the eighteenth century.

More's "EPIGRAMMATA," though much admired in their day, not only in England, but all over Europe, are now only inspected by the curious, who wish to know how the Latin language was cultivated in the reign of Henry VII. The collection in its present form was printed at Basle from a manuscript by Erasmus, consisting of detached copies made by various friends, without his authority or sanction. His own opinion of their merits is thus given in one of his epistles to Erasmus: "I was never much delighted with my Epigrams, as you are well aware; and if they had not pleased yourself and certain others better than they pleased me, the volume would never have been published." The subjects of these effusions are very multifarious—the ignorance of the clergy—the

---

[1] Although he adhered to most of what we call "the errors of popery," it is delightful to find that he was friendly to the circulation of the Holy Scriptures, and that from them he professed to draw his creed. When Erasmus published his admirable edition of the NEW TESTAMENT thus More bursts forth:—

"Sanctum opus, et docti labor immortalis ERASMI,
Prodit, et o populis commoda quanta vehit!
Tota igitur demptis verso est jam denuo mendis,
Atque nova CHRISTI lex nova luce nitet."

foibles of the fair sex—the pretensions of sciolists—the tricks of astrologers—the vices and follies of mankind,—while they are prompted at times by the warmth of private friendship and the tenderness of domestic affection. Many of them were written to dissipate the ennui of tedious and solitary traveling. When rapid movement on the surface of the earth by the power of steam was less thought of than the art of flying through the air with artificial wings, it was the practice of scholars trudging slowly on foot, or toiling along miry roads on a tired horse, to employ their thoughts on metrical composition. Erasmus framed in his own mind, without any assistance from writing materials, his poem upon OLD AGE while crossing the Alps into Italy,—and he devised the plan of the " Encomium Moriæ " during a journey to England, " ne totum hoc tempus quo equo fuit insidendum *amousis* et illiteratis fabulis tereretur." Thus More begins a beauful address to Margaret, Elizabeth, Cicely, and John, " dulcissimis liberis," composed under circumstances which he graphically describes—seemingly very unfavorable to the muses:—

> " Quatuor una meos invisat epistola natos,
>   Servat et incolumes à patre missa salus.
> Dum peragratur itur iter, pluvioque madescimus imbre,
>   Dumque luto implicitus sæpius hæret equus,
> Hoc tamen interea vobis excogito carmen,
>   Quod gratum, quanquam sit rude, spero fore.
> Collegisse animi licet hinc documenta paterni,
>   Quanto plus oculis vos amet ipse suis :
> Quem non putre solum, quem non malè turbidus **aer**,
>   Exiguusque altas trans equus actus aquas,
> A vobis poterant divellere, quo minus omni
>   Se memorem vestri comprobet esse loco ;
> Nam crebrò dum nutat equus casumque minatur,
>   Condere non versus desinit ille tamen."

He then goes on in a very touching manner to remind them with what delight he had caressed them, and treated them with fruit and cakes and pretty clothes, and with what reluctance and gentleness he had flogged them. The instrument of punishment, the application of it, and the effects of it, are all very curious.

> " Inde est vos ego quòd soleo pavisse placento
>   Mitia cum pulchris et dare mala piris.
> Inde quod et Serum textis ornare solebam,
>   Quod nunquam potui vos ego flere pati ;

Scitis enim quàm crebra dedi oscula, verbera rara,
Flagrum pavonis non nisi cauda fuit.
Hanc tamen admovi timideque et molliter ipsam,
Ne vibex teneras signet amara nates.
Ah! ferus est, dicique pater non ille meretur,
Qui lachrymas nati non fleat ipse sui."

As a specimen of his satirical vein, I shall give his lines on an old acquaintance whom he had estranged (seemingly not to his very deep regret) by lending him a sum of money:—

"IN TYNDALEM DEBITOREM.

" Ante meos quàm credideram tibi, Tyndale, nummos,
Quum libuit, licuit te mihi sæpe frui ;
At nunc si tibi me fors angulus afferat ullus,
Haud secus ac viso qui pavet angue, fugis.
Non fuit unquam animus, mihi crede, reposcere nummos;
Non fuit, at ne te perdere, cogar, erit.
Perdere, te salvo, nummos volo, perdere utrumque
Nolo, sat alterutrum sit periisse mihi.
Ergo tibi nummis, aut te mihi redde, retentis :
Aut tu cum nummis te mihi redde meis.
Quod tibi si nutrum placeat, nummi mihi saltem
Fac redeant : at tu non rediture, vale."[1]

[1] The following spirited translation is by the accomplished author of PHILOMORUS:—

" O Tyndal, there was once a time,
    A pleasant time of old,
Before thou cam'st a-borrowing,
    Before I lent thee gold ;
" When scarce a single day did close
    But thou and I, my friend,
Were wont, as often as I chose,
    A social hour to spend.
" But now, if e'er perchance we meet,
    Anon I see thee take
Quick to thy heels adown the street,
    Like one who sees a snake.
" Believe me, for the dirty pelf
    I never did intend
To ask ; and yet, spite of myself,
    I must, or loss my friend.
" To lose my money I consent,
    So that I lose not *thee ;*
If one or other of you went,
    Contented might I be.
" With or without the gold, return,—
    I take thee nothing loath ;—
But, sooth, it makes my spirit yearn,
    Thus to resign you both.
" If neither please, do thou at least
    Send me the money due ;
Nor wonder if to thee I send
    A long and last adieu."

More's controversial writings, on which he bestowed most pains and counted most confidently for future fame, have long fallen into utter oblivion, the very titles of most of them having perished.

But the composition to which he attached no importance,—which, as a *jeu-d'esprit*, occupied a few of his idle hours when he retired from the bar,—and which he was with great difficulty prevailed upon to publish,—would of itself have made his name immortal. Since the time of Plato, there had been no composition given to the world which, for imagination, for philosophical discrimination, for a familiarity with the principles of government, for a knowledge of the springs of human action, for a keen observation of men and manners, and for felicity of expression, could be compared to the *Utopia*. Although the word, invented by More, has been introduced into the language, to describe what is supposed to be impracticable and visionary,—the work (with some extravagance and absurdities, devised, perhaps, with the covert object of softening the offense which might have been given by his satire upon the abuses of his age and country) abounds with lessons of practical wisdom. If I do not, like some, find in it all the doctrines of sound political economy illustrated by Adam Smith, I can distinctly point out in it the objections to a severe penal code, which have at last prevailed, after they had been long urged in vain by Romilly and Mackintosh;—and as this subject is intimately connected with the history of the law of England, I hope I may be pardoned for giving the following extract to show the law reforms which Sir Thomas More would have introduced when Lord Chancellor, had he not been three centuries in advance of his age: He represents his great traveler who had visited Utopia, and describes its institutions, as saying, "There happened to be at table an English lawyer, who took oacasion to run out in high commendation of the severe execution of thieves in his country, where might be seen twenty at a time dangling from one gibbet. Nevertheless, he observed, it puzzled him to understand, since so few escaped, there were yet so many thieves left who were still found robbing in all places.[1] Upon this I said with boldness, there was no

---

[1] "Cœpit accurate laudare rigidam illam justitiam quæ tum illic exercebatur in fures, quos passim narrabat nonnunquam suspendi viginti in una

reason to wonder at the matter, since this way of punishing thieves was neither just in itself nor for the public good; for as the severity was too great, so the remedy was not effectual; simple theft was not so great a crime that it ought to cost a man his life; and no punishment would restrain men from robbing who could find no other way of livelihood. In this, not only you, but a great part of the world besides, initiate ignorant and cruel schoolmasters, who are readier to flog their pupils than to teach them. Instead of these dreadful punishments enacted against thieves, it would be much better to make provision for enabling those men to live by their industry whom you drive to theft and then put to death for the crime you cause."

He exposes the absurdity of the law of forfeiture in case of larceny, which I am ashamed to say, notwithstanding the efforts I have myself made in parliament to amend it, still disgraces our penal code, so that for an offense for which, as a full punishment, sentence is given of imprisonment for a month, the prisoner loses all his personal property, which is never thought of by the Court in pronouncing the sentence. It was otherwise among the Utopians. "Those that are found guilty of theft among them are bound to make restitution to the owner, and not to the prince. If that which was stolen is no more in being, then the goods of the thief are estimated, and restitution being made out of them, the remainder is given to his wife and children."

I cannot refrain from giving another extract to prove that, before the Reformation, he was as warm a friend as Locke to the principle of religious toleration. He says that the great legislator of Utopia made a law that every man might be of what religion he pleased, and might endeavor to draw others to it by the force of argument, and by amicable and modest ways, without bitterness against those of other opinions. "This law was made

cruce, atque eo vehementius dicebat se mirari cum tam pauci elaberentur supplicio, quo malo fato fieret (how the devil it happened) uti tam multi tamen ubique grassarentur." This lawyer reminds me exceedingly of the attorney-generals, judges, and secretaries of state, who in my early youth eulogized the bloody penal code which then disgraced England, and predicted that, if it were softened, there would be no safety for life or property. They would not even like their worthy predecessor here recorded, admit its inefficiency to check the commission of crime.

by Utopus not only for preserving the public peace, which he saw suffered much by daily contentions and irreconcilable heats, but because he thought it was required by a due regard to the interest of religion itself. He judged it not fit to decide rashly any matter of opinion, and he deemed it foolish and indecent to threaten and terrify another for the purpose of making him believe what did not appear to him to be true."[1]

More had in his visits to Flanders—then far more advanced than England in refinement as well as in wealth—acquired a great fondness for pictures, and he was desirous to introduce a taste for the fine arts among his countrymen. He was the patron of Holbein, and it was through his introduction that this artist was taken into the service of Henry VIII. Hence the pains bestowed on Holbein's portraits of the More family, which are the most delightful of his works. More was likewise acquainted with Quintus Matsys, the celebrated painter of Antwerp; and he describes, both in prose and verse, a piece executed for him by this artist. It represented his two most intimate friends, Erasmus and Peter Giles,—the former in act of commencing his "Paraphrase on the Romans," and the other holding in his hand a letter from More, addressed to him in a fac-simile representation of the handwriting of his correspondent.[2]

It is to be regretted that we have so few specimens of More's oratory; his powers as a debater called forth this eulogium from Erasmus: "His eloquent tongue so well seconds his fertile invention, that no one speaks better when suddenly called forth. His attention never languishes, his mind is always before his words, his memory has all its stock so turned into ready money, that without

---

[1] His most wonderful anticipation may be thought that of Lord Ashley's factory measure—by "the Six Hours' Bill," which regulated labor in Utopia. "Nec ab summo mane tamen, ad multam usque noctem perpetuo labore, velut jumenta fatigatus; nam ea plus quam servilis ærumna est; quæ tamen ubique fere opificum vita est exceptis Utopiensibus, qui cum in horas viginti-quatuor æquales diem connumeratâ nocte dividant, sex duntaxat operi deputant, tres ante meridiem, a quibus prandium ineunt, atque a prandio duas pomeridianas horas, quam interquieverunt, tres deinde rursus labori datas cœna claudunt. Etenim quod sex duntaxat horas in opere sunt, fieri fortasse potest. ut-inopiam aliquam putes necessariam rerum sequi. Quod tam longe abest ut accidat, ut id temporis ad omnium rerum copiam, quæ quidem ad vitæ vel necessitatem requirantur vel commoditatem, non sufficiat modo sed supersit etiam."—*Utop.* vol. ii. 68.   [2] Philomorus, 48.

hesitation or delay it supplies whatever the occasion may require."[1]

But by no grave quality does he seem to have made such an impression on his contemporaries as he did by his powers of wit and humor. I therefore introduce a few of his pointed sayings beyond those which have occurred in the narrative of his life. He observed, that "to aim at honor in this world is to set a coat of arms over a prison gate." "A covetous old man he compared to a thief who steals when he is on his way to the gallows." He enforced the giving of alms by remarking, that "a prudent man, about to leave his native land forever, would send his substance to the far country to which he journeyeth." Sir Thomas Manners, with whom he had been very familiar when a boy, was created Earl of Rutland about the same time that More was made Lord Chancellor, and, being much puffed up by his elevation, treated with superciliousness his old schoolfellow, who still remained a simple knight, but would not allow himself to be insulted. "Honores mutant Mores," cried the upstart Earl. "The proper translation of which," said the imperturbable Chancellor, " is, *Honors* change MANNERS."

He once, while Chancellor, by his ready wit, saved himself from coming to an untimely end:—"He was wont to recreate himself on the flat top of his gate house at Chelsea, from which there was a most pleasant prospect of the Thames and the fields beyond. It happened one time that a Tom-of-Bedlam came up to him, and had a mind to have thrown him from the battlements, saying, 'Leap, Tom, leap.' The Chancellor was in his gown, and besides ancient and not able to struggle with such a strong fellow. My Lord had a little dog with him: said he, 'Let us throw the dog down, and see what sport that will be.' So the dog was thrown over. 'This is very fine sport,' said my Lord; 'fetch him up and try once more.' While the

[1] Erasm. Epist. As they had been personally known to each other from the time when More was an undergraduate at Oxford, there can be no truth in the story that the two having met at the Lord Mayor's table, being strangers except by reputation, and conversing in Latin, More having sharply combated some latitudinarian paradox sported by Erasmus,—the latter said, "Aut tu es Morus aut Nullus," to which the answer was, "Aut tu es Erasmus aut Diabolus."

In 1523 Erasmus sent his portrait to More from Basle, and More in return sent Erasmus the famous picture by Holbein of himself and his family, including the Fool, which is still preserved in the town-hall at Basle.

madman was going down, my Lord fastened the door, and called for help; but ever after kept the door shut."[1]

He did not even despise a practical joke. While he held his City office he used regularly to attend the Old Bailey Sessions, where there was a tiresome old Justice, "who was wont to chide the poor men that had their purses cut for not keeping them more warily, saying, that their negligence was the cause that there were so many cut-purses brought thither." To stop his prosing, More at last went to a celebrated cut-purse then in prison, who was to be tried next day, and promised to stand his friend if he would cut this Justice's purse while he sat on the bench trying him. The thief being arraigned at the sitting of the Court next morning, said he could excuse himself sufficiently if he were but permitted to speak in private to one of the bench. He was bid to choose whom he would, and he chose that grave old Justice, who then had his pouch at his girdle. The thief stepped up to him, and while he rounded him in the ear, cunningly cut his purse, and, taking his leave, solemnly went back to his place. From the agreed signal, More knowing that the deed was done, proposed a small subscription for a poor needy fellow, who had been acquitted, beginning by himself setting a liberal example. The old Justice, after some hesitation, expressed his willingness to give a trifle, but finding his purse cut away, expressed the greatest astonishment, as he said he was sure he had it when he took seat in Court that morning. More replied, in a pleasant manner, "What! will you charge your brethren of the bench with felony?" The Justice becoming angry and ashamed, Sir Thomas called the thief and desired him to deliver up the purse, counseling the worthy Justice hereafter not to be so bitter a censurer of innocent men's negligence, since he himself could not keep his purse safe when presiding as a judge at the trial of cut-purses.[2]

[1] Aubrey's Letters, vol. iii. 462.
[2] Sir John Sylvester, Recorder of London, was in my time robbed of his watch by a thief whom he tried at the Old Bailey. During the trial he happened to say aloud that he had forgot to bring his watch with him. The thief being acquitted for want of evidence, went with the Recorder's love to Lady Sylvester, and requested that she would immediately send his watch to him by a constable he had ordered to fetch it.
  Soon after I was called to the Bar, and had published the first No. of my "Nisi Prius Reports,"—while defending a prisoner in the Crown Court, I had occasion to consult my client, and I went to the dock, where I conversed with

I am, indeed, reluctant to take leave of Sir Thomas More, not only from his agreeable qualities and extraordinary merit, but from my abhorance of the mean, sordid, unprincipled Chancellors who succeed him, and made the latter half of the reign of Hedry VIII., the most disgraceful period in our annals.

CHAPTER XXXIV.

LIFE OF LORD CHANCELLOR AUDLEY.

WHEN Sir Thomas More resigned the Great Seal, it was delivered to Sir THOMAS AUDLEY, afterwards Lord Audley, with the title, first of Lord Keeper, and then of Lord Chancellor.[1] There was a striking contrast, in almost all respects, between these two individuals,—the successor of the man so distinguished for genius, learning, patriotism, and integrity, having only common-place abilities, sufficient, with cunning and shrewdness, to raise their possessor in the world,—having no acquired knowledge beyond what was professional and official,—having first recommended himself to promotion by defending, in the House of Commons, the abuses of prerogative,—and for the sake of remaining in office, being ever willing to submit to any degradation, and to participate in the commission of any crime. He held the Great Seal for a period of above twelve years, during which, to please the humors of his capricious and tyrannical master, he sanctioned the divorce of three Queens,—the execution of two of them on a scaffold,—the judicial murder of Sir Thomas More, Bishop Fisher, and many others, who, animated by their example, preferred death to infamy,—the spoliation of the Church and a division of the plunder among those who planned the rob-

---

him for a minute or two. I got him off, and he was immediately discharged. But my joy was soon disturbed; putting my hand in my pocket to pay the "Junior" of the circuit my quota for yesterday's dinner, I found that my purse was gone, containing several bank notes, the currency of that day. The incident causing much merriment, it was communicated to Lord Chief Baron Macdonald, the presiding Judge, who said, "What! does Mr. Campbell think that no one is entitled to *take notes* in Court except himself?"

[1] Rot. Cl. 24 Hen. 8, m. 24.

bery,—and reckless changes of the established religion, which left untouched all the errors of Popery, with the absurdity of the King being constituted Pope, and which involved in a common massacre those who denied transubstantiation and those who denied the King's spiritual supremacy. Luckily for Audley, he has not much attracted the notice of historians; but there can be no doubt that had a considerable influence upon the events which disgraced the latter half of this reign · and we must now inquire into his origin, and try to trace the steps by which he reached, and the means by which he retained, his "bad eminence."

Thomas Audley was born in the year 1488, at the Hay House, in the tenure of the prior of Colne, in Essex.[1] His family was ancient, though, it seems, not entitled to bear arms. His ancestor, Ralph Audley, having been seated at Earl's Colne in that county as early as the 28th of Henry VI., afterwards became possessed of the Hay House, which his descendants continued to inhabit, and which was demolished only a few years ago. But it would appear that they were only of the class of yeomen, and that the Chancellor was the first of them who could boast of heraldic honors.[2]

He had a slender patrimony, and he rose from his own industry and selfish arts. Some accounts represent, that after an indifferent school education he was sent to Magdalene College, Cambridge, of which he afterwards became a benefactor; but the records, both of Oxford and Cambridge, have in vain been searched for his name, and it is doubtful whether he ever had the advantage of being at a university. While still a youth he was entered of the Inner Temple, where he devoted himself very steadily to the study of the the common law, and he is said to have discharged the duties of "Autumn Reader" to the society with some reputation. Being called to the degree of outer

[1] "A.D. 1516. Thomas Audley natus in Colne in Com. Essex. Bergeus." *Oath Book of Corporation of Colchester.*
[2] The original grant of arms to Lord Audley, dated 18th March, 1538, still preserved at Audley End, recites "that not being contynned in nobilitè berynge armes and descended of ancient stock by his auncestors and predecessors by consanguinitè and marriage, and he not willing to use or bere armes that should redound unto damage or reprofe of any of the same name or consanguinitè, or of any other person, he desired the following coat to be assigned to him, &c." The arms differ from those borne by families of the same name, but the motto "*Garde ta Foy*," belonged to Touchet, Lord Audley.

barrister, he early rose into considerable practice from his skill in the technicalities of his profession, and his eager desire to please his clients. He was of a comely and majestic presence; and by his smooth manners and systematic anxiety to give offense to no one, he acquired general popularity, although known to those who had studied his character to be unprincipled, false, and deceitful.

In the 12th year of the reign of Henry VIII. he was called to the degree of Sergeant-at-Law, and, flourishing in Westminster Hall, he became eager for political advancement. Parliament so seldom met during this reign, that aspiring lawyers had but rare opportunities of gaining distinction either as patriots or courtiers. But a parliament being at last called in 1523, Audley contrived to get himself returned a burgess to the House of Commons, in the hope of now making his fortune. This was the parliament at which Sir Thomas More was Speaker of the House of Commons, and gained such distinction by preserving the privileges of the House, and resisting the exorbitant subsidy demanded by Wolsey. Audley strongly took the side of the Court, defended all the Cardinal's proceedings, and bitterly inveighed against all his opponents as disloyal subjects and favorers of heresy. When the lamentation was uttered by Wolsey that More was not at Rome instead of being made Speaker,[1] regret was no doubt felt that Audley had not been placed in the chair; and a resolution was formed, that he should have the Court influence in his favor on a future occasion. In the meanwhile he was made Attorney to the Duchy of Lancaster, and a King's Sergeant.[2]

In the succeeding interval of six years, during which no parliament sat, he distinguished himself by abetting all the illegal expedients resorted to for raising money on the people. No Hampden arose to contest, in a Court of Justice, the legality of the commissions issued under the Great Seal, for levying the sixth of every man's goods; but they excited such deep discontents, that a rebellion was apprehended, and they were recalled. Against such an arbitrary sovereign as Henry, with such tools as Audley, the only remedy for public wrongs was resistance.

On the question of the divorce, Audley was equally subservient to the King's wishes; and he was so high in

[1] See ante, vol i. p. 442. [2] Orig. Jur. 83.

his favor, as not to be without hopes of the Great Seal on Wolsey's disgrace. But though no doubt was entertained of his pliancy, his character for integrity was now very low; and fears being entertained that he would bring discredit upon the government, the more prudent course was adopted of preferring Sir Thomas More.

However, More being appointed to the Great Seal, Audley was named his successor as Chancellor of the Duchy of Lancaster; and, at the meeting of parliament, in the beginning of November, 1529, on the recommendation of the Court, he was elected Speaker of the House of Commons.

Being presented at the bar of the House of Lords, he made an eloquent oration, consisting of two points: first, "that he much praised the King for his equity and justice, mixed with mercy and pity;" secondly, "he endeavored to disable himself, for want of sense, learning, and discretion, for the taking of so high an office, beseeching the King to cause his Commons to resort again to their House, and there to choose another Speaker." To this the Chancellor, by the King's command, replied with the usual courtesy, "that whereas he sought to disable himself in sense and learning, his own elaborate discourse there delivered testified to the contrary; and, touching his discredit and other qualities, the King himself had well known him and his doings, since he was in his service, to be both wise and discreet; and so as an able man he accepted him, and admitted him Speaker."[1]

The King's designs to break with Rome were strongly supported by Audley, and were well received by the Commons: but Fisher, Bishop of Rochester, made a strong speech against them in the Lords, in which he said, that "our Holy Mother, the Church, was about to be brought, like a bondmaid, into thraldom; and that want of faith was the true cause of the mischiefs impending over the State." When the Commons heard of this speech, they conceived great indignation against the Bishop; and not suspecting that there was any irregularity in noticing what was said in debate by a member of the other House, they sent Audley, the Speaker, attended by a deputation of their body, to complain of it to the King, and to let his Majesty know "how grievously they

---
[1] 1 Parl. Hist. 492.

thought themselves injured thereby, for charging them with lack of faith as if they had been infidels or heretics."

The King was well pleased with this interference, which he had most likely prompted, and sent for the Bishop of Rochester to rebuke him for the license he had used to the displeasure of the Commons. The courageous Prelate answered, " that having seat and voice in parliament, he spake his mind freely in defense of the Church, which he saw daily injured and oppressed by the common people, whose office it was not to judge of her manners, much less to reform them." The King advised him " to use his words more temperately."[1]

Audley had more difficulty, as Speaker, to restrain the impetuosity of a party in the Commons, who, having imbibed the new doctrines, wished in earnest for a religious reformation. Trimming his own profession of faith by the personal wishes of his master, he labored to preserve things in their present condition, with the exception of transferring the power of the Pope to the King.

During the session of parliament which began in April, 1532, there was displayed. among the Commons a strong sympathy with Queen Catherine, which the Speaker found it very difficult to restrain within decent bounds. He was compelled to put the question " that an humble address should be presented to the King, praying that his Majesty would be graciously pleased to take back the Queen, and live with her as his wife, according to the admonition of his Holiness the Pope." We have no account of the debate, which, however guardedly conducted, must have been most offensive to the King. The moment he heard of it, in a rage he sent for Audley, and said to him, " That he wondered any amongst them should meddle in businesses which could not properly be determined in their House, and with which they had no concern." His Majesty then condescended to reason the matter with the Speaker, who was to report to the House " that he was only actuated by a regard for the good of his soul; that he wished the marriage with Catherine were unobjectionable, but, unfortunately, the Doctors of the Universities having declared it contrary to the word of God, he could do no less than abstain from her company; that wantonness of appetite was not to be imputed to him, for being

[1] 1 Parl. Hist. 493.

now in his forty-first year, it might justly be presumed that such motions were not so strong in him as formerly;[1] that, except in Spain and Portugal, no one was allowed to marry two sisters; but that for a brother to marry a brother's wife was a thing so abhorred among all nations, that he never heard that any Christian did so except himself; whereat his conscience was sorely troubled."[2]

Audley succeeded in convincing the King that he was not personally to blame in the stirring of the marriage question in the House; and he executed the commission with which he was now intrusted to his Majesty's entire satisfaction.

So much was Henry pleased with his dexterity in managing the House on this occasion, that he was soon after sent for again to Whitehall, to consult about preparing the members for a final rupture with Rome; and he was instructed to inform the House that "his Majesty found that the clergy of his realm were but half his subjects, or scarce so much; every Bishop or Abbot, at the entering into his dignity, taking an oath to the Pope derogatory to that of fidelity to his Sovereign, which contradiction he desired his parliament to consider and take away." The Speaker, at the next sitting of the House, having delivered this message, directed the two oaths to be read by the Clerk at the table, and pointed out the manner in which they clashed so forcibly, that the Commons were ready to renounce the Pope's supremacy whenever this step should be deemed expedient.

Audley was now such a decided favorite at Court that he was destined to be the successor of Sir Thomas More, when the contemplated measures for the King's new marriage and separation from Rome determined that virtuous man to resign the Great Seal. However, a difficulty arose from the disadvantage it would occasion to the King's service if he were immediately removed from the

---

[1] This is one among many proofs that occur, showing that formerly old age was supposed to come on much sooner than at present; but our ancestors began life very early,—often marrying nominally when infants, and actually at fourteen,—and subjecting themselves to very little restraint of any kind. This early decay of the physical powers seems likewise to have prevailed among the Romans in the time of Augustus. Horace says,—

—— " Fuge suspicari,
Cujus *octavum* trepidavit ætas
    Claudere *lustrum*."

[2] 1 Parl. Hist. 518.

House of Commons, where his influence and dexterity had been found so useful. The opinion then was, that if he were made Lord Chancellor, he must immediately vacate his seat in the House of Commons, and take his place on the woolsack as President of the House of Lords; but that merely as Lord Keeper of the Great Seal he might continue a member of the House of Commons, as if he were Chancellor of the Exchequer, or were appointed to any other judicial office usually held by a commoner.

Accordingly Sir Thomas More, having surrendered the office of Chancellor on the 16th of May, 1532, and the Seal having remained four days in the King's hands, enclosed in a bag under the private seal of the late Chancellor, on the 20th of May his Majesty opened the bag and took out the Seal, and after inspecting it, delivered it, with the title of Lord Keeper, to Audley, on whom he then conferred the honor of knighthood.[1]

On Friday, the 5th of June, being the first day of Trinity Term, after a grand procession to Westminstei Hall, he was sworn in and installed in the Court of Chancery—the Duke of Norfolk, who seems always to have acted as master of the ceremonies on such occasions, delivering an oration, in which, after a becoming compliment to the late Chancellor, he highly lauded the abilities and good qualities of the new Lord Keeper. There is no trace to be found of the reply, but we need not doubt that it turned upon the conscientious feelings, humanity and love of true religion which ever dwelt in the royal bosom.

On the 6th of September following, on account of a change in the King's style, the old Great Seal was broken, and a new one delivered to Audley, still with the title of

---

[1] The entry on the Close Roll, after a very circumstantial account of the prior proceedings, thus goes on: "Et post inspccconem illam idem sigillum dilco sibi Thome Audley tradidit et deliberavit cui tunc custodian dci. sigilli sui comisit Ipsmque Thomam Dmm Custodem Magni Sigilli Regii vocari nuncupari et appellari ac omnia et singula facre et singula facre et exercere tam in Cur. Cancellar. dci. Dni. Regis qur in Cama Stellata et Consilio ejusdem Dni. Regis prout Cancellarius Angl. facre et exre solebat, declaravit et expresse mandavit." After stating that he sealed certain letters patent, the entry records that he restored the Great Sealto its bag under his own private seal, "sicque Sigillum illud in custodia ipsius Thome (quem idem Dns. Rex ordine militari tuncinsignavit *) auctoritate regia prdca. remansit et remanet."
—Rot. Claus. 42 H. 8, m. 24, in dorso.

* This distinction must then have been in high repute, as it was not conferred on Audley when made Chancellor of the Duchy or Speaker of the

Lord Keeper.[1] But on the 26th of January, 1533, "about the hour of two in the afternoon, in a chamber near the chapel in the King's manor of East Greenwich, in the presence of the Duke of Norfolk, the Archbishop of Canterbury, the Earl of Wiltshire, the Bishop of Winchester, and other Councillors, the King having ordered the Great Seal to be taken from the bag in which it was inclosed, received it into his hands, and having retained it for the space of a quarter of an hour, divers weighty reasons moving his Majesty thereto, as he then openly declared, he being well pleased with the faithful services of Sir Thomas Audley as Keeper of the Great Seal, then and there constituted him his Chancellor of England.[2]

Sir Humphrey Wingfield was chosen Speaker of the House of Commons in his place; and henceforth till his death in 1544, the Chancellor prompted and presided over the iniquitous measures brought forward in the Upper House, and was the chief agent in the homicides committed by the instrumentality of legal process.

In the proceedings of parliament, and in contemporary writers, I do not discover any censure of him as an Equity Judge. The probability is, that, being regularly trained to the profession of the law, he did his duty efficiently; and that where the Crown was not concerned, and he had no corrupt bias to mislead him, he decided fairly. As a politician he is bitterly condemned by all who mention his name.

At the conclusion of the session in which the act was passed for recognizing the King's marriage with Anne Boleyn, and settling the succession to the Crown on their issue,[3]—the King being seated on the throne, Audley de-

[1] The Close Roll gives a very minute description of the figures on the new Great Seal, "videlt. Dnm. Regem in Majestate sua sedentem et sceptrum in una manu et in altera manu signum Crucis portantem necnom ex utroque latere prefati Dni. Regis ejusdem partis sigilli intersignia Angliæ cum titulo ordinis garterii circa eadem insignia et coronam imperialem supra eadem intersignia stantem ac exaltera parte ejusdem sigilli Dm. Regem armatum manu sua dextera gladium tenentem sedentemque super equum similiter armatum et in scuto suo intersignia Angliæ ferentem ac quandam rosam * in dextro latere insculptam ; necnon sub pedibus regiis canem currentem."

[2] " Sicque sigillum predm. in custodia prefati Thome nunc Cancellarii Angliæ remansit et remanet."   [3] 25 Hen. 8, c. 22.

House of Commons, and not till the Great Seal was delivered to him. He was not raised to the peerage till six years after.

* It would be curious to know whether the rose was gules or argent. If the King regarded his title by descent, he must have preferred the white rose.

livered a warm panegyric on it, saying that "upon the
due observance of it the good and happiness of the kingdom chiefly depended. He then intimated that the King,
by letters patent, had appointed the Lord Chancellor, the
Archbishop of Canterbury, the Duke of Norfolk, and the
Duke of Suffolk, Commissioners to swear the Lords and
Commons, and all others at their discretion, to observe
the act. They immediately, in the King's presence. took
the oath themselves, and administered it to the members
of both Houses, introducing into it words respecting the
original nullity of the King's first marriage, and the
King's supremacy, which the statute did not justify.

We have already seen the part taken by Lord Chancellor Audley, along with the Archbishop of Canterbury
and the Duke of Norfolk, in trying to force the oath upon
Sir Thomas More, and committing him close prisoner to
the Tower of London for refusing to take it:—the acts
which he procured to be passed for the perpetual imprisonment of More and Fisher, and for making the denial
of the King's supremacy high treason; and his various
attempts, by going personally to the Tower, to entrap
More into such denial of the King's supremacy as might be
made the pretense for putting him to death as a traitor.[1]

Audley now issued, under the Great Seal, a special
commission for the trial of Fisher and More,—placing
himself at the head of it. As less skill was apprehended
from the aged prelate in defending himself, and there was
some color of a case against him from the infamous arts
of Rich, the Solicitor General, the wary Chancellor judged
it most expedient to begin with him, although the conviction of the Ex-Chancellor was deemed and object of
still greater importance. Accordingly, on the 17th of
June, Audley, with the other Commissioners, being seated
in the Court of King's Bench in Westminster Hall, Fisher
from age and weakness hardly able to support himself,
was placed at the bar, charged with having traitorously attempted to deprive the King of his title, by maliciously
speaking these words: "The Kyng our Soveraign Lord
is not Supreme Hedd yn Erthe of the Churche of Englande."[2]

The only witness for the Crown was Rich, the Solicitor
General, who, although he was supposed not to have ex-

---

[1] Ante, p. 61 *et seq.*   [2] 26 Hen. 8, c. 1, 13.

ceeded the truth in stating what had passed between him and the prisoner, covered himself with almost equal infamy as when he was driven to commit perjury on the trial of More. He had the baseness voluntarily to swear, that, in a private conversation he had held with the Bishop, when he paid him a friendly visit in the Tower, he heard the Bishop declare "that he believed in his conscience, and by his learning he assuredly knew, that the King neither was nor by right could be supreme Head in Earth of the Church of England."

Fisher, without the assistance of counsel, which could not be permitted against the Crown, objected to Audley and the other Judges, that this declaration ought not to be received in evidence, or be considered as supporting the charge in the indictment, considering the circumstances under which it was elicited from him. "Mr. Rich," said he, "I cannot but marvel to hear you come and bear witness against me of these words. This man, my Lords, came to me from the King, as he said, on a secret message, with commendations from his Grace declaring what good opinion his Majesty had of me, and how sorry he was of my trouble, and many more words not now fit to be recited, as I was not only ashamed to hear them, but also knew right well that I could no way deserve them. At last he broke to me the matter of the King's supremacy, telling me that the King, for better satisfaction of his own conscience, had sent him unto me in this secret manner to know my full opinion in the matter for the great affiance he had in me more than any other. When I had heard this message, I put him in mind of the new act of parliament, which, standing in force as it does, might thereby endanger me very much in case I should utter anything against its provisions. To that he made answer, 'that the King willed him to assure me, upon his honor, and on the word of a King, that whatsoever I should say unto him by this his secret messenger, I should abide no peril for it, although my words were ever so directly against the statute, seeing it was only a declaration of my mind secretly as to his own person.' And the messenger gave me his solemn promise that he never would mention my words to living soul save the King alone. Now, therefore, my Lords, seeing it pleased the King's Majesty to send to me thus secretly to know my poor advice and opinion, which I most gladly was and ever will be ready to offer to him when so commanded, methinks it very hard to allow the same as sufficient testimony against me to prove me guilty of high treason."

Rich did not contradict this statement, observing only that " he said no more to him than his Majesty commanded," and then, as Counsel for the Crown, argued that, assuming the statement to be true, it was no discharge in law against his Majesty for a direct violation of the statute.

Audley ruled, and the other Judges concurred, " that this message or promise from the King neither did nor could, by rigor of law, discharge him, but in so declaring his mind and conscience against the supremacy, yea, though it were at the King's own request or commandment, he committed treason by the statute, and nothing could save him from death but the King's pardon."

Fisher still argued, that as the statute only made it treason *maliciously* to deny the King's supremacy, he could not be guilty by merely expressing an opinion to the King himself by his own order;—to which Audley answered, that *malice* did not mean spite or ill-will in the vulgar sense, but was an inference of law; for if a man speak against the King's supremacy by any manner of means, that speaking is to be understood and taken in law as *malicious*.

The right reverend prisoner then took an objection, which seems to have rather puzzled the Court—that here there was but one witness, which in treason is insufficient.

Audley and the Judges, after some hesitation, answered that as this was a case in which the King was personally concerned, the rule requiring two witnesses did not apply; that the jury would consider the evidence, the truth of which was not disputed, and as they believed or disbelieved it the prisoner should be acquitted or condemned. " The case was so aggravated to the jury, by my Lord Chancellor making it so heinous and dangerous a treason, that they easily perceived what verdict they must return ; otherwise heap such danger on their own heads as none of them were willing to undergo." Yet many of his hearers, and some of his judges, were melted to tears, to see such a venerable father of the Church in danger of being sentenced to a cruel death upon such evidence, given contrary to all faith and the promise of the King himself.

The jury having withdrawn for a short time, brought in a verdict of *guilty*. The Bishop prayed to God to forgive them: but the Lord Chancellor, "framing himself to a solemnity of countenance," passed sentence of death upon him in the revolting terms used on such occasions; ordering that his head and four quarters should be set up where the King should appoint, and piously concluding with a prayer, that God might have mercy on his soul. This wicked Judge had not the apology of having any taste for blood himself, and he would probably have been much better pleased to have sustained the objections, and directed an acquittal; he was merely a tool of the tyrant, who, hearing that Pope Paul III. had sent Fisher a Cardinal's hat, exclaimed, "I will take care that he has not a head to put it upon."

Audley's demeanor on the trial of Sir Thomas More, which took place a fortnight afterwards, we have already commemorated.[1]

The merit has been ascribed to him of favoring the Reformation; but, in reality, he had no opinions of his own, and he was now acting merely as an instrument in the hands of the most remarkable adventurer to be met with in English history; whose rise more resembles that of a slave, at once constituted Grand Vizier in an Eastern despotism, than of a minister of state promoted in a constitutional government,—where law, usage, and public opinion check the capricious humors of the sovereign.

Thomas Cromwell, the son of a fuller,[2] having had a very slender education,—after serving as a trooper in foreign armies, and a clerk in a merchant's counting-house at Antwerp, had picked up a little knowledge of the law in an attorney's office in London,—had been taken into the service of Cardinal Wolsey as a steward,—had obtained a seat in parliament,—had acquired a great ascendency in the House of Commons by his energy and volubility,—had insinuated himself into the favor and confidence of Henry

---

[1] Ante, p. 70.
[2] He is often called the son of a blacksmith, but whoever has curiosity to investigate the point, will clearly see that his father was a fuller.' A true life of Thomas Cromwell might be made as interesting as a fairy tale.

VIII. by his pliancy and dexterity in business;—and having been successively made Clerk of the Hanaper in the Court of Chancery, Master of the Jewel House, Chancellor of the Exchequer, a Knight and a Privy Councillor, was now Lord Chamberlain, Chief Justice in Eyre beyond Trent, Lord Privy Seal, Baron Cromwell of Okeham, in the county of Rutland, Vicar-General and Vicegerent of the King as Head of the Church, with precedence in parliament above all temporal and spiritual Peers, and with absolute power in all the civil affairs of the realm. To such subordination was the office of Lord Chancellor reduced, that Audley, unless by some extraordinrry ebullition of baseness, seems to have attracted little notice from his contemporaries; and his name is hardly mentioned by the general historian. Yet in the detail and execution of the measures which were brought forward by the Vicar-General, the Lord Chancellor took a very active and important part. He framed the bills for completing the separation from Rome, and punishing those who went farther than the King, and favored the doctrines of Luther. He was very efficient in the suppression of the monasteries. his zeal being influenced by the hope of sharing in the plunder. He recommended the commissions, under the Great Seal, for inquiring into the immoralities and abuses alleged to exist in those institutions; and he approved of the plan of first granting to the King the revenues of all under £200 a year, and then of all above that amount. There was never any difficulty in carrying such bills through parliament. Ministers, in those days, instead of triumphing in a good working majority, could command an absolute unanimity in both Houses. It is a curious fact, that against bills respecting religion, which must have been most highly distasteful to the great body of the prelates, and to many lay peers,—after the execution of Fisher there was not a dissentient voice, or the slightest audible murmur of opposition.[1]

[1] Some of these bills passed both Houses after being read only once in each House. There was then no certain number of times necessary for a bill to be read according to parliamentary usage before passing; a bill was sometimes read four, five, six, seven and even eight times, before it passed or was rejected. Journ. vol. i. 26, 49, 52, 55, 56. But the marvel is that such bills as those for the dissolution of the monasteries and the transfer of the Pope's supremacy to the King passed the House of Lords at all, considering that from the reign of Edward II. till 1539 the spiritual peers were much more

Audley had his difficulties, but they arose from the King's conjugal inconstancy. He thought that after witnessing the dissolution of the King's first marriage by the sentence of Archbishop Cranmer, and his union with her to whom, in spite of all obstacles, he had been for six years a devoted lover, and an act of parliament setting aside the Princess Mary and settling the succession on the infant Princess Elizabeth,—holding the Great Seal, he was to enjoy peace and freedom from care for the rest of his days, with nothing to think of but his own aggrandisement.

Henry, however, had seen Jane Seymour, one of Anne's maids, more beautiful and attractive than herself, and had resolved that there should be a vacancy in the office of Queen, that his new favorite might be advanced to it.

Audley conformed without hesitation to the royal will, and took a leading part in the proceedings against the unfortunate Anne, from the first surmise against her at Court till she was beheaded on Tower Hill. He formed one the Committee of Council to whom the "delicate investigation" was intrusted, and he joined in the report, founded on the mere gossip of the Court, or the representations of suborned witnesses, "that sufficient proof had been discovered to convict her of incontinence, not only with Brereton, Norris, and Weston of the Privy Chamber, and Smeaton the King's musician, but even with Lord Rochford, her own brother."

After secretly examining and committing to prison some of the supposed paramours, Audley planned the arrest of the Queen herself at the tilting match at Greenwich, and next day in his proper person went down the river, that he might accompany her to the Tower, and try to extract something from her which might be perverted into evidence of her guilt. Having met the barge in which she was coming up as a prisoner, he informed her that she had been charged with infidelity to the King's bed, and intimated to her that it would be better for her to confess; but, falling on her knees, she prayed aloud, that, "if she were guilty, God might never grant her pardon;" and no advantage being then obtained over her,

---

numerous than the temporal. Then twenty-six mitred abbots and two priors being disfranchised, there were forty-one temporal to twenty spiritual peers. But Bishop Fisher's fate had such an effect on the nerves of the prelates, that they offered no opposition to the bills which they abhorred.

she was given in ward to Kingston, the Lieutenant of the Tower.

Having been active as her prosecutor, Audley sat as her Judge. The trial was nominally before the Court of the Lord High Steward,—the Duke of Norfolk, her uncle, being appointed Lord High Steward, as Audley was not yet raised to the peerage; but he sat as assessor at the Duke's right hand during the trial, and directed all the proceedings.[1] The only symptom of humanity exhibited was in reluctantly granting the indulgence of a chair to the Queen s dignity or weakness. Unassisted by counsel, she repelled each charge with so much modesty, temper, and natural good sense, that before an impartial tribunal she must have been acquitted; for though she had undoubtedly fallen into some unjustifiable levities, the evidence to support the main charge, consisting of hearsay and forced confessions by accomplices not produced, was such as is in our days could not be submitted to a jury. Yet, under the direction of Audley, she was unanimously found guilty by the Peers " upon their honor; " and the iron Duke of Norfolk, with tears in his eyes, condemned her to be " burnt or beheaded at the King's pleasure."[2]

The next proceeding is, if possible, still more discreditable to Audley and the other instruments of Henry's vengeance. Not satisfied with knowing that she whom he had so passionately loved was doomed in her youth to suffer a violent and cruel death, he resolved before her execution to have a sentence pronounced dissolving his marriage with her, and declaring that it had been null and void from the beginning,—not seeing, in the blindness of his rage, that in this case she could not have been guilty of adultery or treason. Nevertheless, in a divorce suit which lasted only a few hours, which Audley sanctioned, and in which Cranmer personally pronounced the sentence,—some say on the ground of a pre-contract with the Earl of Northumberland, which he on his oath denied, —some on the ground that Henry had cohabited with Mary Boleyn, the sister of Anne,—that marriage was declared

---

[1] In all accounts of the trial, he is represented as one of the Queen's Judges, along with the twenty-six peers who constituted the Lord High Steward's Court; but being only a commoner, it is impossible that he should have voted.   [2] 1 St. Tr. 409.

null and void, which Cranmer himself had solemnized, and which had been declared valid by an act of parliament then remaining on the Statute Book. It is well that Henry did not direct that Audley should officiate as executioner, with Cranmer as his assistant; for they probably would have obeyed sooner than have given up the seals or the primacy.

The day after the execution the King was married to Jane Seymour, and for a short time his happiness was without alloy; but he was reminded that by statute the Crown was still settled on the issue of his last mariage, whom he had resolved to bastardize; and he called a new parliament to meet at Westminster on the 8th of June, 1537, for the purpose of registering the edicts which the altered state of affairs rendered necessary.

On the day appointed, the King being seated on the throne, and the Commons being in attendance, Lord Chancellor Audley delivered a very singular harangue, of which the following is said to be a correct outline :—

" First he told them, that at the dissolution of the last Parliament it did not enter into the King's mind that he should so soon have occasion to call another; but that for two especial causes, very necessary, both for easing the King's scruples and conducive to the good of the whole kingdom, he had issued a fresh summons for calling this Parliament. The one was concerning the heirs and successors of the King's Majesty, who, knowing himself obnoxious to infirmities, and even death itself (a thing very rare for kings to think of [1]), and, besides, considering the state of the whole kingdom, depending, as it were, upon his single life; but willing, above all things, to have it free from all dangers to posterity, he had called this parliament to appoint an heir apparent to the Crown, who, when the present King had resigned to fate, without children lawfully begotten, might, by their own consent, happily reign over them.—The second cause for which the present parliament was summoned was for repealing a certain act made in the last, by the tenor and force of which this whole realm is bound to be obedient to the Lady Anne Boleyn, the King's late wife, and her heirs be-

---

[1] This reminds us of a dialogue between the Dauphin and his tutor, when to the question, " Les rois meurent-ils?" the answer was, "Quelquefois, monseigneur."

tween them lawfully begotten. Also, by the force of the
said act, whoever should say or do any ill against her or
her issue should be condemned for high treason.—But
now, he said, that they might more rightly understand
the reasons of this summons, his counsel was according
to these three proverbs of Solomon (to whom our most
excellent Prince here may be most justly and worthily
compared), 'Operabimini quibus admonemur: 1. præter-
ita in memoria habere; 2. præsentia intueri; et, 3. obventura providere.' And as to the first, they very well
remembered what great anxieties and perturbations of
mind their most invincible Soverign suffered on account
of his first unlawful marriage, which was not only judged
so in all the Universities in Christendom, but declared
unlawful by the general consent of the kingdom in a late
act of parliament. So also ought they to bear in mind
the great perils and danger their Prince was under when
he contracted his *second* marriage, in regard to the second
of Solomon's proverbs, by considering in what a situation
this realm is in by reason of the oath then made and taken
for the support of the said Anne and her issue. Which
said Lady Anne and her accomplices had been since justly
found guilty of high treason, and had received their due
reward for it. What man of middle condition would not
this deter from marrying a third time? When he remem-
bers that the first was a vast expense and great trouble of
mind to him, and the second ran him into great and imminent dangers, which hung over him during the whole
time of it,—yet this, our most excellent Prince, on the
humble petition of the nobility, and not out of any carnal
lust or affection, again condescends to contract matrimony,
and hath at this time taken unto himself another wife,
whose age and fine form denotes her most fit and likely
to bring forth children. And, therefore, according to the
third proverb of Solomon, *obventura provideamus*, we are
now met by the King's command, with unanimous consent, to appoint an heir apparent to the Crown, that if
this our Prince (which God avert) should leave this mortal
life without children lawfully begotten, the heir so appointed may lawfully rule and govern this kingdom after
him. Lastly, let us humbly pray to God that he would
bless this our most excellent Prince with some offspring;
at the same time giving him thanks that he has hitherto

preserved him from so many and such imminent dangers. Because, it is his whole study and endeavor to rule us all in perfect peace and charity during his life, and to transmit the same happiness to posterity."

The Commons were then ordered to withdraw and choose a Speaker. To reward the services of Richard Rich, the Solicitor General, as counsel, and still more as witness at the late state trials, he was recommended by the Government to fill the chair, and, as a matter of course, was elected.

When presented at the bar on a subsequent day, he was determined to eclipse the Chancellor in his adulation of the King, and to show himself worthy to succeed to the Seals on the first fitting opportunity. After repeating the heads of the Chancellor's discourse, explaining the reasons for calling the parliament, and extolling his Majesty's consideration for the good of his people, " he took occasion to praise the King for his wonderful gifts of grace and nature, and compared him for justice and prudence to Solomon, for strength and fortitude to Samson, and for beauty and comeliness to Absalom." He concluded by observing that the Commons, having chosen him, the most unworthy of them all, for Speaker, he besought his Majesty that he would command them to withdraw again and elect another, for he had neither learning, experience, nor boldness fit for the office.

To this, Lord Chancellor Audley, by the King's command, replied, " that his Majesty had well heard his speech, and was glad to understand by the first part of it, that the members of the House of Commons had been so attentive to the Chancellor's declaration. That as to the praises and virtues ascribed to himself, his Majesty thought proper to disavow them, since, if he really had such virtues, they were the gifts of Almighty God."[1] Lastly, added he, " as to your excuses, Richard, which the King hath heard, that you have neither learning, experience, nor boldness, fit for such an office, his Majesty hath commanded me to reply, that if he did not know that you had all these qualifications, he would not, amongst so many urgent matters as are now depending, admit you

---

[1] This is a plain admission on the part of his Majesty, that by the gift of God he had the wisdom of Solomon, the strength of Sampson, and the beauty of Absalom.

into the office, and therefore he does not look upon your excuses as just."

Audley immediately prepared a bill which rapidly passed both Houses, the most arbitrary and unconstitutional that had ever yet been put upon the rolls of parliament. By this, the sentence of divorce nullifying the King's marriage with Anne Boleyn *ab initio* was confirmed, and she and all her accomplices, were attainted ;—the children of both marriages were declared illegitimate, and it was even made treason to assert the legitimacy of either of them ; —to throw any slander on the King, Queen Jane, or their issue, was subjected to the same penalty ;—the Crown was settled on the King's issue by his present or any subsequent wife,—*in case he should die without legitimate children he was empowered by his will or letters patent to dispose of the Crown;*—whoever being required should refuse to answer upon oath to a belief of every article of this act, was declared to be guilty of treason, so as to establish a political inquisition into conscience ;—and the King was empowered, by will or letters patent, to create new principalities, and thereby to dismember the kingdom.[1]

At the close of the session there was another contest between the Chancellor and the Speaker in praising the King in his presence, Rich making Audley rather uncomfortable by comparing his Majesty to the Sun, " who exhales all the noxious vapors which would otherwise be hurtful to us, and cherishes and brings forth those seeds, plants, and fruits, so necessary for the support of human life." [2]

Henry was soon after thrown into ecstacy by the birth of a son, in the midst of which he felt not very severely the loss of his Queen, Jane Seymour, who, although married to him, had the felicity to die without violence or disgrace. Audley was much disappointed at not being included in the batch of Peers made a few days after on the creation of the infant Prince of Wales ; but in the following year his ambition was gratified by becoming Baron Audley, of Walden, in the county of Essex.

This honor was conferred upon him that he might preside as Lord High Steward at the trial of Courtenay Marquess of Exeter, and De la Pole Lord Montague, who

[1] Stat. 28 Hen. 8, c. 7.   [2] 1 Parl. Hist. 534.

were particularly obnoxious to Henry as his cousins, and whom he wished to have condemned for high treason on a charge of being in correspondence with another cousin of his, Cardinal Pole, now considered by him his capital enemy. Courtenay was grandson to Edward IV., by his daughter Catherine, and the Poles were grandsons of the Duke of Clarence, the brother of Edward, by his daughter the Countess of Salisbury. For this reason both families were regarded with peculiar affection by the adherents of the house of York, and extreme jealousy by the reigning Sovereign. Baron Audley, of Walden, presiding as High Steward, the Marquess and Lord Montague were arraigned before their Peers on an indictment for high treason. The overt act was, that the former had been heard to say, and the latter abetted him in saying, "I like well of the proceedings of Cardinal Pole: I like not the proceedings of this realm. I trust to see a change in the world. I trust once to have a fair day on the knaves which rule about the King. I trust to give them a buffet one day." The natural construction of such language is, that they did not approve of the policy of the government, and that by an active opposition they hoped to bring about a change of ministers; but the Lord High Steward held that it showed a conspiracy to use physical force to bring about a revolution and to dethrone the King. Both were found guilty, condemned to suffer death as traitors, and executed accordingly.[1]

Lord Audley was very desirous of having a reward for his services from the plunder of the monasteries, and wrote many letters upon the subject to Cromwell, who had the distribution of it. The reader may be amused with a specimen of his epistolary style: My Lord Chancellor had been favored with a sight of the young Prince Edward, then a baby of a few months old, sent to Havering in Essex for change of air; and in the hope that his begging letter might be shown to the King, he thus addresses the Vicar-General:—

"After my right harty comendations to your good Lordship, with my most harty thankes for your last gentill letters, I am required by the Erle of Oxford and Master Chauncelour, to desire your good Lordshipp in all our names, to make our moost humble recommendations to

[1] 1 St. Tr. 479.

the kynges mageste, and to render ouer most harty
thankes to his Highness for our licens to visite and see
my lord pryncess grace, whom, accordyng to our desires
and duteez, we have seen to our most rejoise and comfort,
next the kynges mageste. And I assure your Lordshipp
I never saw so goodly a childe of his age, so mery, so
plesaunt, so good and lovyng countenaces, and so ernest
an eye, as it were a sage juggement towards every person
that repayreth to his grace ; and as it semyth to me,
thankes be to our Lord, his grace encresith well in the
ayer that he ys in. And albeyt a litell his graces flesche
decayeth, yet he shotyth owt in length, and wexith ferme
and stiff, and can stedfastly stond, and wold avaunce hym-
self to move and go if they would suffir hym ; but as me
semyth they do yet best, consideryng his grace is yet
tendir, that he should not streyn himself as his owen corage
would serve hym, till he cum above a yere of age. I can
not comprehend nor describe the goodly towardly quali-
teez that ys in my Lord princes grace. He ys sent of al-
myty Good for all our comfortes. My dayly and contynual
prayer ys and shalbe for his good and prosperus preservation, and to make his grace an olde prince, besechyng
your good lordeshipp to render to the kynges mageste
thankes in al our names, as ys above sayd."

He then proceeds to the real object of his letter, to obtain a grant of two abbeys in Essex,—St. John's and St.
Osyes'. Deprecating them much, as "St. Johns lakkyth
water, and St. Osyes stondyth in the mersches ;" he offers
to give £1000 apiece for them. In a "*Postscripta*" he
adds, that to recruit from the labors of the Court of Chancery, he was then going on a sporting party, "to mete the
Duke of Norfolk, at Framyngham, to kyll sum of his
bukkes there."[1]

But the grand object of his ambition was to get the
site and lands of the dissolved abbey at Walden, in
Essex. For this purpose he writes to Cromwell with
much earnestness, and it must be owned with much candor and simplicity, showing that some extraordinary recompense was due him for having sacrificed even his
character and conscience in the King's service. "I be-
seche your good Lordshipp, be my good Lord in this my
sute, yf it shall plese the Kyng's Mageste to be so good

[1] Letters on Suppression of Monasteries, by Camden Society, p. 245.

and gracius lord to me, it shall sett forth as moche my poor estymacion as the valu of the thynge. In the besy world I susteyned damage and injury, and this shall restore me to honeste and comodyte."[1] Afterwards he urges his claim on this ground with still more force and naiveté. "I have in this world susteyned *greate damage and infamie* in serving the Kynge's Highness, which this grant shal *recompens*."[2]

This appeal was felt to be so well founded, that in consideration of the bad law laid down by him on the trials of Fisher, More, Anne Boleyn, Courtenay, and De la Pole, and of the measures he had carried through parliament to exalt the royal prerogative and to destroy the constitution, and of the execration heaped upon him by the whole English nation—as well as by way of retaining fee for future services of the like nature, and recompense for farther infamy,—he reccived a warrant to put the Great Seal to the desired grant.

But Henry, never contented with showering favors on those who pleased him, till, changing his humor, he doomed them to destruction, likewise bestowed upon him the site and precinct of the Priory of the Canons of the Holy Trinity of Christ Church, Aldgate, in the city of London, where the Chancellor erected for himself a commodious town mansion, with gardens and pleasure grounds. This was described by a contemporary wag as " the best cut at the feast of Abbey lands, a dainty morsel and an excellent receipt to clear his voice, and make him speak well for his master."

Still insatiable, he wrote to Cromwell "that his place of Lord Chancellor being very chargeable, the King might be moved for addition of some more profitable offices unto him."[3] There was no rich sinecure that conveniently could be bestowed upon him at that moment, but a vacant Blue Riband was offered him to stay his importunity, and he was installed Knight of the Garter with all due solemnity,—being the first Lord Chancellor of England who, while in office, had ever reached that dignity. Decorated with the Collar, George, and Garter, Audley showed himself, if possible, more eagerly desirous to com-

---

[1] Letters on Suppression of Monasteries, by Camden Society, p. 245.
[2] Dugdale's Baronage, tit. "Audley."   [3] Ibid.

ply with the humors, whether arbitrary, fantastical, or cruel, of his royal benefactor.

On the 28th of April, 1539, a new parliament met to confirm the dissolution of the monasteries, and to provide severe punishments for those inclined to adopt the reformed opinions, which were as distasteful to Henry as a denial of the supremacy.[1] The Chancellor's speech on the first day of the session is not preserved; but the Journals state, that on the 5th of May he informed the House of Lords "that it was his Majesty's desire, above all things, that the diversities of opinions concerning the Christian religion in this kingdom should be with all possible expedition plucked up and extirpated." A select committee was therefore appointed, with the Vicar-General at their head, who were to report what was fit to be done to produce uniformity of faith among all his Majesty's loving subjects.

On the 30th of May, the Lord Chancellor declared before the Lords, that not only the Bishops and other spiritual Peers, but even the King's Majesty, had taken great pains, and labored incessantly, to bring about an union, and had at last completed it. Therefore, it was his Majesty's pleasure "that some penal statute should be enacted to compel all his subjects who were anywise dissenters to obey the articles agreed on."

On the 7th of June, "the bloody Bill of the Six Articles" was brought into the House by Lord Chancellor Audley,[2] himself secretly inclined to the new opinions, and subjecting all who should venture to profess them to be burnt or beheaded. By the first article,—to question the doctrine of transubstantiation, or to say that after the consecration of the elements in the sacrament of the Lord's Supper there remaineth any substance of bread or wine, was heresy, punishable with burning and forfeiture of lands and goods, as in case of high treason. The second was leveled against the doctrine that communion in both kinds was good for the souls of the laity; the third enjoined the celibacy of the clergy; the fourth the observance of monastic vows; the fifth the efficacy and propriety of private masses;—and the sixth auricular confession. Each of these four last mentioned dogmas was enforced by the milder penalty of death by hang-

[1] 1 Parl. Hist. 537.   [2] Ibid. 538.

ing, with forfeiture of lands and goods, as in the case of felony.

The Chancellor's bill was so arbitrary and cruel, that Cranmer even had the courage to oppose it; but it was carried through the House of Lords in three days; and, being sent down to the Lower House by the Attorney and Solicitor General, it passed there with equal rapidity. The finishing hand was now put to the dissolution of the monasteries, and twenty-eight mitred Abbots and Priors were ejected from parliament.

There having been some grumbling in the House of Lords on account of the precedence given to Cromwell, the Lord Chancellor brought in a bill enacting, that he should have place in parliament and in the Privy Council next after the blood royal, and regulating the precedence of the Peers and officers of state as it now exists.[1]

But to save all future trouble in calling parliaments, or managing them when refractory, the Chancellor crowned the labors of the session by bringing in and passing a bill whereby the King's proclamation, issued with the assent of his Council, was to have the force and effect of an act of parliament.[2]

A new session began on the 12th of April, 1540;[3]—through all the perils of which Audley steered with his usual cunning and success,—but which proved fatal to Cromwell. A few months previously, Henry, by his Vicegerent's advice, after remaining a widower two years, and being disappointed in a negotiation for a French Princess, had married Anne of Cleves; but cruelly disappointed in her person and manners, and determined not to live with her as his wife, he conceived a deep resentment against the man who had "put his neck into the yoke." To render the fall of the favorite more grievous, he was created Earl of Essex, and a Knight of the Garter; and the King seemed to trust him with more than wonted confidence.

On the first day of the session the Chancellor com-

---

[1] 31 Hen. 8, c. 10, which is the only restraint on the power of the Crown to grant precedence, but does restrain that power both in the House of Lords and in the Privy Council.

[2] 31 Hen. 8, c. 8. This was followed by 34 Hen. 8, c. 23, appointing a tribunal consisting of nine privy councillors, with power to punish in a summary manner all transgressors of such proclamations. To our surprise we find there was not perfect unanimity with respect to this bill, and Bishop Gardyner says, in a letter preserved by Burnet, that it did not pass without 'many large words."—Ref. ii. 114.   [3] 1 Parl. Hist. 542.

plained, in the King's name, of the great diversity of religions which still prevailed among his subjects; a grievance, he affirmed, which ought to be the less endured, because the Scriptures were now published in English, and ought universally to be the standard of belief to mankind. But the King, he said, had appointed some Bishops and divines to draw up a list of tenets to which the people were to assent; and he was determined that Christ, the doctrine of Christ, and the truth, should have the victory.

Cromwell, sitting on the Bishops' bench, on the King's right hand, above the Archbishop of Canterbury, made another speech in the King's name; and the Peers, believing him to be still in high favor, bestowed great flattery on him, saying, "that, by his desert, he was worthy to be Vicar-General of the universe."[1]

But Henry's aversion to his new Queen increasing daily, and, at last, breaking all restraint, prompted him to seek the dissolution of a marriage so odious to him, and to ruin the minister who had been the author of it. On the morning of the 10th of June the Vicar-General attended in his place in the House of Lords, neither himself nor those about him suspecting that he was in any peril. At three o'clock in the afternoon of the same day, while attending a meeting of the cabinet, he was arrested for high treason by the Duke of Norfolk, and committed to the Tower of London.

Lord Chancellor Audley immediately engaged zealously in the prosecution of his colleague and chief, whom the King resolved to bring immediately to the block; for at that time it was considered almost a matter of course in England that a minister should lose his head with his office, in the Turkish fashion,—only that, instead of the bow-string applied by a mute, the instrument of vengeance was the verdict of a packed jury, or an act of attainder passed by a servile parliament.

About a year before, Cromwell, to please Henry, had extorted an opinion from the Judges, in the case of the Countess of Salisbury, that persons might be lawfully attainted by bill without being heard in their defense; and Audley now recommended that this precedent should be acted upon against Cromwell himself, as awkward disclosures might take place if he should be tried by the

[1] 1 Parl. Hist. 548.

House of Peers, or in the Court of the Lord Steward; or if he should be permitted to plead at the bar against the bill of attainder. It contained a strange medley of charges, few of which even savored of high treason;— "That he had received bribes, and encroached on the royal authority by issuing commissions, discharging prisoners, pardoning convicts, and granting licenses for the exportation of prohibited merchandise; that as Vicar-General he had betrayed his duty, by not only holding heretical opinions himself, but also by protecting heretical preachers, and promoting the circulation of heretical books; and that he had expressed a resolution to fight against the King, if it were necessary, in defense of his religious opinions."[1] He wrote to the Chancellor, demanding a public trial: but all that was conceded to him was, that he should be privately heard to defend himself before Commissioners appointed by the Crown, who should express their opinion on his case to the two Houses.

After a timid attempt by Cranmer to soften the King on account of past services, the Bill passed through the House of Lords unanimously, Cranmer himself attending and voting for the second and third reading; and the Peers with one voice, at the request of the King conveyed by the Chancellor, thought proper, without trial, examination, or evidence, to doom to a cruel and ignominious death a man whom, a few days before, they had declared worthy to be "Vicar-General of the Universe." It can hardly be supposed that Henry insidiously gave him the Garter to make him more obnoxious to the nobility, but all accounts agree in stating that they were more incensed against the fuller's son, the trooper, the merchant's clerk, and the attorney, when they saw him bearing the decoration hitherto reserved for nobles and warriors, than by thinking of the enormities by which he had risen to greatness. A bill of attainder against Audley himself, proposed by Cromwell, if the King had so willed, would have passed with equal unanimity.

The projector of the marriage with Anne of Cleves being disposed of, Audley, by the King's orders, took the necessary measures for having the marriage itself dissolved, although there was no better pretext for questioning its

[1] St. Tr. 433.

validity than that Henry had been deceived by Holbein's too flattering portrait of Anne;—that he thought her a Flanders mare;—that when he did consent to marry her after he had seen her, he withheld assent in his own mind in going through the ceremony;—that he suspected she was not a true maid;—that she could speak no language but high Dutch;—and his assertion that though they slept in the same chamber for many weeks, he had only lived with her as a friend.

On the 6th of July the Lord Chancellor, addressing the House of Lords, said, "their Lordships very well knew what bloody and cruel slaughter had formerly been acted in this kingdom by reason of various contentions occasioned by dubious titles to the succession of this Crown, and since, by the grace of God, all these controversies were ceased, and all those titles were united by the Divine benevolence in the single person of his most serene Majesty, so that no occasion of discord could arise, unless their only hope, the noble Prince Edward, undoubted heir to his father's kingdoms, should by some sinister accident, be taken from them. In that case (which God avert) it was necessary for the general safety that some other future heir, by the Divine goodness, should be born to them in true and lawful wedlock; and since this was very doubtful from the marriage lately contracted between his Majesty and the most noble Lady Anne of Cleves, because of some impediments which upon inquiry, might arise to make the validity of that marriage dubious,—for the quietness and concord of the kingdom in succeeding times, he therefore recommended that a committee of both Houses should be appointed to wait upon his Majesty, humbly opening to him, as far as decency would admit, their doubts and scruples in this matter, and humbly entreating that he would please to acquaint them whether the aforesaid marriage was valid or not." He concluded with a motion that a message be sent to the Commons by certain members of the House, requesting them to deliberate upon the subject, and that they would send back six of their body to inform their Lordship of the result of their consultation.[1]

The Chancellor's motion was carried with the usual unanimity; and the Commons forthwith announced that

[1] 1 Parl. Hist. 546.

they had appointed a committee of twenty to co-operate with the Lords in the proposed application to his Majesty. All the temporal Lords and this committee accordingly awaited on the King, when the Chancellor told him they had a matter of great moment to communicate, if his Majesty would pardon their presumption. Henry having desired them "to speak their minds freely," the Chancellor delivered the address of both Houses, "praying his opinion upon the validity of his present marriage." The answer was, "that he would refer the question to the judgment and determination of grave, learned, honest, and pious ecclesiastics, viz. the Archbishops and Bishops."

This business was very soon concluded; for, to the unspeakable disgrace of Cranmer and the other prelates, whether inclining to the old or the new religion,—on the 10th of June they declared to the House of Lords that they had examined into the affair of the marriage, by virtue of the King's commission directed to them, and that, both by divine and human law, they found it invalid. They then handed to the Chancellor a sentence of nullity; which, on the Chancellor's motion, being read and approved of, it was sent down by two Bishops to the House of Commons. The next day the Chancellor brought in a bill to dissolve the marriage between his Majesty and the Lady Anne of Cleves; and, without hearing what she had to say against it, or receiving any evidence, it was passed unanimously the following day, and sent down to the Commons, where it experienced an equally favorable reception. In a few days more it received the royal assent; and Henry, who had always another wife ready on the divorce, dishonor, or beheading of a former, was publicly married to the Lady Catherine Howard, niece to the Duke of Norfolk.

As Eastern despotism was now established in England, there was introduced a near approximation to the Eastern custom of prostration before the Sovereign. We are told that on the last day of this session, as often as any piece of flattery peculiarly fulsome was addressed to the King by the Speaker or the Chancellor, "every man stood up and bowed themselves to the throne, and the King returned the compliment by a gracious nod from it."[1]

By the King's commands the Chancellor now dissolved

---

[1] 1 Parl. Hist. 547.—"et totum nutu tremefecit Olympum."

the parliament, which had sat above six years, and went by the name of the "Long Parliament," till another obtained that name, and utterly abolished monarchy as this had subverted all the free institutions of the country.

Audley was too cautious ever to aim at the station of "prime favorite and minister," which, after the fall of Cromwell, was for a time filled by the Duke of Norfolk. This stern sire of a most accomplished son, inclining strongly to Romanism, commenced a furious persecution against the Protestants; and the law of "the Six Articles" was executed with frightful rigor. Audley would have screened those of his own way of thinking if he could have done so without danger of offending the King; but, while he saw crowds led to the stake for questioning transubstantiation, he took care, in the impartial administration of justice, that no mercy should be shown to Catholics who denied the King's supremacy, beyond favoring them with a gibbet instead of surrounding them with fagots; so that a foreigner then in England said with reason, that "Henry's subjects who were against the Pope were burned, and those who were for him were hanged."[1]

Things went on smoothly enough with Audley, and all who, like him, had the prudence to conform to the prevailing fashions in religion, till the autumn of the following year, when a discovery was made which again threw the whole kingdom into confusion. The present Queen had, "by a notable appearance of honor, cleanness, and maidenly behavior, won the King's heart;"[2] for more than twelve months he lavished upon her proofs of his affection; he had publicly in his chapel returned solemn thanks to Heaven for the felicity which the conjugal state now afforded him; and he directed the Bishop of Lincoln to compose a form of prayer to the like effect, to be used in all churches and chapels throughout the kingdom. But before the general thanksgiving took place, Archbishop Cranmer came one morning to the Chancellor, and announced that information had been laid before him, which he could not doubt, that the Queen, both before and since her marriage, could be proved to have been and to be one of the most dissolute of her sex. By Audley's advice a written statement upon the subject was put into the

[1] Fox, vol. ii. p. 529.   [2] Herb. 532.

hands of the astonished husband. He was particularly mortified at the thought that the world would now question that upon which he so much piqued himself in the case of Anne of Cleves—his skill in discovering a true maid; but when he had recovered from the shock, he directed the necessary steps to be taken for the Queen's conviction and punishment.

In consequence, the Chancellor assembled the Judges and Councillors in the Star Chamber, and laid before them the evidence which had been obtained. With respect to Catherine's incontinence before marriage no difficulty arose, for this she did not deny, although she tried to mitigate her misconduct, by asserting that "al that Derame did unto her was of his importune forcement, and in a manner violence, rather than of her fre consent and wil;"[1] but this did not amount to an offense for which she could be punished by any known law, and she maintained her entire innocence since the time when a departure from chastity amounted to treason. However, it appeared that since her marriage she had employed Dereham as her secretary, and that she had allowed Culpepper, a maternal relation and gentleman of the Privy Chamber, who had likewise formerly been her lover, to remain in company with her and Lady Rochford from eleven at night till two in the morning. The Judges being asked their opinion, replied that, considering the persons implicated, these facts, if proved, formed a satisfactory presumption that adultery had been committed.

Fortified with this extra-judicial opinion, Audley immediately caused these two unfortunate gentlemen to be brought to trial before a jury, and, without any additional evidence, they were both convicted and executed.

But it was impossible to deal with the Queen herself and the other parties accused, without that commodious instrument of tyranny, a bill of attainder, which obviated the inconvenient requirements of proofs and judicial forms. Accordingly a new parliament was summoned to meet at Westminster, on the 16th of January, 1542.

The Lord Chancellor's speech on the first day of the session is commemorated in a most extraordinary entry on the Journals by the clerks of the House of Lords, the only reporters of those days,—stating that "Thomas Lord

[1] Archbishop Cranmer's letter to the King.—Stat. Pap. Off.

Audley, the Lord Chancellor, opened the cause of the summons in a grave and eloquent speech, but of such *uncommon and immoderate length*, that the clerks being busy on different affairs could not attend even to take the heads of the whole speech, which would take three hours to write down and one to read, and therefore they gave an imperfect *compendium orationis*. First, the Chancellor declared in what manner David began his reign over the people of God, the Israelites; he did not pray that honor and riches might be heaped upon him, but only that his understanding and wisdom might be enlarged, —*Give me understanding that I may search thy law*, as it is in the Psalms. This understanding he asked for, that he might the better learn things equally necessary for both prince and people. Such was the case also in our Sovereign Lord the King, who, when he first came to the Crown, wished for nothing more ardently or fervently than that God would bestow on him wisdom and understanding. The Almighty anointed him with the oil of sapience above his fellows, 'above the rest of the kings in the earth, and above all his progenitors, so that no king of whom history makes mention could be compared to him.' At which words all the Peers, as well as Commons, stood up and bowed to the throne with that reverence as plainly showed with what willing minds they owned his empire over them, and what they owed to God who had committed the government of the kingdom to such a Prince." But the entry breaks off abruptly just as the orator was coming to the pith of his oration,—the cause of parliament being then called. Some have ingeniously conjectured that this was done by design, that the Queen's shame and the King's misfortune might not be blazoned on the Journals.[1]

A bill was forthwith brought in by the Lord Chancellor to attaint of high treason the Queen, and Lady Rochford as her accomplice, and to subject to forfeiture and perpetual imprisonment the Duchess of Norfolk, her daughter the Countess of Bridgewater, Lord William Howard and his wife, and several others of inferior rank, on the ground that they had been aware of Catherine's antenuptial errors, and still had allowed the King to marry her.

For once in his life Audley was now guilty of an indis-

[1] 1 Parl. Hist. 550.

cretion, by yielding to the dictates of humanity and justice, and declaring after the first reading of the bill, "how much it concerned all their Honors not to proceed to give too hasty a judgment; they were to remember that a Queen was no mean or private person, but an illustrious and public one; therefore her cause was to be judged with that sincerity that there should be neither room for suspicion of some latent quarrel, or that she should not have liberty to clear herself if perchance, by reason or counsel, she was able to do it, from the crime laid to her charge. For this purpose, he though it but reasonable that some principal persons, as well of the Lords as Commons, should be deputed to go to the Queen, partly to tell her the cause of their coming, and partly in order to help her womanish fears, by advising and admonishing her to have presence of mind enough to say anything to make her cause better. He knew for certain it was but just that a Princess should be judged by equal laws with themselves, and he was sure that the clearing herself in this manner would be highly acceptable to her most loving husband." A committee was accordingly appointed to wait upon the Queen, and a resolution passed to suspend further proceedings on the bill till they had made their report.[1]

But Henry seems to have considered this proceeding very presumptuous; for two days afterwards the Chancellor was obliged to declare to the Lords openly, that the Privy Council, on mature deliberation, disliked the message to be sent to the Queen, and that the parliament might have leave to proceed to give judgment, and to finish the Queen's cause, that the event might be no longer in doubt, and that the King would give his assent to the bill by letters patent under the Great Seal.

The bill was accordingly rapidly run through both Houses, and the Commons attending in the House of Lords, the Lord Chancellor produced it signed with the King's own hand, with his assent to it signified under the Great Seal,—and holding it forth in both hands that all the Lords and Commons might see it, he declared that from thenceforth it had the full force and authority of law. Then, upon the true principle of "Castigatque auditque dolos subigitque fateri," the Duke of Suffolk stated that the Queen had openly confessed and acknowledged the

[1] 1 Parl. Hist. 550.

great crime she had been guilty of against the most high God and a kind Prince, and, lastly, against the whole English nation.[1]

On the third day after this ceremony the unhappy Catherine and her companion, Lady Rochford, were led to execution,—bidding the spectators take notice that they suffered justly for "their offenses against God from their youth upward, and also against the King's royal Majesty very dangerously." It must be observed that, according to the ideas of the age,—for the sake of surviving relatives, it was not customary or reckoned becoming for persons, however unjustly condemned, to say any thing at their execution which could be offensive to the King, and we cannot fairly take these words as a confession of more than the irregularities imputed to Catherine before she had mounted a throne.

To obviate the difficulties now experienced if a similar case should again occur, the Chancellor, by the King's special orders, wound up the whole affair by bringing in a bill, which quickly passed both Houses, and received the royal assent from the King in person,—whereby it was enacted, that every woman about to be married to the King, or any of his successors, not being a true maid, should disclose her disgrace to him under the penalty of treason; and that all other persons knowing the fact, and not disclosing it, should be subject to the lesser penalty of misprison of treason.[2]

The law, which was afterwards repealed, as "trespassing too strongly as well on natural justice as female modesty,"[3] continued in force during the remainder of this reign, and so much frightened all the spinsters at Henry's court, that instead of trying to attract his notice, like Anne Boleyn, Jane Seymour, and Catharine Howard, in the hope of wearing a crown, they shunned his approach as if he had been himself the executioner; and they left the field open for widows, who could not, by any subtlety of Crown lawyers, be brought within its operation.[4] When the act

---

[1] 1 Parl. Hist. 553.   [2] Statutes of Realm, iv. 859.   [3] 1 Bl. Com. 222.
[4] See Lodge, vol. i. *Cath. Par.*—" In concluding another match he found a difficulty; for as it had been declared death for any whom the King should marry to conceal her incontinency in former time, so few durst hazard to venture into those bonds with a King who had, as they thought, so much facility in dissolving them. Therefore they stood off as knowing in what a slippery

passed, it had been foretold that the King, notwithstanding his passion for maids, would be obliged by it to marry a widow, and accordingly, on the 12th of July, 1543, he did marry, for his sixth and last wife, Catherine Par, who had been twice before led to the hymeneal altar,—first by Edward Lord Borough of Gainsborough, and secondly, by Neville Lord Latimer.

She was inclined to the new doctrines, and the marriage gave great satisfaction to Audley, Cranmer, and others of the same way of thinking; while it alarmed the Duke of Norfolk, Gardyner, and Wriothesley, now considered champions of the ancient faith.

The standard of orthodoxy, however, for the rest of this reign, was "The King's Book," which, with the exception of the Pope's supremacy, rigidly inculcated all the doctrines of the Church of Rome, and it would have been most dangerous for Queen or Chancellor to question anything which it contained.

On the 14th of January, 1544, began the last session of parliament which Audley ever saw; for, though not advanced in years, he was now pressed with infirmities, and he was threatened by an inexorable King, bearing a dart for his sceptre, whom no prayers or artifice or subserviency could appease.

The Chancellor's opening speech is no where to be be found, so that we have lost his felicitations to the King on this occasion, and we know not to what Saint or Hero he compared him for the extraordinary proof his Majesty had given of his love for his people in marrying a sixth time.

After a bill had passed ordaining that the royal style should be "King of England, France, and Ireland, Defender of the Faith, and of the Church of England and Ireland in earth the Supreme Head," the Chancellor, by the King's orders, introduced a measure of very great importance to regulate the succession to the Crown. As the law stood, the Princesses Mary and Elizabeth were both excluded as illegitimate, and it was highly penal to say that the mother of either of them had ever been lawfully married to the King. In default of his exercising his power of appointing a successor by deed or will,—

estate they were, if the King, after receiving them to bed, should through any mistake declare them no maids."—*Lord Herbert.*

after Prince Edward the right would have been in the issue of the King's eldest sister, Margaret, married to the King of Scots, and then in the issue of Mary, his youngest sister, married to the Duke of Suffolk. The bill now introduced, without saying anything expressly of the King's first two marriages, enacted that in default of Prince Edward and the heirs of his body, and of heirs by the King's present marriage, the Crown should go to the Lady Mary, the King's eldest daughter, and the heirs of her body; and then to the Lady Elizabeth, the King's younger daughter, and the heirs of her body, the power of appointment by deed or will being still reserved to the King;—with a proviso that an oath should be required to maintain the King's supremacy and the succession according to this act under the penalties of treason, and that whoever should say or write anything contrary to this act, or to the peril or slander of the King's heirs limited in the act, should be adjudged a traitor.[1] It immediately passed both houses, and was a suitable conclusion to Lord Chancellor Audley's performances in the legislative line, as in one moment he made it high treason to deny that which the moment before it was high treason to assert, respecting the legitimacy of the King's children and their right to succeed to the Crown,—he himself having brought in the bill which bastardized Mary, and settled the Crown on Elizabeth, and the bill which bastardized Elizabeth as well as Mary, and made it treason to assert the legitimacy of either.

On the 20th of March, the day when the session was closed,[2] Audley was on his death-bed, and the closing speech was made by the Duke of Norfolk, who referred to the Lord Chancellor's illness, and regretted the necessity imposed upon himself of dissolving the parliament in the King's name.

Audley's disease gaining upon him, and the business of Easter Term in the Court of Chancery requiring despatch, on Monday, the 21st of April, 1544, he (if we may believe all that is said in the entry in the Close Roll) *spontaneously* sent the Great Seal to the King by Sir Edward North and Sir Thomas Pope,—humbly praying that his Majesty would deign to accept the resignation of it, as, from bodily infirmity he was no longer able to perform the

[1] 35 Hen. 8, c. 1.   [2] 1 Parl. Hist. 559.

duties of the office, which by his Majesty's bounty he had so long held. His resignation was graciously accepted, but out of delicacy to him, and holding out a hope that he might recover and be reinstated in his office, the Great Seal was delivered to Sir THOMAS WRIOTHESLEY merely as Lord Keeper and to be held by him as Lord Keeper only during the illness of Lord Chancellor Audley.[1]

The following letter, which was lately discovered in the Augmentation Office, exhibits a curious picture of the dying Chancellor's plans and anxieties. It is written by his secretaries, who afterwards were his executors, to Sir Anthony Denny,—who did, as proposed, obtain the wardship of the Lady Margaret after her father's decease, although the projected match did not take place, and she formed much higher alliances:

"After owre righte hartie commendacions we shall like yow tunderstande the phisicons dispaire very mouche in

[1] Mem. qd vicesimo primo die Aprilis, &c. Thomas Audley Miles Dns Audley de Walden tunc Cancellarius Anglie infirmitate corporis debilitatus et considerans se ipm ex occone non valere excere et facre ea que ad officium suum tam in ministrando leges dci Dmni Regis justiceam qm in supervidendo pcessum per magnum sigillum dcti Dni Regis sigillandum dcum in manibus ipsius Thome, Dmni Cancellarii adtunc existens prfto Dno Regi per Edwardum North Militem et Thomam Pope Militem misit. Qui quidem Edwardus et Thomas Pope sigillum illud in quadam baga de albro corio inclusum et sigillo dci Dni Cancellarii munitum regie Majestati apud novum palacium suum Westm. in camera sua privato circa horam terciam post meridiem in presentia Thome Heneage, &c., presentarunt et obtulerunt humiliter suppliantes ex parte dci Thome Dni Cancellarii eandem regiam majestatem quatenus idem Dns Rex sigillum suum prdm recre et acceptare dignr Qui Dns Rex sigillum illud per manus ipsorum Edwardi et Thome Pope recepit et acceptavit et penes se retinuit usque in diem proxm. videlt, &c. Quo die circa horam terciam post meridiem prftus Dns Rex sigillum suum prdm apud palacium suum prdm in cama prta in presentia Antonii Denny, &c. Thome Wriothesley militi, Dno Wriothesley custodiendum et exercendum durante infirmitate dci Thome Dni Audley Dni Cancellarii comisit ipsumque Thomam Dn Wriothesley magni sigilli regii durante infirmitate dci Dni Cancellarii ibidem constituit et ordinavit cum auctoritate excendi et facdi omnia et singula que Dns Cancellarius Angle prtextu officii sui prdci facre et exre potuisset et valeret, &c. The circumstantiality of the Close Roll historiographer of the Great Seal is very amusing, as he not only tells the day, the hour, the house, the room in the house, and in whose presence the transfer was made, but the color of the leathern bag in which the Great Seal was contained.

or good Chauncellor his helthe: and suerly for or parts we thinke his Lordship to be in greate danger, and that there is small hoope of his recoverye. Wherfore, forasmouche as before this tyme, we knowing his Lordship's ernest disposition and hartie good wille to joyne withe yow in mariage betwixte your sonne and his eldest doughter wherin yt hathe pleased hym oftentymes to use oure poore advise,—we have therfore thought goode to signifie his state to yowe to thentente yow may further declare the same unto the Kings ma^{tie}; and therupon to be an humble suter unto his highness for the prefermente of his saide eldest doughter, whome we beleve he coulde be contente right hartilye amongest other his legasies to bequethe unto yow, so he mighte dispose her as he maye other his possessions and moveables. And thus mooste hartily fare yow well. From Crechurche, this Wedynsdaye. Your own, most assuredlye,

"EDWARD NORTH,
"THO. POPE."

On the 30th of April following, Audley expired in the 56th year of his age.

He is a singular instance of a statesman, in the reign of Henry VIII., remaining long in favor and in office, and dying a natural death. Reckoning from the time when he was made Speaker of the House of Commons, he had been employed by Henry constantly since the fall of Wolsey,—under six Queens,—avoiding the peril of acknowledging the Pope on the one hand, or offending against the Six Articles on the other. He enjoyed great power, amassed immense wealth, was raised to the highest honors and dignities, and reaped what he considered a full recompense for his "infamy."

Such a sordid slave does not deserve that we should say more of his vices or demerits. It has been observed, that the best apology for Wolsey was the contrast between the early and the latter part of Henry's reign; and Audley's severest condemnation must be a review of the crimes which, if he did not prompt, he abetted. He might have been reproached by his master in the language of a former tyrannical sovereign of England,—

"Hadst thou but shook thy head, or made a pause,
Or turn'd an eye of doubt upon my face,
Deep shame had struck me dumb."

But no eunuch in a seraglio was ever a more submissive tool of the caprice and vengeance of a passionate and remorseless master than was Lord Chancellor Audley.

According to a desire expressed in his will, he was buried at Saffron Walden, in the chancel of the parish church which he had erected. There an altar tomb of black marble was raised to him with the following inscription, which some suppose that, in imitation of his immediate predecessor, he had himself composed; and which Fuller quaintly enough calls "a *lamentable* epitaph."

"The stroke of deathe's inevitable Dart . Hath now alas of lyfe beraft the hart . Of Syr Thomas Audeley of the Garter Knight . Late Chancellour of England under owr Prince of might . Henry Theight wyrthy high renowne . And made by Him Lord Audeley of this Town. Obiit ultimo die Aprilis, Anno Domini 1544, Regni Regis Henrici 8, 36, Cancellariatus sui 13, et suæ Ætatis 56."

The Chancellor espoused Lady Mary Grey, one of the daughters of Thomas, second Marquis of Dorset. Any one might have supposed that he would have been sufficiently proud of such a noble alliance, whereas he actually sued the King for further recompense, as he expresses himself, "*for reparation of my pour marriage, wherein his Majestè was the principall doer.*"[1]

Lady Audley, who survived her husband many years, bore to him two daughters; Mary, who died in childhood, and Margaret, who became sole heir to her father's vast possessions. She married first, Lord Henry Dudley, who fell at the battle of St. Quintin's; and, secondly, Thomas, fourth Duke of Norfolk, by whom, amongst other issue, she had Thomas, afterwards created Earl of Suffolk, who built Audley End, in honor of his maternal grandfather,[2] and from whom are descended the Earls of Suffolk and Berkshire, and Carlisle, the Earls and Marquises of Bristol, and the Lords Howard de Walden, besides the Earls of Bindon and Lords Howard of Escrick, whose titles are extinct.

Lord Audley has been always considered as the founder of Magdalene College, Cambridge, which he endowed with large estates. He also authorized the society to use his arms; and appointed " his heirs, the possessors of the late

[1] Cottonian MSS.
[2] "A stately palace," says Dugdale, "not to be equalled, excepting **Hampton Court**, by any in this realm."—*Bar.* tit. "Audley."

monastery, of Walden, visitors of the College *in perpetuum*, with the right of nominating the masters;" which privileges are still exercised by Lord Baybrooke, the present owner of Audley End.[1]

CHAPTER XXXV.

LIFE OF LORD CHANCELLOR WRIOTHESLEY FROM HIS BIRTH TILL THE DEATH OF HENRY VIII.

THE new Chancellor displayed very different qualities from his predecessor, being a man of principle; but he was, if possible, a worse minister; for, when invested with power, he proved narrow-minded, bigoted, and cruel. Fortunately, he was likewise rash and headstrong, so that his objects were generally defeated, and his political career was short.

Thomas Wriothesley was sprung from a family long distinguished in "*Arms*," for they were Heralds. John, his grandfather, was Garter King at Arms to Edward IV. Thomas, his uncle, filled the same office under Henry VII. William, his father, was Norroy King at Arms to that Sovereign.

Thomas, the future Peer and Chancellor, early initiated in heraldic lore, was not contented with the prospect of wearing a tabard, making visitations, examining pedigrees, and marshalling processions. He therefore abjured the Heralds' College, took to the study of the common law, and was called to the bar. He was a diligent student, and made considerable proficiency in his legal studies, but he does not seem ever to have risen into much practice as an advocate; and he showed a preference of politics to law. In 1535, having recommended himself to Lord Chancellor Audley, through his interest an office of considerable emolument was conferred upon him in the Court of Common Pleas. Three years after he was made Secretary of State, a post beginning to be important, but still

---

[1] I am exceedingly indebted to this descendant of the illustrious House of Neville (several members of which held the office of Lord Chancellor) for information enabling me considerably to improve my memoir of Lord Audley.— *Note to 2nd Edition.*

very inferior to its present rank, as then the Lord Chancellor conducted foreign negotiations, and attended to the internal administration of the country. He was a warm adherent of the old faith, to which Henry himself was sincerely attached, except in as far as the "supremacy" was concerned; and with the Duke of Norfolk and Gardyner, he formed the party actually opposed to the Reformation, who procured the passing of "the Six Articles."

He was now in such high favor, that he was employed in the embassy sent by Henry during his widowhood, after the death of Jane Seymour, to negotiate a marriage for him with Christiana, the Duchess Dowager of Milan, then in Flanders, at the Viceregal Court. This negotiation failed, and so did another of the same kind, in which Wriothesley was engaged for an alliance with Mary of Guise, who preferred the youthful King of Scotland, James V., Henry's nephew. The negotiator, in consequence, was some time in disgrace; but luckily for him he had strenuously opposed a match with a German Princess, from the dread of the introduction of Lutheranism; and the sight of Anne of Cleves obtained for him warm thanks for the advice he had given.

After the fall of Cromwell, Wriothesley might be considered prime minister; for Audley did not aspire higher than to remain in office to execute the measures of others. As the chief in the King's confidence, he went abroad to negotiate in person the treaty with the Emperor Charles V., which, to his great delight, led to the restoration of the Princess Mary to her place in the line of the royal succession, and opened the prospect of the suppression of Lutheranism.

The bounties of the Crown were now lavished upon him. On the death of Robert Earl of Sussex, he was made Chamberlain of the Exchequer, and Constable of Southampton and Porchester castles; the possessions of the dissolved abbey of Tichfield were granted to him, and he was raised to the peerage by the title of Baron Wriothesley of Tichfield, in the County of Hants.

The disgrace of Queen Catherine Howard had been a heavy affliction to him and to all true Roman Catholics, as she was an avowed protectress of the old faith; and very anxious to have seen another of the same ecclesiastical opinions succeed her as consort to the sovereign, he from time to time recommended alliances with reigning houses in Europe who remained true to Rome. He was exceedingly surprised and shocked, therefore, when he was told one morning by the King that he had resolved to marry the Lady Catherine Par, a widow of unimpeached private character; but, in religion, regarded as little better than a Lutheran. He was very much alarmed by apprehension of the influence she might acquire, and the advantage she might give to the cause of the Reformation, which in spite of frequent executions for heresy, was daily gaining ground in England. He did not venture upon the idle task of combating the King's inclination; and he passively saw the ceremony of the marriage performed by Gardyner, Bishop of Winchester, in the Queen's Privy Closet at Hampton Court, although Cranmer, actuated by contrary feelings,—to hasten and secure the match, had granted a special license, dispensing with the publication of banns and all contrary ordinances.

Wriothesley, nevertheless, under the influence of misguided zeal, resolved, for the good of the Church, to take the earliest opportunity of making the new Queen share the fate of her predecessors;—sanguine in the hope that *she* would be indiscreet, and that the King would be relentless.

The declining health of Lord Audley showed that a vacancy in the office of Chancellor was at hand, and Wriothesley, without hesitation, agreed to accept it; for its duties were not considered at all incompatible with those of prime minister; and the patronage and emoluments peculiarly belonging to it, made it always an object of the highest ambition.

Audley's resignation taking place on the 22nd of April, 1544, we have seen that on the same day the Great Seal was delivered to Wriothesley, with the modest title of "Lord Keeper during the illness of the Chancellor." Having gratefully received it from the King at Whitehall, he carried it to his house in Cannon Row, and there, the following day, " he held a Seal."[1]

On Friday, the 30th of April, the first day of Easter Term, while Audley was breathing his last, the Lord Keeper publicly took the oaths in the Court of Chancery

[1] Rot. Cl. 36 Hen. 8.

in Westminster Hall. His abjuration of the Pope was very ample, and must have cost him a severe pang, unless he had a dispensation for taking it:—

"I, Thomas Wriothesley, Knyght, Lord Wriothesley, Lorde Keeper of the Brode Seale, havynge now the vaile of darkness of the usurped power, auctoritie, and jurisdiccion of the See and Bishoppes of Rome clearly taken away from myne eyes, do utterly testifie and declare in my conscience, that neyther the See, nor the Bishop of Rome, nor any foraine potestate, hath nor ought to have any jurisdiccion, power, or auctoritie within this realme, neither by Godd's lawe, nor by any other juste lawe or meanes; and though by sufferance and abusions in tymes passed, they aforesaide have usurped and vindicated a fayned and unlawful power and jurisdiccion within this realme, whiche hath ben supported tyll fewe yeres passed, therefore, by cause it myght be denied, and thought thereby that I toke or take it for just and good, I therefore nowe do clerely and frankeley renounce, refuse, relinquish, and forsake the pretended auctoritie, power, and jurisdiccion both of the See and Bishop of Rome, and of all other foraine powers; and that I shall never consent nor agre that the foresaid See or Bishop of Rome, or any of their successours, shall practise, exercise, or have any manner of auctoritie, jurisdiccion, or power within this realme, or any other of the Kynge's realmes or domynions, nor any foraine potestate, of what estate, degree, or condiccion soever he be, but that I shall resiste the same at all tymes to the utmost of my power, and that I shall accepte, repute, and take the Kynge's majestie, his heyres, and successors, when they or any of them shall enjoy his place, to be the only supreme Head in earth, under God, of the Churche of England and Ireland, and of all other his Hignesse's dominions; and in case any other hathe ben made by me to any person or persons in maintenance, defence, or favour of the See or Bishop of Rome, or his auctoritie, jurisdiccion, or power, I reporte the same as vague and adnihilate, and shall holly and trewely observe and kepe this othe. So help me God, all Sainctes, and the Holy Evangelists."[1]

The old Duke of Norfolk, who had so often officiated on such occasions, attended this installation, but we have

[1] Rot. Cl. 36 Hen. 8.

no account of any orations delivered, and probably the ceremony was made as short and simple as possible, out of delicacy to the dying Audley.

On the third day after his death the Lord Keeper brought the Great Seal to the King at Whitehall, and resigned it into his hands. His Majesty, sitting on his throne, having accepted it, re-delivered it to him, with the title of "Lord Chancellor," making a speech very complimentary both to the deceased and the living Chancellor.[1]

There was then a grand procession from the Palace to Westminster Hall; and in the Court of Chancery the Duke of Norfolk, by the King's command, again administered the oaths to the new Chancellor, and installed him in his office.

Although bred to the law, he had never been thoroughly imbued with its principles nor versed in its forms; and his scanty legal learning had been almost entirely forgotten by him since he had abandoned professional for political pursuits.

He accordingly found himself very inadequate to the discharge of the judicial duties of his office, and the public complained loudly of his delays and mistakes. He continued to sit during Easter and Trinity Terms, pelted by motions which he knew not how to dispose of, and puzzled by causes the bearings of which he could hardly be made to understand;—perplexed by the conflicting assertions of the opposite counsel as to the doctrine and practice of the Court;—his chief solicitude being to conceal his ignorance from the bar and the by-standers;—desirous to do what was right both for his own conscience and his credit,—but with constant apprehensions that his

---

[1] "Dms Rex in solio suo regali sedens et sigillum prdum in baga predicta inclusum manu sua tenens *post verba ad prftum Thomam Wriothesley et alios ibidem prestes habita*, sigillum illud prefto Thome Dno Wriothesley tanqm Dno Cancellario Anglie tradidit et redeliberavit ipsumque Thomam Dmm Wriothesley Cancellarium suum Anglie constituit." The entry then goes on to specify the names of the Master of the Rolls, and a large assemblage present, and to state that the Chancellor having opened the bag and taken out the seal, sealed a writ with it and restored it to the bag, carried it off with him, and describes the ceremony of his swearing in; but instead of again setting out the oath of supremacy, merely says, " I, Thomas Wriothesley, Knight, Lorde Wriothesley, Lorde Chancellor of England, havynge now the vaile of darkness," &c., ut supra.

decisions were erroneous, and that he was ridiculed in private, even by those who flattered him in his presence. At length the long vacation came to his relief, during which, in those times, the tranquillity of the Chancellor was little disturbed by motions for injunctions or summary applications of any sort.

He now applied himself to the study of the few cases in the recent Year Books as to where "a subpœna lies," and tried to gain information from the officers of the Court to qualify him for a more satisfactory performance of his part in "the marble chair;" but as Michaelmas Term approached, his heart failed him, and he resolved not again to expose himself to the anxieties and indignities he had before suffered. Nevertheless, he by no means intended to resign the Great Seal, and with the King's consent, on the 9th of October, 1544,[1] he issued a commission to Sir Robert Southwell, Master of the Rolls, and several others, to hear causes in the Court of Chancery during his absence. He afterwards took his seat in court occasionally, as a matter of form: but on these Commissioners he, in reality, devolved all the judicial business of his office, and during the remainder of the reign of Henry VIII. he devoted himself entirely to matters of state and religion.

There was no profound peace with France and the Emperor, and the public attention was absorbed by the struggle between the favorers and opposers of the new doctrines. The Chancellor was at the head of the latter party, and showed the qualities of a Grand Inquisitor, rather than an enlightened minister to a constitutional King.

Henry, his pride and peevishness increasing as his health declined, was disposed to punish with fresh severity all who presumed to entertain a different speculative notion from himself respecting religion, particularly on any point embraced by the "Six Articles" framed against Lutheranism; and the Chancellor, instead of restraining and soothing, urged on and inflamed his persecuting spirit.

In spite of all these efforts the reformed doctrines gained ground, and were even becoming fashionable at Court under the secret countenance of the Queen. The alarm was given by the indiscretion of Anne Ascue, one of her

[1] Rot. Cl. 36 Hen. 8.

maids, a young lady of great beauty, of gentle manners, and warm imagination, who had had the temerity to declare in a large company, "that in her opinion, after a consecration of the elements in the sacrament of the Lord's Supper, the substance of bread and wine still remains in them." This conversation being reported to the King and the Chancellor, she was summoned and examined before the Council. Being menaced by Bonner, who was beginning to show that disposition which proved so formidable in a succeeding reign, she recanted to a certain degree, but still under qualifications which were not satisfactory, and she was committed to prison on a charge of heresy. This severity only heightened her enthusiasm: she now saw the crown of martyrdom within her reach, and she resolved to court it by boldly asserting her religious principles. A letter which she wrote to the King, saying, "as to the Lord's Supper, she believed as much as Christ himself had taught or the Catholic Church required, but that she could not assent to his Majesty's explication of the doctrine," was considered a fresh insult, and as it was suspected that she was countenanced by the leaders of the Lutheran party at Court, the Lord Chancellor went himself in person to interrogate her in the hope of obtaining some evidence against Cranmer, or against the Queen. Anne freely answered all the Chancellor's questions respecting her own faith, but she maintained an inviolable fidelity to her friends, and would give no information as to her instructors or participators in the heretical opinions she expressed. According to a custom then common, defended by high authority as necessary to religion and good government, and not entirely abolished in England for near a century afterwards, she was thereupon ordered to be put to the torture. This being applied with great barbarity without extorting any confession, the Chancellor ordered the Lieutenant of the Tower to stretch the rack still further. The refractory officer refused compliance, though repeatedly ordered by the highest Judge in the land, and menaced with the King's displeasure and the utmost vengeance of the law. Thereupon (such are the enormities which may be prompted by superstitious zeal!) Wriothesley,—on ordinary occasions a humane man,—now excited by resistance, and persuading himself that discoveries might be obtained which would do service to

God,—put his own hand to the rack and drew it so violently, that he almost tore asunder the tender limbs of his youthful and delicately formed victim. Her constancy still surpassed the barbarity of her persecutor, and he was obliged to withdraw, baffled and discomfited, lest she should die under his hands without the form of trial.[1]

When he made complaint, as he had threatened, of the clemency of the Lieutenant of the Tower, it should be recorded that Henry approved of the conduct of this officer, and refused to dismiss him. It was resolved, however, to proceed against Anne Ascue, according to the existing statutes; and she was brought to trial, with several others, for denying the real presence. A clear case was proved against them; and, under the law of the Six Articles, they were duly sentenced to be burnt. Anne was still so much dislocated by the rack, that she was carried in a chair to the place of execution.

The Chancellor, in the hope of saving the criminals, or of aggravating their guilt, made out of a conditional pardon to them, to which, with the King's consent, he affixed the Great Seal; and when they had been tied to the stake,—before the torch was applied to the fagots which were to consume them, he communicated to them that the pardon which was shown them should be instantly handed to them if they would deserve it by a recantation. Anne and her companions only considered this offer a fresh garland to their crown of martyrdom; and continuing their devotions, calmly saw the devouring flames rise around them.[2]

Wriothesley soon after thought that he had got into his power a nobler victim, and that he might offer up a still more acceptable sacrifice. It should be borne in mind that, during this reign, the situation of Queen was considered an office at Court to be struggled for by contending factions. The Catholics were most active in the prosecution of Anne Boleyn, and the divorce of Anne of Cleves; the Reformers had been equally active in the divorce of Catherine of Aragon, and the prosecution of

---

[1] I am sorry for the honor of the law to say that Griffin, the Solicitor General, was present at this scene, and, instead of interceding for Anne, recommended himself to the Chancellor by tightening the rope with his own hand to add to her torture. This is said to be the only instance of a woman being put to the torture in England.—See Jardine's Reading on Torture, p. 65.

[2] Fox, vol. ii. p. 578. Speed, p. 780. Baker, p. 299.

Catherine Howard. Now, the Catholics were eager to pull down Catherine Par, in the hope that a true Catholic might take her place on the throne. What no saint would promise to the supplicating Wriothesley, and what the rack would not accomplish for him, he thought that chance, or rather the good providence of God, had unexpectedly brought to pass.

Gardyner came to him one morning to announce that the King had been gravely complaining to him of the Queen for abetting Lutheran doctrines in their *tete-à-tete* conversations, and for secretly sinning against the Six Articles; and that his Majesty had favorably listened to the remarks he had hazarded to make to him, " that such misconduct could not be winked at by a King anxious for preserving the orthodoxy of his subjects." The Chancellor flew into the royal presence to take proper advantage of this disposition, and eagerly represented, "that the more elevated the individual was who was made amenable to the law, and the nearer to his person, the greater terror would the example strike into every one, and the more glorious would the sacrifice appear to posterity." Henry was so much touched by these topics, that he directed articles of impeachment to be drawn up against his consort, so that she might forthwith be brought to trial and arraigned; and ordered that the following day she should be arrested by the Chancellor himself, and carried to the Tower of London. Wriothesley joyfully drew the articles, and brought them to the King for his royal signature; without which it was not deemed regular or safe to take any further step in the prosecution. Henry signed the paper without hesitation, and the execution of another Queen seemed inevitable.

By some means the contents of this paper became known to a friend of Catherine, who instantly warned her of her danger. She fainted away at the intelligence. On recovering her senses, she uttered frightful shrieks, and she well might have anticipated, after a mock trial, a speedy death on Tower Hill; for hitherto the King had never relented in any capital prosecution once commenced against wife or minister. She was told that her only chance of escape was to seem ignorant of his intentions, and to try to soothe and to disarm him before there should publicly be taken against her any step from which he could not recede without risking his reputation for firmness and courage. She showed much presence of mind, and went to pay the King her usual visit with a tranquil and cheerful air. He began, as he had lately done, to challenge her to an argument on divinity, thinking he should obtain a still plainer avowal of her heterodoxy. But she said, " She humbly hoped she might be permitted to decline the conversation, as such profound speculations were ill-suited to the natural imbecility of women, who, by their first creation, were made subject to men, the male being created after the image of God, the female after the image of the male; it belonged, therefore, to the husband to choose principles for his wife, the wife's duty being, in all cases, to adopt implicitly the sentiments of her husband. As for herself, it was doubly her duty, being blest with a husband who was qualified by his learning and judgment, not only to prescribe articles of faith for his own family, but for the most wise and knowing of every nation." This speech, so artfully adapted to his peculiar notions of female submission and his own fancied superiority, delivered with such apparent sincerity,—for he did not suspect that she was at all aware of the pending prosecution,—so pleased him that he exclaimed, " Not so! by St. Mary; you are now become a doctor, Kate, and better fitted to give than to receive instruction."

She followed up her success by meekly observing, that she was little entitled to such praise on the present occasion, as the sentiments she now expressed she had ever entertained; that, though she had been in the habit of joining in any conversation proposed by his Majesty, she well knew her conceptions on any topics beyond domestic affairs could only give him a little momentary amusement; that, finding their colloquy sometimes apt to languish when not quickened by some opposition, she had ventured to feign a difference of opinion, in order to give him the pleasure of refuting her, and that all she purposed by this artifice, which she trusted he would deem innocent, was to engage him in discussions, whence she had herself derived profit and instruction. "And is it indeed so, sweetheart?" replied the King; "then we are perfect friends."

Luckily for her, there was no fair maid of hers on whom he had cast an eye of affection, and whom he had destined for Queen, or all Catherine's eloquence would not have saved her from the penalties of heresy and treason ; but having no other inclination, and having been pleased with has as a companion and a nurse, he sent her away with assurances of his kindness and protection.

Next day Henry and Catherine were conversing amicably in the garden, when the Lord Chancellor, ignorant of the King's change of intention, appeared with forty poursuivants to arrest her and carry her to the Tower. She withdrew to some distance, saying that she supposed that the Chancellor wished to speak with his Highness on public business. From where she stood she could hear the appellations of "*Fool, knave,* and *beast,*" bestowed with great emphasis upon the Chancellor, and an order at last given to him by the King, in a resentful tone, *to depart his presence.* When Wriothesley was gone, Catherine ran up to the King, and tried to soothe him by putting in a good word for the object of his anger. "Poor soul, cried he, "you little know how ill entitled this man is to your kind offices."

The orthodox Chancellor was still on the watch to find an occasion to do an ill turn to her whom he justly suspected of being in her heart Lutheran ; but Catherine, cautious after narrowly escaping so great a peril, never more offended Henry's humor by any contradiction, and remained in his good graces to the end of his life.

Wriothesley was now employed as a Commissioner to conclude a treaty with Scotland, and conducted the negotiation so much to Henry's satisfaction, that he was installed a Knight of the Garter, being the second Chancellor who had reached this dignity.

On the 23d of November, 1546, met the only parliament called while Wriothesley was Chancellor. We do not find anywhere his speech at the opening of the session; but if we may judge of what took place at the prorogation, it had not been much applauded; and certainly it had not flattered the King to his liking.

The first act of the session was to take away from the Chancellor a patronage which, the preamble recites, had been greatly abused, of appointing the Custos Rotulorum in every county, and to provide that the appointment thereafter shall be directly by the King.[1] But the great

---
[1] 37 Hen. 8, c. 1.

object of the King was to have made over to him by parliament certain colleges, chantries, and hospitals, with very extensive possessions, which were supposed to be connected with the Pope as their religious head, and were now dissolved.[1] The plunder of the monasteries was all dissipated, and notwithstanding large subsidies, the Exchequer was empty. But this new fund, managed by the Court of Augmentations under the Chancellor's superintendence, brought in a tolerably sufficient revenue during the remainder of Henry's reign.

At the close of the session, after the Speaker of the House of Commons had delivered his oration, the King himself made the reply, beginning in a manner not quite complimentary to Chancellor Wriothesley. "Although my Chancellor for the time being hath before this time used very eloquently and substantially to make answer to such orations, yet is he not able to open and set forth my mind and meaning, and the secrets of my heart, in so plain and ample a manner as I myself am and can do." His Majesty then, with modest vanity, disclaims the praises bestowed upon him; but in such language as shows that he conceived they were well merited. "But of such small qualities as God hath endued me withal, I render to his goodness my most humble thanks, intending, with all my art and diligence, to get and acquire to me such notable virtues and princely qualities as you have alleged to be incorporate in my person."[2]

This was the last time that Henry ever appeared upon the throne before Parliament. He had now grown immensely corpulent; he was soon after unable to stir abroad, and in his palace he could only be moved from one room to another by machinery. All began to look forward to a new reign, and there was intense anxiety as to the manner in which Henry would exercise the power conferred upon him by parliament to provide for the government of the country during the minority of Prince Edward, and to direct the succession to the Crown on the death of his own children without issue.

Wriothesley, the Chancellor, had the most constant access to him, and was eager that a settlement should be made the most favorable to the Catholic faith; but he was thwarted by the Seymours, the young Prince's uncles,

[1] 37 Hen. 8, c. 4. [2] 1 Parl. Hist. 562.

who were strong favorers of the Reformation, and determined, upon the accession of their nephew, to engross the whole royal authority into their own hands. The King's will, drawn by Wriothesley, was at last executed, but whether with the forms required by law is still a matter of controversy.[1] By this will Wriothesley himself was appointed one of the sixteen Executors, to whom was entrusted the government of the realm till the Prince, then a boy nine years old, should complete his eighteenth year, and he counted, with absolute certainty, upon the Great Seal remaining in his hands during the whole of that interval.

Through the agency of the Chancellor, Henry's reign had a suitable termination in the unjust prosecution of the Duke of Norfolk and the Earl of Surrey, the greatest subjects in the kingdom, the father deserving respect for his devoted services to the Crown, not less than for his illustrious birth; and the son, distinguished by every accomplishment which became a scholar, a courtier, and a soldier, refining the language and softening the manners of the age,—uniting the brilliant qualities of chivalry with the taste and cultivation of modern times,—celebrating the praises of his mistress in the tournament, as well as in the sonnet and the masque. It can hardly be supposed that Wriothesley planned their downfall, for they were of the same religious faith with himself, unless it may be conjectured that he himself wished to be the head of the party, and to guide all its measures in the succeeding reign. But admitting, what is more probable, that the Seymours, dreading the influence of the House of Howard, were the original instigators of this prosecution, Wriothesley, instead of resisting it, sanctioned and promoted it,—making himself accessory to the murder of the son,—and not having likewise to answer for that of the father, only

---

[1] On the question, whether the power given to Henry to appoint to the succession was duly executed, depended in strictness the right of the Stuarts to the throne; for he excluded them, preferring the issue of his younger sister, married to the Duke of Suffolk, whose descendants still exist. The better opinion seems to be that the signature by the stamp, though affixed by the King's command, was defective. Wriothesley was not by any means an accurate lawyer, and in the hurry in which the instrument was executed there is no improbability in supposing that the conditions of the power were not strictly fulfilled. At all events, after a lapse of 300 years, and the subsequent acts of settlement, our allegiance cannot much depend on this nicety.—See *Hall. Const. Hist.* vol. i. p. 393.

by being suddenly freed from the inhuman master whose commands he was afraid to disobey or question. He concurred in the commitment of both of them to the Tower on the same day. Surrey being a commoner, a commission under the Great Seal was issued for his trial before a jury; and this hope of his country, a man of undoubted loyalty and unsullied honor, being convicted of high treason on no better evidence than that he had quartered the arms of Edward the Confessor on his scutcheon,—by authority of a warrant signed by the Chancellor, was immediately executed.[1]

It was necessary to deal with the Duke of Norfolk as a Peer. A session of parliament being called on the 14th of January, 1547, on the 18th a bill was brought inio the House of Lords for his attainder, and passed that House on the 20th. The overt act of treason was, that he had said that "the King was sickly and could not hold out long, and the kingdom was likely to fall into disorders through the diversity of religious opinions." The bill being returned passed by the House of Commons on the 24th, the Lord Chancellor on the 27th having ordered all the Peers to put on their robes, and the Commons, with their Speaker, to attend at the bar, declared to both Houses that his Majesty wishing the bill for the attainder of the Duke of Norfolk to be expedited, that his office of Earl Marshal might be filled up by another, and being hindered by sickness from coming to give his royal assent to it in person, he had directed a commission to pass the Great Seal, authorizing him and other Peers to give the royal assent to it in the King's name, The commission being read, the Lord Chancellor commanded the clerk of parliament to pronounce the words, *Soit fait comme il est désiré*; and so it being passed into a law, a warrant was issued for the execution of Norfolk on the 29th of January.[2] But early in the morning of that day news was brought to the Tower that Henry had expired in the night, and the lieutenant gladly suspended the execution of a sentence so unjust and tyrannical.

In the reign of Mary the attainder was reversed, on the ground that the offense of which he was accused was not treason, and that Henry had not signed the commission,

---

[1] 1 St. Tr. 453.   [2] 1 St. Tr. 457. 1 Parl. Hist. 561.

in virtue of which his pretended assent had been given to the act of parliament.

On the 31st of January the Lord Chancellor formally announced the King's death to both Houses: and, says the Journal, "the mournful news was so affecting to the Chancellor and all present that they could not refrain from tears!"[1] It is impossible that there should not have been a general joy at the deliverance of the country from the rule of such a heartless tyrant.[2]

A few sentences will be sufficient to notice the state of the equitable jurisdiction of the Court of Chancery, and the changes in the law, during this reign. By the Statute of Uses, 27 H. 8, c. 10, it was proposed to confine all controversies respecting land to the Courts of common law, by preventing a severance between the legal and beneficial estate; but the conveyancers and the Judges repealed the act of parliament by the addition of three words to a deed; and "uses" being revived under the name of "trusts," the jurisdiction of the Court of Chancery over land was confirmed and extended. The Statute of Wills, 32 H. 8, c. 1, for the first time gave a general power of devising real property; and the Statute of Limitations, 32 H. 8, c. 2, conferred an indefeasible right to it after an adverse possession of sixty years.

The first Special Commission for hearing causes in Chancery was granted in this reign, while Cardinal Wolsey was sitting on the trial of Catherine's divorce. It was directed to the Master of the Rolls, four Judges, six

[1] Several of the successors of St. Swithin have been much given to *crying*, and we shall hereafter see one of them weeping so as to recall " the iron tears which rolled down the cheeks of Pluto."

[2] I must express my astonishment and regret to find the character and conduct of Henry defended by such an able writer and excellent man as Mr. Sharon Turner, who thus apologises for his worst acts:—" None of these severities were inflicted without the due legal authority. The verdict of juries, the solemn judgment of the Peers, or attainders by both Houses of parliament on offenses proved to its satisfaction, pronounced all the convictions, and produced the fatal sentence. Every one was approved and sanctioned by the cabinet council of the government. The King is responsible only for adopting the harsh system, for not interposing his prerogative of mercy, and for signing the death warrants which ordered the legal sentences to be put in force. He punished no one tyrannically without trial or legal condemnation."—*Turner's Hist. of Eng.* vol. x. p. 532. What difference is there between procuring a house of parliament or a jury to convict an innocent man of a capital charge, and hiring an assassin to take away his life? The most dangerous species of murder is that which is committed under the forms of law.

Masters, and ten others, and authorized them, or any four of them, two being the Masters of the Rolls, Judges, or Masters, to hear, examine, and finally determine all causes in Chancery committed to them by the Chancellor, and to order execution thereon.[1]

Although there are some valuable reports of common law cases in this reign, there is no trace of any of the decisions of Chancellors Warham, Wolsey, More, Audley, or Wriothesley; and the rules by which they guided their discretion still remained vague or unknown.

In this reign there were several instances of the Court of Chancery pronouncing decrees for divorces; and there seemed a probability that it would assume a jurisdiction to decree the specific performance of a contract to marry, and a restitution of conjugal rights; but it was afterwards held, that the Ecclesiastical Court alone has cognizance of marriage and divorce.[2]

CHAPTER XXXVI.

CONCLUSION OF THE LIFE OF LORD CHANCELLOR WRIOTHESLEY.

ON the same day that Henry died the young King was proclaimed; and the sixteen Executors assembled in the Tower to commence their government in his name.

Wriothesley thought he had so arranged matters that the chief power would be in his own hands. Archbishop Cranmer was the first on the list; but he was not expected to mix much with secular affairs. Next came the Chancellor, who would naturally be looked up to as the real head, and would be enabled to guide the deliberations of the body. He therefore was most anxious that the King's will should be strictly observed; and as soon as they had taken their places at the board, and the will had been read, he moved " that it be resolved not only to stand to

[1] Rym. xiv. 299. This commission has since been followed as a precedent for delegations of the judicial authority of the Chancellor.
[2] See Tothill, 124. De Manniville v. De Manniville, 10 Ves. 60. In America the Court of Chancery still decides in matrimonial suits.

and maintain the testament of their master the late King, and every part and article of the same to the uttermost of their power, wits, and cunning, but also that every one of them present should take a corporal oath for the more assured and effectual accomplishment of the same." This resolution could not be decently objected to; the oath was taken, and the Chancellor thought himself secure.

But the ceremony of swearing had hardly been concluded, when the Earl of Hertford, the King's uncle, who, as Lord Chamberlain, was only fourth in precedence in the Council, but who was determined to get all power into his own hands, suggested that, for the despatch of business, for the facility of communicating with foreign ambassadors, and for the purpose of representing on other occasions the person of the young Sovereign, it would be necessary to elect one of the Council to preside, with such title as might be agreed upon; and that he himself would willingly submit to any one whom a majority might prefer. Thereupon, according to a concerted plan, a creature of Hertford's moved that he, as nearest in blood to the King, and not in the line of succession to the throne, and eminent for his abilities and virtues, should be appointed governor of the King's person, and Protector of the realm.

Wriothesley rose, and with fury opposed a measure which he saw would reduce himself to insignificance. He insisted that it would be a direct infringement of the late King's will, which, being made under a statute, had all the force of an act of the legislature, and could not be altered but by the same authority which had established it. By the words and the spirit of the instrument under which they were there assembled, all the Executors were equal, and were intended to remain so during the King's minority; and it would be monstrous to place one of them over the rest as Protector,—an undefined and ill-omened title, which the chronicles showed was always the forerunner of broils and civil war.

To his astonishment and consternation, however, he found that he made no impression upon his audience, and that a majority had been secured by his rival, who had been lavish of his promises in case he should be elected. Wriothesley was likewise personally unpopular, and his

adherence to the old religion was strongly against him,—
the current now running very strong in favor of the
Reformation. Seeing that opposition would be vain, he
abstained from calling for a division ; and he pretended to
be contented with an assurance, which he knew would
prove fallacious, that the new officer should in no case act
without the assent of a majority of the Council.

All the Lords, spiritual and temporal, were now assembled in the Chamber of Presence, into which the Executors conducted the young Edward. Each in succession
having kissed his hand kneeling, and uttered the words
" God save your grace !" the Chancellor explained to the
assembly the dispositions in the will of their late Sovereign, and the resolution of the Executors to put the Earl
of Hertford at their head,—without hinting at his own
disapproval of this step. All present unanimously signified their assent ; the new Protector expressed his gratitude " for the honor which had been so *unexpectedly* conferred upon him ;" and Edward, pulling off his cap, said,
" We heartily thank you, my Lords all ; and hereafter, in
all that ye shall have to do with us for any suit or causes,
ye shall be heartily welcome."

In the next measure of the new government, there was
the greatest respect professed for the late King, and it had
the unanimous support of all the Executors. There was
a clause in Henry's will, requiring them " to see that all
the promises he had made in his lifetime should be fulfilled after his death,"—without any statement in writing
what those promises were. According to the precedent
of Anthony, acting as executor under the will of Cæsar,—
they asserted that what was convenient to themselves had
been promised by the testator. Three gentlemen of his
privy chamber, with whom he had been most familiar, and
who knew that their assertion would not be questioned,
being called before the Board of Regency, declared they
had heard Henry say, shortly before his death, that he intended to make Hertford Duke of Somerset, Wriothesley
Earl of Southampton,—and so to confer on all of them
the titles in the peerage which they coveted—down to
Sir Richard Rice, who was to be made Baron Rich ;—with
suitable grants to all of them to support their new dignities. It should be recorded, to the honor of two of the
Council, St. Leger and Danby, that they declined the

proposed elevation; but all the rest accepted it, and our Chancellor became Earl of Southampton.[1]

Though he gained his title, he speedily lost his office. Notwithstanding a seeming reconciliation, as often as he and the Protector met in council, it was evident that there was a bitter enmity between them. Wriothesley, under pretense that nothing was to be done by the Protector without the authority of a majority of the Executors, tried to form a party against him, and thwarted him in all his measures. Somerset, feeling that he then had a decided majority in the Council, but doubtful how long with such intrigues it might last, was resolved, as soon as possible, to get rid of so dangerous a competitor.

The Chancellor soon furnished him with a pretence. We have seen how, in the time of Henry VIII, disliking judicial business, and feeling himself unfit for it, he issued, with the King's consent, a commission to the Master of the Rolls and others to sit for him in the Court of Chancery.[2] Now, that he might enjoy ease, and devote himself to his ambitious projects, he of his own mere motion, without royal warrant, or the authority of the Board of Regency, issued a similar commission to four lawyers, empowering them to hear all manner of causes in his absence; and giving to their decrees the same force as if they had been pronounced by himself, provided that, before enrollment, they were ratified by his signature.

Upon the Commissioners taking their seats in the Court of Chancery, there were murmurs among the barristers; and these coming to the ears of the delighted Somerset, he secretly suggested that a petition upon the subject should be presented to the Council. This being received as the spontaneous complaint of "the undersigned, actuated by a great respect for the constitution, and the due administration of justice," a reference was made to the Judges to pronounce upon the validity of the commission, and the nature of the offense committed by issuing it, if it were illegal. The Chancellor did not resist this proceeding, being in hopes that the Judges would take part with the head of the profession; but they, anticipating his downfall, returned for answer, that "the Chancellor having affixed the Great Seal without sufficient warrant

[1] However, he is not known in history by this title, and I shall continue to call him by his family name.   [2] Ante, p. 128.

to the commission, the commission was void, and that he had been guilty of an offense against the King, which, at common law, was punishable with loss of office, and fine and imprisonment, at the King's pleasure." He called for a second reference to them, on the ground that they had not properly considered the question, thinking that he might procure some of them to retract. They counted on the firmness of the Protector, and all adhered to their former opinion. A motion was now made in council to pronounce judgment against him, of deprivation of his office of Chancellor, and to sentence him to fine and imprisonment. He spoke boldly and ably in his defense, treating the opinion of the Judges with great contempt; and arguing that the commission was fully justified by former precedents. But if it were illegal for want of any form, he contended that the Council could only revoke it; and to avoid dispute, he was willing that it should at once be cancelled. He added, that if they hesitated to allow him the assistance enjoyed by former Chancellors, he was himself ready to do all the duties of the office in person; but that, holding the office by patent, and the late King's will, made under an act of parliament, having confirmed the grant, he could not be deprived of it during the minority of Edward. If there were any charge against him, he appealed to parliament, which alone could deal with his case.

He found, however, a most determined resolution against him in a majority of the Council, and he knew not to what extremities they might resort if he continued to defy them. To avoid going to the Tower, he said he should submit to their pleasure, and begged permission (which was granted) that he might return to his house in Ely Place, Holborn, while they deliberated upon his fate.

It was instantly resolved that he should be removed from the office of Chancellor and his seat in the Council. The same evening the sentence was communicated to him, with an intimation that he must remain a prisoner in his house till, upon further deliberation, the amount of his fine should be ascertained. Lord Seymour of Sudeley, the Protector's brother, Sir Anthony Brown, and Sir Edward North, were immediately sent to demand the Great Seal from him. He quietly surrendered it to them, and they carried it to Somerset, who, on receiving it into his hands, said to himself, "I am at last Lord Protector."[1] But, freed for a time from all rivalry, he played such fantastic tricks that he raised up fresh enemies, disgusted the nation, and, before long, was himself brought to the block.

No sooner was Wriothesley removed than the Protector caused the Great Seal to be affixed to letters patent, formally setting aside the King's will, and conferring on himself the whole authority of the Crown. A new Council was appointed, from which Wriothesley was excluded, with power to the Protector to add to their number, and to select from the whole body such individuals as he should think fit to form the Cabinet; but he was not bound to follow their advice, and he was empowered in every case to decide according to his own judgment till the King should have completed his eighteenth year.

Wriothesley was not further molested, and remained quiet for two years, till the Protector, by the execution of his brother, Lord Seymour, the contempt with which he treated all who approached him, and the imbecility and rashness of his measures of government, had rendered himself universally odious, and was tottering to his fall.

The Ex-Chancellor now contrived to get himself reinstated in the Council, and he associated himself with Dudley, Earl of Warwick, a man, from his energy and want of

---

[1] The entry of this transaction in the Close Roll is very curious. "Mem. qd Die Dnica videlt, &c. Magnum Sigillum ipsius Dni Regis in custodiâ Thome Comitis Southampton tunc Cancellar. Anglie existens per mandatum ejusdem Dni Regis de avisamento Dni Ducis Somerset psone regie Gubernatoris ac Regn. Protectoris necnon aliorum de consilio suo in manus ejusdem Dni Regis resumptum es idemque Comes adtunc de officio Cancellarii Angl. *ob offens. et transgress. pr. ipsum perpetrat.* et alias justas et ronabiles causas exonatus et amotus fuit. Sup. quo idem Mag. Sigill. in quadam baga de corio inclusum et coopt. alia baga de velveto rubeo * insigniis regiis ornat.

per eundem Comitem prtextu mandati prdci apud Hospit. ejusdem Comitis in Holbourn London vocat. Ely Place in quadam interiori Camera ibidem circa horam septimam post meridiem ejusdem diei nobil. viris Thome Seymour sacri ordinis garteri militi Dno. Seymour de Sudley, &c. libatum fuit Rusquidem Thomas Dns. Seymour, &c. Sigillum prdm. in baga predicta inclusum et sigillo ips. Comitis munitum demanibus ips Comitis recipiet illud circa horam nonam post meridiem prci diei in prsencia Wolli Paulet, &c. prnobili viro Edwardo Duci Somerset Dno Protectori prdco in Camera sua infra nov. Palac. West. prfto Dno Regi prstand. libaverunt."

* This is the first mention I find of the *red velvet bag*, with the royal arms, in which the Great Seal is now enclosed.

principle, rising into consequence, and destined soon to fill a great space in the eyes of mankind. They formed a party, to which they drew in the Earl of Arundel, Lord St. John, and several other members of the Council, and, holding their meetings at Ely House, prepared measures for depriving Somerset of all his authority.

At last the crisis arrived. The Councillors assembled in Holborn, assumed to themselves the functions of government, and professed to act under the powers conferred upon them as executors under the late King's will.

The Protector carried off the King from Hampton Court to Windsor Castle, under an escort of 500 men, and issued orders to the adjoining counties to come in for the guard of the royal person. A manifesto was issued, prepared by Wriothesley, forbidding obedience to these orders, detailing the misconduct of the Protector, and accusing him of a design, after the destruction of the nobility, to substitute himself in the place of the young Sovereign. The Lord Mayor and citizens of London took part with the Council; most of the executors joined them; the Protector found himself deserted at Windsor; and Secretary Petre, whom he had dispatched with a threatening message to Ely House, instead of returning, sent him word that he adhered to the lawful government.

Somerset was as abject in his adverse fortune as he had been insolent in prosperity. He submitted unconditionally to all the demands of his adversaries, abdicated the Protectorship, allowed himself to be quietly committed to the Tower, and there signed a confession of the articles of charge which his enemies had drawn up against him.

These proceedings had been chiefly conducted by the advice of Wriothesley, who was now in a state of ecstasy, not only from the prospect of being reinstated in his office of Chancellor, but (what he really valued more, though a man of great personal ambition) of being now able to check the Reformation, which Somerset had so much favored, and of bringing back the nation to the true faith. Warwick had hitherto pretended to be of the same religious principles, and he reckoned, without any misgiving, on his co-operation,—resolved to retain his own ascendency. But he suddenly found that he had been made the tool of a man of greater intrigue, who was not embarrassed by any regard to principle or consistency. He saw himself at once drop into insignificance, and the Reformation received a new impulse. Warwick had the great advantage of being a man of the sword, and he had acquired considerable reputation by his military exploits. He was, besides, of captivating address, while the manners of the Ex-Chancellor were cold and repulsive. The councillors, the nobility, and the common people, therefore, did not hesitate, at this juncture, to hail him as leader, and his power was absolute. He is believed really to have been in favor of the Romish religion; but finding that the young King was deeply imbued with the new doctrines, and that they were becoming more and more popular, he suddenly turned round, and professed a determination steadily to support all the ecclesiastical reforms introduced since the commencement of the present reign.

Wriothesley, in anguish, made several bold attempts at resistance; but meeting with no support, and Warwick, who thought he might become a dangerous rival, taking every opportunity to affront him, he withdrew from the Council, and through disappointment and vexation he fell into a dangerous illness, from which he did not recover. Never again taking any part in public affairs, he languished till the end of the year 1550, and then died of a broken heart.

Shortly before his death he made his will, by which he left his rich collar of the garter to the King, all his garters and Georges to the Earl of Pembroke, and his large landed estates to his sons.

Expiring in his town house, where Southampton Buildings now stand, he was buried in the church of St. Andrew, Holborn; but there is no monument or inscription to mark the spot where his dust reposes.

In estimating his character, it would be most unjust to apply to it the standard of modern times. In his age toleration was as little sanctioned by the followers of the Reformation as by the adherents to the Papal supremacy; and though we deplore the extremes to which he was carried by his mistaken zeal, we must honor the sincerity and constancy by which he was distinguished from the great body of the courtiers of Henry VIII., and the leaders of faction in the reign of Edward VI., who were at all times disposed to accommodate their religious faith to their personal interest. Even Burnet says, that "although he was fiercely zealous for the old superstition, yet was he otherwise a great person."[1]

His descendants continued to flourish in the male line for three generations, and were men of note both under the Tudors and the Stuarts. His great-grandson, the Earl of Southampton, the personal friend of Charles I., and Lord Treasurer to Charles II., having no male issue, the heiress of the family was married to the unfortunate Lord Russell, and was the famous Rachel Lady Russell who behaved so heroically on the trial of her husband, and whose virtues extolled by Burnet, are best illustrated by her own simple, sweet, and touching letters. The present Bedford family thus represent Lord Chancellor Wriothesley, resembling him in sincerity and steadiness of purpose, but happily distinguished for mildness and liberality instead of bigotry.

CHAPTER XXXVII.

LIFE OF SIR WILLIAM PAULET, LORD PAULET OF ST. JOHN BASING, EARL OF WILTSHIRE, AND MARQUESS OF WINCHESTER, LORD KEEPER OF THE GREAT SEAL.

AS this individual held the Great Seal of England in his own right above seven months,—according to the plan of this work, I am called upon here to introduce a sketch of his life; but as he had little connection with the law, and was not a very interesting character, although for long tenure of high office he exceeded all the statesmen of the century in which he lived, —my memoir of him shall be very brief. He accounted for his not being upset by any of the storms which assailed him, by saying that he was "a willow, and not an oak," and there would be no great pleasure or instruction in minutely observing his *bendings*.

He was born about the year 1476, and was the only son of Sir John Paulet, of a very ancient family in Somerset-

[1] Reform. i. 342.
[2] Dugd. Baron. tit. "Southampton." Wiffen's " History of the House of Russell."

shire. One of his ancestors was a sergeant-at-law in the reign of Henry V.[1] Having studied at the University, he was removed to the inns of Court,—but more with a view to general education than to qualify him for the law as a profession; and it is doubtful whether he was ever called to the bar.

He was of a cheerful temper, pleasing manner, moderate abilities, and respectable acquirements. Exciting no envy or jealousy, he had every one's good word, and accommodating himself to the humors of all, all were disposed to befriend him.

By his family interest he was soon introduced at Court, gaining the favor of Henry VIII., was made by him Comptroller and Treasurer of the Household. He was thus near the person of the Sovereign, and had occasionally the honor to tilt with him and to play with him at primero,—taking care always to be worsted, after a seeming exertion of his utmost skill. So successful were these arts, that without any greater service, on the 9th of March, 1539, he was raised to the Peerage by the title of Baron St. John of Basing, and three years after he was made a Knight of the Garter.

He accompanied the King as an amusing courtier rather than as a military officer, in the expedition into France, in which Paris might easily have been surprised, but which terminated in the capture of Boulogne, and the fruitless siege of Montreuil. He was soon after promoted to the office of Grand Master of the Household.

When Henry's will was to be made for arranging the government of the country during the approaching minority, both parties counted with confidence on the co-operation of Lord St. John; and his name was inserted with general approbation in the list of the Executors.

Guided by his principle of siding with the strongest, on the accession of the new Sovereign he supported the election of Somerset as Protector, and concurred in the measures by which Wriothesley was deprived of the office of Chancellor, and banished from the Council.

The Protector, having got the Great Seal into his hands, was in great perplexity as to how he should dispose of it. Wishing to depress the clergy, he was unwilling to recur to the practice of giving it to an ecclesiastic; and he was

[1] Rot. Cl. 3. Hen. 5, m. 20.

determined to advance the Reformation, with the principles of which the blending of civil and spiritual employments were deemed incompatible. Besides, Archbishop Cranmer certainly would not have accepted the office of Chancellor himself, and probably would not have liked to see it bestowed on any other prelate who might thus have eclipsed him. Rich, who had gained such unenviable notoriety on the trials of Bishop Fisher and Sir Thomas More,—a cunning and experienced lawyer,—had become Lord Rich, and one of the Executors;—but there was the greatest reluctance to promote him farther, from his general bad character, and the special reasons which convinced Somerset that no confidence could be reposed in his fidelity.

There being no other producible lawyer belonging to the party, Somerset resolved to take time for consideration, and in the meanwhile to place the Great Seal in the hands of some one who might do its routine duties, who could not be formidable to him, and from whom he might resume it at pleasure. Such a man was Paulet Lord St. John.

Accordingly, on the 7th of March, 1547, the Protector having received the Great Seal from the messengers he had sent to demand it from Wriothesley, went through the ceremony of presenting it to the infant King, and then, in his Majesty's name, delivered it to St. John, with the title of "Lord Keeper,"—to be held by him for a fortnight, with all the powers and emoluments belonging to the office of Lord Chancellor.[1]

In a few days after, the Lord Keeper, by order, put the

[1] The entry on the Close Roll, after stating the King's acceptance of the Great Seal (which must have been shown to him as a toy), thus proceeds:— "Quo die circa horam primam post meridiem prefatus Dus Rex Sigillum suum prum apud Palm suum prum in sua privata camerâ in presencia &c. prîto nobili viro Willo Seynt John per spacium quatuordecim dierum prx sequent, scdm beneplacitum regium custodiend. exercend. et utend. comisit et tradidit, ipsumque Willm Dum Seynt John adtunc et ibidem custodem Magni Sigilli Regii fecit ordinavit et constituit Hend pr termino et per spacm quatuordecim dier. scdm beneplacitum regium cum omnibus et singulis auctoritatibus, &c. que Cancellariis Anglie prtu officii sui fcre et excre consuerat posset et valeat." It then goes on to record that the new Lord Keeper, in the King's presence, having taken the Seal from the bag and sealed a *dedimus potestatem* with it, returned it into the bag and carried it off with him.—R. Cl. 1 Ed. 6, m. 14.

Great Seal to the letters patent, setting aside the will of Henry VIII., and constituting Somerset Protector, with unlimited power, till the young King should reach his majority; and proving an apt instrument, as far as politics were concerned, there were successive grants to him of the office of Lord Keeper—till the 26th of May,—till the 6th of July, and till the Feast of All Saints;—he, on each occasion, going through the ceremony of returning the Seal into the King's hands, and receiving it back again for the extended time.[1]

But at last, the complaints of the suitors and the public voice, which even then could not long be entirely disregarded, required that some new arrangement should be be made to despatch the judicial business of the Court of Chancery, for which the Lord Keeper, with all his plausibility, had shown himself to be quite incompetent. He contrived to get through Easter and Trinity terms by postponing the hearing of causes, and taking time to consider his judgments, and pretending that it was necessary for him to leave the Court of Chancery that he might sit in the Star Chamber, or attend the Council. The long vacation came to his relief; but Michaelmas term was approaching, and he himself, with his usual discretion, begged that he might be permitted to resign.

The Protector had no longer any choice; and, on the 23rd of October, 1547, before All Saints' day arrived, Lord St. John resigned the Great Seal into the King's hands at Hampton Court, and it was delivered to RICH, with the title of Lord Chancellor.[2]

Lord St. John, after his resignation, remained true to his party till the Protector's fall was certain; and then going over to Wriothesley, attended the meetings of the Executors, held in Ely Place, which brought about a revolution in the government. He hesitated for a moment

---

[1] These are the only instances I find of the Great Seal being granted for a term certain,—the grant, where not during pleasure, having been for life or upon a contingency, such as the illness or absence of the Chancellor.

[2] "Idemque Dmns Rex de avisamento et consensu precarissimi avunculi sui Edwardi Ducis Somers prne sue Regie Gubernatoris et Regn. et subditor. suor. Protectoris cetmq. consilm surum, tunc et ibidem Sigillum illud in baga prea ut erat inclusum spectabili et honorabili viro Rico Riche militi Dno Riche custodiend. utend. et exercend. tradidit et libavit ipsmq. Ricum Riche Cancel larium suum Anglie adtunc et ibidem fecit, &c."—Rot. Cl. 1 Ed. 6.

between the rival chiefs of the victorious party, but, seeing that Dudley Earl of Warwick was the more powerful, he joined in those measures which drove Wriothesley from the Council, and broke his heart.

The Ex-Lord Keeper was rewarded with the office of Lord High Treasurer, which he contrived to hold under three successive reigns, while there was sometimes a Protestant and sometimes a Roman Catholic Sovereign on the throne, and while many of his colleagues were disgraced, imprisoned, beheaded, or burnt.

In 1551 he showed his aptness for office by presiding, as Lord High Steward, on the trial of his benefactor the Duke of Somerset, who, having escaped from the great peril which first assailed him, and having been pardoned and discharged from the Tower on paying a large fine, had again incurred the resentment of his rival, now become Duke of Northumberland, and had excited great jealousy by the marks of returning favor bestowed upon him by the youthful King.

His death was therefore determined upon. On the 17th of October, 1551, he was committed to the Tower on a charge of treason, and he was brought to trial, before the Lord High Steward, on the 1st of December following. According to usage, Rich, the Lord Chancellor, ought to have presided; but although he had given an opinion upon his guilt in the Star Chamber, he managed to throw the odious and unprofitable task of trying him upon Paulet, who, having been before made Earl of Wiltshire, was now gratified with the title of Marquess of Winchester.

The trial took place in Westminster Hall, the Lord High Steward, "sitting under the cloth of state, upon a bench between two posts three degrees high."[1]

The only evidence produced consisted of the written depositions of witnesses who could not be brought to state more than that Somerset had engaged in a plot to imprison the Duke of Northumberland, the Marquess of Northampton, and the Earl of Pembroke. An objection was made by the prisoner, that these three ought not to sit as Judges on his trial, the charge being for practices against them; but the Lord High Steward ruled that "no challenge lies against a Peer of England, who, giving his

[1] 1 St. Tr. 518.

verdict, without oath, on his honor, must be presumed to be absolutely free from favor or affection, hatred or malice."

The prisoner required to be confronted with the witnesses ; but he was told that, according to well-considered precedents, "where the King was concerned, the written depositions of witnesses taken privately by the King's Council, in whose good faith, impartiality, and cunning the law reposes entire confidence, were sufficient."

A difficulty still remained, supposing the witnesses were believed,—to make out the plot to be treason. Although the counsel for the Crown argued, "with much bitterness," that this was a case within 25 Ed. III., Northumberland himself declared "he would never consent that any practice against him should be reputed treason."

The Lord High Steward decided, that "if it was not treason, it was felony." Thereupon all the Lords acquitted Somerset of treason, a majority found him guilty of felony, and the Lord High Steward sentenced him to be hanged.[1]

Burnet says, "it was generally believed that all the pretended conspiracy, upon which he was condemned, was only a forgery ; and, indeed, the not bringing witnesses into Court, but only the depositions, and the parties sitting Judges, gave great occasion to condemn the proceedings against him."[2] But, according to the notions of the times, the Ex-Lord Keeper was not much worse thought of for this specimen of his judicial powers, and he continued to enjoy a pretty fair reputation,

On the death of Edward VI. he first took part with Lady Jane Grey; but by the unerring instinct which ever guided him, he was the first to leave her party, and go over to Queen Mary, who was so much pleased, that she forgave him, and renewed his patent of Lord High Treasurer. During her reign he remained very quiet, and taking example by the fate of Cranmer and others, he conformed very rigidly to the reigning religion, and without actively urging persecution would by no means run any risk of giving offense by trying to restrain or soften it.

On the accession of Elizabeth he avoided the scandal of an abrupt change of religion ; but he soon fell in with the system established by her; and though she placed all her confidence in Cecil, she allowed the wily old courtier

[1] Ibid. 520. [2] Burn. Ref. ii. 186.

still to enjoy his place of Lord Treasurer till his death in 1572, when he was in his 97th year, and had 103 descendants to attend him to the grave.

It was shortly before his death, that, being asked "how he did bear up in those dangerous times wherein great alterations were made both in Church and State," he returned the noted answer, "By being a willow, and not an oak." No one, however, will be seduced to follow his example who has any regard for posthumous fame, for his existence is now known only to dull biographers, genealogists, and antiquaries, and is discovered only to be contemned;—while the name of Sir Thomas More will continue to be familiar as household words in the mouths of all Englishmen, and will be found honored and revered to the latest generations.[1]

The Marquess of Winchester married Elizabeth, daughter of Sir William Capel, Lord Mayor of London, and by her had four sons and four daughters, who were all married, and left a numerous progeny. His descendants distinguished themselves highly in the civil and military service of their country. The sixth Marquess was, in the reign of William and Mary, created Duke of Bolton. After a succession of six Dukes, this title became extinct in 1794, by the death of Harry Duke of Bolton without male issue; but the Marquisate was inherited by the father of the present gallant representative of this illustrious house, who, lineally descended through males from the Lord Keeper, is the premier Marquess in the peerage of England.[2]

---

[1] Sir James Mackintosh, when speaking of "the versatile politicians who had the art and fortune to slide unhurt through all the shocks of forty years of a revolutionary age," says, "the Marquess of Winchester, who had served Henry VII., and retained office under every intermediate government till he died in his 97th year, with the staff of Lord Treasurer in his hands, is perhaps the most remarkable specimen of this species preserved in history."* But more scandal was excited in his own time by William Herbert, whom Henry VIII. created Earl of Pembroke. Having followed all the fantasies of that monarch, and obtained from him the dissolved monastery of Wilton, he was a keen Protestant under Edward VI., and one of the first to acknowledge and to desert Queen Jane. Mary having restored Wilton to the nuns, he is said to have received them "cap in hand;" but when they were suppressed by Elizabeth, he drove them out of the monastery with his horsewhip, bestowing upon them an appellation which implied their constant breach of the vow they had taken.

[2] See Grandeur of Law, p. 15.

---

* Mackintosh's History of England, vol iii. p. 155.

CHAPTER XXXVIII.

LIFE OF LORD CHANCELLOR RICH.

WE now come to a Chancellor of whose infamy we have already had several glimpses, and who was through life a very consistent character in all that was base and profligate, RICHARD RICH was descended from a commercial family that had flourished in the city of London from the time of Henry VI.,—the founder having acquired great opulence as a mercer, and served the office of Sheriff of London and Middlesex in the year 1441. This worthy citizen's epitaph, in the church of St. Lawrence Poultney, shows more piety than poetry:—

"Respice quod opus est præsentis temporis ævum
Omne quod est nihil est præter amare Deum."

His son followed his trade, and was well esteemed as a substantial tradesman, not wishing for more dignity than to be elected deputy of his ward. The grandson, however, who is the subject of this memoir, early displayed an aspiring genius, and a determination to have all the pleasures of life without patient industry, or being very scrupulous about the means employed by him to gain his objects.

He was born in the city of London, in a house near that occupied by Sir John More, Judge of the Court of King's Bench, and he and young Thomas More were intimate, till, on account of his dissipated habits, all who had any regard to character were obliged to throw him off. While yet a youth, he was "esteemed very light of his tongue, a great dicer and gamester, and not of any commendable fame."[1]

He does not seem ever to have been at any University; but his father, finding there was no chance of his applying to the business of the counting-house, agreed to his request, that he might be bred to the bar, and entered him of the Middle Temple. For some time there was no amendment of his life; and instead of attending "readings" and "moots," he was to be found in the ordinaries, gaming-houses, and other haunts of profligacy in White

[1] Speech of Sir Thomas More on his trial.—More, 265.

Friars, which had not yet acquired the name of "*Alsatia*," though infamous for all sorts of irregularities.

Nevertheless, he had occasional fits of application; and being of quick and lively parts, he laid in a small stock of legal learning, which, turned to the best account, enabled him to talk plausibly on black letter points in the presence of attorneys, and to triumph at times over those who had given their days and nights to Bracton, Glanville, and the Year Books. In the 21st of Henry VIII. he was appointed "Autumn Reader" of his house, and acquitted himself with applause. He was still in bad odor with his contemporaries; for besides his dissolute habits, no reliance could be placed on his honor or veracity. By evil arts, he rose into considerable practice; and while Sir Thomas More was Chancellor, recommending himself to the Duke of Norfolk, and the party who were hurrying on a breach with Rome, he was, in 1532, appointed for life Attorney General of Wales. The Great Seal being transferred to Audley, Rich was taken regularly into the service of the Crown, and was ever ready to assist in imposing the new-fangled oaths, or examining state prisoners before trial, or doing any dirty work by which he might recommend himself to promotion. So successful was he, that in 1533 he, was appointed Solicitor-General to the King, and the most dazzling objects of ambition seemed within his reach.

We have seen how he laid a trap to betray Bishop Fisher and Sir Thomas More under the guise of friendship;—how he disgraced himself at the trial of the former by disclosing what had been communicated to him in private confidence;[1]—and how he perjured himself on the trial of the latter by inventing expressions which had never been used, when mere breach of confidence, and his skill as a counsel, could not obtain the required capital conviction.[2]

I know not whether, like Lord Chancellor Audley, he ever openly urged "the *infamy* he had incurred in the service of the government" as a claim to favor; but there can be no doubt that this was well understood between him and his employers, and in 1535 he was rewarded with the wealthy sinecure of Chirographer of the Common Pleas.

In 1537, an insult was put upon the House of Com-

[1] Ante, p. 93.   [2] 1 St. Tr. 385.

mons, which shows most strikingly the degraded state to which parliament was reduced in the reign of Henry VIII. On the recommendation of the Court, Rich, whose bad character was notorious, and who was hardly free from any vice except hypocrisy, was elected Speaker. We have seen how he repaid this promotion by comparing the King, on the first day of the session, for prudence to Solomon, for strength to Samson, and for beauty to Absalom; and, on the last, "to the sun, that warms, enlightens, and invigorates the universe."[1]

While Speaker, he rendered most effectual service in reconciling the Commons to the suppression of the greater monasteries, and the surrender of all their possessions to the King.

These were now put under the management of a royal commission, and Rich was placed at the head of it, with the title of "Chancellor of the Court of Augmentations." His first care was to augment his own fortune; and he got a grant of the dissolved priory of Lighes, in Essex, and of other abbey-lands of immense value, which were found a sufficient endowment for two Earldoms, enjoyed simultaneously by his sons.

He gave himself no trouble about the religious controversies which were going forward, and, except that he became the owner of such a large portion of church property, it could not have been suspected that he was a friend of the new doctrines more than of the old.

He felt some disappointment at not succeeding to the Great Seal on the death of Audley, though greatly comforted by the increased means he enjoyed of amassing wealth. He had been a spendthrift in his youth, but cupidity grew with his riches, and he was become saving and penurious. In 1544, he was made Treasurer of the King's wars in France and Scotland, an office by virtue of which the whole of the expenditure for the pay and provisioning of the army passed through his hands, and which afforded ample scope for his propensity to accumulate. Soon after the capture of Boulogne, he was one of the Commissioners who negotiated the peace between France and England.

He was now in high personal favor with Henry, conforming himself to all his caprices, and assisting at the

[1] Ante, p. 102, 103.

Council board in examining and committing Lutherans for a violation of the Six Articles, and Roman Catholics for hesitating to acknowledge the King's spiritual supremacy. When the King's will was made, he was appointed one of the sixteen Executors who were to carry on the government during the minority of Edward,—both parties being suspicious of him, but each party expecting from his professions to gain him.

On the demise of the Crown the Great Seal seemed within his reach, if it could be made to fall from the hand which held it, and he did his utmost to widen the breach between the Chancellor and the Protector. He was supposed to suggest the expedient of bringing the charge against Wriothesley of issuing the illegal commission to hear causes in Chancery, and to refer to the Judges the question of its validity, and the nature and punishment of the offense of fabricating it. He had been included in the great batch of Peers, along with most of the Executors,—who ennobled themselves, or took a step in the Peerage, under pretense that these honors were intended for them by the late King. Most of the Commoners now promoted took new and high sounding titles; and it might have been expected that the witness against Fisher and More would have become "Lord of *Lighes;*" but whether he was afraid that some scurvy jests might have been passed upon this title as personal rather than territorial, he preferred to be "Lord Rich,"—and by this title he was made an English Baron.

When the Great Seal had actually been wrested from the fallen Wriothesley, the new Lord thought that, as a matter of course, it must at once be handed over to him, and he was exceedingly indignant to find it intrusted to Paulet, who was no lawyer, and who had never done, and was never likely to do, any very signal service to the Crown. He made no open remonstrance, even when the ceremony of the delivery of the Great Seal to Paulet as Lord Keeper was from time to time repeated; but he privately complained of the appointment, and procured others to complain of it as insulting to the profession and detrimental to the public. Paulet's real insufficiency gave effect to these cabals. The Protector doubted some time whether such an unscrupulous intriguer would be more dangerous to him as an opponent or as a colleague.

Timid councils, or a love of present ease, prevailed, and on the 23d of October, 1547, Richard Lord Rich was appointed Lord Chancellor of England.[1]

The ceremony of delivering the Great Seal to him took place at Hampton Court, in the presence of the infant King, in whose name the Lord Protector declared "the royal pleasure that the new Chancellor should hold the office, with all powers and profits that had ever belonged to any of his predecessors." I do not find any account of his swearing in or installation in Westminster Hall.[2] The old Duke of Norfolk, who had so often presided at such ceremonies, could not have been present, for, although he survived, by the seasonable death of King Henry VIII., he was still kept a prisoner in the Tower, from the apprehensions of both parties,—and his attainder was not reversed till the following reign.

Lord Chancellor Rich displayed considerable ability as well as dexterity in discharging the duties of his office, and in combating the difficulties he had to encounter in the conflicts of contending factions. He presided himself in the Court of Chancery, and despatched the whole of the business without assistance till the end of the year 1551,[3] when a commission was issued to Beaumont, the Master of the Rolls, and others, to hear causes in his absence.

Although he had retired from the bar a good many years, he had kept up his professional knowledge by attending the mootings in the Middle Temple, by associating with the Masters of the Bench of that learned Society, and by acting as Chancellor of the Court of Augmentations, where he had, from time to time, to hear and decide various legal questions. With discretion to conceal ignorance, a little law goes a great way on the bench,— and the new Chancellor, who was much superior to his immediate predecessor, was pronounced "a great Judge' by the dependents and expectants who surrounded him,— and believed to be "a tolerably good one" by the public in general. In a few terms he nearly cleared off the

[1] Cl. R. 1 Ed. 6.
[2] The entry in the Close Roll concludes with merely stating that having joyfully received the Seal, and extracted it from the bag, he sealed a commission, "Sicque prcus Ricus Dns. Riche curam et custodiam ejusdem Magni Sigilli ac officium Cancellarii Anglie super se assumens Sigillum illud penes se retinuit et retinet in presenti." [3] Nov. 26, 1551.

arrears which he found in the Court; but he afterwards became more remiss, and complaints arose of his delays, notwithstanding his liberal compliance with the usage beginning to gain ground of referring matters of difficulty to the Masters, who were often very expert officers, and although still generally churchmen, were well acquainted with the civil law, and much more familiar with the practice of the Court than "the Keeper of the Royal Conscience." During the last year he held the Great Seal, he seems to have found sitting in Court very irksome, or he was much absorbed by political intrigue, for he left the hearing of causes chiefly to the Master of the Rolls and the other Commissioners, whom he appointed to supply his place.[1] But during the whole time of his continuance in office we are to regard him much more as a minister of state than as a dispenser of justice.[2]

A few days after his appointment, the first parliament of the new reign was to assemble; and, to gratify the vanity of his patron, he put the Great Seal to a patent directing, in the King's name, that the Protector should be placed in the House of Lords on a stool, on the right hand of the throne, under the cloth of state, "*non abstante* the statute 31 H. 8, by which all Peers were to have place and precedence according to their rank in the peerage."

When the first day of the session arrived, the infant King being placed on the throne, and the Protector on his stool, the Commons were summoned to the bar; but, unfortunately, we are disappointed in our wish to know the rest of this interesting ceremony, for the Parliament Roll abruptly terminates with these words, "The Lord Rich, being Lord Chancellor, began his oration to the effect as follows.—" We may conjecture that, after some compliments to the humane temper and mild rule of the late sovereign, and the hopeful virtues of his living image, warm congratulations were offered upon the abili-

---

[1] There having been a king's warrant for putting the Great Seal to this commission, it was free from the objection for which Lord Chancellor Wriothesley was deprived of the Great Seal.

[2] Some of his decrees, rather of an arbitrary character, are to be found in the Registrar's Book; *e. g.* "Cope *v.* Watts:—It is ordered by the Lord Chancellor that the plaintiff shall upon his knees ask forgiveness of the defendant, at Daventry, openly, upon such market day as the Lord Chancellor by his letters to some justice of the peace there abouts to be directed shall appoint." Then follows a direction for payment of £10 by the plaintiff to the defendant by instalments of five marks. Reg Lib. A., 3 & 4 Ed. 6, f. 44.

ties and worth of the Lord Protector, by whose stool the throne was now propped, and to whom the exercise of the royal prerogatives had been deputed till his Majesty should be of maturer years.

In justice to the Lord Protector and the Lord Chancellor it should be mentioned, that they began with repealing some of the most fantastical and tyrannical of Henry's statutes respecting treason,[1] and modifying an act whereby any King of England coming to the throne during his minority might, on reaching the age of twenty-four, vacate *ab initio* all statutes assented to in his name. It was provided, that henceforth there should. only be a power to repeal such statutes, leaving untouched all that had been done under them.

But the grand object was to further the Reformation. Lord Rich, since the grant to him of *Lighes* and the other dissolved abbeys, had become a sincere reformer, and was anxious that the breach with Rome might be widened as much as possible, so that there might be no danger of his share of the plunder of the church being wrested from him by a counter revolution in religion. He therefore zealously supported the measures which were brought forward under the auspices of Cranmer for introducing the Lutheran system with modifications into England. Successively he laid on the table bills for establishing the King's power to appoint Bishops; for dissolving chantries; for repealing the bloody act of the Six Articles; for allowing priests to marry, still with a recital that "it were more commendable for them to live chaste and without marriage, whereby they might better attend to the ministry of the Gospel, and be less distracted with secular cares;" and a bill for uniformity of service and administration of the sacraments, whereby the mass book was purified of its errors, and the beautiful Liturgy of the Church of England was established nearly such as it has subsisted down to our own days.

The Lord Chancellor had, ere long, to determine with

---

[1] The bill for this purpose being considered of great importance, it was referred to a joint Committee of both Houses. "They were appointed to meet *at two o'clock after dinner*, in order to treat and commune on the purport of the said bill."- 1 Parl. Hist. 384. The hour of dinner, which had been eleven in the good old times, was now twelve, and sometimes as late as one. It was not then foreseen that a time would come when the two Houses meeting for public business at five, and half-past seven being the hour of dinner,—at seven the one House would break up, and the other would be deserted.

which of the two brothers he would side, the Duke of Somerset or Lord Seymour of Sudeley; for a mortal rivalry had sprung up between them. That quarrel was begun by their wives. Lord Seymour having married the Queen Dowager so soon after the King's death, that had she immediately proved pregnant it was said, a doubt would have arisen to which husband the child belonged,—the Lady Protectoress professed to be much shocked at this indecorum, but was, in reality, deeply mortified that the wife of a younger brother should take the *pas* of her, and raised the question whether, by a disparaging alliance, the reginal precedence was not lost?

This controversy was terminated by the death of the Queen Dowager in childbed. But Lord Seymour himself was ambitious and presumptuous, and dissatisfied with the power he enjoyed as Lord High Admiral,—being now a widower, he aspired to marry the Lady Elizabeth, who was certainly attached to him, and whose reputation had been a little scathed by the familiarity to which she had admitted him.[1] He likewise insisted that Somerset could not, according to constitutional principles, be Protector of the realm and guardian of the royal person; and during Somerset's absence in the Scottish war, he prevailed upon the young King to write a letter to the two Houses, intimating his wish to be put under the care of his younger uncle. But the Protector arriving from the North, and expressing a determination to crush his rival, notwithstanding the ties of blood,—Lord Rich at once agreed to concur in the necessary measures for that purpose.

On the 19th of January, 1549, the Admiral was committed to the Tower of London by order of the Council, and,

[1] From the indignant denial by Elizabeth of the reports then circulated, they are believed to be untrue; but certainly the courtship was not conducted with much delicacy. Her governess being examined upon the subject stated that the moment he was up he would hasten to Elizabeth's chamber, "in his nightgown and bare-legged;" if she were still in bed "he would put open the curteyns, and make as though he wold come at hir;" "and she wold go farther in the bed so that he cold not come at hir." If she were up, he "wold ax how she did, and strike her upon the back or the buttocks famyliarly." Parry the cofferer also says, "she told me that the Admirale loved her but too well;" at one time as he came into her room while she was beginning to make her toilette, she was obliged to run behind the curtains, "her maidens being there;" that "the Quene was jelowse on hir and him, and that suspecting the often accesse of the Admirale to her, she came sodenly upon them wher they were all alone, he having her in his armes."—See 7 Ling. 34 *n*. The council deemed it prudent to dismiss her governess.

according to the usage of the times, the Chancellor and other Councillors went there to interrogate him upon the charges brought against him. He repelled them with disdain, and required that he should be confronted with his accusers, or, at least, have a copy of their depositions; but he was told that the demand was unprecedented, unreasonable, and inadmissible. Under the directions of the Lord Chancellor, articles were regularly drawn up against the Admiral for treason,—chiefly on the ground that, with the aid of one Sharington, the Master of the Mint at Bristol, who was to coin false money for him, he had laid a plan to carry off the King and to change the present form of government. He, denying the fact, insisted that the charge did not amount to treason; for the Protector's power being usurped, contrary to the will of the late King founded on an act of parliament, resistance to it was lawful.

A bill of attainder against Seymour was, however, laid on the table by the Lord Chancellor. To take from himself the responsibility and odium of the proceeding, he then summoned the Judges and King's Council,[1] and a question was put to them "whether the charges, or any of them, amounted to treason?" The expected answer was given, "that some of them amounted to treason," and the bill proceeded.

The principal evidence consisted of Sharington's conviction, on his own confession; and several Peers, rising in their places,—to please the Protector, who was present in the House, repeated evidence which they had previously given before the Council, to show the Admiral's dangerous designs. The bill passed the Lords without a division or dissenting voice, but met with a very unexpected opposition in the Commons. There the first principles of natural justice were beginning to be a little attended to, and several members, to the horror of the old courtiers, contended that it was unfair to legislate by bill of attainder without evidence, and to condemn a man to death who had not been heard in his defense. The Peers hearing of this factious opposition, twice sent a message to the Commons, "that the Lords who were personally acquainted with the traitorous designs of the Admiral would, if required, repeat their statement to the

[1] Viz. the King's Serjeants, and the attorney and Solicitor General.

nether House." There were a few ultra-radical members still not satisfied. Thereupon another power in the state, to resist which no one was yet so hardy as to venture, was called into action, and the Protector sent a message to the Common's, in the King's name, declaring it to be the opinion of his Majesty that it was unnecessary to hear the Admiral at the bar of the House, and repeating the offer of the evidence which had been considered so satisfactory by the Lords. On receipt of this message there was a cry of " Divide! divide!" and a division immediately taking place, the bill was passed by a majority of nearly 400. There were only nine or ten members who had the courage to vote against it.[1]

Three days after the bill had received the royal assent the Lord Chancellor, at the Protector's request, called a Council to deliberate about carrying it into effect. The Protector withdrew, "out of natural pity," during the deliberation, well knowing it would be resolved that his brother should die on the Wednesday following. He actually signed the warrant for the execution on that day. The second signature was that of Archbishop Cranmer, to whom it probably cost a pang to be concerned in such an affair of blood. The third was that of Lord Chancellor Rich, who rejoiced in the belief that his official life was now likely to be smooth and secure. The Admiral's offense certainly did not amount to more than an attempt to deprive Somerset of usurped authority, and his death added to the list of English legislative murders. There was retribution in respect to some of the most culpable agents in it. Somerset, before long, found verified the prophecy uttered at the time, that "the fall of one brother would prove the overthrow of the other." Cranmer himself perished miserably by an unjust sentence; and perhaps Rich suffered more than either of them, when, from the fear of similar violence, he resigned all his employments, and gave himself up to solitary reflection on the crimes he had committed. Seymour's execution was not looked upon with great horror at the time when it took place; and Bishop Latimer immediately preached a sermon before the King, in which he highly applauded it.

The Chancellor was grievously disappointed in ex-

[1] 2 & 3 Ed. 6, c. 18. Burnet, vol. ii. p. 99. 1 Parl. Hist. 587. 1 St. Tr. 497.

pecting quiet times from the bloody termination to the struggle for power which we have described. The Protector became more vain, presumptuous, and overbearing, and to the members of the Council, who, under the late King's will ought to have been his equals, he behaved as a haughty master to his slaves. He had likewise brought much odium upon himself by the sacrilege and rapine through which he had obtained the site and the materials for his great palace, Somerset House; and general discontents had caused insurrections in various parts of England.

In a few months after Seymour's death, Lord Rich was again thrown into the perplexity of making his election between rival factions. As we have before related,[1] the discontented members of the Council, headed by Ex-Chancellor Wriothesley, and Dudley Earl of Warwick, taking advantage of Somerset's unpopularity and weakness, had established a rival government at Ely House, in Holborn. Rich was at this time with the Protector at Hampton Court, and accompanied him to Windsor when the young Edward was removed thither, in the hope that "the King's name might be a tower of strength;"—but when he saw that Somerset was deserted by all parties in the country, and that his power was rapidly crumbling to pieces, he joined the malcontent Councillors, carrying the Great Seal along with him, and took an active part in supporting their cause.

Being born and bred in London, being free of one of the companies, being related to some of the principal merchants, and the livery and apprentices being proud of his elevation, the Lord Chancellor, in spite of his bad private character, had great influence in the City, which then constituted the metropolis, and took the lead in every political convulsion. Having summoned the Lord Mayor, Aldermen, and principal members of the Common Council to Ely House, he made them a long and powerful speech, showing how Somerset had usurped the Protectorship contrary to the will of the late King—how he had abused the power which he had unlawfully acquired—how he had mismanaged our foreign affairs, by allowing the infant Queen of Scots to be married into the royal family of France—how at home he had oppressed both the no-

[1] Ante, p. 144.

bility and the people—and how the only chance of rescuing the King from the captivity in which he was then held, and of saving the state, was for the Chancellor's fellow-citizens, ever distinguished in the cause of loyalty and freedom, to rally round the enlightened, experienced, and independent Councillors there assembled; in whom, by the law and constitution, was vested the right of governing the country in the King's name, till his Majesty had completed his 18th year. This speech was received with the most rapturous applause, and cries of "Down with the Protector!—Long live the King!—Long live the Council!—Long live the Lord Chancellor!"

A proclamation was immediately framed, which Rich was the first to sign, and which was the same day posted all over the city, calling upon all the true subjects of the King to arm in his defense, to obey the orders of his faithful Councillors, assembled at Ely House, and to take measures to prevent the Crown from being taken from his head by a usurper. When news of this movement reached Windsor, Somerset saw that his cause was desperate; he surrendered at discretion, and in a few days he was a prisoner in the Tower.

This is the only occasion where Rich played more than a secondary part; and presently he was acting under the directions of the Earl of Warwick, with whom he had no difficulty in siding against Ex-Chancellor Wriothesley; for if this stern Roman Catholic had gained the ascendency, not only would he have striven for a reconciliation with Rome, but he would himself have resumed the custody of the Great Seal. Rich therefore heartily concurred with Warwick in those proceedings after the fall of Somerset which were meant to mortify Wriothesley, and which deeply wounded his spirit, and brought him to the grave.

Ere long he gained a complete insight into the character of Warwick, and felt himself very uncomfortable and insecure; perceiving that his new master, with an open and captivating manner, was dark, designing, immoderately ambitious, and wholly unscrupulous and remorseless. He could not tell how soon his own turn might come to be transferred to the Tower; and he knew well that, notwithstanding all his services in the late crisis, if it should at any time be desirable to have a vacancy in the office of Chancellor, there would be no hesitation in creating it by cutting off the head of the Chancellor.

In the meantime Rich felt that his only chance of safety was passive obedience,—while he secretly hoped that there would be another revolution in the political wheel, and that Warwick might be precipitated from his present height of power. He accordingly took an active part in those proceedings against Somerset, which terminated in his being dismissed from the Protectorship. He presided at the examinations of his former patron before the Council,—drew up the articles against him,—obtained his confession,—and brought in the bill of pains and penalties, by which he was deprived of all his offices, and sentenced to forfeit land to the value of £2,000 a year.

We cannot but admire, though puzzled to explain, the mildness of this proceeding. According to all precedent, Somerset ought now to have been attainted of high treason, and could not hope to leave his cell in the Tower till he was led out to execution. Let us charitably suppose that Rich, finding he could do so without endangering himself, put in a good word for the life of the man who had made him Lord Chancellor,—urging upon Warwick that Somerset, if pardoned, would thenceforth be powerless, and that the present chief of the state might add to his own influence, both with the young King and with the nation, by an act of clemency rather than of vengeance. When Somerset was afterwards pardoned, and restored to the Privy Council, Rich must, from selfish motives, at any rate, have been pleased with the prospect of some check hereafter arising to the unbounded sway which Warwick seemed otherwise destined permanently to enjoy.

While fresh political feuds were engendered, the Chancellor was for some time engaged in enforcing the new regulations respecting religious belief and religious worship. The Council, under his presidency, took cognizance as well of those who departed too far from the ancient standard of orthodoxy, as of those who adhered to it too rigidly; and a few Anabaptists and Arians were burnt, to show that the Reformers had a just abhorrence of heresy. But the principal difficulty was to deal with the numerous class of Roman Catholics, who had the Lady Mary, the heiress presumptive to the throne, at their head. A positive order was issued that the mass should not be celebrated; and Dr. Mulet, her chaplain, was committed to close custody in the Tower because, under her sanction, he disobeyed this order. Mary demanded the enlargement of her chaplain; the Chancellor wrote to her in the name of the Council, requiring her to obey the law. As she still remained intractable, the Chancellor, by order of the Council, paid her a visit at Copped Hall, in Essex, where she then resided, and delivered into her hand a letter from the King, peremptorily requiring her "to take a more earnest regard to the reformation of her family."[1] She received the King's letter on her knees as Rich delivered it—explaining, that the respect was paid to the writer, and not to its contents.

Rich declared the determination of the cabinet, that "she should no more use the private mass, nor do any other divine service than the law prescribed." She told him, "she would obey the King in any thing that her conscience permitted, and would gladly suffer death to do him good, but preferred to lay her head on a block rather than use any service different from that established at her father's death." She added, "I am sickly: I would not willingly die, but will do the best I can to preserve my life; but if I shall chance to die, you of the Council will be the cause of my death."

She then took her ring from her finger, and, on her knees, gave it to the Chancellor to present to the King as a token of her regard and duty. As the Chancellor was waiting in the court-yard to depart, she accosted him from the window in a style not quite so dignified, but which gives us a favorable opinion of her frankness and good humor. "Send me back my comptroller," said she, "whom you have taken from me because he obeyed my commands; for since his departing I take the accounts myself of my own expenses, and have learned how many

---

[1] See the letter at full length, 1 St. Tr. 549, with the King's instructions to the Lord Chancellor and those who were to accompany him on this occasion. They were "to pursuade her Grace that this proceeding cometh only of the conscience the King hath to avoid the offense of God, and of necessary counsel and wisdom to see his laws in so weighty causes executed." But they were "in the King's Majesty's name most strictly to forbid the chaplains either to say or use any mass or kind of service other than by the law is authorized." "Item, if ye shall find either any of the priests or any other person disobedient to this order, ye shall commit them forthwith to prison as ye shall think convenient." Surely it is rather unreasonable to expect that Mary should afterwards herself act on the principles of toleration.

loaves be made of a bushel of wheat. But my father and mother never brought me up to baking and brewing; and, to be plain with you, I am weary of mine office, and therefore, if my Lords will send mine officer home they shall do me pleasure; otherwise, if they will send him to prison, I beshrew him if he go not to it merrily." In spite of these remonstrances Rich did nothing to gratify her; the comptroller and others of her servants were committed to the Tower, and continued in close confinement till a new Chancellor had been appointed,—when her solicitations, aided by the interference of the Emperor, procured their discharge, with the relaxation in her favor of being permitted to worship God according to her conscience, which, when upon the throne, she was too little inclined to grant to others.[1]

Nearly a year of tranquillity was now enjoyed by Lord Rich, during which there was seeming harmony between Somerset and Warwick,—and even matrimonial alliances were contracted between their families;—but a terrible crisis was at hand, which so much shook the nerves of the Chancellor that in a panic he renounced his office, and fled into obscurity. Somerset had always been regarded with favor by the common people, whose part he took against the landed aristocracy in the disputes about enclosures and the clearing of estates; his haughty carriage to the nobles was forgotten in the superior insolence of Warwick, who, being merely the son of an Attorney-General, hanged for extortion, was regarded as an upstart, and the young King had recently shown some distrust of his present minister, and a returning regard for his uncle.

Somerset resolved to avail himself of this favorable juncture to recover his office of Protector, without being guilty of any disloyalty to his nephew, who, he doubted not, would sanction all that he projected when it was accomplished. He was urged on by his rival procuring himself to be created Duke of Northumberland, and manifesting a determination to tolerate no one at Court who, even by a look, expressed any dissatisfaction with his autocracy. Somerset, therefore, as a measure of self-preservation, engaged in a plot with a few associates to get possession of the person of the new Duke, to seize the Great Seal, to induce the King to throw himself into the

[1] Strype, 457, 458. Ellis's Letters, vol. ii. p. 179-182.

arms of the uncle to whom he had been so much attached, and to issue a proclamation calling on all his faithful subjects to rally round him, and to take arms in his defense.

This scheme might very possibly have succeeded if it had been kept secret till the day when it was to be carried into execution, and Northumberland might have finished his career by the sentence of the law in the reign of Edward, instead of Mary; but Sir Thomas Palmer, one of the confederates, revealed it to him and Somerset was soon a close prisoner in the Tower, his execution being delayed only till the ceremony should have been gone through of a mock trial. There is a curious contrast between the history of France and of England, that assassination, so common in the one country, was hardly ever practiced in the other ; but I know not whether our national character is much exalted by adherence to the system of perpetrating murder under the forms of law.

For some reason, not explained to us, it was thought more convenient to bring Somerset to trial before his Peers and a Lord High Steward—rather than (according to the practice introduced by Lord Cromwell, and followed against himself) to call a parliament and proceed by bill of attainder, without hearing the accused in his defense. Perhaps alarm was taken at the sentiments of humanity and justice expressed by a very small minority of the Commons in the case of Lord Seymour.

Rich was now in a state of great consternation. Regularly, being Lord Chancellor, he ought to have been created Lord High Steward to preside at the trial; but he was not free from suspicion of being himself implicated in the conspiracy, and there was no saying what disclosures might take place. He therefore feigned sickness; to give greater color to the pretense, he issued a commission authorizing the Master of the Rolls, and others, to hear causes for him in Chancery; he obtained Northumberland's consent that another Lord High Steward should be appointed; and he caused it to be privately intimated to Somerset that he absented himself from the trial out of tenderness to his ancient friend.

The Ex-Chancellor Paulet, now created Marquess of Winchester, was fixed upon as Lord High Steward, and the trial took place before him, as I have related in his life.[1]

[1] Ante, p. 149, 150.

To Rich's great relief a conviction took place without his name being mentioned in the course of the proceedings, but a very difficult and delicate question arose as to the execution of the sentence. Being acquitted of high treason, though convicted of felony—on leaving Westminster Hall the populace who were assembled in Palace Yard observed that the edge of the axe was not turned towards the prisoner, and concluded that there had been a general verdict of *not guilty* in his favor. They immediately raised a shout of exultation which was heard beyond the village of Charing, and risings were apprehended both in the city of London and in the provinces, if the idol of the people should be destroyed. It was likewise said that the King, who, notwithstanding his youth, now took a lively interest in the affairs of the state, wavered, and not only would not consent to sign the death-warrant of his uncle, but was disposed to take him again into favor.

Rich saw that whichever side prevailed, he himself, if he remained in office, must be exposed to the greatest peril, for, by his trimming policy, he had made himself odious to both: " Having accumulated to himself a very fair fortune (like a discreet pilot, who, seeing a storm at hand, gets his ship into harbor), he made sute to the King, by reason of some bodily infirmities, that he might be discharged of his office."[1]

He shut himself up in his town mansion, in Great St. Bartholomew's, and wrote to Northumberland that he was struck with a mortal disorder; that he was unable even to stir abroad as far as Whitehall or St. James's to deliver up the Great Seal in person to the King; and praying that messengers might be sent to him to receive it, so that he might now devote all his thoughts to preparations for a better world. Accordingly, on the 21st of December, 1551, the Duke of Northumberland himself, the Marquess of Winchester and others, authorized by letters of Privy Seal signed by the King, came to Lord Rich's house between eight and nine in the morning, and received from him the surrender of the Great Seal, which they forthwith carried and delivered to the King at Westminster.[2] We have no particulars of

[1] Dugdale's Baronage.
[2] The Close Roll, after reciting the authority to Northumberland, &c.

this interview, but we may fairly conjecture that the Chancellor appeared to be in a dying condition, and that, after well-acted regrets on both sides, it was speedily brought to a conclusion.

However this may be, we know that Rich, lightened from the anxieties of office, had a wonderful recovery, and lived sixteen years after his resignation. But so frightened was he by the perils he had gone through, that he never again would engage in public business. He spent the rest of his days in the country, in the management of his great estates, and the accumulation of wealth, —preferring the pleasures of avarice to those of ambition. Instead of ending his career, as was once so probable, amidst countless thousands on Tower Hill,—after he had long sunk from public notice, he expired at a small country-house in Essex—the event, when known in London, hardly causing the slightest public sensation.

His two sons, both amply provided for, were created Earls of Warwick and of Holland,—but his descendants after making a distinguished figure for some generations are now extinct.[1] They could not have looked with much pride on the character of the founder of their family, who, though he had pleasant manners, and was free from cant and hypocrisy, was, in reality, one of the most sordid, as well as most unprincipled men who have ever held the office of Lord Chancellor in England.

"Magnum Sigillum Dni Regis apud Hospicium ejusdem Dni Riche in Greate Saynte Bartilemewes in quadan interfori camera ibm intr. horas octavam et nonam ante meridiem ejusdem diei in quadam baga de corio inclusum et coopt alia baga de velueto rubeo insigniis Regiis ornat. per dcum Dnm Riche dcis nobilibus viris liberat. fuit."

[1] By one of them was erected Holland House, so famed as the residence of Addison when married to the dowager Countess of Warwick, and as the center of intellectual and refined society under the family of Fox, who succeeded to it.

CHAPTER XXXIX.

LIFE OF LORD CHANCELLOR GOODRICH.

THE Duke of Northumberland having the Great Seal so unexpectedly surrendered to him, was very much at a loss on whom he should bestow it. There was no lawyer in whom he could place entire confidence; and he began to have aspiring projects to which a lawyer with any remaining scruples of conscience must object. After a little deliberation he therefore resolved to recur to the old practice of putting an ecclesiastic at the head of the law,—taking care to select a man of decent character, who would not disgrace the appointment, and of moderate abilities, so as not to be dangerous to him. Such a man was THOMAS GOODRICH, Bishop of Ely, elevated because he was in no way distinguished—whose name would hardly have come down to us if at that time he had been less obscure.

On the 22d of December, 1551, the day after Lord Rich's resignation, the Great Seal was delivered by the King, in the presence of Northumberland and other grandees, to the Bishop, with the title of Lord Keeper.[1]

I do not find any account of his origin.[2] His name is often spelt Goodrick; but from the following epigram upon him, indicating that he had emerged from poverty, it must have been pronounced Goodrich:

> "Et bonus et dives, bene junctus et optimus ordo ;
> Præcedit bonitas ; pone sequuntur opes."

He was a pensioner of Benn'et College, Cambridge, and afterwards a fellow of Jesus College; and was said to have made considerable proficiency in the civil law as well as in Divinity. He took, however, only the degree of D.D. He early felt an inclination in favor of the reformed doctrines ; which he openly avowed, when it was safe for him to do so, in the reign of Edward VI. He was ac-

---

[1] Rot. Cl. 5 Ed. 6, p. 5.
[2] My friend Mr. Pulman has found for me, by searches in the Herald's College, that he was the son of Edward Goodrich, of East Kirby, in the county of Lincoln, and grandson of John Goodrich of Bolingbroke 3rd edition.

cordingly employed to assist in revising the translation of the New Testament, and in compiling the Liturgy, and, as a reward for his services, was made Bishop of Ely. But he was a quiet, bookish man, not mixing with state affairs.

While he held the Great Seal he was a mere cipher in the Council; and his appointment was a contrivance of Northumberland to have the power and patronage of Lord Chancellor in his own hands. It was thought, however, that this object would be more effectually gained if Goodrich were treated with apparent respect; and on the 19th of January following, he delivered up the Great Seal to the King, and received it back with the title of Lord Chancellor.[1]

On the previous day a commission had passed the Great Seal, authorising Beaumont, the Master of the Rolls, and others, to hear causes; and upon them devolved all the judicial business of the Court of Chancery while Goodrich was Chancellor.

The grand object now was to obtain the royal warrant for the execution of the illustrious convict lying under sentence of death in the Tower. Access to the King's presence was strictly denied to all who were suspected of being friendly to Somerset; and the new Chancellor, probably conscientiously, gave an opinion that he was guilty, and that the safety of the state required that the law should take its course. After a long delay Edward was induced to sign the fatal instrument, and the Protector was executed on Tower Hill, amidst wishes construed into prophecies that Northumberland might soon share his fate.

Parliament met a few weeks after, and a bill was introduced to confirm the attainder of the Duke of Somerset, and to set aside an entail of estates upon his family. It easily passed the Lords, but it was thrown out by the

---

[1] This ceremony took place "apud Greneweche in quodam interiori deambulaterio sive galerio ibidem inter horas secundam et terciam post meridiem." The entry, without stating any swearing in or installation, thus concludes:—
"Et superinde predicus Reverendus Pater Sigillum prcum de manibus dci Dni Regis gratutent. accipiens illud extra bagam in qua repositum erat in presencia predica extrahi et quidam brevia ibidem sigillari mandavit deindeque in bagam prcam iterum reponi et sigillo suo prpro muniri fecit ac curam et custodian ejusdem spr se assumpit et illud penes se retinuit et retinet."—I Rot. Cl. 5 Ed. 6.

Commons. Thereupon the Chancellor, in the name of the King and by command of Northumberland, dissolved the parliament which had now lasted about five years.[1]

In the beginning of the following year a new parliament was summoned, which Northumberland was determined should be more subservient, and for this purpose he caused the Chancellor to send, along with the writs, a letter, in the King's name, to each Sheriff, which, after setting forth the importance of having able and experienced representatives to serve in the House of Commons, concluded in these words:—"Our pleasure is, that where our Privy Council, or any of them, shall recommend men of learning and wisdom, in such case their directions be regarded and followed, to have this assembly to be of the most chiefest men in our realm for advice and good counsel."[2] This extraordinary breach of privilege passed without complaint.

On the 1st of March the parliament met in the palace of Whitehall, the King, on account of declining health, not being able to go to the usual place of meeting in London or Westminster. The Lords spiritual and temporal being assembled in their robes, in the King's chapel, Ridley, Bishop of London, preached a sermon to them, and they received the communion. They then adjourned to the King's great chamber, which was fitted up as a House of Lords, "the King sitting under his cloth of state, and the Lords in their degrees." The Commons being called in, Lord Chancellor Goodrich made a speech in the King's name, which is said to have been "brief on account of the King's sickness,"—and no part of it is preserved.

The object of the summons was chiefly to obtain a subsidy, and this being granted, and the Commons showing symptoms of discontent with the existing rule, the Lord Chancellor, at the end of a month, dissolved the Parliament, the King being present, and then seen the last time in public by his subjects.[3]

This Sovereign, of so great promise, was now drawing to his untimely end, and Northumberland wished to be at liberty, without the control of Parliament, to carry on his machinations for changing the succession,—well knowing that if the Lady Mary, who was next heir both by right of blood and by parliamentary settlement, should be

---

[1] 1 Parl. Hist. 590.   [2] Ibid. 591.   [3] Ibid. 602.

placed on the throne, his power would be gone, and his personal safety would be compromised. Although a majority of the nation had become attached to the Reformation, there was no chance of a parliament being induced to disturb the succession. Mary could not, with any show of reason, be set aside in favor of Elizabeth; a regard for hereditary right and respect for the memory of Henry VIII., who had always been a favorite with the common people, would have been strongly opposed to any attempt to set aside both. Northumberland himself was daily becoming more unpopular; and the last House of Commons, which he had taken such pains to pack, had shown considerable hostility to him. He resorted, therefore, to another expedient.

A statute of the realm had conferred on Henry VIII. personally a power to dispose of the Crown by will,—and a will had accordingly been made by him, under this statute, by which he excluded the Scottish line, and called the issue of his younger sister to succeed after his own children. Edward had no such power, but Northumberland pretended that it belonged to him by the common law, and was in hopes that the nation would not nicely inquire into the distinction.

He had easily succeeded in inculcating this doctrine on the debilitated mind of the dying King, through the medium of the Chancellor and other creatures, whom he employed for that purpose. They represented to Edward that both his sisters having been declared illegitimate by parliament, and their legitimacy never having been restored—though they were nominally put into the succession, they could not constitutionally succeed;—that being of the half blood to him, according to a well-known rule of law, they were not his heirs;—that the succession of Mary would be the restoration of Popery;—that the Scottish line had already been justly set aside as aliens;—that the true heiress was the Marchioness of Dorset, daughter of Mary the Queen-dowager of France;—that, as she waived her rights, the next to succeed was her eldest daughter, the Lady Jane Grey, married to Northumberland's fourth son, a young lady of rare beauty and accomplishments, and a zealous Lutheran; and that to secure Edward's fame with posterity, and his salvation in another world, he should exercise the power which belonged to him, by securing that glorious reformation of religion which he had established.

The sick Prince was so far misled by this sophistry, that with his own hand he drew a sketch of a will settling the Crown, if he should die without issue, on "the Lady Jane and her heirs masles," and by direction of the Chancellor (who in the whole of this transaction was under an apprehension of the penalties of treason) he put his royal signature to this instrument above, below, and on each margin.

But to give validity to the settlement the Chancellor insisted that it must be approved of by the Council, and being reduced into due form, must pass under the Great Seal,—adding that in a matter of such importance he could not act without the opinion of the Judges. On the 11th of June, 1553, Sir Edward Montague, Chief Justice of the Common Pleas, and two or three other Judges who were supposed to be most complying, together with the Attorney and Solicitor General, were summoned to Greenwich, where the Court then lay. They were immediately conducted by the Chancellor into the royal presence, and Edward made them a formal speech to the effect, "that he had seriously weighed the dangers which threatened the laws and liberties and religion of the country if the Lady Mary should inherit the Crown and marry a foreign Prince; that, to prevent so great an evil, he had determined to change the order of the succession; and that he had sent for them to draw up a legal instrument according to the instructions which he produced to them."

Being quite unprepared for such a proposal, they were thrown into the greatest perplexity. They expressed doubts to which the King listened with impatience; but they at last obtained a respite that they might peruse the various acts of succession which had been passed in the preceding reign, and consider the best mode of accomplishing the object which his Majesty for the good of his people had in view.

On deliberation they were more convinced of the entire illegality of the scheme, and of the personal peril in which they would themselves be involved by assisting in it. Accordingly, two days after, at a Council over which the Chancellor presided, and from the commencement of which Northumberland chose to be absent,—being asked for the instrument they had been ordered to prepare, they boldly answered that such an instrument would be a flat violation of the statute of the 35th of the late King, and would subject both those who should draw it and those who had advised it to be prosecuted for high treason. Northumberland, who had been within hearing in an adjoining room, finding that the persuasions of the Chancellor could make no impression upon them, and that his project was in danger of instantly blowing up, rushed into the Council Chamber with the most indecent violence, threatened to proceed against them as traitors, and declared that "he was ready to fight in his shirt with any man in so just a quarrel."[1] They still considered there was less peril in disobedience, and they departed expressing a resolute refusal.

Northumberland was not thus to be baulked. Gryffith, the Attorney-General, was supposed to be the chief instigator of the opposition. He was therefore dismissed,[2] and the others were again summoned to Greenwich the following day. Edward, prompted by Northumberland, sternly asked them "why his command had not been obeyed?" The Chief Justice answered, that to obey would have been dangerous to them, and of no service to his Grace: that the succession having been settled by parliament, could only be altered by parliament; and that nothing could be done but to call a parliament and introduce a bill for that purpose. The King replied that he intended to follow that course, but that in the mean time he wished to have the deed of settlement prepared which should be ratified in the parliament to be held in September. The Chancellor and the whole Council who were attending in a body joined in the request,—with a hint of their power to commit to the Tower for a breach of allegiance.

Montague at last agreed,—on condition that the Chancellor would make out a commission under the Great Seal to draw the instrument, and a full pardon under the Great Seal for having drawn it. This arrangement still was not

[1] This language would not appear so indecorous then as now, for instead of proposing a prize fight according to the rules of the ring, it referred to judicial combats, which at that time occasionally took place before the Judges.

[2] He was rewarded for his fidelity by being re-appointed by Mary, while Mr. Solicitor was dismissed.

satisfactory to Gosnald, the Solicitor-General, but means were found to bring him over the following day; and the Chancellor having made out the commission and the pardon in due form, the official instrument was engrossed on parchment, settling the Crown on the Lady Jane Grey.

The Chancellor himself now began to waver, and he refused to set the Great Seal to it unless it was signed not only by the King, but by all the Judges and all the members of the Council. The Judges all signed it except Sir James Hales, a Justice of the Common Pleas, who, although a zealous Protestant, could not be prevailed upon by any solicitations or threats to derogate from the rights of the Princess Mary, the lawful heir to the Crown.[1] The Councilors all readily signed except Cranmer, who at last had the weakness to yield (as he confessed) against his own conviction.[2] Goodrich then affixed the Great Seal to the patent, and Northumberland, having got possession of it, confidently expected forthwith to reign under the name of his daughter-in-law.[3]

Edward's strength henceforth declined so rapidly as to create a strong suspicion that poison assisted in hastening his end,—probably without foundation, for his feeble constitution had been undermined by consumption, which the nation had for some time foreseen must disappoint the hopes entertained of the coming felicity of his reign. He expired on the 6th of July, but his death was kept secret for three days, while preparations were made for the accession of Queen Jane, and steps were taken to get the Ladies Mary and Elizabeth into the power of Northumberland, the usurper.

Goodrich was allowed to retain the Great Seal as Chancellor, without any fresh appointment, and he heartily

---

[1] He had a very unsuitable return for his fidelity when Mary was upon the throne.—See *Life of Gardyner*, post.

[2] The Archbishop's signature appears the first, and then the Chancellor's; that of Cecil (afterwards the celebrated Burleigh) was the last, and it was so placed as to give him the pretext to which he resorted, that he signed only as a witness.—*Burnet*, vol. vi. pp. 275, 276.

[3] Upon his trial for high treason in Mary's reign, although he could not contend that Jane had been so far sovereign *de facto* as to entitle him to the benefit of the statute of Hen. VII., he tried to defend himself by this commission under the Great Seal, which he contended amounted to a pardon; but the Court held that it had no force, being contrary to an act of parliament, and that it could not pardon future treason to be committed after the King's death.—See *Burn*. xi. 243.

concurred with Northumberland in all the steps which were taken to carry into effect the new settlement of the Crown. The Lord Mayor, six Aldermen, and twelve principal citizens of London were privately summoned before the Council, and he read to them the patent for changing the succession, explained its provisions, and enforced its validity. He then required them to take an oath of allegiance to the new Sovereign, and dismissed them with an injunction not to betray the secret, and to watch over the tranquillity of the city.

On the fourth morning the Chancellor rode with the other Lords of the Council to Sion House, to do homage to Queen Jane, who was herself still entirely ignorant of her cousin's death, and of her approaching elevation. The Duke of Northumberland having announced to her the astounding intelligence, the Chancellor and other Councillors all fell on their knees,—declared that they took her for their Sovereign, and swore that they were ready to shed their blood in support of her right. When she had recovered from the swoon into which she fell, they intimated to her that she must, according to the custom of English Sovereigns on their accession, repair to the Tower of London, there to remain till her coronation; and they accompanied her down the Thames in a grand state barge which had been prepared for her, all the great officers of the Court and the principal part of the nobility joining in the procession. In the evening a proclamation was published superscribed by Jane as Queen, and countersigned by the Chancellor, setting forth her title; and she was proclaimed by the heralds without any opposition, but without any acclamations from the people.

A messenger arriving next day from Mary, as Queen, commanding the Council, on their allegiance, to give immediate orders for her proclamation, the Chancellor and twenty-one Councillors, Cranmer being of the number, sent an answer, directed to the "Lady Mary," requiring her to abandon her false claim, and to submit, as a dutiful subject, to her lawful and undoubted Sovereign. They likewise sent a mandate to the Lord Lieutenant of the county of Essex, where Mary was now mustering forces, which, after cautioning him against assisting the rebels, thus concluded: " Requiring your Lordship nevertheless, like a nobleman, to remain in that promise and steadiness to our Sovereign Lady Queen Jane's service as ye shall find us ready and firm with all our force to the same, which neither with honor, nor with safety, nor yet with duty, we may now forsake."[1]

But intelligence was in a few days received at the Tower that the Duke of Northumberland, who had marched with an army to suppress the insurrection, was deserted by his troops; and that the nobility, the gentry, and the commons, satisfied with a declaration of Mary, that she did not mean to change the national religion, were flocking from all quarters to her standard, and joyfully acknowledging her as Queen.

The Chancellor and other Councillors, in great alarm, now left the Tower under the pretence of receiving the French Ambassador at Baynard's Castle, but, in reality, with the intention of sending in, as speedily as possible, their adhesion to Queen Mary, in the hope of pardon. Having summoned the Lord Mayor and a deputation of Aldermen, the discussion was commenced by the Earl of Arundel, who declaimed against the ambition of Northumberland, and asserted the right, by birth and statute, of the two daughters of Henry VIII. The Earl of Pembroke then drew his sword, exclaiming, "If the arguments of my Lord of Arundel do not persuade you, this sword shall make Mary queen, or I will die in her quarrel." He was answered with shouts of approbation.

Goodrich thereupon declining to act any longer as Chancellor, delivered up the Great Seal to the Lords Arundel and Paget, that they might carry it to Queen Mary to be disposed of as her Grace should deem proper.[2] They immediately framed a recognition of Mary as their lawful Sovereign, which was signed by all present, including the Duke of Suffolk, who had joined them, and the whole body rode through the streets in procession, proclaiming Queen Mary at Paul's Cross, and all the principal stations of the city.

The Earl of Arundel and Lord Paget immediately af-

[1] The date is " Tower, July 19." The signatures are,—
"Cranmer."   "Lord W. Paget."
"T. Ely, Chancellor."   "Marq. Winchester,"
"The Earls of Suffolk,   and nine Knights.
   "Pembroke.   *Strype*, 913.
   "Arundel.
[2] Rot. Cl. 1 Mary, p. 7.

terwards set off for Framlingham, where Mary then was, and riding post all night, next morning delivered into her hands the Great Seal, the *clavis regni*, and she was so pleased with the gift and the accompanying news that she immediately granted them forgiveness. At the same hour Jane, leaving the Tower, returned to Sion House after a nine days' dream of empire.

By some historians she is reckoned among the Sovereigns of England. Goodrich most undoubtedly acted as her Lord Chancellor, although there was not time to make a new Great Seal with her style and insignia upon it.

He was beset with great terrors from the part he had ostensibly taken in concocting the patent to change the succession; but, partly from his sacred character and partly from his real insignificance, he was not molested, and he was permitted to retire to his diocese. His zeal for the Reformation now so far cooled that he offered no opposition to the restoration of the old religion effected by Mary, and he retained his bishopric till his death, which occurred on the 10th of May, 1554. In the lottery of life some high prizes are appropriated to mediocrity, and he was the holder of a fortunate ticket.

We ought here to take a retrospect of changes in the law, and of the administration of justice during the short reign of Edward VI. In the history of our religious establishment, it is the most memorable in our annals, for now indeed the Reformation was introduced, and it may be important to remember that this was done by the legislature, without any concurrence of convocations, and against the almost unanimous wish of the heads of the church.

The criminal law was improved by repealing a number of Henry VIII.'s fantastical treasons, and by enacting that in every prosecution for treason the overt act should be proved by two credible witnesses.[1] At the commencement of the reign an act passed from which no very favorable inference can be drawn as to the morals, habits, or accomplishments of the English nobility in the middle of the 16th century. Housebreaking by day or by night, highway robbery, horse stealing, and the felonious taking of goods from a church, having being made capital offences. it was provided, " that any Lord or Lords of the parlia

[1] 1 Ed. 6, c. 12. 5 & 6 Ed. 6, c. 11.

ment (to include Archbishops and Bishops), and any Peer or Peers of the realm having place and voice in parliament, being convicted of any of the said offenses for the first time, upon his or their request or prayer, *though he cannot read*, be allowed benefit of clergy, and be discharged without any burning in the hand, loss of inheritance, or corruption of blood."[1] It seems strange to us that this privilege of peerage should have been desirable, or should have been conceded; but it continued in force till taken away by an act passed after the trial of Lord Cardigan in the reign of Queen Victoria.

Edward's Chancellors, without any statute for that purpose, took upon themselves, in many instances, the exercise of legislative power. Thus, in April, 1549, Lord Chancellor Rich issued a proclamation under the Great Seal, addressed to all justices of the peace, enjoining them "to arrest all comers and tellers abroad of vain and forged tales and lies, and to commit them to the galleys, there to row in chains during the King's pleasure;" and by similar proclamations rates were fixed for the price of provisions,— penalties were imposed on such as should buy bad money under its nominal value, and the melting of the current coin was prohibited under pain of forfeiture.[2]

The attainder of the Seymours shows that the ruling faction could still perpetrate any atrocity through parliamentary or judicial forms. Nevertheless, in this reign, able judges presided in Westminster Hall, and between party and party justice was equally administered. The prejudices against the equitable jurisdiction of the Court of Chancery subsided, and although hardly any of the decisions of the Chancellors are preserved, they appear to have been satisfactory to the public till nearly the close of the reign, when there were heavy complaints of the inexperience of Goodrich.[3]

[1] 1 Ed. 6, c. 12, s. 10 14.   [2] 2 Strype, 147, 149, 341, 491.
[3] Dyer's Rep. Moore's Rep.

CHAPTER XL.

LIFE OF STEPHEN GARDYNER, LORD CHANCELLOR OF ENGLAND, FROM HIS BIRTH TO THE END OF THE REIGN OF HENRY VIII.

WE pass from a Chancellor appointed on account of his insignificance, that he might be a tool in the hands of others, to a man of original genius, of powerful intellect, of independent mind,—at the same time unfortunately of narrow prejudices and a relentless heart,—who had a powerful influence upon the events of his age, and left a distinguished name to posterity. Thomas Goodrich was succeeded by the celebrated STEPHEN GARDYNER.

The extraction of this extraordinary man has been matter of great controversy. The common statement is, that he was the natural son of Lionel Woodville, Bishop of Salisbury, brother of Elizabeth, the Queen of Edward IV.; while others insist that "he came of poor but honest parents." So much we know, that he was born at Bury St. Edmunds in the year 1483, under the reign of Richard III.

No account has reached us of his schooling, and the first notice of his education represents him as a most diligent student at Trinity Hall, Cambridge. There he made great proficiency in classical learning, devoting himself to the school of the "Ciceronians," then in high fashion. At the same time he laid the foundation of his future advancement by the profound skill he acquired in the civil and canon law. In 1520 he was admitted a Doctor in both faculties, and soon after he was made Master of Trinity Hall. Having a son of the Duke of Norfolk under his care, he acquired the friendship of that great noble, and was introduced by him to Wolsey, then in the plenitude of power as Chancellor to Henry VIII. The Cardinal was much pleased with the manners and accomplishments of the academic,—and, with his usual discernment, concluded that he might be made useful in the public service. Gardyner was very willing to change his career, for even with a view to advancement in the church there was then no such certain road for churchmen as secular employment.

He began with being the Cardinal's private secretary, and showed dexterity in managing the public correspondence and the private affairs of his patron. We may judge of the confidence reposed in him from the terms in which he is spoken of by Wolsey, who calls him "primarium secretissimorum consiliorum secretarium, mei dimidium, et quo neminem habeo cariorem."[1] The treaty of alliance with Francis I. in 1525 being projected, Gardyner was employed to draw up the *projet*, and the King coming to his house at Moor Park, in Hertfordshire, found him busy at this work. Henry looked at it, liked the performance well, the Secretary's conversation still better, and his fertility in the invention of expedients best of all. From this time Gardyner was consulted about the most secret affairs of State. Soon after he was made Chaplain to the King, and speedily Almoner, when he was admitted to Henry's closest familiarity and intimacy.

The question of the divorce from Catherine of Aragon coming up, Gardyner's consequence was much enhanced from his high reputation as a jurist and canonist. Misled by his ambition, and eager to conform to the King's humors, he now, and for several years afterwards, took a part of which he deeply repented when he became the great supporter of Papal power in England, and the Chancellor and Prime Minister of the daughter of Catherine. He not only gave a strong opinion as to the invalidity of Henry's first marriage, but he devoted the whole of his energies to the object of obtaining the formal dissolution of it. Having assisted in preparing questions upon the subject for the Universities at home and abroad, and in procuring favorable answers, he was himself sent as ambassador to the Court of Rome for the purpose of furthering the divorce. As a bribe to Clement VII., he was to procure from the Venetians the restoration to the Roman see of Ravenna and Servia, and then to extort from the gratitude or timidity of the Pope the bull and dispensation which would enable Henry to get rid of the wife of whom he was tired, and to marry her of whom he was then so deeply enamored. No better proof can be given of his high favor with Henry than that, in his embassy, he

[1] Burnet, Ref. No. VIII.

wrote him private letters not to be seen by Wolsey, whose good faith in the negotiation began to be suspected, He failed in the object of his mission, but he managed well while at Rome in advancing his own fortunes; for by rendering a service to the Bishop of Norwich, he was made Archdeacon of Norfolk; by intriguing for Wolsey's promotion to the popedom, he recommended himself more than ever to his patron;[1] and by the zeal and dexterity with which he conducted the secret correspondence in which he was engaged, he entirely won the heart of Henry.

As the divorce suit was now to be tried in England before a court consisting of Cardinal Campeggio, sent over as legate for that purpose, and Cardinal Wolsey associated with him, the King immediately retained Dr. Gardyner as his counsel, and desired him to hurry home to prepare for the trial. The keen advocate, on his arrival, was indefatigable in getting up the proofs of the consummation of Catherine's marriage with Prince Arthur, and the other facts relied upon to show the nullity of the dispensation of Pope Julius, under which that marriage was solemnized. After long delays, the suit was brought to a hearing, and Gardyner pleaded for his royal client with great learning and ability. But when a favorable judgment was expected, the cause was evoked to Rome to be decided by the Pope in person, assisted by the conclave. This step led to the fall of Wolsey. Of Gardyner's sincerity no doubts were entertained; and it was thought that he would have then been appointed to succeed as Chancellor, had it not been that, from the arrogance of the great Cardinal, and the manner in which, from his ecclesiastical character, it was supposed he had been able to thwart the King's inclinations, a fixed resolution had been formed that the Great Seal should not again be intrusted to a churchman.[2]

But although Sir Thomas More was preferred as Chancellor, he generally confined himself to the discharge of

[1] While Gardyner was at Rome Clement was dangerously ill, and he so won over the cardinals, that if a vacancy had occurred it is believed that Wolsey must have succeeded. When his masterly dispositions were related, Wolsey, thinking the triple crown already on his head, exclaimed, "O inestimable treasure and jewel of this realm!"

[2] So pleased was Anne Boleyn with his zeal, that she was in private correspondence with him, and thus addressed him: "I thank you for my letter, wherein I perceive the willing and faithful mind you have to do me pleasure." —*Letter in State Paper Office.*

his judicial duties; and Gardyner, now Secretary of State, was the chief adviser of the measures of the government. In 1531 he was appointed to the see of Winchester; and hitherto Cranmer and he, who afterwards took such different courses, and proved such mortal enemies, concurred in throwing off allegiance to Rome. While Sir Thomas More sacrificed first his office, and then his life, to his consistency, Gardyner, more flexible, not only acknowledged the King's supremacy, but wrote a book in defense of it, entitled " De verâ et falsâ Obedientiâ." He was always a determined enemy of the general Lutheran doctrines; but for a while he made his creed so far coincide with his interest, as to believe that the Anglican Church, rigidly maintaining all its ancient doctrines, might be severed from the spiritual dominion of the Pope, and flourish under a laymen as its head. At this time, so completely was he attached to the Antipapal faction, that he actually sat on the bench with Cranmer, and concurred in the sentence when the marriage between Henry and Catherine was adjudged null and void.

However, he joined himself with the Duke of Norfolk and the party opposed to any further innovation in religion, and was ever on the watch to counteract the efforts of Cranmer, supposed to be abbetted by Lord Chancellor Audley, to extend the Reformation. It was whispered that he had obtained absolution from the Pope for his past backsliding on the question of the supremacy, with a dispensation to yield silent obedience to this law while it existed,—on condition of his strenuous resistance to the new opinions, and his promise to take the earliest opportunity of bringing England back to full communion with the true Church.

Being sent on an embassy to Germany, he took occasion, on his return, to detail to the King the excesses of the Anabaptists, and to point out to him the importance of preserving uniformity of faith for the safety of the state. He likewise urged upon him, that it was impolitic farther to offend the Pope, by reason of the power of the Holy See itself, and because the Emperor and other orthodox Princes would break off all commerce with him if he went to extremities against the Roman Catholic religion. These representations produced "the bloody act of the

Six Articles," and the deaths of the numerous *sacramentaries*, who suffered under it for denying the real presence.

But what he chiefly watched was the manner in which the situation of Queen-consort was filled,—judging that upon this depended a good deal what should be the national religion. Although he had contributed to the elevation of Anne Boleyn, he rejoiced in her fall, and was supposed to have hastened it.[1]

Death delivered him from the apprehensions he entertained of the ascendancy of Jane Seymour. Then arose a mortal struggle between him and Cromwell for supplying the vacancy thus occasioned. The Vicar-General had a temporary triumph from the flattering portrait, by Holbein, of the Protestant Anne of Cleves; but Anne herself arrived; Henry was disgusted with her, and he was enraged against the man who had imposed her upon him In a few months Anne was divorced, and Cromwell was beheaded.

Nothing could exceed the exultation of Gardyner at this catastrophe, for Cromwell, who was the author of the dissolution of the monasteries, and himself deeply tainted with the new doctrines, had entered into secret engagements with the Protestant Princes of Germany, and was supposed to have a plan, in conjunction with some of the nobility, to make still further inroads on the property of the Church.

There was much anxiety till it was seen what choice the King would make, but Gardyner considered the true faith forever established when he had placed upon the throne the young and beautiful Catherine Howard, the niece of the Duke of Norfolk, and herself a rigid Roman Catholic.

For a year he went on contentedly, and had the satisfaction of alarming Cranmer so much, that the Archbishop, in great consternation, sent back his German wife to her own country, lest he should be subjected to the severe penalties enacted to enforce the celibacy of the clergy. But a cruel mortification awaited Gardyner in the discovery of the profligate character of the new Catholic

---

[1] "*Gardyner.* —— It will ne'er be well
Till Cranmer, Cromwell, her two hands and she,
Sleep in their graves."—*Shaksp. Hen. VIII.*

Queen. He at first resisted the proofs of her guilt, and contended that they were fabricated by Cranmer.

After her execution, his earnest desire was to assist in elevating to the throne a lady not only of pure morals but of pure orthodoxy, who should at once be faithful to the King and to the Pope. After the act passed making it high treason for any women who was not a true maid to marry the King without disclosing her shame, there was, as we have seen, much shyness among all the young ladies of the Court when his Majesty seemed to make any advance towards them; but Gardyner still hoped for an alliance with some sovereign family on the Continent that was leagued against the new heresy.

What must have been his astonishment and consternation when, in the morning of the 12th of July, 1543, being in attendance on the King at Hampton Court, he was ordered forthwith to celebrate a marriage between his Majesty and the Lady Catherine Par, the widow of the Lord Latimer, and well known to be a decided Lutheran, although, from the discretion which always marked her conduct, she had taken care not to give offense to those of opposite opinions! Of the mature age of thirty-five, she was by no means without personal attractions; but no one had ever dreamed of Henry putting up with a widow after his many declarations, both to parliament and in private society, that he could have nothing to say to any woman who he could not be sure, from his superior science, was an untouched virgin.

When Gardyner had recovered his speech, he made an objection, that the forms of the Church must be observed even by crowned heads; and that the proposed marriage, at that moment, would be irregular and uncanonical. But his astonishment and mortification were redoubled when the King, saying he had foreseen the difficulty, produced to him a license from Archbishop Cranmer, dispensing with the publication of banns, and allowing the ceremony to be performed at any hour and in any place, " for the honor and weal of the realm." The wily prelate perceived that he had been completely outwitted, and that, as a piece of wicked pleasantry, it was intended to make him the instrument of bringing about a matrimonial union, which it was known would be so distasteful to him. But he could no longer resist the King's commands; and being led into a small private chapel in the Palace, there he found the Lady Catherine and all requisite preparations for the marriage ceremony. Henry having gone through this for the sixth time, in a few minutes the widow Latimer was Queen of England.[1]

Gardyner, who had always a great command of himself, behaved with decency; but he felt that he had been insulted, and secretly vowing revenge, he resolved to "bide his time."

He took every opportunity of instilling suspicion into the King's mind respecting Cranmer's principles and purposes; and at last Henry gave consent that the Archbishop should be examined before the Council, and that they should take such steps respecting him as the safety of the state might require. But it had been intended from the beginning to play off another trick upon Gardyner; or the King, upon farther consideration, resolved to disappoint and to mortify him; for his Majesty gave Cranmer a ring, to be shown, in case of necessity, as a proof that he was still in full favor.

It was supposed that the Archbishop was at last to share the fate of Fisher, More, and Cromwell. Being summoned as a criminal before the Council,—after he had been kept waiting for some hours at the door among the populace, he was called in and underwent a strict interrogatory respecting his opinions. Gardyner then said in a stern tone: "My Lord of Canterbury, you must stand committed to the Tower." The Archbishop showed the royal signet; and the King himself suddenly coming in, sharply reprimanded Gardyner and Chancellor Wriothesley for their harsh conduct to a man to whom he owed such obligations, and whom he was determined to protect.[2]

---

[1] Chron. Catal. 238.

[2] Shakespeare gives a very lively and just representation of this scene in the fifth Act of Henry VIII.,—only that, by his usual pardonable disregard of dates, he supposes it to have happened in the lifetime of Anne Boleyn, at least twelve years sooner. Gardyner's speech is very characteristic:—

"My Lord, because we have business of more moment,
We will be short with you. 'T is his Highness' pleasure
And our consent, for better trial of you,
From hence you be committed to the Tower;
Where being but a private man again,
You shall know many dare accuse you boldly,
More than I fear you are provided for."
"Receive him
And see him safe i' the Tower."—*Hen. VIII.* act v. sc. 2.

In the following year, Gardyner thought that the hour of vengeance had at last arrived. The King, of his own accord, complained to him of the Queen,—representing, "that he had discovered, to his great concern, that she entertained most suspicious opinions concerning the real presence, and other points comprised in the Six Articles; and that, forgetting the modesty of her sex, and the subjection of the wife to the husband (to say nothing of what was due to himself as Sovereign and Defender of the Faith), she had actually been arguing with him on these essential heads of theology, and had been trying to undermine his orthodoxy, and to make him a convert to the damnable doctrines of Luther, which, in his youth, he had refuted with so much glory." Gardyner eagerly laid hold of the opportunity to inflame the quarrel; and strongly inculcated upon the King his duty to forget every private consideration, and to set a bright example of piety and Christian courage by prosecuting the sharer of his bed and throne for thus violating the law of God and a statute of the realm. The King, exasperated by these exhortations, agreed that the matter should be mentioned to Wriothesley; and (as we have seen in the life of that Chancellor), had it not been for the accident of the articles of impeachment being clandestinely read, and secretly communicated to the Queen before they were acted upon, —so as to give her an opportunity for a dexterous explanation which soothed the King's wrath—she would certainly have been sent to the Tower,—and, probably, ending her career on Tower Hill, Henry would have made a seventh attempt to have a wife both chaste and orthodox.[1]

During the rest of this reign Gardyner was out of favor at Court, and obliged to confine himself to the discharge of what he considered his duties as a prelate. In this capacity he took an active part in the persecution of Anne Ascue, Nicholas Boleman, John Lassels, and others, who were burnt for denying the real presence; while he could not save an equal number of stanch Papists who suffered at the instance of the opposite party for denying the King's supremacy. But his chief object was to check the

[1] Ante, p. 130-133. Some historians think that in this affair Henry was again mystifying Gardyner. I have no doubt that, in the present instance he was serious and sincere.

translation of the Bible, and its circulation among the laity, which he considered the grand source of heresy and insubordination to just spiritual authority. Having tried ineffectually to render the translation unintelligible, by retaining a large mixture of Latin words from the Vulgate, for which he contended there were no equivalent terms in the English tongue,[1] he succeeded in introducing a clause into an act of parliament upon the subject, confining the use of the translation to gentlemen and merchants, with a preamble, "that many seditious and ignorant persons had abused the liberty granted them of reading the Bible, and that great animosities, tumults, and schisms had been occasioned by perverting the sense of the Scriptures."[2]

He still made ineffectual attempts to recover the King's favor. Having prevailed on the Convocation to grant rather a liberal subsidy, he hurried with the news to Windsor. The King taking horse on the terrace to ride out a hawking, saw Gardyner standing in a group with Lord Chancellor Wriothesley and other Councillors, and calling out to the Lord Chancellor said, "Did not I command you he should come no more amongst you?" The Lord Chancellor answered, "An it please your Grace his coming is to bring word of a benevolence given to your Majesty by the clergy." The King exclaimed, "Ah! let him come hither;" "and so," observes the narrator of this scene, of which he was an eye-witness, "he did his message, and the King went straight away."[3] Being anxious to keep up a belief with the multitude that he still enjoyed the King's confidence, it is related that Henry, lying ill in bed, and having summoned a Council, Gardyner attended, but was not admitted into the royal presence. "Thereupon he remained in the outer Privy Chamber until the Council came from the King, and then went down with them,—to the end, as was thought, to blind the world withal."[4]

The prosecution of the Duke of Norfolk and the Earl of Surrey, at the close of the reign, still further weakened the Catholic party; but a great struggle was made by

---

[1] Among these were *ecclesia, pænitentia, pontifex, contritus, holocausta, sacramentum, elementa, ceremonia, mysterium, presbyter, sacrificium, humilitas, satisfactio, peccatum, gratia, hostia, charitas.*—Burnet, vol. i. p. 315.
[2] 33 Hen. 8, c. 1.
[3] Sir Anthony Lenny. See Fox, Mart. 1 St. Tr. 56c.   [4] Ibid.

them to have Gardyner included in the list of Henry's Executors, to whom the government was to be intrusted during the minority of his son. Sir Anthony Brown, "a principal pillar of the Romanists," having at all times access to the King, as being of the Privy Chamber, knelt down, Henry lying sick in bed, and said, "My Lord of Winchester, I think by negligence, is left out of your Majesty's will, who hath done your Highness most painful, long, and notable service, and one without whom the rest shall not be able to overcome your great and weighty affairs committed unto them." "Hold your peace," quoth the King, "I remembered him well enough, and of good purpose have left him out. For surely, if he were in my testament, and one of you, he would cumber you all, and you should never rule him, he is of so troublesome a nature. I myself could use him and rule him to all manner of purposes as seemed good unto me, but so shall you never do, and therefore talk no more of him to me in this behalf." Sir Anthony was urged on again to press the point, as everything was felt to depend upon it; but Henry, well prepared by the Seymours and Catherine Par, who had got complete possession of him, put an end to all farther attempts, by exclaiming, "Have you not yet done to molest me in this manner? If you will not cease to trouble me, by the faith I owe unto God I will surely despatch thee out of my will also, and therefore let us hear no more of it."[1]

On the accession of the new Sovereign, Gardyner, though excluded from the Council, set himself openly and fearlessly to oppose the measures brought forward under the Protector, to change the established religion;—and there can be no doubt that he had the law on his side. Before a parliament was called, the Council, disregarding the "Act of the Six Articles" which was still in force, issued orders for changing the ceremonial of Divine worship,—published a book of homilies to be read by all priests, inculcating the new doctrines,—and appointed ministers to go into every diocese to see that the new regulations were observed. Gardyner expressed his firm resolve that if the visitors came into his diocese he should proceed against them, that they might be restrained and punished. He made representations on the subject to the

[1] Fox, Mart.

Protector, and tried to show both the illegality and the inexpediency of these proceedings. "'Tis a dangerous thing," said he, "to use too much freedom in researches of this kind. If you cut the old canal, the water is apt to run further than you have a mind to. If you indulge the humors of novelty, you cannot put a stop to people's demands, nor govern their indiscretions at pleasure. To speak my mind and to act as my conscience directs, are two branches of liberty which I can never part with."

He forcibly urged that Edward was too young and that the Protector was too much occupied to study subjects of controversy; that it was imprudent to run such a risk of disturbing the public peace during a minority; that injunctions issued in the King's name could not invalidate acts of parliament; and that as Cardinal Wolsey had incurred a premunire though he acted under royal license, so all clergymen who taught the doctrines in the homilies would be liable to the penalties enacted by the statute of the Six Articles,—which he himself was determined to enforce for the honor of God and the good of the Church.[1] He likewise wrote in a contemptuous tone to Cranmer, defying him to prove the truth of certain doctrines inculcated in the book of homilies, and reproaching him with duplicity in now reprobating the opinions which he had appeared zealously to countenance during the life of the late King.

Gardyner was in consequence summoned before the Council, and required to promise obedience to the royal injunction. He appealed to the approaching parliament. The Protector's party became afraid of the resistance which, as a member of the House of Peers, he might offer to their measures, and they were still more alarmed at the flame he was beginning to kindle out of doors by addressing himself to the religious feelings of the people. Therefore, though he could not be charged with any offense against the law, he was in the most arbitrary manner forthwith committed to the Fleet, and detained a close prisoner till the end of the session.

Attempts were made in vain during his confinement to gain him over to the new plan of reform. On one occasion, Cranmer, finding he could make no impression upon him, exclaimed testily, "Brother of Winchester, you like

---

[1] Strype. See the correspondence at full length. 1 St. Tr. 55.

not anything new unless you be yourself the author thereof." "Your Grace wrongeth me," replied the true conservative; "I have never been author yet of any one new thing, for which I thank my God."

An intriguing subordinate was afterwards sent to him to hint, that if he would soften his opposition, he might have a place in the Council, and be restored to his see. But he answered indignantly, "that his character and conscience forbade it; and that if he agreed on such terms he should deserve to be whipped in every market town in the realm, and then to be hanged for an example, as the veriest varlet that ever was bishop in any realm christened."[1]

At the end of the session which had been so much smoothed by his absence he was set at liberty, and ordered by the Council to preach at Paul's Cross before the King on the feast of St. Peter,—with an injunction that he should not touch on any controverted question. He declared to a friend that this was perhaps the only opportunity the young Prince might have of hearing the truth, and that he was determined, whatever might be the consequences, to explain to him the true Catholic doctrine with respect to the mass and the eucharist. He kept his word; but the next day he was committed to the Tower.

During his absence from parliament the statute of the Six Articles was repealed, and bills were passed allowing the clergy to marry;—for the administration of the Sacrament of the Lord's Supper to the laity in both kinds;—for uniformity of worship, and for the use of the new Liturgy.[2] Still certain bishops, animated by Gardyner's example, refused to conform; and after he had been confined for two or three years, a resolution was taken to deprive him and them of their bishoprics, so that the reformed church might be complete.

The method of procedure against him was violent, and was hardly disguised by any color of law or justice. A deputation from the Council were sent to tempt him with questions. Finding him more compliant than they expected, they rose in their demands; and at last insisted on unconditional submission, and an acknowledgment of

---
[1] Strype. 1 St. Tr. 551.   [2] Stat. 1 Ed. 6.

past errors. Perceiving that it was their purpose either to dishonor or to ruin him, or perhaps both, he determined not to gratify them by any further compliance. He therefore refused to answer any questions till he should recover his liberty; but he asserted his innocence, and desired a fair trial. In a few days he was brought before the Council, when certain articles were read, and, in the King's name, he was required to subscribe them. He replied that "in all things his Majesty could lawfully command he was most ready to obey; but forasmuch as there were divers things required of him that his conscience would not bear, therefore he prayed them to have him excused." Immediate sequestration of his ecclesiastical revenue was pronounced, with an intimation that, if he did not submit within three months, he should be deprived of his bishopric.

At the end of that time a commission was issued to the Metropolitan, three Bishops and six laymen, to bring him judicially to trial. Having protested against the validity of the commission, which was not founded on any statute or precedent, he defended himself with vigor; but Cranmer, on the twenty-second day of the proceedings, before the close of the defendant's proofs, which occasioned some disagreeable disclosures,—on the ground that he was contumacious, pronounced sentence against him that he should be deprived of his bishopric. He appealed to the King, but his appeal was not regarded, and he was now shut up in a meaner cell in the Tower,—with instructions from the Council that no man should see him but one of the warders; that all his books and papers should be taken from him; and that he should be refused the use of pen, ink, and paper. There he lay, in solitary confinement, without any mitigation of his sufferings, till the accession of Queen Mary, when he was made Lord Chancellor and Prime Minister to that Sovereign.

Such was the seclusion in which Gardyner had been kept that he had not heard of the death of Edward VI., the proclamation of Lady Jane Grey as Queen, or the manner in which the nation had taken up the cause of the rightful heir to the Crown,—when, on the morning of the 31st of July, 1553, he was told of those events,—with the additional news that Queen Mary, accompanied by her sister Elizabeth, was actually making a triumphal procession through the streets of London, on her way to the Tower.

It happened that in this fortress there were confined four other state prisoners, who had never been allowed to communicate with each other, and had been subjected to equal rigor,—the old Duke of Norfolk, attainted in the last days of Henry VIII., and saved from the block by the opportune death of that tyrant,—the Duchess of Somerset, who had been committed at the same time, with her husband, as an accomplice in his treasons,— Courtenay, son of the Marquis of Exeter, who, without being charged with any crime, had been shut up ever since his father's execution, in the year 1538,—and Tunstal, Bishop of Durham, who, imitating the firmness of Gardyner, had likewise been deprived and sentenced to close imprisonment. As the procession approached amidst the deafening acclamations of the people, these five illustrious captives were liberated: and having immediately met and appointed Gardyner to deliver an address of congratulation to the new Queen in their names, they all knelt down on the green inside the great gate leading from Tower Hill. As she entered, Gardyner, still on his knees, pronounced his address in terms and in a tone the most affecting. Mary burst into tears, called them *her* prisoners, bade them rise, and having kissed them, restored them to complete liberty.

If Gardyner's fall from power had been precipitate, much more sudden and striking was his reinstatement. He was the Queen's chief favorite and adviser from their first interview, and, taken from a dungeon, he was invested with the supreme power of the state. We have seen, in the life of Lord Chancellor Goodrich, that the Great Seal, which he renounced on the dethronement of Queen Jane, was carried by the Lords Arundel and Paget to the Queen at Framlingham.[1] She brought it with her to London, as an emblem of her sovereignty, and she immediately delivered it to Gardyner, as Lord Keeper, till he might be more regularly installed; at the same time swearing him of her Privy Council. At the end of three weeks she constituted him Lord Chancellor, with an intimation that he should use the Great Seal which bore the name and

---

[1] Ante, p. 179.

style of her deceased brother, till another, bearing her own name and style, should be made. It is curious to observe, that she herself assumed the title of "Supreme Head of the Church."[1]

CHAPTER XLI.

LIFE OF LORD CHANCELLOR GARDYNER, FROM THE ACCESSION OF QUEEN MARY.

IT must be admitted that the earliest measures of Mary's reign, prompted by Gardyner, were highly praiseworthy. The depreciated currency was restored; a new coinage came out of sovereigns and half-sovereigns, according to the old standard; the subsidy extorted from the late parliament was remitted; and, to discountenance puritanical severity, the festivities which distinguished the Court in the time of Henry VIII. were restored. No complaint could as yet be made of undue severity in punishing the late movement in favor of Queen Jane; for though she and her youthful husband, and various others, were convicted of treason, Northumberland only and two of his associates were actually executed.

The privilege of crowning the Sovereigns of England, we have seen, belongs to the Archbishops of Canterbury; but Mary would have considered it an insult to her mother's memory, and little less than sacrilege, to have permitted Cranmer to perform this rite, and he was in no situation to assert the claim of his see, as he was at present liable to be prosecuted as a traitor for signing the settlement to disturb Mary's succession, and for having actually supported the title of Queen Jane. The honor of anointing the Queen and placing the crown upon her head was

[1] "Memd. qd die Mercurii videlt vicisemo tertio die Augusti anno regni Dne Marie Dei Gra. Angl. Franc. et Hiber. Regine Fidei Defensoris *et in Terra ecclie Anglicane et Hibernie supremi capitis* primo circa horam quintam post meridiem ejusdem diei Magnum Sigillum ipsius Domne Regine quondamque sigillum excellentissimi Principis Edward Sexti nuper Regis Anglie Angl. defunct. fris prce Dne Regine percharissimi apud Richemount in sua privata cra ibidem sigillum illud in quadam baga, &c. Reverendo in Xro Pri Sta Stepho Winto Epo deliberavit ad sigillandum et excendum ut Magnum Sigillum ipsius Dne Regine quousque aliud Magnum Sigillum cum nome et titulo Regine insculptum fabricari et de novo fieri possit, &c."—Rot. Cl. 1 Mar.

conferred on Lord Chancellor Gardyner, who had been restored to his see of Winchester.

To please the people, he took care that the ceremony should be performed with great magnificence, ancient precedent being strictly adhered to in the religious part of it; and the banquet in Westminster Hall gave high satisfaction to all who partook of it, whether Romanists or Reformers. Gardyner deserved still more praise for publishing, the same evening, a general pardon under the Great Seal (with a few exceptions) to all concerned in treasonable or seditious practices since the Queen's accession.

Hopes were entertained that his elevation to power had mitigated the sternness of his character, and that moderate and humane counsels would continue to distinguish the new reign. These hopes, probably, would not have been disappointed, had not the Chancellor formed a strong opinion that it was essentially necessary for the safety of the state that the new doctrines should be utterly suppressed, and that church government should be restored to the same condition in which it was before the rupture with Rome. He was no enthusiast; he was not naturally cruel; he was not bigoted in his creed, having several times shown that he could make profession of doctrine bend to political expediency. But even in the reign of Henry VIII. he had come to the conclusion that the privilege of free inquiry in religion was incompatible with the peace of society, and that the only safe policy was to enforce the established standard of faith. His own sufferings during the reign of Edward VI. had, no doubt, strengthened these views, and he was now prepared resolutely to carry through the most rigorous measures, any temporary display of liberality being intended only to facilitate the attainment of his object. He resolved, at the same time to proceed with caution, and to wait till he had brought about a reconciliation with Rome and the restitution of the Catholic religion by authority of parliament, before resorting to the axe and the stake as instruments of conversion.

Meanwhile he himself and the other Bishops deprived during the last reign being restored, the heretical Archbishop of York and the Bishops of London, Exeter, and Gloucester were sent to prison. Cranmer and Latimer soon followed them. It should be recorded however that when some zealous Catholics urged the imprisonment of the celebrated foreign reformer, Peter Martyr, Gardyner, to his honor, pleaded that he had come over by an invitation from a former government, and furnished him with supplies to return to his own country in safety.

Parliament meeting on the 5th of October, the Chancellor, after celebrating a solemn mass of the Holy Ghost according to the ancient ritual, delivered, in presence of the Queen and the two Houses, an eloquent oration, in which he celebrated the piety, clemency, and other virtues of the reigning Sovereign, and called upon the legislature to pass the laws which were required, after the late dissensions and disturbances, for the good of the Church and the safety of the realm.

The first act which he proposed was most laudable, as it swept away all the newly created treasons, although it was considered by some an insidious attempt to restore the authority of the Pope. He had little difficulty in changing the national religion as to doctrine and worship; but there was a great alarm at the thought of restoring Papal supremacy, as this might draw along with it a restoration of the church lands, with which the nobles and gentry had been enriched.

In the Lords, there was no show of opposition to any proposed measure; but, notwithstanding great pains taken by Gardyner to manage the elections, there were symptoms of discontent exhibited in the House of Commons, which rendered it prudent that several bills brought in should be postponed.

The most strenuous opponent of the Catholic counter-revolution was that same Sir James Hales, the Judge of the Common Pleas, who, at the close of the reign of Edward VI., had risked his life by refusing to join in the illegal scheme for setting Mary aside from the succession to the Crown.

In vacation time he resided in Kent, where he acted as a magistrate; and presiding as chairman at the Michaelmas Quarter Sessions, held for that county, he gave charge to the grand jury to inquire of all offenses touching the Queen's supremacy and religious worship, against the statutes made in the time of Henry VIII. and Edward VI., which he told them remained in full force, and parliament alone could repeal. In consequence, an indictment being found for the unlawful celebration of mass, contrary to the form of the statute in such case made and provided, Hales tried, convicted, and sentenced the defendant as the law required.

On the first day of the following term, the Judges were to be sworn in before the Chancellor in Westminster Hall, under their appointment by the new Sovereign; and Hales having, with the rest, presented himself to his Lordship, the following dialogue took place between them, highly characteristic of the individuals and of the age. *Lord Chancellor.*—" Master Hales, ye shall understand, that like as the Queen's Highness hath heretofore conceived good opinion of you, especially for that ye stood both faithfully and lawfully in her cause of just succession, refusing to set your hand to the book, among others that were against her Grace in that behalf; so now, through your own late deserts against certain her Highness's doings, ye stand not well in her Grace's favor, and, therefore, before ye take any oath, it shall be necessary for you to make your purgation." *Hales, J.*—" I pray you, my Lord, what is the cause?" *Lord Chancellor.*—" Information is given that ye have indicted certain priests in Kent for saying mass." *Hales, J.*—" My Lord, it is not so; I indicted none: but, indeed, certain indictments of like matter were brought before me at the last sessions there holden, and I gave order there as the law required. So I have professed the law, against which in cases of justice, I will never, God willing, proceed, nor in any wise dissemble, but with the same show forth my conscience; and if it were to do again, I would do no less than I did." *Lord Chancellor.*—" Yea, Master Hales, your conscience is known well enough; I know you lack no conscience." *Hales, J.*—" My Lord, you may do well to search your own conscience, for mine is better known to myself than to you; and to be plain, I did as well use justice in your said mass case by my conscience as by law, wherein I am fully bent to stand in trial to the utmost that can be objected. And if I have therein done any injury or wrong, let me be judged by the law; for I will seek no better defense, considering chiefly that it is my profession." *Lord Chancellor.*—" Why, Master Hales, although you had the rigor of the law on your side, yet ye might have regard to the Queen's Highness's present doings in that case. And further, although ye seem to be more than precise in the law, yet I think ye would be very loth to yield to the extremity of such advantage as might be gathered against your proceedings in the law as ye have sometimes taken upon you in place of justice, and if it were well tried, I believe ye should not be well able to stand honestly thereto. *Hales, J.*—" My Lord, I am not so perfect but I may err for lack of knowledge. But, both in conscience, and such knowledge of the law as God hath given me, I will do nothing but I will maintain and abide in it; and if my goods, and all that I have, be not able to counterpoise the case, my body shall be ready to serve the turn, for they be all at the Queen's Highness's pleasure." *Lord Chancellor.*—" Ah, sir, ye be very quick and stout in your answers. But as it should seem that which you did was more of a will favoring the opinion of your religion against the service now used, than for any occasion or zeal of justice, seeing the Queen's Highness doth set it forth as yet, wishing all her faithful subjects to embrace it accordingly; and where you offer both body and goods in your trial, there is no such matter required at your hands, and yet ye shall not have your own will neither." *Hales, J.*—" My Lord, I seek not wilful will, but to show myself, as I am bound, in love to God, and obedience to the Queen's Majesty, in whose cause willingly, for justice sake, all other respects set apart, I did of late, as your Lordship knoweth, adventure as much as I had. And as for my religion, I trust it be such as pleaseth God, wherein I am ready to adventure as well my life as my substance, if I be called thereunto. And so in lack of mine own power and will, the Lord's will be fulfilled." *Lord Chancellor.*—" Seeing you be at this point, Master Hales, I will presently make an end with you. The Queen's Highness shall be informed of your opinion and declaration. And as her Grace shall thereupon determine, ye shall have knowledge. Until such time, ye may depart as you came without your oath; for as it appeareth, ye are scarce worthy the place appointed." *Hales, J.*—" I thank your Lordship; and as for my vocation being both a burden and a charge more than ever I desired to take upon me, whensoever it shall please the Queen's Highness to ease me thereof, I shall most humbly, with due contentation, obey the same."[1]

[1] Somers' Tracts, 2 Coll. vol. xcv. 1 St. Tr. 714.

In this witty recontre it must be confessed that the Chancellor had the worst of it; but the poor Puisne ere long had reason to regret his triumph, for not only was he dismissed from his office of Judge, but in a few days after he was committed to the King's Bench prison, where he remained in close custody till Lent in the following year, when he was transferred to the Compter in Bread Street. He was then sent to the Fleet, where he was frightened to such a degree by stories which the keeper told him of the torments in preparation for those who denied the supremacy of the Pope, that he attempted to commit suicide by stabbing himself; and when he was at last discharged, his mind was so much weakened by the hard usage he had undergone, that he drowned himself in a river near his own house in Kent.[1]

Gardyner incurred greater odium by advising, as a discouragement to the Reformers, the execution of the Lady Jane Grey, and her youthful husband, Lord Guilford Dudley. a cruelty not palliated by Wyatt's rebellion, with which they had no privity. He behaved generously, however, to the Princess Elizabeth, and procured her release from the Tower, perhaps because she had, about this time, been induced to conform to the Catholic worship. " The Protestant schoolmaster of Jane Grey and of Elizabeth was likewise protected by the Popish Chancellor of Mary; and the grateful testimony of Ascham in memory of his protector, who in days of danger had guarded 'the Muses' bower,' is recorded in a spirit which Milton would not have disdained."[2]

---

[1] The coroner's jury very unjustly brought in a verdict against him of *felo de se*, which gave rise to the famous question whether, "if a man kills himself, the crime of suicide is to be considered as complete in his lifetime or not?" He held an estate as joint tenant with his wife, which it was contended was forfeited to the Crown by his felony. The counsel for Lady Hales argued ineffectually that a man cannot kill himself in his lifetime. The legal reasoning in Judge Hales's case (which is reported in Plowden *) is copied almost word for word in the dialogue between the gravediggers in Hamlet upon the parallel case of Ophelia:—

1st Clo. " Here lies the water; good : here stands the man; good: If the man go to this water and drown himself, it is, will he, nill he, he goes : mark you that. But if the water come to him and drown him, he drowns not himself. Argal, he that is not guilty of his own death, shortens not his own life."

2nd Clo. "But is this law?"

1st Clo. " Ay, marry is 't, crowner's quest law."

[2] Ed. Review, April, 1846.

* Hales *v.* Patit Plowd. 253.

Where religion was not concerned, Gardyner showed himself a wise and even patriotic statesman. When the important question of the Queen's marriage came to be discussed, he strongly recommended to her choice a handsome Englishman, Courtenay, Earl of Devonshire, so that the liberties and independence of the nation might not be endangered by an alliance with a foreign prince. Mary was at first inclined to take his advice, till, piqued by the preference which Courtenay showed to Elizabeth, and alarmed by his dissolute character, she formed a determination to marry her cousin, Philip of Spain, from which Gardyner in vain labored to divert her. She declared that "she would prove a match for all the cunning of the Chancellor;" and having sent for the imperial ambassador, kneeling at the altar, she, in his presence, pledged her faith to Philip, and vowed that while she lived, she never would take any other man for her husband.

Gardyner contrived to get an address voted to her from the House of Commons, which, after earnestly pressing her to marry, expressed strong apprehension of a foreign alliance. When told of it, she said she would answer it with her own mouth. Accordingly, when the speaker had read the address, and it was expected that the Chancellor, as usual, would answer in her name, she herself replied, "that for their expressions of loyalty, and their desire that the issue of her body might succeed her on the throne, she sincerely thanked them; but in as much as they pretended to limit her in the choice of a husband, she thanked them not. The marriage of her predecessors had always been free, nor would she surrender a privilege which they had enjoyed."[1]

Finding her immovable, Gardyner took care that the articles of marriage should be as favorable as possible for the interest and security of England, by stipulating, that though Philip should have the title of King, the administration should be entirely in the Queen; that no foreigner should be capable of enjoying any office in the kingdom; that no innovation should be made in the English laws, customs, and privileges; and that Philip should not carry the Queen abroad without her consent, nor any of her children, without the consent of the nobility. As soon as the treaty was signed, the Chancellor called a meeting

[1] Noailles, 269.

of the Lord Mayor, Aldermen, and citizens of London,
at Guildhall, and, in an eloquent discourse, explained to
them the many and valuable benefits which he anticipated
from an union between their Queen and a Prince, the apparent heir of so many rich and powerful states.

Parliament assembling, the Chancellor opened the session by a speech in which he dwelt on the Queen's hereditary title to the Crown, maintained her right of choosing
a husband for herself,—observed how proper a use she
made of that right by giving the preference to an old ally
descended from the house of Burgundy,—and, remarking
the failure of Henry VIII.'s posterity, of whom there now
remained none but the Queen and the Lady Elizabeth,
added, that in order to obviate the inconveniences which
might arise from different pretenders, it was necessary to
invest the Queen by law with a power of disposing of the
Crown, and of appointing her successor, which had belonged to her father.

Both parties ratified the articles of marriage, but they
refused to pass any such law as the Chancellor pointed
out to them, and it is supposed that he made the suggestion only to please the Queen; for the power might have
been used not only by setting aside the Lady Elizabeth,
at which he would have rejoiced, but by appointing Philip
to succeed, to which he never would have consented.

The royal bridegroom at last arrived at Southampton,
and in the cathedral church of Winchester the Lord Chancellor himself celebrated the marriage between him and
Mary, which he had done all in his power to prevent, and
which turned out so inauspiciously. His power, however,
was if possible increased; for the Emperor Charles having
the highest opinion of his wisdom, had strongly exhorted
Philip in all things to be guided by his counsels.

The passionate wish of the Court now was to consummate the reconciliation with Rome, and for this purpose
a parliament was summoned to meet in November. To
ensure a favorable House of Commons, Gardyner sent
circulars in the Queen's name to the Sheriffs, who were
all Catholics, desiring them to use their influence that no
favorer of heresy might be elected.

On the day of meeting there was a grand procession to
Westminster Abbey, led by the Commons,—the Peers
and Prelates following,—the Chancellor being last; then

came Philip and Mary, in robes of purple, the King on a Spanish genet, richly caparisoned, attended by the Lords of his household, the Queen on a litter, surrounded by her ladies of honor. A religious ceremony after the ancient fashion being performed, and all being duly ranged in the Parliament Chamber, the Chancellor from his place in front of the throne addressed the two Houses. "The Queen's first parliament," he said "had re-established the ancient worship,—the second had confirmed the articles of her marriage,—and their Majesties expected that the third, in preference to every other object, would accomplish the re-union of the realm with the universal Church."

The bills brought in for this purpose passed the Lords unanimously, and were opposed only by two Members of the House of Commons. Cardinal Pole, having been appointed Archbishop of Canterbury and Legate *à latere* from the Pope, had a few days before arrived in England, and on his landing had been received with great distinction by the Chancellor. His attainder being reversed, he was now introduced into parliament, and the King and Queen being present, the Chancellor spoke as follows:—

"My Lords of the Upper House, and you my masters of the Nether House here present, the Right Reverend Father in God, my Lord Cardinal Pole, Legate *à latere*, is come from the Apostolic See from Rome as ambassador to the King's and Queen's Majesty, upon one of the weightiest causes that ever happened in this realm, and which pertaineth to the glory of God and your universal benefit. The which ambassade their Majesties' pleasure is to be signified unto you all by his own mouth, trusting that you receive and accept it in as benevolent and thankfulwise as their Highnesses have done, and that you will give attentive and inclinable ears unto his Grace, who is now ready to declare the same."[1]

The Cardinal, after saying that "the cause of his repair hither had been most wisely and gravely declared by my Lord Chancellor," delivered a long oration on the sin of schism and the wickedness of the proceedings in England which had brought about the disruption from the true Church, and proclaimed his readiness, on due submission, to restore them to her bosom.

[1] 1 Parl. Hist. 618.

Both Houses agreed in an address, expressing their deepest contrition for what they and their fathers had done against the Pope, and praying that his supremacy might be re-established as the true successor of St. Peter and Head of the universal Church.

On the feast of St. Andrew, the Queen having taken her seat on the throne, the King seated on her left hand, the Legate, at a greater distance, and a degree lower, on her right, the Chancellor read the address, and the Cardinal, after a speech of some duration, absolved "all those present and the whole nation, and the dominions thereof, from all heresy and schism, and all judgments, censures, and penalties for that cause incurred, in the name of the Father, Son, and Holy Ghost." The Chancellor called out *Amen!* and this word resounded from every part of the hall.[1]

The Legate making his public entry into the City, the Lord Chancellor preached at Paul's Cross, and lamenting in bitter terms his own misconduct under Henry VIII., exhorted all who had fallen through his means to rise with him and seek the unity of the Catholic Church.

Had Gardyner died that night, he would, upon the whole, have left a fair fame to posterity; he would have been the unqualified boast of the Roman Catholics; and Protestants could not have refused to do honor to his firmness and courage,—making due allowance for the times in which he lived, and comparing him with Cranmer, their own hero, who had been much more inconsistent, and almost as vindictive;—but his existence being unfortunately prolonged for another year, during which, under his direction, the fires blazed without intermission in Smithfield, and the founders of the reformed church in England suffered as martyrs,—Roman Catholics are ashamed of him, and his name, coupled with that of Bonner, whom he employed as his tool, is still used to frighten the children of Protestants.

He deliberately formed the plan of entirely crushing the Reformation in England, by using the necessary degree of force for that purpose. However much we may abhor the cruel and relentless disposition evinced by such a plan, we ought not, from the event, rashly to condemn

[1] This precedent is now probably frequently consulted by those who wish to bring about a similar reconciliation.

it as foolish. The blood of martyrs is said to be the seed of the Church; nevertheless persecution, in a certain proportion to the numbers and spirit of those who are to be subdued, may prove effectual.

Thus the Lutheran heresy was completely suppressed in Spain and in Italy by the Inquisition. In England the higher ranks and the great bulk of the nation had so easily conformed to the religious faith or ecclesiastical caprice of the Sovereign for the time being, that a reasonable expectation might be entertained that there would be a general acquiescence in the renewed connection with Rome, and that strict inquiry into the profession of heretical opinions, with some terrible examples of severity when they were obstinately adhered to, might, in a short time, produce uniformity of faith throughout the realm. Cardinal Pole, though a much more sincere believer than Gardyner, took the opposite side, and wished that reason and persuasion only should be used to bring about the return to the Church of those who had erred.

The matter being debated in the Council, and the conflicting opinions being submitted to Mary,—after she had consulted with Philip, she returned to the Chancellor the following answer, which was a warrant to him, under very easy conditions, to proceed to any extremities:—" Touching the punishment of heretics, we think it ought to be done without rashness,—*not leaving in the meantime to do justice to such as by learning would seem to deceive the simple*, and the rest so to be used that the people might well perceive them not to be condemned without just occasion; by which they shall both understand the truth, and beware not to do the like. And especially within London I would wish none to be burnt" (how mild and merciful!)—"without some of the Council present, and both there and everywhere good sermons at the same time."

Gardyner having got all the old laws against Lollardy and the denial of transubstantiation revived, vigorously began his great enterprise. For the trial of heretics under those statutes he constituted a Court, of which he, as Lord Chancellor, was made the presiding Judge.

On the 22nd of January, 1555, he mounted his tribunal, assisted by thirteen Bishops and a crowd of Lords and Knights, and he ordered to be placed at the bar Hooper, the deprived Bishop of Gloucester,—Roger, a prebendary

of St. Paul's,—Saunders, rector of Allhallows, in London,—
and Taylor, rector of Hadley, in Suffolk,—all charged with
denying the Papal supremacy now re-established by law.
They tauntingly replied, that the Lord Chancellor, before
whom they were tried, had himself taught them to reject the authority of the Bishop of Rome, in his unanswerable treatise "De verâ Obedientia," which had been so
much approved by the Queen's royal father, that renowned
sovereign, Henry VIII. This *argumentum ad hominem* did
not prevail, and the Lord Chancellor said they ought to
have been reconverted by his subsequent treatise entitled
"Palinodia dicti Libri," which he now recommended to
their perusal; and a delay of twenty-four hours was given
them for consideration. At the end of that time, as they
stuck to the text of the Lord Chancellor's earlier work,
they were condemned to the flames. He, with professions
of mercy, made out a conditional pardon for each of them,
under the Great Seal, to be offered them on recantation
at the stake. Those protomartyrs of the Reformed Church
of England all displayed an equal constancy, and scorned
to purchase the continuance of life by feigning an assent
to doctrines which they did not believe.

Gardyner did not personally preside at the subsequent
trials; but he felt no hesitation in persevering in the line
of policy he had adopted, and (perhaps with a view to a
favorable contrast) he was represented in Court by Bonner, Bishop of London, the most brutal and bloody persecutor who ever appeared in this island; but the Chancellor himself actively directed almost all the arrests, examinations, and punishments of the Protestants. Cranmer, Ridley, and Latimer now suffered under circumstances familiar to us all from early infancy; and in the
course of a few months, by Gardyner's orders, there
perished at the stake, as heretics, in different parts of
England, above seventy persons, some of them of the
softer sex, and some of tender years.

Not satisfied with punishing those who taught, or openly
dogmatized contrary to the established creed, men's
thoughts were scrutinized; and, to do this more effectually, Gardyner issued a commission, bearing a close resemblance to the Spanish Inquisition, authorizing twenty-one
persons, or any three of them, "to search after all heresies,
the bringers in, the sellers, and the readers of all heretical

books, to punish all persons that did not hear mass or come to their parish church to service, or that would not go in processions, or would not take the holy bread or holy water, and to force all to make oath of such things as ought to be discovered, and to put to the torture such obstinate persons as would not confess." [1]

While these atrocities were going forward, an occurrence took place, of which Gardyner took immediate advantage to further his designs. Mary supposing herself pregnant, he pronounced the prospect of an heir to be the reward of Heaven for her piety; and as she fancied that she felt the infant stir in her womb when the Pope's Legate was introduced to her, he compared it to what happened to the mother of John the Baptist at the salutation of the Virgin. The Chancellor, with nine others of the Cabinet Council, immediately addressed a letter to Bonner, as Bishop of London, ordering "Te Deum" and masses to be celebrated on the occasion; he sent messengers to foreign courts to announce the event; and he settled the family of the young prince, as he confidently predicted the child would be a male. Some have said that he was aware from the beginning that Mary's infirmities rendered her incapable of having children, and that he resorted to a political artifice for the purpose of strengthening his power. He certainly kept up the delusion in the nation long after the physicians had declared that her Majesty's increased size arose from a dropsy. It was probably a knowledge of her real condition which induced him very readily to oblige her, by bringing in and supporting a bill constituting Philip, in case of her death, unlimited Regent during the minority of her son. What might have been the effect of this system of persecution on the Reformation in England, had Gardyner long survived to carry it into vigorous execution, we cannot tell. His career was near its close.

On the 21st of October parliament again met, and Mary, now deserted by her husband, rode to the parliament-house all alone in a horse-litter, to be seen of every one. The Lord Chancellor, by her direction, produced a Papal bull confirming the grants of Church property, and delivered a speech to both Houses, detailing the great exertions of the government for the good of the Church, and explain-

[1] Burnet, vol. iii. p. 243, 246.

ing the wants of the Crown and Clergy. It was remarked that on this and the following day, when he was again in his place, he displayed uncommon ability in unfolding and defending his measures.[1] But on his return from the House, on the second day, he was suddenly taken ill in his chamber, and, without being ever able to leave it, on the 12th of November he expired. Strange and groundless stories were propagated respecting the nature of his malady; and in the next age it was said he had been struck by it, as a judgment from Heaven, on the day that Bishop Ridley and Bishop Latimer were burnt, when, waiting for the joyful news, though the old Duke of Norfolk was to dine with him, he would not go to dinner till the unexampled hour of four in the afternoon;[2] but on an examination of dates, it will be found that these victims had been offered up before the opening of parliament, and before he had so much distinguished himself by his eloquence.[3]

He felt deep penitence in his last moments. The passion of our Saviour being read to him, when they came to the denial of Peter he bid them stay there, for, saith he, " *Negavi cum Petro, exivi cum Petro, sed nondum flevi cum Petro.*" This remorse arose not from the cruelties he had inflicted, but from the temporary renunciation of his allegiance to the Pope.

To the hour of his death he was in possession of the Great Seal, and the entire confidence of his Sovereign.

In those times religious controversy so completely absorbed the attention of mankind, that we read little of him

---

[1] " His duobus diebus ita mihi visus est non modo seipsum iis rebus superasse quibus cæteros superare solet, ingenio, eloquentia, prudentia, pietate, sed etiam ipsas sui corporis vires."—Bale.

[2] " At this time it was a mark of gentility and fashion to dine *early* instead of late. With us the nobility, gentry, and students do ordinarily go to dinner at eleven before noon, and to supper at five, or between five and six at afternoon. The merchants dine and sup seldom before twelve at noon and six at night. The husbandmen also dine at high noon as they call it, and sup at seven or eight; but out of term in our universities the scholars dine at ten."—Hall, *descr. G. Brit.* These hours were probably reckoned rather late, for Froissart mentions that having himself called on the Duke of Lancaster at five o'clock in the afternoon, he found that supper was over. Down to this time, the Courts of law meeting at seven in summer and eight in winter, never sat later than eleven in the forenoon; though some Chancellors, like Sir Thomas More, had sittings again after dinner.

[3] Ridley, Latimer, and Collier suffered at Oxford on the 16th of October, and parliament did not meet till the 21st.

as a Judge; but, in the absence of all complaint, we may fairly infer that he acquitted himself with ability and impartiality. The profound knowledge of jurisprudence which he early acquired, he kept up and extended by continual study, and his practice in the Ecclesiastical Courts must have well initiated him in judicial procedure. It had been intended that the equitable jurisdiction of the Court of Chancery over landed property should be, in a great measure, abolished by the Statute of Uses;[1] but by a decision of the common-law Judges, while Gardyner was Chancellor, it was held that a use could not be limited on a use,[2] so that the doctrine of uses was revived under the denomination of trusts, and a statute made on great deliberation, and introduced in the most solemn manner, in the result had little other effect than to introduce a slight alteration in the formal words of a conveyance.[3]

As a statesman, he is to be praised for discernment and vigor. He had even a regard for the liberties as well as independence of his country, and on several memorable occasions gave constitutional advice to the Sovereigns whom he served.[4] But whatever good inclinations he had,

[1] 27 Hen. 8, c. 10.
[2] Jane Tyrrel's case, Dyer, 152. See Bl. Com. 336. 4 Reeves, Hist. of Law, 520.
[3] There is to be found in the Registrar's Book a very curious decree of Lord Chancellor Gardyner, pronounced with a view to enforce the celibacy of the clergy. He held that a lease granted by an incumbent, after he had, "contrary to his vow, and contrary to the ecclesiastical laws, married a wife," was void, and he granted an injunction against the lessee continuing in possession.—*Hinkersfield* v. *Bailly*, Reg. Lib. 16 June, 5 P. & M., p. 18.
[4] "The Lord Cromwell," says Gardyner in one of his letters, "had once put in the King's head to take upon him to have his will and pleasure regarded for a law; and thereupon I was called for at Hampton Court. And as he was very stout, '*come on my Lord of Winchester,*' quoth he, '*answer the King here; but speak plainly and directly, and shrink not, man. Is not that,*' quoth he, '*that pleaseth the King a law? Have you not that in the civil law,* QUOD PRINCIPI PLACUIT, &c.?' I stood still, and wondered in my mind to what conclusion this would tend. The King saw me musing, and with gentle earnestness said, '*Answer him whether it be so or no.*' I would not answer the Lord Cromwell, but delivered my speech to the King, and told him that '*I had read of kings that had their will always received for law, but that the form of his reign to make the law his will was more sure and quiet; and by this form of government ye be established,*' quoth I, '*and it is agreeable with the nature of your people. If you begin a new manner of policy, how it may frame no man can tell.*' The King turned his back, and left the matter." Fox, ii. 65.

In Mary's time the Spanish Ambassador submitted a plan to her by which she should be rendered independent of parliament. Sending for Gardyner she made him peruse it, and adjured him, as he should answer at the judgment-

they were all under the control of ambition, and never obstructed his rise. In the various turns of his fortune he displayed a happy lubricity of conscience, which surmounted or evaded every obstacle, convincing him that his duty coincided with his interest. Though his strong sense and persuasive manners gave him an appearance of sincerity, he had an insidious cast of his eye, which indicated that he was always lying in wait; and he acquired at last such a character for craft and dissimulation, that the saying went, " My Lord of Winchester is like Hebrew, *to be read backwards.*"

He lived in great style at Winchester House in Southwark, where he had a number of young gentlemen of family as his pages, whose education he superintended. His establishment was the last of this sort in England, for Cardinal Pole did not live long enough to form a great household at Lambeth, and after the Reformation the Bishops' palaces were filled with their wives and children. He daily came up the river Thames in his splendid state barge to Whitehall and Westminster. An immense library which he had collected was destroyed by the mob during Wyat's rebellion, " so that a man might have gone up to his knees in the leaves of books cut out and thrown under foot."[1]—He was interred with much pomp in the cathedral at Winchester.

Although, being an ecclesiastical Chancellor, we have nothing to say of his descendants, we must not forget the progeny of his brain. He was a voluminous and popular author, but none of his writings have preserved their celebrity; not even his "Defense of Holy Water," which had a prodigious run for some years. He entered keenly into the dispute which raged in Cambridge in his time respecting the right pronunciation of Greek; and when he was chosen Chancellor of that University, notwithstanding his conservative notions, he patronized the new studies which were there introduced in rivalry to Aristotle and

seat of God, to speak his real sentiments respecting it. "Madam," replied the Chancellor, "it is a pity that so virtuous a lady should be surrounded by such sycophants. The book is nought; it is filled with things too horrible to be thought of." She behaved better than her father, as above related, for she thanked him, and threw the paper into the fire.—Burnet, ii. 278.

[1] *Stow's Annals.* This reminds us of the destruction of Lord Mansfiel l's library in the riots of 1780.

Aquinas. Had he lived in happier times, he might have left behind him a reputation for liberality of sentiment and humanity of conduct.[1]

CHAPTER XLII.

LIFE OF LORD CHANCELLOR HEATH.

THE sudden death of Gardyner was a heavy blow to Queen Mary, in the absence of Philip;—and she was exceedingly perplexed in the choice of a successor. She might easily have selected an eminent lawyer from Westminster Hall, but she at once resolved that "the Keeper of her Conscience" must be an ecclesiastic. According to the common course of promotion, the Great Seal ought to have been offered to her cousin, Cardinal Pole, appointed Archbishop of Canterbury on the deprivation of Cranmer, and after the example of Wolsey, his legatine functions could have been no obstacle to this arrangement. Though Pole was not much versed in juridical practice, he was intimately acquainted with the civil as well as canon law; and, with good advice, he might have presided very reputably as an equity judge. Mary had a great personal regard for him, and the highest respect for his learning and piety, but she placed no reliance on his civil wisdom, and was greatly shocked by his leaning in favor of toleration. In some respects Bishop Bonner would have been much more agreeable to her; but, notwithstanding his claims as a furious zealot and remorseless persecutor, he was so brutally ignorant, his manners were so offensive and he was so generally abhorred, that she was afraid to add to the odium she was sensible her government had already incurred, by placing such a man at the head of the administration of justice. The episcopal bench furnished no other individual of whom she could entirely approve. But it was now the middle of Michaelmas term; and some arrangement must be made for trans-

[1] It seems unaccountable that there has never hitherto been a separate life of Gardyner, although he made such a distinguished figure in three reigns, and in one most interesting reign was not only Lord Chancellor but Prime Minister, with power almost as great as that of Wolsey.

acting the business of the Court of Chancery. In this perplexity, to obtain time for further deliberation, she issued a commission to Sir Nicholas Hare, the Master of the Rolls, and others, to hear causes and to issue writs under the Great Seal, on account of the death of Lord Chancellor Gardyner, till a successor to him should be appointed.[1]

She, at length, fixed upon the least exceptional person presented to her choice; and

"On Friday, the 1st of January, in the second and third year of the reign of Philip and Mary, by the Grace of God, of England, France, Naples, Jerusalem, and Ireland, King and Queen, Defenders of the Faith," [not Heads of the Church,] "Prince and Princess of Spain and Sicily, Archduke and Archduchess of Austria, Duke and Duchess of Milan, Burgundy and Brabant, Count and Countess of Hapsburg, Flanders, and the Tirol, between the hours of four and six in the afternoon, the Great Seal of the said King and Queen, being in the Queen's custody, inclosed in a bag of leather, covered with a bag of red velvet, at Greenwich, in her inner private chamber there, was delivered by her to the most Reverend Father in God, Nicholas, Archbishop of York, whom she then and there constituted her Chancellor of England."[2]

This choice was made on the ground that the object of it was a man of spotless moral character, of undoubted orthodoxy, of respectable learning and ability, and of a quiet, passive disposition; so that if he would not originate, he would not obstruct the necessary measures for consummating the reconciliation with Rome, and extinguishing the Lutheran heresy in England.

NICHOLAS HEATH was the son of a citizen of London, and born there in the early part of the reign of Henry VII. He was educated at St. Anthony's school, in

[1] Rot. Par. 2 & 3 Ph. & M.

[2] R. Cl. 2 & 3 Ph. & M. "Et superinde prcus Revdiss. Pater N. Ebor. Archs sigillum prm de manibus ipsius dne Regne tunc gratulr accipiens in nobilium virorum W. Marchionis Winton. &c. prcia, curam et custodiam ejusdem Magni Sigilli Anglie de offic Cancellar Angl. sup se assumens sigillum illud penes se retinuit et retinet in prsi." The entries now are silent as to swearing in the Chancellor, and this entry is a rare instance of omitting to state that the new Chancellor took the Seal from the bag and sealed with it some writ or patent in the presence of the Sovereign.

Threadneedle Street, famous at that time for its discipline, and for the great men it turned out; among whom were two Lord Chancellors.[1] He was entered a student at Christ College, Cambridge; and after taking his degrees with distinguished credit, he was elected a fellow of Clare Hall. During one of Wolsey's visits to this University, Heath was presented to him as a great proficient in classical and theological learning. The Cardinal, who was always ready to patronize merit, took a fancy to him, made him one of his own chaplains, and afterwards chaplain to the King. Heath subsequently succeeded to be almoner to Henry; and although he never actively enlisted himself in any of the factions which divided the Court, he was successively promoted by that Sovereign to the sees of Rochester and Worcester. Like every other Bishop in England, he was compelled to acknowledge the King's ecclesiastical superiority; but he was supposed to have a secret understanding with Rome, and he steadily concurred with Lord Chancellor Wriothesley, the Duke of Norfolk, and Bishop Gardyner, in resisting any further innovation.

During the Protectorate of the Duke of Somerset he voted in the House of Lords against all the bills for bringing about a change of religion; but, conducting his opposition with moderation, occasion could not be found for taking any violent proceedings against him till the act was passed for a new "ordinal," or form of ordination of the clergy, which was to be framed by twelve Commissioners, to be appointed by the Crown. Although he had expressed his dissent to the measure, he was insidiously named one of the Commissioners, along with eleven stanch reformers. They proposed a form, which they contended preserved whatever according to Scripture was necessary for the ordination of Bishops, Priests, and Dea-

---

[1] Here, as we have before related, Sir Thomas More received the rudiments of his education. Stow, after celebrating the scholastic dispensations he had witnessed in the churchyard of St. Bartholomew, "where upon a bank boarded about under a tree some one scholar hath stepped up, and there hath apposed and answered till he were by some better scholar overcome and put down,—and then the overcomer taking the place did the like as the first," says, "I remember there repaired to these exercises among others the masters and scholars of the free schools of St. Paul's in London, of St. Peter's at Westminster, of St. Thomas Acon's hospital, and of *St. Anthony's hospital*, whereof the last named commonly presented the best scholars, and had the prize in those days."—Stow's *London*, p. 75.

cons. He insisted that it made no material distinction between these orders; that it had carefully omitted what was requisite to impart the sacerdotal character; and that if it were adopted, there would be a breach in the apostolical succession in the Church. The Council nevertheless peremptorily required him to subscribe it; and, on his refusal, committed him to prison for a contempt.[1]

Not satisfied with this, they soon after resolved to deprive him of his bishopric if he would not conform; and they cunningly examined him with respect to the proper construction of altars, and the mode of placing them in churches,—a subject on which he was known to be particularly sensitive. But he was resolute, telling them that "of other mind he thought never to be, and that consent he would not, if he were demanded to take down altars and set up tables." Being threatened with deprivation if he did not submit within two days, he replied "that he could not find in his conscience to do it, and should be well content to abide such end, either by deprivance or otherwise, as pleased the King's Majesty." He was sent back to prison; a commission of delegates pronounced sentence of deprivation against him, and he was kept in close custody till the commencement of the next reign.

Upon the accession of Mary he was liberated and restored to his benefice, along with the other deprived Roman Catholic Bishops, and he was justly considered, by reason of his constancy and private virtues, a great ornament to the ancient faith, he was soon after promoted to the archbishopric of York. It was supposed that he secretly coincided in opinion with Cardinal Pole in disapproving the violent measures of persecution to which Gardyner now resorted; but he had not the boldness openly to oppose them. A just estimate had been formed of his character when he was selected as Gardyner's successor; for however much he might wish that reason and persuasion alone might be relied upon for making converts to the true Church,—after his appointment the fires of Smithfield continued to blaze as before.[2]

---

[1] Burnet, ii. 143.
[2] We have a statistical table, on the authority of Lord Burghley, of burnings by Mary and her cabinet, rather favorable to the memory of Gardyner:—

In 1555 (Gardyner, Chancellor)	71
1556 (Heath, Chancellor)	89

He took his seat in the Court of Chancery on the first day of Hilary term, 1556; and was found as a Judge to display patience and good sense, and to act with impartiality and integrity; but, never having had any training whatever in jurisprudence, he got through his judicial business in a most unsatisfactory manner; and the clamor of the bar, and the suitors, and the public, which was thus raised, prevented the appointment of any other ecclesiastic to hold the Great Seal till Bishop Williams, the very last of his order who ever sat in the marble chair, was appointed Lord Keeper by James I.

The parliament which was sitting at the death of Gardyner was dissolved, in presence of the Queen, by Ex-Chancellor the Marquess of Winchester, then Lord Treasurer; and another parliament was not called till the beginning of the year 1558.

This was opened by a speech from Lord Chancellor Heath;[1] but we have no account of his topics, except that he pressed for an aid to her Majesty. We may conjecture that he touched upon the loss of Calais, which had caused such universal consternation, and that he held out a hope, if sufficiently liberal supplies were voted, of wiping off this national disgrace.

He had immediately after to decide a question of parliamentary privilege. Thomas Eyms, burgess for Thirsk, complained to the House of Commons that, while in attendance as a member, a subpœna had been delivered to him to appear in Chancery, and that if engaged in a Chancery suit he could not discharge his duty as a representative of the people. The House, in great indignation, immediately ordered Sir Clement Higham, and the Recorder of London to go to the Lord Chancellor, and require that the process should be revoked,[2]—and the writ was quashed.[3]

Acts, proposed by the Lord Chancellor, having been passed—to take away clergy from accessories in petty

```
In 1557 (Heath, Chancellor) . . . . . . 88
   1558 (ditto     ditto   ) . . . . . . 40
                                         ---
                                         288
```

However, it was Chancellor Gardyner who set the wheel of persecution in motion, and it continued to revolve when his hand had been withdrawn from it.

[1] 1 Parl. Hist. 629.   [2] Ibid. 630.   [3] Hats. Præc. 1 Parl. Hist. 630.

treason and murder,—to allow a *tales de circumstantibus* in the case of the Queen,—and to punish such as should forcibly carry off maidens under sixteen,[1] he, by the Queen's command, prorogued the parliament to the 5th of November.

When this day arrived Mary was approaching her end,—in a state of the greatest mental dejection from the irremediable loss of Calais, the neglect of her husband, the discontent of her subjects, the progress of the reformed religion in spite of all her cruelties, her despair of children, and the prospect of a Protestant succession. Being unable to attend in person, a commission passed the Great Seal, authorizing the Chancellor and others to hold the parliament in her name; and he delivered a speech pointing out the necessity for some measure to restrain the evils of licentious printing, whereby sedition was now spread abroad, and showing that, from the destitute state of the exchequer, the Queen's forces could not be kept on foot, and the safety of the realm was endangered. He accordingly introduced a bill, enacting that "no man shall print any book or ballad unless he be authorized thereunto by the King and Queen's Majesties' license under the Great Seal of England." The art of printing had not been known in this country much more than half a century, and was already found a most formidable instrument for guiding public opinion, and assailing or supporting the Government. During the recess a proclamation had been issued, stating that books filled with heresy, sedition, and treason were daily brought from beyond the seas, and were covertly reprinted within the realm, and ordering that "whatsover should be found to have any of the said wicked and seditious books should be reputed a rebel, and executed according to martial law."[2] But this was such a stretch of authority as, even in those days, caused great complaint, and probably the Judges, dependent as they were, would have resisted it. The Chancellor's bill, having passed through its previous stages, was appointed to be read the third time on the 16th of November,—but when that day arrived the Queen was at the point of death, and all public business was suspended.

Meanwhile some very curious proceedings were going on in the Lower House respecting the supply. The

[1] 4 & 5 Ph. & M. c. 5, 7, 8.   [2] Strype, iii. 459.

Commons, finding that the Queen had impoverished the exchequer by restoring property to the Church, and by new religious endowments, would not open their purse-strings. On the 7th of November, Mary, ill as she was, sent for the Speaker, and ordered him "to show to the Commons the ill condition the nation was in; for, though a negotiation was going on for a peace with France, prudence required that the nation should be put into a state of defense, in case it should miscarry. Still the Commons were so dissatisfied, that, after a week's deliberation, they could come to no resolution.

As a last effort, on the 14th of November, Lord Chancellor Heath, accompanied by the Duke of Norfolk, the Lord Treasurer, and several other Peers and Bishops, went down to the Commons, walked into the House, and "seated themselves in that place where the Privy Councillors used to sit,"—which we now call "the Treasury Bench." The Speaker left his chair, and he, with the Privy Councillors in the House, came and sat on low benches before them. The Lord Chancellor then made them a speech, proving the necessity for granting a subsidy to defend the nation both from the French and the Scots. Having concluded, he with the other Lords immediately withdrew to their own chamber.[1]

This proceeding does not seem to have been considered any breach of privilege, but it had not the desired effect. The two following days the Commons continued the debate. On the afternoon of the third day, while they were still in deliberation, they received a summons requiring the Speaker and their whole House to come to the bar of the Upper House, when they should hear certain matters that the Lords had to communicate to them.

Upon their arrival the Lord Chancellor Heath, in a solemn tone, announced "that God had taken to his mercy their late Sovereign, the Lady Mary, and had given them another in the person of her sister, the Lady Elizabeth, whom he prayed God to preserve and bless." He then recommended that they should all assemble in Westminster Hall, where the Lords would come and cause her to be forthwith proclaimed Queen of England.

Elizabeth was accordingly proclaimed, first in Palace Yard before the members of the two Houses, and again at

---
[1] 1 Parl. Hist. 631.

Temple Bar, in the presence of the Lord Mayor, Aldermen, and Companies of the city, amidst the deafening acclamations of the people.

The new Sovereign was then at Hatfield, in Hertfordshire, where she had been living for some time in great seclusion. Early next morning, the Lord Chancellor and most of the Council waited upon her there, in a body, to give in their allegiance. Heath, as first in dignity, addressed her, congratulating her upon her accession to the throne, and the unanimity and joy with which her title was acknowledged by all classes of her subjects.

Cecil had been beforehand with them, and had already gained her entire confidence, notwithstanding the part he had taken in Northumberland's treason on the death of Edward VI., by which she would have been set aside, and notwithstanding his wary conformity during the whole of Mary's reign. He had prepared an answer for her which she now delivered, to the effect that "she was struck with amazement when she considered herself and the dignity to which she was called; that her shoulders were too weak to support the burden, but it was her duty to submit to the will of God, and to seek the aid of wise and faithful advisers; that for this purpose she would, in a few days, appoint a new Council; that it was her intention to retain several of those who had been inured to business under her father, brother, and sister; and if the others were not employed, she would have them to believe that it was not through distrust of their ability or will to serve her, but through a wish to avoid that indecision and delay which so often arise from the jarring opinions of a multitude of advisers."

Heath then on his knee tendered her the Great Seal,—rather expecting that she would desire him to take it back and to become her Lord Chancellor. At this moment it was quite uncertain what part she was to take in religion; and although there was a suspicion that she had an inclination in favor of the reformed doctrine, her conformity to the established ritual and her famous answer when questioned about her belief in the real presence,[1] led

---

[1] "Christ was the Word that spake it,
He took the bread and brake it;
And what the Word did make it,
That I believe and take it."

Heath and the Catholic party to hope that she would now declare in their favor. To his surprise and chagrin, however, having received the Great Seal into her hand, she immediately delivered it to Sir Ambrose Cave to carry it to her private chamber, there to remain till she should otherwise direct.[1]

Nevertheless she spoke very courteously to the Ex-Chancellor, and retained him as member of her Privy Council, along with twelve others who had served her sister,—adding eight new members. In truth, her policy, though not yet avowed, was determined upon, and she had resolved that, Cecil being her minister, she should without violence restore the Reformation introduced under her brother, and put herself at the head of the Protestant party in Europe. It is lucky for us that she considered this to be for her interest, and that she was already afraid of all true Roman Catholics questioning her legitimacy, and preferring the title of her cousin Mary, Queen of Scots,—so that she felt the necessity for having the support of the Protestant States against this claim. She herself, as well as Cecil and her principal advisers, were far from being bigoted on the Protestant side, and if they had taken a different view of the question of expediency, England might have remained to this day under the spiritual dominion of the Pope.

The remainder of the career of Ex-Chancellor Heath, though not marked by any very striking events, was most honorable to his character, and ought to make his memory revered by all denominations of Christians. Instead of following the example of the "willow-like" Marquis of

[1] "Memorandum Qd die Veneris XVIII. die Novembr anno primo Dne Elizabeth Regine, eadem Dna Regina existens apud Hatfield Regia in Com. Hert. in Domo ejusdem Dne Regine ibidem, inter horas decimam et undecimam ante meridiem ejusdem diei, in camera presencie, tunc ibidem, presentibus Edwardo Comte Derb, &c. ac aliis Magm Sigillm Angle in custod Reverendissimi in Christo Pris Nichi Archp Ebor adtunc Cancellar Angl. existens prfte Dne Regine pr prftum Revssim. Prem deliberat, erat ac eadem Dna Regina Magnum Sigillum prdm de manibus predi Revssimi Pris accipies Ambrosio Cave militi deliberabat ac prftus Ambrs Cav, Miles, pr mandatum ipsius Dne Regine Magnum Sigillum prftum in privatam Cameram prfte Regne secum ferebat ibidem pr prftam Dnam Reginam custodiend. quousq. eadem Regina alitr duxrit deliberand."—Rot. Cla. 1 Eliz.

Winchester, and adopting the new fashion in religion, he steadily though mildly adhered to that system in which he had been educated, and which he conscientiously believed to be divine; sacrificing not only his high civil office, but his ecclesiastical dignity of Archbishop, and contentedly retiring to poverty and obscurity.

His first open difference with the Queen was upon the occasion of her coronation. Although, for a short time after her accession, she observed a studied ambiguity, and kept the hopes of the Catholics alive by assisting at mass, receiving the communion in one kind, burying her sister with the solemnities of the Romish ritual, and ordering a solemn requiem for the soul of the Emperor Charles V.; her determination to change the national religion was soon made manifest by her appointments of Protestants to places of power and profit, by her order forbidding the elevation of the host in her private chapel, and by a proclamation allowing the observance of the established worship " until consultation might be had in parliament by the Queen and the three estates." The primacy not yet being filled up since the death of Cardinal Pole, who survived his cousin, Queen Mary, only a few hours, Heath, Archbishop of York, was the highest functionary in the Church, and he called a meeting of all the Prelates, to consider what was now fit to be done. A motion was made, and unanimously carried, that till satisfied of her adherence to the Church, none of them would put the crown on her head, or attend her coronation. This was considered a masterly move; for, though a change had taken place in the opinions of the people from the times when a king's reign only dated from his coronation, and he was supposed to have no right to allegiance till he had been anointed,—coronation was still considered an essential right, and there had been no instance of an uncrowned Sovereign meeting parliament and making laws. But the Queen was relieved from this great embarrassment by the defection of one prelate, Oglethorpe, Bishop of Carlisle, who agreed to crown her—on condition that she should take the accustomed oath to preserve the liberties of the Church, receive the sacrament under one kind, and conform, during the ceremony, to all the observances of the Catholic Pontifical.

The Queen was accordingly crowned: parliament was

opened by her, and a bill was introduced to declare her "Head of the Church." On the second reading of this bill, in the House of Lords, Heath, rising from the Archbishop's bench, delivered a very long oration, of which it may be worth while to give an extract, as a specimen of the style of debating which then prevailed. He thus began: "My Lords all, with humble submission of my whole talk unto your honors, I purpose to speak to the body of this act touching the supremacy." Then dividing and subdividing his discourse into heads, he first handled the objection, that this measure would be a relinquishing of the see of Rome. He spoke rather freely of Paul IV., who had recently denied the Queen's title, and had shown himself "a very austere, stern father unto us ever since his first entrance into Peter's chair;" but it was not a personal question with him, but by forsaking Rome they should fly from four things:—1st, All General Councils:—2ndly, All Canonical Laws of the Church of Christ:—3rdly, The Judgment of all Christian Princes:—4thly, and lastly, "we must forsake and fly from the unity of Christ's Church; and by leaping out of Peter's ship, hazard ourselves to be overwhelmed and drowned in the waters of schism, sects, and divisions." Each of these heads he discusses, with many quotations and illustrations from the Old and New Testament, and the Fathers; and concludes with the observation that, as we had received our doctrine, faith, and sacraments, entirely from the Church of Rome,—in forsaking that church as a malignant church, the inhabitants of this realm shall be forced to seek for another gospel of Christ, other doctrine, faith and sacraments, than we hitherto have received. He next considers the meaning of the words "supreme Head of the Church of England;" if they meant temporal power, *that* her Highness had without statute; and if spiritual power, neither could Parliament confer it, nor was her Highness capable of receiving it. How could they say to her, "Tibi dabimus claves regni cœlorum?" or "Pasce, pasce, pasce?" He then touches a very delicate topic—that however it might be with a King, at all events a Queen, by reason of her sex, was incapable of being the Head of the Church. "That her Highness, being a woman by birth and nature, is not qualified, by God's word, to feed the flock of Christ, appeareth most plainly, by St. Paul's saying, '*Taceant mulieres in ecclesiis; non enim permittatur eis loqui sed subditas esse.*' Again, says the same great Apostle, '*Turpe est mulieri loqui in ecclesiis.*' '*Docere autem mulieri non permitto neque dominari in virum sed in silentio esse.*' To preach or minister the holy sacraments, a woman may not; neither may she be supreme Head of the Church of Christ. Christ, ascending into heaven, gave the whole spiritual government of his Church to men. '*Ipse dedit ecclesiæ suæ quosdam apostolos alios evangelistas, alios pastores et doctores in opus ministerii in ædificationen corporis Christi.*' But a woman in the degrees of Christ's church is not called to be an apostle nor evangelist, nor to be a shepherd, neither a doctor or preacher." He thus concludes: "So much I have here said, Right Honorable and my very good Lords, against this act of supremacy, for the discharge of my conscience, and for the love, dread, and fear that I chiefly owe unto God and my Sovereign Lady the Queen's Highness, and unto your Lordships all; when otherwise, and without mature consideration of these premises, your Honors shall never be able to show your faces before your enemies in this matter; being so rash an example and spectacle in Christ's church as in this realm only to be found, and in none other. Thus humbly beseeching your good Honors to take in good part this rude and plain speech that I have used, of much good zeal and will, I shall now leave to trouble your Honors any longer."[1]

After a second reading of the Bill, the expedient was resorted to of a conference between five Roman Catholic Bishops and three Doctors to argue against it, and eight reformed divines on the other side,—Heath as Ex-Chancellor, and Sir Nicholas Bacon, the new Lord Keeper, being appointed moderators. This conference ended in the commitment of two of the Bishops to the Tower, and binding over the other six Catholic disputants to appear before the Council. The Supremacy Bill, and another in favor of the new book of Common Prayer, passed the Lords by a small majority, but were supported almost

---

[1] Parl. Hist. 660. Ibid. 643. This speech shows, among other curious particulars, that the expletives "My Lords" and "Your Lordships," now so copiously introduced almost into every sentence by most speakers in the House of Lords, were then nearly unknown.

unanimously in the House of Commons, to which, by Cecil's management, very few Catholics were returned.

Heath was now called upon to conform to the law, and himself to take the oath of supremacy. He pleaded conscience and the divine commandment as superior to all human law. He was therefore deprived of his archbishopric, and the difficulty being surmounted of consecrating new Bishops, a successor was appointed to him. He retired to a small property of his own at Cobham, in Surrey, where he devoted the rest of his days to study and devotion. He was here compared to Abiathar, sent home by Solomon to his own field, and he was said to have found himself happier than he had ever been during his highest elevation. Queen Elizabeth herself, remembering how promptly he had recognized her title when he was Lord Chancellor, and believing that he afterwards acted from conscientious motives, was in the frequent habit of visiting him in his retreat, and, with a certain hankering after the old religion, she probably, in her heart, honored him more than she did Archbishop Parker, whom she found living splendidly at Lambeth, with a lady whom she would neither call his " mistress " nor his " wife."

Heath survived till the year 1566, when he died deeply lamented by his friends, and with the character of a good, if not of a great man.[1]

Before proceeding with the Lord Keepers and Lord Chancellors of Elizabeth, we ought to take a glance at the juridical history of the preceding reign. It was begun with an act of parliament, which we should have thought unnecessary,—to declare that a Queen Regnant has all the lawful prerogatives of the Crown, and is bound by the laws of former Kings.[2] Change of religion afterwards completely occupied the attention of the people, this change being still effected by acts of the legislature.

The law of treason was now brought back to the consti-

---

[1] A most beautiful panegyric is pronounced upon him by Hayward, an original historian, whose " Annals of Queen Elizabeth " have been lately published by the Camden Society. Speaking of the changes upon the accession of Elizabeth, he says, " Among thes Doctor Heath, Archbishop of Yorke, was removed from being Lord Chancellour of England, a man of most eminent and generous simplicity, *who esteemed any thing privately unlawfull which was not publickelye beneficial and good.* But as it is noe new thing for merchants to breake, for saylers to be drowned, for soldiers to be slayn, so is it not for men in authority to fall."—Hayward's *Annals of Elizabeth*, p. 13.

[2] 1 Mary. sess. 3, c. 1.

tutional basis on which it had been placed by the celebrated statute of Edward III., and where religion was not concerned the Queen and her ministers showed considerable respect for the rights of the people.[1]

Much obloquy was brought upon the two Chancellors, Gardyner and Heath, for the furious religious persecution which they prompted or sanctioned; but the former gained popularity by his resistance to the Queen's matrimonial alliances with Philip of Spain, and the latter was respected for the general moderation of his character and his personal disinterestedness. They issued writs, under the Great Seal, for the election of representatives to the House of Commons to fourteen places, of very small population, which had not before sent members to parliament,—imitating the conduct of Edward's Chancellors, who, to strengthen the Reformation, had enfranchised no fewer than twenty-two similar boroughs. None of their judicial decisions have been handed down to us.

CHAPTER XLIII.

LIFE OF LORD KEEPER SIR NICHOLAS BACON.

WE now come to the life of a man who held the Great Seal above twenty years, but whose selected motto being "*Mediocria firma*," was of very moderate ambition, aiming only at the due discharge of

---

[1] During this reign the lawyers devoted much of their attention to the regulation of their own dress and personal appearance. To check the grievance of "long beards," an order was issued by the Inner Temple "that no fellow of that house should wear his beard above three weeks' growth on pain of forfeiting 20s." The Middle Temple enacted "that none of that society should wear great breeches in their hose made after the Dutch, Spanish, or Almain fashion, or lawn upon their caps, or cut doublets, under a penalty of 3s. 4d., and expulsion for the second offense." In 3 & 4 P. & M. it was ordained by all the four Inns of Courts, "that none except knights and benchers should wear in their doublets or hose any light colors, save scarlet and crimson, nor wear any upper velvet cap, or any scarf or wings in their gowns, white jerkins, buskins, or velvet shoes, double cuffs in their shirts, feathers or ribbons in their caps, and that none should wear their study gowns in the city any farther than Fleet Bridge or Holborn Bridge; nor, while in Commons, wear Spanish cloaks, sword and buckler, or rapier, or gowns and hats, or gowns girded with a dagger on the back." *

* 1 Dug. Or. Jur. 148.

his judicial duties, and desirous to avoid mixing himself up with any concerns which were not connected with his office. Till we reach the Earl of Clarendon, we shall not again find the holder of the Great Seal Prime Minister,— and in the interval it will not be necessary for us to enter minutely into historical events, as these were guided by political chiefs under whom the individuals whose lives we have to narrate acted only a subordinate part.

The business of the Court of Chancery had now so much increased, that to dispose of it satisfactorily required a Judge regularly trained to the profession of the law, and willing to devote to it all his energy and industry. The Statute of Wills, the Statute of Uses, the new modes of conveyancing introduced for avoiding transmutation of possession, the questions which arose respecting the property of the dissolved monasteries, and the vast increase of commerce and wealth in the nation, brought such a number of important suits into the Court of Chancery, that the holder of the Great Seal could no longer satisfy the public by occasionally diverting a few hours from his political occupations to dispose of bills and petitions, and not only was his daily attendance demanded in Westminster Hall during term time, but it was necessary that he should sit, for a portion of each vacation, either at his own house, or in some convenient place appointed by him for clearing off his arrears.

Elizabeth having received the *Clavis Regni* from Lord Chancellor Heath on the day after her accession, she kept it in her own possession rather more than a month before she determined how she should dispose of it. At last, on the 22nd of December, 1558, " between the hours of ten and eleven in the forenoon, at the Queen's Royal Palace of Somerset House, in the Strand, the Queen, taking the Great Seal from its white leather bag and red velvet purse before the Lord Treasurer and many others, delivered it to Sir NICHOLAS BACON, with the title of Lord Keeper, and all the powers belonging to a Lord Chancellor; and he, gratefully receiving it from her Majesty, having sealed with it a summons to the Convocation, returned it into its leathern bag and velvet purse and carried it off with him, to be held during the good pleasure of her Majesty."[1]

This new functionary had not passed through any dan-

[1] See all this and much more of the ceremony related, Rot. Cl. 1 Eliz.

gers or difficulties, or interesting vicissitudes before his advancement ;—without being once in prison or in exile, or engaged in foreign embassies,—much less having, like some of his predecessors, led armies into the field,—he had risen in the common-place track of the legal profession as dully as a prosperous lawyer of the eighteenth or nineteenth century, who going through Eton or Westminster, Oxford or Cambridge, and a special pleader's or an equity draughtsman's office, is called to the bar, pleases the attorneys, gets a silk gown, and is brought into parliament by a great nobleman to whom he is auditor, there to remain quietly till for some party convenience he is farther promoted.

Nicholas Bacon was of a respectable gentleman's family long seated in the county of Suffolk. He was the second son of Robert Bacon, of Drinkston, Esquire, and was born at Chislehurst, in Kent, in the year 1510. He received his education under his father's roof till he was sent to Corpus Christi College, Cambridge. Having taken his degree, he traveled for some time in France.

On his return he studied the law diligently at Gray's Inn, and without brilliant talents, by industry and perseverance he gained considerable practice at the bar. When the dissolution of the monasteries took place, he was appointed by Henry VIII. to the lucrative post of Solicitor to the Court of Augmentations, a board established for managing the church property which came to the Crown,— and like most others concerned in the management of it, he contrived to have a grant of a portion of it for his own use.[1]

Along with all the other grantees of church property he became a favorer of the Reformation, but he took care to give no offense by going openly beyond the limits of the departure from Rome which the law permitted. He now presented to the King a splendid plan for the endowment from the spoils of the monasteries of a great seminary in London, after the model of a University,—for the study of the law, and for the training of ambassadors and statesmen.[2] It is much to be regretted that, owing to the ra-

---

[1] He got the manors of Bottesdale, of Ellingham, and of Redgrave, where he afterwards received Queen Elizabeth.

[2] Besides the study of the common and civil law, the objects of the projected institution were to cultivate the knowledge of Latin and French, and

pacity of the courtiers, this effort was abortive, as, down to our own time, London remained the only metropolis in Europe (except Constantinople) without a University, and English lawyers, though very acute practitioners, have rather been deficient in an enlarged knowledge of jurisprudence.

Nicholas Bacon was, in this reign, further promoted by being appointed Attorney to the Court of Wards, an important situation during the subsistence of military tenures, and affording ample scope for corruption and oppression. But he conducted himself in it with integrity as well as diligence, and he was allowed to retain it both by Edward IV. and Queen Mary. He was a brother-in-law of Sir William Cecil, afterwards the celebrated Burghley, now rising into eminence, and already known for his prudence and craft; but although in close intimacy with him, he was not sufficiently eminent to share with him in the plot for bringing in Lady Jane Grey,[1] and he still remained in his subordinate situation when Cecil had gained the confidence of Mary, and was himself in high office.

During her reign both brothers acquiesced in the reconciliation with Rome, and quietly conformed to the reigning religion, although they had actively supported the Reformation under Edward. A satirical writer, referring to this period of Nicholas Bacon's life, bitterly says, "His Lordship could neither by the greatness of his beads, creeping to the cross, nor exterior show of devotion before the high altar, find his entrance into high dignity in Queen Mary's time.

Notwithstanding the seeming warmth of the Roman Catholic zeal he now displayed, Queen Mary had some suspicion of his sincerity, and forbade him to go beyond

in those languages to write and debate on all questions of public policy; to form historical collections, and publish new treaties relating to domestic institutions and foreign diplomacy; and the students were finally to perfect their knowledge of political science as *attachés*, traveling in the suits of the King's ambassadors on the Continent.

[1] It has always seemed to me a strong proof that Northumberland's scheme was by no means so foolish and desperate as has been generally supposed,—that it was supported by a man of the sagacity of Cecil.

[2] It is very curious that his son in defending him against this libel does not at all deny his ostentatious profession of the Roman Catholic religion to please Queen Mary, but contends that he was a great favorite with her "in regard of his constant standing for her title," and that he might have had great promotion under her if he had been so minded. Lord Bacon's Works, ed. 1819, vol. iii. p. 96.

sea, because "he had a great wit of action," and she was afraid he might enter into the plots that were formed against her among the Protestants of Germany.—He owed his elevation to his brother-in-law. Cecil, while Secretary to Mary, had a private understanding with Elizabeth, who looked up to him for securing her succession, and he had been the first to repair to Hatfield to announce to her that she was Queen. She employed him to compose the speech she was to deliver at her first council, and he became her sole adviser in the formation of her ministry.

For the Great Seal he recommended his near connection, Nicholas Bacon, wishing to favor him, and considering him competent to the duties of the office, without any ambitious or intriguing turn which might render him dangerous as a rival. The Queen hesitated for some time, as the office of Chancellor or Lord Keeper had hitherto generally been given either to a dignified prelate, or some layman who had gained distinction by civil service; and Bacon was only known in his own profession as a plodding lawyer, and for having industriously done the duties of attorney to the Court of Augmentations and the Court of Wards. She saw the necessity for the appointment of a lawyer, and the accounts she received of the respectable and useful qualities of Bacon induced her to yield; but sparing of honors from the commencement of her reign, she would only give him the title of "Lord Keeper," and would only knight him instead of raising him to the peerage. He was perfectly contented—often repeating his motto, "*Mediocria firma.*" He was sworn of the Privy Council, however, and admitted to the public deliberations of this board.

For some time he used the Great Seal of Philip and Mary, but on the 26th of January, 1559, this seal was broken by the Queen's commands, and she delivered to him another, with her own name and insignia.[1] From the

[1] See a very circumstantial account of this ceremony in the Cl. Roll, 1 Eliz., which, after narrating the delivery of the old Seal to the Queen in her private chamber at Westminster, her order that it should be broken, the execution of this order in an outer room, the production of another Seal, "imagine armis et titulis honoris Domine Regine tantumdo insculptum." the delivery of this to Sir Nicholas as Lord Keeper, thus concludes, "Ipseque prdm nov. Sigill. de Dna Regna adtunc et ibidem in presencia eordm nobilium virorm gra .ulentr recipiens in exteriorem cameram prdcam recessit, ac illud in quan-

first he gained the confidence of the youthful Queen, who, says Camden, "relied upon him as the very oracle of the law."

Parliament met on the 25th of January,[1] when, the Queen being seated on the throne, the Lord Keeper opened it with a speech beginning thus: "My Lords and Masters all, the Queen's most Excellent Majesty having summoned hither her high Court of Parliament, hath commanded me to open and declare the chief causes and considerations that moved her thereunto." This discourse is very long and tedious. He compares Elizabeth to the good King Hezekiah and the noble Queen Hester, and extols her desire for the amendment of the laws and the promotion of true religion. But the only part worth transcribing is his advice as to the manner in which the debates were to be conducted in both Houses. "You will also clearly forbear, and as a great enemy to good council fly from all manner of contentious reasonings and disputations, and all sophistical, captious, and frivolous arguments and quiddities, meeter for ostentation of wit than consultation of weighty matters; comelier for scholars than councillors, and more beseeming the schools than parliament houses."[2]

The Lord Keeper is said to have now given very discreet advice respecting the Queen's title. On the accession of Mary, an act was passed declaring void the divorce between Henry and Catherine of Aragon, which virtually bastardized Elizabeth, although the statute of 36 Henry VIII., putting her into the succession to the Crown, remained unrepealed. He laid down for law, that the descent of the Crown of itself removed all disabilities; and

---

dam perulam de corio poni et sigillo suo pprio muniri et sigillari fecit, ac sic munitum et sigillatum in quendam sacculum velveti rubei insigniis regiis decoratum posuit illudque penes se retinuit et retinet."

[1] Parliament was called under writs dated the 1st of December, and it would appear that between her accession and the 22nd of December, when the Queen delivered the Great Seal to Bacon, she affixed it to all instruments which required it with her own hand.

[2] It must be remembered that such an oration was not like a modern Queen's speech delivered by Lords Commissioners,—which is supposed to be the language of her Majesty, advised by her cabinet,—but was delivered as the extempore composition of the orator. On this occasion the Lord Keeper makes many apologies for his own imperfections, and regrets his "want of ability to do it in such sort as was beseeming for her Majesty's honor, and as the great weightiness and worthiness of the matter did require."

she was contented with an act to acknowledge her title, without reversing the attainder of her mother.¹

Bacon was now called upon to act in a capacity that would seem strange to a Lord Chancellor or Lord Keeper of our time—as a moderator in the grand public disputation held by the Queen's command, between the champions of the two religions, his predecessor, Ex-Chancellor Heath, acting for the Catholics, being his colleague.

There is much reason to fear that the Lord Keeper, become an avowed and zealous Protestant, was by no means impartial; for entirely superseding the other moderator, and taking upon himself the management of the conference, he insisted, each morning, that the Catholic disputants should begin, and he would not allow them to reply upon the Protestants. At last the five Bishops and three Doctors of Laws on the Catholic side declared they would argue no longer, and that they would withdraw. The Lord Keeper, highly incensed, put the question to them successively, "whether they would not stay?" All except one insisted on departing, and thereupon he dismissed them with these ominous words; "For that ye would not that we should hear you, perhaps you may shortly hear of us." Accordingly, their abrupt departure being declared to be a contempt of the Queen's authority, the Bishops of Winchester and Lincoln were committed to prison, and the rest were bound over to appear before the Council, and not to go beyond the cities of London and Westminster without leave.

As a Judge the Lord Keeper gave the highest satisfaction, and it was universally acknowledged, that since the time of Sir Thomas More justice had never been so well administered in the Court of Chancery. Thoroughly imbued with the common law, he soon became familiar with the comparatively simple system of equitable jurisprudence then established. He was slow to enlarge his own jurisdiction, interfering very cautiously with common-law actions,—always respecting the principles of the common law, and consulting the common-law Judges upon any question of difficulty which arose before him. On the

---

¹ This was a very delicate question; and from Elizabeth not wishing to stir it, there is reason to fear that the proofs of Anne's guilt were formidable. It was remarked that although she was constantly boasting of being the daughter of Henry VIII., she hardly ever made any allusion to her mother.

bench he was patient and courteous, and it was remarked that the parties against whom he decided, if not convinced by his reasons, never doubted his honesty, and admitted that they had had a fair hearing. More fortunate in this respect than his greater son, he was never once accused or suspected of bribery or corruption, either by his contemporaries or by posterity.[1]

Soon after he was in office, doubts were raised respecting his judicial authority. He had been appointed by the Seal having been merely delivered to him as Keeper; and some said that though a Chancellor might be created by "tradition" of the emblem of his jurisdiction, the only regular mode of making a Lord Keeper was by patent. On the 14th of April a patent was passed, by the Queen's warrant, giving him the same powers in all respects as if he was Lord Chancellor, and ratifying all that he had done as Lord Keeper. Still difficulties arose in his own mind, or cavils were made by others, respecting the extent of his powers, the Custos Sigilli having been originally only a deputy of the Lord Chancellor; and finally, an act of parliament was passed, declaring that:

"The common law of this realm is, and always was, and ought to be taken, that the Keeper of the Great Seal of England for the time being hath always had, used, and executed, and of right ought to have, use, and execute, and from henceforth may have, perceive, take, use, and execute, as of right belonging to the office of the Keeper

[1] I find an order of his in the Registrar's Book, which, though pronounced somewhat irregularly, shows his great good nature.
"17 Nov. 1577.
"Between
LAWRENCE DANYELL, Plaintiff,
RICHARD JACKSON, Defendant.

"Whereas the matter in variance between the said parties was the 5th of this month dismissed for such causes as are in the order expressed, and the Plaintiff adjudged thereby to pay to the Defendant 30s. costs: *Forasmuch as the Plaintiff being a very poor boy, in very simple clothes and bare-legged, and under the age of twelve years,* came this present day into this Court and desired that he might be discharged of the said costs, it is therefore, in consideration as well of his age as also of his poverty and simplicity, ordered that (upon an affidavit made that he is the same Lawrence Danyell named Plaintiff herein) he be discharged of the said 30s. costs, and no process to issue out against him for the same." This is a rare instance of the advantage of a suitor pleading his own cause.—There is another entry showing that a poor man having followed him on foot from London to Windsor, he there patiently examined the case, and referred him to the Court of Requests. Rayley *v.* Dyon, Reg. Lib. A. 5 & 6 Eliz. 1565, f. 471.

of the Great Seal of England for the time being, the same and the like place, authority, pre-eminence jurisdiction, execution of laws, and all other customs, commodities, and advantages as the Lord Chancellor of England for the time being lawfully used, had and ought to have, use. and execute, as of right belonged the office of the Lord Chancellor of England for the time being, to all intents, constructions, and purposes as if the same Keeper of the Great Seal for the time being were Lord Chancellor of England."[1]

The Protestant faith being established, and the government settled in the session of parliament held soon after the Queen's accession, the Lord Keeper was not at all diverted by politics from the regular dispatch of judicial business till the beginning of the year 1563, when the Queen's exchequer being empty from the assistance she rendered to the French Huguenots, she found herself reluctantly obliged to summon a new parliament for the purpose of obtaining a supply.

On the day on which the writs were returnable, the Queen being indisposed, the Lord Keeper, by virtue of a commission, postponed the meeting till the following day. He then joined a grand procession from Whitehall to Westminster Abbey, the Queen riding on horseback, clad in crimson velvet, with the Crown on her head,—twenty-two Bishops riding behind her in scarlet, with hoods of minever down their backs,—followed by all the temporal Lords in their parliamentary robes. After service and sermon they proceeded to the parliament chamber; and the Queen being seated on the throne, the Commons attending at the bar, the Lord Keeper stationed on her right hand, a little beside the cloth of estate, and somewhat back and lower than the throne, by her Majesty's orders delivered a speech, which thus began: " My Lords and others of this honorable assembly, you shall understand that my most dread and sovereign Lady the Queen's

---

[1] 5 Eliz c. 18. This assertion of former usage is correct, where there had been a Lord Keeper without a Lord Chancellor; but the framer of the statute was probably not aware of what we, from the examination of records, now know, that in early ages there were frequently a Chancellor and Keeper of the Great Seal at the same time,—when the latter could only act by the special directions of the former. There could not after 5 Eliz. have been a Chancellor and Keeper at the same time, but all occasion for such an arrangement is now obviated by the multiplication of Vice-Chancellors.

Majesty here present hath commanded me to declare the occasion of this assembly, which I am not able (but unmeet) to do as it ought to be done among such a noble, wise, and discreet company. Howbeit, knowing the experience of her Majesty bearing with such as do their good wills, and your Honors' patience, in bearing with me in the like afore this time, it encourageth me the better herein." It must be confessed that he put the patience of her Majesty and their honors to a considerable trial; for his speech was very prolix and pointless, and they must have been greatly relieved when he at last said—" And for that the Nether House being so many, of necessity must have one to be a mouth-aider or instructor unto them, for the opening of matters, which is called the Speaker;—therefore, go and assemble yourselves together, and elect one,—a discreet, wise, and learned man; and on Friday next the Queen's Majesty appointeth to repair hither again for to receive the presentment of him accordingly." [1]

On that day the Queen again attended, and the Speaker-elect then exceeded the former length and dullness of the Lord Keeper, who, on this occasion, contented himself with disallowing the disqualification pleaded, and conceding to the Commons all their ancient privileges.[2]

This was considered a very laborious session, and did not end till the 10th of April. On that day the Speaker touched upon the several bills which they had passed, and after comparing Elizabeth to three most virtuous British Queens (not very generally known),—PALESTINA, who reigned here before the deluge; CERES, who made laws for evil-doers some time after that event; and MARCA, wife of Bathilicus, mother to King Stelicus,—in the name of the Commons strongly exhorted her to marry, so that the nation might hope to have her issue to reign over them; and if she were resolutely determined to die a maid, earnestly entreated that she would name a successor.

The Queen thereupon called the Lord Keeper unto her, and commanded him, in her name, to answer the Speaker. Sir Nicholas accordingly, *more suo*, went over all Mr. Speaker's topics till he came to the last; when it appeared that she had considered this rather too delicate

[1] 1 Parl. Hist. 664.   [2] Ibid. 685.

for him to be trusted with. He thus proceeded: "And touching your request aforetime made to her for her marriage and succession, because it is of such importance whereby I doubted my opening thereof, I therefore desired her Majesty that her meaning might be written, which she hath done, and delivered to me." He then read the paper: "For my marriage, if I had let slip too much time, or if my strength had been decayed, you might the better have spoken therein; or if any think I never meant to try that life, they be deceived; but if I may hereafter bend my mind thereunto, the rather for fulfilling your request, I shall be therewith very well content. As to the succession after me, the greatness thereof maketh me to say and pray that I may linger here in this vale of misery for your comfort, wherein I have witness of my study and travail for your surety; and I cannot with 'Nunc dimittis' end my life without I see some foundation of your surety after my gravestone."

The royal assent was then given to the acts of the session, and the Lord Keeper prorogued the parliament.[1]

Whether the Queen ever had any serious thoughts of marriage is uncertain; but she successively flattered the hopes of Philip of Spain, Charles of Austria, Eric of Sweden, Adolphus of Holstein, the Earl of Arran, and her own subject, Robert Dudley, Earl of Leicester. The nation at last became most seriously and justly alarmed about the succession. She had been dangerously ill, and if she had died, a civil war seemed inevitable. The heir by blood was the Queen of Scots; but she was a Catholic, and set aside by the will of Henry VIII., or at least postponed to the House of Suffolk descended from his younger sister. There was some doubt who was the legitimate heir of that house, and there was another claimant in the Countess of Lennox, descended from Margaret, the eldest sister of Henry by a second marriage.

Another attempt was made, in which the Lord Keeper took a more active part than was consistent with his usual caution, to induce the Queen either to marry, or to allow that her successor should be declared. After a conference between the two Houses, the Lords resolved upon an address to her Majesty, to be presented by Lord

[1] 1 Parl. Hist. 703.

Keeper Bacon, and the address bears strong marks of having been prepared by the Lord Keeper himself.

It is said to have been delivered by him to her Majesty in parliament, and she seems to have come down to the House of Lords to receive it on the throne. It is very long, after the Lord Keeper's manner; but a few extracts of it may be amusing. After a tiresome preface, he says, " The Lords petition, 1st, that it would please your Majesty to dispose yourself to marry when it shall please you, with whom it shall please you, and as soon as it shall please you: 2ndly, that some limitation may be made how the imperial Crown of this realm may remain if God calls your Highness without heir of your body (which our Lord defend), so as these Lords and Nobles, and other your subjects then living, may sufficiently understand to whom they owe their allegiance." He then handles each head separately with many subdivisions, enumerating no fewer than ten reasons why her Highness should take husband. Lest she should have made a vow of perpetual celibacy, he tells her it may be laudably broken, " for it appeareth by histories that in times past persons inheriting to Crowns being votaries and religious, to avoid such dangers as might have happened for want of succession to kingdoms, have left their vows and monasteries, and taken themselves to marriage,— as Constantia, a nun, heir to the kingdom of Sicily, married after fifty years of age to Henry VI., Emperor of that name, and had issue, Frederick II. Likewise Peter of Aragon, being a monk, married, the better to establish and pacify that kingdom." He next tries to inflame her by the desire of having children. "Antoninus Pius is much commended, for that, not two days before his death, he said to his Council, *Læto animo morior quoniam filium vobis relinquo.* Pyrrhus is of all godly men detested for saying he *would leave his realm to him that had the sharpest sword.* What, but want of a successor known, made an end of so great an empire as Alexander the Great did leave at his death?—God, your Highness knoweth, by the course of Scriptures, hath declared succession, and having children, to be one of the principal benedictions in this life; and, on the contrary, he hath pronounced contrarywise; and therefore, Abraham prayed to God for issue, fearing that Eliazar, his steward, should have been his heir, and had promise that kings should proceed of his body. Hannah, the mother of Samuel, prayed to God with tears for issue; and Elizabeth (whose name your Majesty beareth), mother to John the Baptist, was joyous when God had blessed her with fruit, accounting herself thereby to be delivered from reproach."

Bacon's harangue being at last brought to a close, the Queen returned a short answer, which has all the appearance of being unpremeditated. She was much nettled at some of the illustrations which she thought referred to Mary, Queen of Scots, then lately delivered of a hopeful son. "I thought it had been so desired, as none other trees' blossom should have been minded, or ever any hope of any fruit had been denied you. And yet by the way, if any here doubt that I am by vow or determination bent never to trade in that kind of life, put out that kind of heresy, for your belief is therein awry. For though I can think it best for a private woman, yet I do strive with myself not to think it meet for a Prince, and if I can bend my liking to your need I will not resist such a mind." After a few evasive generalities she withdrew, and the Lords declared themselves contented.[1]

The subject was renewed at the close of the session, when the Queen having come in her barge from Whitehall, and being placed on the throne, the Lord Keeper standing by the rail a little behind her on the right, Onslow, the first Speaker of that name, appearing at the bar, was marched through the House of Lords, making his obeisances, to the rail near the Lord Keeper, and delivered a tremendously long address to her Majesty, which he thus concluded:—" God grant us that as your Majesty hath defended the faith of Abraham, you may have the like desire of issue; and for that purpose that you would shortly embrace the holy state of matrimony, when and with whom God shall appoint and best like your Majesty; and so the issue of your own body by your example rule over our posterity."

The Lord Keeper returned an answer, but in such a very unsatisfactory manner, that the Queen stopped him and herself took the word, saying that, " as a periphrasis, she had a few words farther to add, notwithstanding she had not been used to speak, nor loved to do it in such open

[1] 1 Parl. Hist. 708

assemblies." She then gave them a good scolding. "I have in this assembly found so much dissimulation where I always professed plainness, that I marvel thereat; yea, two faces under one hood and the body rotten, being covered with two visors, SUCCESSION and LIBERTY. But, alas! they began to pierce the vessel before the wine was fined. Do you think I am unmindful of your surety by succession, wherein is all my care, considering I know myself to be mortal? No, I warrant you. Or that I went about to break your liberties? No, it was never my meaning—but to stay you before you fell into the ditch. All things have their time. Although, perhaps after me you may have one better learned or wiser, yet none more careful over you; and however that be, beware you prove that Prince's patience as you have mine."[1]

She was in such dudgeon that she ordered the Lord Keeper instantly to dissolve parliament, which he did, and no other was called for a period of five years.

But in the meantime the nation was in a state of great excitement on the question of the succession, and various pamphlets were published in support of the rights of the different claimants. Among these was one which professed to be indited by "John Hales, Clerk of the Hamper in the Court of Chancery,"—strongly espousing the cause of the House of Suffolk, which rested on the will of Henry VIII., alleged to be duly executed under the authority of an act of parliament,—violently disparaging the Stuart line, whose pretensions were denounced as inconsistent with the religion and independence of England,—and calling loudly for a parliamentary declaration of the right of the true heir. On the complaint of the Scottish ambassador, Hales was committed to prison; but upon his examination great was the astonishment—deep the indignation of the Queen, when the truth came out that the real author of this pamphlet, pretending to be the production of a subordinate officer in the Court of Chancery, was no less a person than the chief of the Court himself, whose religious zeal, fortified by the threats of the Catholics that they would revoke all the grants of Church property, for once had overcome his prudence.

Elizabeth, although restrained by jealousy of a rival Queen she concealed her real sentiments, had secretly de-

[1] 1 Parl. Hist. 722.

termined that the Stuarts should succeed, and she had an extreme antipathy to the Hertford blood. The Lord Keeper would at once have been deprived of the Great Seal, and sent to the Tower, had there not been a very serious difficulty about appointing a successor to him; but his name was immediately struck out of the list of Privy Councillors, and he was strictly enjoined to meddle with no business whatever except that of the Court of Chancery. It seems strange to us that the first Judge of the land should be so far disgraced, and still permitted to retain his office. Leicester, whose aspiring project to share the throne he had thwarted, attempted to incense the Queen further against him; but Cecil, who was suspected of sharing his sentiments on the succession question, and even of having contributed to the obnoxious pamphlet, steadily supported him, and in little more than a twelvemonth he was again sworn of the Privy Council, and entirely restored to Elizabeth's favor.

The next affair of importance, in which Lord Keeper Bacon was engaged, was the inquiry into the conduct of the Queen of Scots, respecting the murder of her husband. The unhappy Mary, after the battle of Langside, having sought refuge in England from her rebellious subjects, was now a prisoner in Bolton Castle, under the care of Lord Scrope; and Elizabeth, with a view to make herself arbitress of the affairs of Scotland, having refused to see her till she had proved her innocence of the great crime imputed to her, both parties had submitted themselves to the judgment of the English Queen. A commission passed under the Great Seal, appointing the Lord Keeper and others to act for Elizabeth in this investigation. The conferences took place at Hampton Court,—Murray, the Regent of Scotland, assisted by Buchanan, the famous poet and historian, appearing as accuser, and Mary being represented by Lord Herries, and Lesley, Bishop of Ross.

Bacon is said to have conducted himself, on this occasion, with dignity and propriety. He gained the friendship of the Bishop of Ross, who ever after spoke of him in terms of respect and esteem,—and of Buchanan, who recorded his high admiration of him in a Latin epitaph, inscribed on his tomb in St. Paul's Cathedral. But the casket being produced containing Mary's letters and sonnets, addressed to Bothwell, which, if genuine, clearly established her guilt, and proof being offered that they were in her handwriting, by comparing them with letters addressed by her to Elizabeth, her commissioners refused to give in any answer, and the conferences were broken off, without any judgment being pronounced,—Mary still protesting her innocence, and desiring to be permitted to justify herself before Elizabeth in person.

In about two years after, the negotiations were renewed at York House, the residence of the Lord Keeper. The English commissioners now demanded, as the price of Mary's liberty, that some of the chief nobility, and several of the principal fortresses of Scotland, should be placed in Elizabeth's hands. The pride of the Scotsmen was much wounded by this proposal, which they denounced as insulting. But thereupon the Lord Keeper broke up the conference, saying, "All Scotland—your prince, nobles, and castles, are too little to secure the flourishing kingdom of England."[1]

The next occasion of the Lord Keeper appearing before the public in his political capacity, was at the meeting of parliament, on the 2d of April, 1571. On that day the Queen went to Westminster Abbey, for the first time in a coach—which was drawn by two palfreys, covered with crimson velvet, embossed and embroidered very richly; but this was the only carriage in the procession, the Lord Keeper and the Lords spiritual and temporal, attending her on horseback.

Her Majesty being seated on the throne, and the Commons attending,—after a few complimentary words from her own lips, "looking on the right side of her, towards Sir Nicholas Bacon, Knight, Lord Keeper, standing a little beside the cloth of estate, and somewhat back, and lower from the same, she willed him to show the cause of the parliament." His most eloquent flight was in celebrating the Queen's economy. "What need I to remember unto you how the gorgeous, sumptuous, super-

---

[1] This speech may well account for the great enmity afterwards entertained against him in Scotland, and the libels published against him at Edinburgh:

An interesting account of this negotiation will be found in the lately-published Despatches of De la Mothe Fénélon, then French Ambassador at the English Court. He designates Sir Francis Bacon "Milord *Quiper*, Garde des Sceaux," and records in a very lively manner his dialogues with the Bishop of Ross [called *l'evesque de Roz*], representative of Mary (*la Royne d'Escoce*).— *Note to 4th Edition.*

flious buildings of time past be for the realm's good, by her Majesty in this time turned into necessary buildings and upholdings?—the chargeable, glittering, glorious triumphs, into delectable pastimes and shows?—ambassades of charge into such as be void of excess, and yet honorable and comely? These imperfections have been commonly Princes' peculiars, especially young. One free from these was anointed *rara avis*, &c., and yet (God be thanked!) a phœnix, a blessed bird of this kind God hath blessed us with." He concluded by supposing they were all heartily sick of his tediousness. "Here I make an end, doubting that I have tarried you longer than I promised, or meant, or perchance needed."[1]

He delivered another speech a few days after, approving of the choice of Speaker; in which he told the Commons, by the Queen's command, that "they should do well to meddle with no matters of state but such as should be propounded unto them."

This injunction, however, was by no means universally obeyed; and several members brought forward motions about the abuse of the prerogative in granting monopolies, and the necessity for settling the succession to the Crown. They were called before the Council, when the Lord Keeper reprimanded them for their temerity; and one refractory member was committed to prison.

At the close of the session the Lord Keeper highly extolled the discretion and orderly proceedings of the Upper House, which redounded much to their honor and much to the comfort and consolation of her Majesty; but he inveighed heavily against the popular party in the Commons "for their audacious, arrogant, and presumptuous folly, thus by superfluous speech spending much time in meddling with matters neither pertaining to them nor within the capacity of their understanding."[2] The importance of the Commons was now rapidly rising, and that of the Lords sinking in the same proportion.

The last notice we have of Sir Nicholas Bacon's appearance in public was at the close of the session of parliament in the year 1575, when a scene took place which

---

[1] 1 Parl. Hist. 724. In the course of his speech he cites the maxim "Frustra fit per plura quod fieri potest per pauciora" which he never much regarded, for he is a very verbose and vapid orator.
[2] 1 Parl. Hist. 766.

must have caused a good deal of internal tittering among the bystanders, if all due external gravity was preserved in the royal presence. Her Majesty had reached an age at which according to the common course of nature she could hardly be expected to bear children: yet the Speaker of the House of Commons (perhaps to flatter her now—as she had formerly in her younger days been annoyed by such requests) proceeded humbly to petition her Majesty to make the kingdom further happy in her marriage, that so they might hope for a continual succession of those benefits in her posterity." The Lord Keeper, after conferring with the Queen, made answer,—

"In this her Majesty conceiveth the abundance of your inward affection grounded upon her good governance of you to be so great, that it doth not only content you to have her Majesty reign and govern over you, but also you do desire that some proceeding from her Majesty's body might by a perpetual succession reign over your posterity also—a matter greatly to move her Majesty (she saith) to incline to this your suit. Besides, her Highness is not unmindful of all the benefits that will grow to the realm by such a marriage, neither doth she forget any perils that are likely to grow for want thereof. All which matters considered, her Majesty willed me to say, that albeit of her own natural disposition she is not disposed or inclined to marriage, neither could she ever marry were she a private person, yet for your sakes and benefit of the realm, she is contented to dispose and incline herself to the satisfaction of your humble petition, so that all things convenient may concur that be meet for such a marriage, whereof there be very many, some touching the state of her most royal person, some touching the person of him who God shall join, some touching the state of the whole realm; these things concurring and considered, her Majesty hath assented."[1]

Parliament was not again called during the life of Sir Nicholas Bacon. He continued in a quiet manner to have considerable influence in public affairs. From the time of his restoration to the Council he was its legal adviser, and Cecil, now Lord Burghley, had been much influenced by him respecting the measures proposed to the legislature on the part of the government. Not being a Peer,

[1] 1 Parl. Hist. 806.

he could not take a share in the Lords' debates; but presiding as Speaker on the Woolsack, he exercised a considerable influence on their deliberations. He was supposed to have framed the acts aimed at the Queen of Scots and her supporters. Although death saved him from the disgrace of being directly accessory to the death of this unfortunate Princess, he is chargeable with having strongly supported the policy which finally led to that catastrophe, by urging the continuation of her captivity and rigorous treatment,—by assisting in the efforts to blacken her reputation,—by resisting the recognition of her right and that of her son to succeed to the crown,—and by contending, that though a captive sovereign, she ought to be treated as a rebellious subject.

Being a Commoner, he could neither act as Lord Steward, nor sit upon the trial of the Duke of Norfolk, who was the first to suffer for favoring Mary's cause; but as he put the Great Seal to the commission under which this mockery of justice was exhibited, and must have superintended and directed the whole proceeding, he is to be considered answerable for such atrocities as depriving the noble prisoner of the use of books, and debarring him from all communication with his friends from the time of his commitment to the Tower,—giving him notice of trial only the night before his arraignment,—keeping him in ignorance of the charges against him till he heard the indictment read in court,—and resting the case for the Crown on the confessions of witnesses whom the Council had ordered "to be put to the rack that they might find the taste thereof."[1] The religious zeal of the Lord Keeper and the Protestant ministers was now greatly exasperated, and they were eager by any expedients to crush the believers in those doctrines which they themselves had openly professed in the preceding reign.

Sir Nicholas, from his family connection with Burghley, continued opposed to the party of Robert Dudley, Earl of Leicester. Through the ill offices of this favorite he had been expelled from the Privy Council, and a great coldness ever after subsisted between them.

Although the Queen's reputation never suffered from her attentions to this old, fat Lord Keeper, as it did when she danced and flirted with his young and handsome

[1] 1 St. Tr. 958. Ellis, ii. 261. Jardine's Criminal Trials, i. 121.

successor, Sir Christopher Hatton, she was latterly very kind to him, and visited him in her progresses at Redgrave and Gorhambury. It was on one of these occasions that she remarked to him that his house was too small for him, and he answered, "Not so, Madam, your Highness has made me too great for my house." During another visit, Frank, with his curly locks, was introduced to her, and the lad showing from his earliest years the extraordinary genius which afterwards immortalized him, she, captivated by his manners and his answers to her questions, called him "her young Lord Keeper."

Old Sir Nicholas had grown exceedingly corpulent, insomuch that when he had walked the short distance from the Court of Chancery to the Star Chamber, it was some time after he had taken his place on the Bench there before he had sufficiently recovered his breath to go on with the business,—and the Bar, before moving, waited for a signal which he gave them by thrice striking the ground with his staff.

When unable to attend the meetings of the Council, he was in the habit of writing long letters to the Queen, explaining his views on public affairs. Thus he begins one of these, respecting the troubles in Scotland and in the Low Countries:—

"MY MOST GRACIOUS SOVEREIGN, I with all humbleness pray pardon of your Majesty that I presume by letter to do that, which bounden duty and service requireth to be done in person. O good Madam, not want of a willing heart and mind, but an unable and an unwieldy body, is the only cause of this. And yet the body, such as it is, every day and hour is, and ever shall be, at your Majesty's commandment; and so should they be, if I had a thousand as good as any man hath, mine allegiance and a number of benefits hath so sundry ways bounden me."

He had enjoyed remarkably good health, and he might still have done the duties of his office satisfactorily for years to come, had it not happened that in the beginning of February, 1579, while under the operation of having his hair and his beard trimmed, he fell asleep. The awestruck barber desisted from his task, and remained silent. The contemporary accounts state, that from "the sultriness of the weather, the windows of the room were open," which, considering the season of the year, I do not exactly understand. However this may be, the Lord Keeper continued long asleep in a current of air, and when he awoke he found himself chilled and very much disordered. To the question, "Why did you suffer me to sleep thus exposed?" the answer was,—"I durst not disturb you." Sir Nicholas replied,—" By your civility I lose my life." He was immediately carried to his bed, and in a few days he expired.

He was buried in St. Paul's Cathedral, where a monument to his memory stood till the great fire of London,—with the following epitaph from the pen of his friend, George Buchanan :—

> " Hic Nicolaum ne Baconum conditum
> Existima illum, tam diu Britannici
> Regni secundum columen, exitium malis,
> Bonis asylum ; cæca quem non extulit
> Ad hunc honorem sors, sed æquitas, fides,
> Doctrina, pietas, unica et prudentia.
> Neu morte raptum crede, quia unica brevi
> Vita perennes emeruit duas ; agit
> Vitam secundam cælites inter animus ;
> Fama implet orbem vita quæ illi tertia est.
> Hac positum in ara est corpus olim animi domus
> Ara dicata sempiternæ memoriæ."

The character of Lord Keeper Bacon, by Camden, is very flattering, notwithstanding the sneer at his obesity :[1] —" Vir præpinguis, ingenio acerrimo, singulari prudentia, summâ eloquentiâ, tenaci memoriâ et sacris conciliis alterum columen."

His son bears the most honorable testimony to his sincerity of mind and straightforward conduct—abstaining from ascribing to him brilliant qualities which he knew did not belong to him:—" He was a plain man, direct and constant, without all finesse and doubleness, and one that was of a mind that a man in his private proceedings, and in the proceedings of state, should rest on the soundness and strength of his own courses, and not upon practice to circumvent others, according to the sentence of Solomon, *Vir prudens advertit ad gressus suos; stultus autem divertit ad dolos,*—insomuch that the Bishop of Ross, a subtle and observing man, said of him that he could fasten no words

---

[1] The Lord Keeper's figure seems to have been the subject of much jesting at Court. The Queen herself, alluding to it, said, "Sir Nicholas's soul lodges well," whereat, no doubt, the lords with white staves and the ladies in waiting laughed consumedly. Fuller describes him as a man " cui fuit ingenium subtile it corpore crasso."

upon him, and that it was impossible to come within him, because he offered no play; and the Queen mother of France, a very politic Princess, said of him that he should have been of the Council of Spain, because he despised the occurrents and rested on the first plot."[1]

The most valuable tribute to his memory is from the faithful Hayward, who describes him "as a man of great diligence and ability in his place, whose goodnesse preserved his greatnesse from suspicion, envye, and hate."[2]

Amidst the drudgery of business and the cares of state, he kept up his classical learning, and was a patron of learned men, who repaid him for his condescension by their flattery. "I have come," said one of them, "to the Lord Keeper, and found him sitting in his gallery alone with the works of Quintilian before him. Indeed he was a most eloquent man, of rare wisdom and learning as ever I knew England to breed, and one that joyed as much in learned men and good wits—from whose lips I have seen to proceed more grace and natural eloquence than from all the orators of Oxford and Cambridge."[3]

In his own time he was "famous for set speeches, and gained the reputation of a witty and weighty orator;" but I have been obliged to express my opinion, that the specimens of his eloquence transmitted to us are exceedingly dull and tiresome, having neither the point and quaintness of the preceding age, nor showing any approach to the vigor and eloquence which distinguished the latter half of the reign of Elizabeth.[4]

No judicial decision of his, either in the Court of Chancery or in the Star Chamber is reported, although we meet with much general commendation of his conduct as a Judge. He had the admirable qualities of patience and regularity: and he would often say, "Let us stay a little that we may have done the sooner,"—truly thinking that an irregular attempt to shorten a cause generally makes it last twice as long as it would have done if regularly heard to its conclusion. When Lord Bacon, in his admirable essay "on Judicature," draws the picture of a good

---

[1] Observations on a Libel. Bac. Works, ed. 1819, vol. iii. p. 96.
[2] Hayward's Annals of Elizabeth, published by Camden Society, p. 13.
[3] Puttenham.
[4] There are references to a MS. collection of his speeches said to be in the public library at Cambridge; but after a most diligent search, which I have caused to be made, it is not to be found.

Judge, he is supposed to have intended to delineate his sire. The old gentleman's manner, however, seems to have had about it something of the ridiculous, for the saying went, "some seemed wiser than they were, but the Lord Keeper was wiser than he seemed."[1]

[1] There are a good many decrees of Sir Nicholas Bacon to be found in the Registrar's Book. I will give an abstract of one of them, which may amuse my female readers, and will strikingly illustrate the manners of the times. Who would have thought of a courtship being carried on under the directions of the Lord Keeper? Two powerful Cheshire families, the Traffords and the Boothes, had had a violent feud respecting a marriage between young Edward Trafford and Margaret Boothe. "It therefore pleased her Highness the Queen, for the speedy end and quieting thereof, to direct her special warrant to her Lord Keeper, commanding him to hear and determine the same." The young lady's father alleged "that neither there was nor could be any such liking between the said Edward and Margaret as were convenient to have a marriage between them, and that the said Margaret could not in her heart like well of the said Edward." "Whereupon the said Lord Keeper, understanding the said Margaret to have accomplished the full age of *twelve years*, and wishing to be informed of the truth of this objection before he should proceed to any decree, doth require and enjoin Thomas Stanley, Esq. [ancestor of the present Lord Stanley of Alderley], in whose indifferent custody the said Margaret now is, to suffer the said Edward to have access to the house of the said Thomas Stanley, and that the said Edward and Margaret shall there have meeting, talk, and conference the one with the other, two or three several times before the term of St. Michael next coming, in the presence of the said Thomas Stanley, and thereupon the said Thomas Stanley shall diligently examine and try, by such convenient and good means as he can, what liking the said parties shall have each of other, and shall advertise the said Lord Keeper of his doings and proceedings in that behalf, and what liking he shall find in the said parties." Mr. Stanley certified to the Lord Keeper that "he had permitted the said Edward and Margaret to have meeting and talk together at his house and in his presence, on the 6th day of August and on the 19th day of September, on which last day the said Thomas Stanley, after that the said Edward and Margaret had had some talk and conference the one with the other, took the said Edward apart and demanded of him what liking he had of this gentlewoman? who answered that he had very good liking of her. And thereupon taking the said Margaret also apart, demanded of her what liking she had of the said Edward? Who likewise did answer that she had very good liking of him." He then gives a similar account of another meeting which the lovers had on the 26th of September, when "the said Edward declared that he could be very well content to marry the said Margaret, and the said Margaret declared that she could be very well content to marry the said Edward with a free good will, and farther that she had not been persuaded nor dissuaded to have liking or disliking of the said young Trafford." Thereupon the Lord Keeper, by his final decree, bearing date the 8th of November, 15 Eliz., "ordered and directed that the said Margaret should be delivered by the said Thomas Stanley into the custody of the father of the said Edward, to the end that a marriage may be had between the said Edward and Margaret, and that nothing shall be done to hinder the delivery of the said Margaret into such custody to the intent aforesaid." The decree then goes on to order certain sums of money to be paid by their relations for the benefit of the young couple, "all the several payments aforesaid to be made at or in the south porch of the parish church of

He wrote "A Treatise of Treason," and other works which have deservedly perished. Only two of his publications are extant to reconcile us for the loss of the rest:— 1. "An argument to show that the persons of noblemen are attachable by law for contempts in the High Court of Chancery;" and, 2. "A Palinode, proving the right of succession to the Crown of England to be in the family of the Stuarts descended from Henry VII., exclusive of Mary Queen of Scots, who had forfeited her rights."

His *bon mots* have had better luck, for several of them which have been preserved show that, for a Keeper of the Great Seal, he was by no means a contemptible jester.

Being asked his opinion, by the Earl of Leicester, concerning two persons of whom the Queen seemed to think well, "By my troth, my Lord," said he, "the one is a grave Councillor; the other is a proper young man, *and so he will be as long as he lives.*"[1]

At a time when there was a great clamor about monopolies created by a license to make a particular manufacture, with a prohibition to all others to do the like,—being asked by Queen Elizabeth what he thought of these monopoly licenses, he answered, "Madam, will you have me speak the truth? *Licentiâ* omnes deteriores sumus. We are all the worse for Licenses."

Once going the Northern Circuit as Judge, before he had the Great Seal, he was about to pass sentence on a thief convicted before him, when the prisoner, after various pleas had been overruled, asked for mercy on account of kindred. "Prithee," said my Lord Judge, "how comes this about?" "Why, if it please you, my Lord, your name is *Bacon*, and mine is *Hog*, and, in all ages, *Hog* and *Bacon* have been so near kindred that they are not to be separated." "Ay, but," replied the Judge, "you and I

Manchester, in the county of Lancaster, between the hours, &c." But there is a proviso that the young lady shall still have free choice to take or refuse her suitor "without any threatenings or other constraints to be used to her;" and that if she should change her mind before the marriage was celebrated, she should be delivered back into the custody of her own father. Reg. Lib. A. 1573, p. 71.—This proceeding reminds us of the decrees of the French parliaments for a CONGRESS to see if the parties *well liked of each other*—after marriage.

[1] This sarcasm (indifferent as it is) was stolen from Sir Thomas More, who, when his wife last had a son who turned out rather silly, observed to her that she had so long prayed for a *boy*, he was afraid her son would continue *a boy as long as he lived.*

can not be kindred except you be *hanged*, for *Hog* is not *Bacon* until it be well *hanged*."

He used to tell a story which he was supposed to have invented or embellished,—that a notorious rogue, about to be arraigned before him, hoping that he might have some chance from my Lord Judge's love of humor,—instead of pleading, took to himself the liberty of jesting; and, as if the Judge having some evil design, he had been to swear the peace against him,—exclaimed, "I charge you in the Queen's name to seize and take away that man in the red gown there, for I go in danger of my life because of him."

At times he had a slight hesitation, which impeded his utterance. A certain nimble-witted counsellor at the bar having often interrupted him, he at last said, "There is a great difference between me and you,—a pain for me to speak, and a pain to you to hold your peace." There was then a *glimpse of silence*, of which the Lord Keeper took advantage to finish his sentence.

On a bill exhibited to discover where lands lay, being told that the plaintiffs had a certain quantity of land, but could not set it forth, he was wont to say, "And if you can not find your land in the country, how do you expect me to find it for you in the Court of Chancery?"[1]

Soon after his death, a wag at the Chancery bar, to expose the practice beginning to prevail too much of referring everything to the Master (then called "the Doctor," from the Masters being all Doctors of the civil law), feigned a tale that Sir Nicholas, when he came to Heaven's gate, was opposed in respect of an unjust decree which he had made while Lord Keeper. He desired to see the order, and, finding it to begin "Veneris," &c., "Why," saith he, "this being done on a Friday, I was then sitting in the Star Chamber: it concerns the Master of the Rolls: let him answer it." Sir William Cordell, M. R., who died soon after, following, he was likewise stayed upon it. Looking into the order, he found it ran thus: "Upon reading the report of Dr. Gibson, to whom this cause stood referred, it is ordered," &c. And so he put it upon Dr. Gibson, who next coming up, said that the Lord Keeper and his Honor, the Master of the Rolls, were the parties who ought

[1] Lord Bacon's Apophthegms. Works, ii. 401.

to suffer, for not doing their own work;—whereupon they were all three turned back.

Considering that he held the Great Seal above twenty years, he left behind him a very moderate fortune, which was chiefly inherited by his eldest son,—Francis and the younger children being but slenderly provided for. His town residence was York House, near Charing Cross, where he splendidly exercised hospitality. After the visit from Queen Elizabeth, he added wings to his house at Gorhambury, and laid out large sums of money in planting and gardening there. The decorations of his grounds, however, displayed the bad taste of the age. For example, in a little banqueting house there was a series of pictorial designs emblematic of the LIBERAL ARTS,—to wit, GRAMMAR, ARITHMETIC, LOGIC, MUSIC, RHETORIC, GEOMETRY, and ASTROLOGY, with hideous portraits of their most celebrated professors, and each one with a barbarous Latin couplet. Over the hall door was an inscription, which marks the period of the erection as the 10th year of his Keepership (1568):

> "Hæc cum perfecit Nicholaus tecta Baconus
> Elizabeth regni lustra fuere duo.
> Factus Eques, magni custos erat ipse sigilli;
> Gloria sit solo tota tributa Deo
> MEDIOCRIA FIRMA."

He was extremely popular with the English nation, but particularly odious in Scotland, from the part he took in the continued imprisonment of Queen Mary, and the reports spread of his dislike to all the inhabitants of that country. Gross libels against him were printed at Edinburgh, and circulated industriously in London. The Queen issued a proclamation ordering them to be burnt, and highly commending the services of the Lord Keeper.

Sir Nicholas Bacon was twice married: first to Jane, daughter of William Fernly, Esq., of West Creding, in Suffolk, by whom he had several sons and daughters; and, secondly, to Anne, daughter of Anthony Cooke, Esq., of Giddy Hall, in Essex, by whom he had two sons, Sir Anthony,—and Francis, the immortal Lord Verulam, Viscount St. Alban's. It was by this latter marriage that the connection was created between the Cecils and the Bacons.

The subject of this memoir would probably have filled

a greater space in the eyes of posterity had it not been for the glory of his son; but one of the grounds on which we ought to admire and to respect him is the manner in which he assisted in forming a mind so supereminent; he pointed out the path by which FRANCIS BACON reached such distinction in literature and eloquence, and became the first philosopher of any country or any age.[1]

CHAPTER XLIV.

LIFE OF SIR THOMAS BROMLEY, LORD CHANCELLOR OF ENGLAND.

ON the sudden death of Lord Keeper Bacon, great perplexity existed with respect to the appointment of his successor. On the day he expired the Queen sent Lord Burghley and Lord Leicester to York House for the Great Seal, and they having received it from Lady Bacon, his widow, in a bag sealed with his private signet, took it to the Queen, who was in her palace at Westminster. She retained it in her own keeping above two months, while she considered with whom she should intrust it. Luckily this period was in the interval between Hilary and Easter terms, so that the delay in filling up the office did not cause any serious interruption to the despatch of business in the Court of Chancery. The sealing of writs and patents was accomplished under the Queen's immediate orders. To show her impartiality, she handed it over for this purpose, alternately, to the heads of the two opposite parties, Burghley and Leicester; except that on one occasion, the latter being absent to prepare for receiving a royal visit at Kenilworth, Secretary Walsingham was substituted for him. The Close Roll records, with much circumstantiality, no fewer than seven instances of the Great Seal being so used between the 20th of February and the 26th of April.[2]

---

[1] See Rawley's Life of Bacon. Baconiana. Lord Bacon's Works, ii. 407, 422, 426; iii. 96; vi. 368.

[2] I shall copy as a specimen of this entry the recovery of the Great Seal on Sir N. Bacon's death, and the first instance of its being used while in the Queen's custody. "Memdum qd die Veneris &c. (Feb. 20, 1 Eliz.) circa

There being now an outcry that no injunctions could be obtained, and that the hearing of causes was suspended, the Queen, who personally made all such appointments, and sometimes vacillated much about them, was informed that Westminster Hall could go on no longer without a Lord Chancellor or Lord Keeper. She was determined that the clergy should be kept to their spiritual affairs; a mere politician could not be fixed upon without great scandal, and there was no lawyer whom she considered eligible. Sir Gilbert Gerrard had been Attorney General ever since her accession to the Crown; but although he was well learned in his profession and very industrious, he was awkward and ungainly in his speech and manner, and not considered fit for such a place of representation and dignity. Yet there was a reluctance to pass over a man of approved service. Sir Thomas Bromley, the Solicitor General, was inferior to him in legal acquirements, but was much more a man of the world, and had shown himself a most zealous partisan, and ready, without scruple, to perform any task that might be assigned to him. After much intriguing, the friends of Mr. Solicitor prevailed with the Queen; and on a suggestion that, on account of

horam nonam ante meridiem ejusdem diei Magnum Sigillum suum regium post mortem egregii viri Nichi Bacon militis tunc nuper Custodis ejusdem Magni Sigilli exist. in quadam baga de corio inclus. et signato ejusdem Nichi sigillatum et cooperta alia baga de velueto rubeo insigniis regiis ornat. nobilibus viris Willo Dno Burghley Dno Thesaurario Angl. et Robo Comiti Leicester ex mandato ejusdem Dne Regne apud Hospicium ejusdem Nichi vocatum Yorke Place prope Charing Crosse in quadam interiori Camera ibidem per dominam Annam Bacon Viduam nuper uxem ejusdem Nichi liberatum fuit; Quiquidem Wills Ds Burghley et Robertus Comes Leicestr sigillum predictum in baga predicta inclusum et sigillo ipsius Nihi ut predicitur munitum de manibus ejusdem Dne Anne Bacon recipien. illud circa horam decimam ante meridiem predicti diei prfe Dne Regne in sua privata Camera infra palacium suum Westmon. ibidem juxta ipsius Dne Regne benepltum obtulerunt et presentaverunt ac eadem Dna Regina," &c. (received the Seal and kept it till Feb. 24, when she delivered it to Burghley and Leicester), "pro tempore utend. et exercend. Quo accepto iidem Wills Dns Burghley et Comes Leicester tunc immedi ate usque Magnam Cameram Concilii infra palacium prdm asportari fecerunt et sigillum illud ibidem extra bagam prm adtunc extrahi fecerunt et eodem sigillo sic extracto divers. literas patentes processus et brevia de communi cursu Regni Angl. in presencia Thom. Poole, &c. sigillari fecerunt." Then comes a statement of their having, at seven o'clock, restored the Seal o its integuments, and given it to the Queen in her private chamber, and that the Queen kept it there till the 8th of March,—the whole history being repeated *toties quoties.*

his inferior rank, there might be a disposition not to treat him with proper respect, she added to their triumph by delivering the Great Seal to him, with the title and rank of " Lord Chancellor."[1]

Sir Gilbert Gerrard, the Attorney General, was consoled with a promise of the office of Master of the Rolls, which was actually given to him on the 30th of May, 1581.

Although Sir THOMAS BROMLEY held the Great Seal during eight years, he would hardly have been known to history, had it not been from the part he acted in the proceedings against the unfortunate Mary Stuart; but he will be remembered to the latest times as the person who framed the measures intended to bring her to the scaffold, and who actually presided at her mock trial in the hall of Fotheringay Castle.

He was the son of George Bromley and Jane, daughter of Sir Thomas Lacon of Whitley, and was born in the year 1530 at Bromley, in the county of Salop, where the family had been seated many ages, their name being territorial.[2] I do not find any information respecting his school or academical education. He was bred to the law in the Inner Temple, and was there remarkable for his proficiency and the regularity of his conduct. Rapidly rising to eminence at the bar, he was, in 1566, elected Recorder of London, and having secured the good opinion and patronage of Lord Keeper Bacon, in 1570 he was made Solicitor General.[3]

His first great public appearance in his official character was on the trial of the Duke of Norfolk for high treason, before the Court of the Lord High Steward. The Counsel for the Crown was Barham, the Queen's Sergeant, Gerrard, the Attorney General, Bromley, the Solicitor General, and Wilbraham, the Queen's Attorney of the Court of Wards. We have a short-hand writer's report of the trial, which is extremely curious, and shows that Bromley was exceedingly zealous in bringing about the conviction.[4] The Court consisted of the Earl of Shrewsbury, appointed Lord High Steward, the Great Seal being

---

[1] Rot. Cl. 21 Eliz. p. 201.
[2] As we say in Scotland, " Bromley of that ilk." This family produced several other distinguished lawyers; among these were Sir Thomas Bromley, made a Judge of the King's Bench, 36 H. 8—and Sir George Bromley, a brother of the Chancellor, a Justice of North Wales. Dugd. Or. Jur.
[3] Pat. 11 Eliz. Or. Jur. s. 3.   1 St. Tr. 957.

in the keeping of a Commoner,—and twenty-six Peers triers, attended by all the common-law Judges as assessors. The indictment had been settled at a conference of all the Judges before it was preferred to the grand jury. No regularity was observed, much of the time being occupied with dialogues between the prisoner and the Judges, and interlocutory speeches by the Lord High Steward, the Lords Triers, the Judges, and the counsel. The French fashion of interrogating the prisoner then prevailed in England, and the Duke was frequently asked to admit or to deny certain facts,—to explain his conduct on particular occasions,—and to reconcile the evidence adduced against him with his alleged innocence.[1]

Barham, the Queen's Sergeant, holding an office which had precedence of that of the Attorney General till the regency of George IV., began, and gave in evidence copies of letters, examinations, and confessions, mixing them up with speeches from himself and questions addressed to the prisoner, to show that the Duke persisted in his design to marry the Queen of Scots after his promise not to do so, and that he was engaged in a plot to further her escape. Mr. Attorney having followed in the same strain, Bromley, Solicitor General, thus began :—" For that the time is spent, and your Lordships, I think, are weary, I will not now make any collection what hath been gathered of the attempt of marriage with the Scottish Queen ; only I will deal with the matter of Rodolph's message, and the effect thereof; and the Duke's adhering to the Queen's enemies and rebels, shall be another part." He then proceeded, at considerable length, to detail the supposed plan of invading the kingdom by the intrigues of Rudolfi, an Italian banker, with the Duke of Alva, and gave in evidence a deciphered copy of a letter from Rudolfi to the Duke, alleged to have been delivered to him by one Barker, who was supposed to have taken the copy.—
Duke. " It may be Barker received this letter as you spake of, and that it was decyphered, and that it contained the matters that you allege, but it may be that they kept

---

[1] He was first very artfully asked " whether he knew that the Scottish Queen pretended title to the present possession of the crown of England," and wishing to evade the question, he is pressed, " did you know that she claimed the present possession of the Crown ?—that she usurped the arms and royal style of this realm—and that she made no renunciation of that usurped pretense ?"

that letter to themselves, and might bring me another letter containing only such matter as I was contented with."—*Solic.* "An unlikely matter! But thus you see the Duke confesseth the receipt of the letter; he only denieth it was to this effect." *Duke.* "I know not. Barker presented me the letter out of cypher, and I had not the cypher nor saw any such letter as you allege."—*Solic.* "The Pope sent letters to the Duke and the Scottish Queen, that he liked well of their enterprise. Would Rudolph have gone to the Pope and procured letters if he had not had instructions accordingly? The Duke himself hath confessed such a letter."—*Duke.* "Barker indeed brought me about six or seven lines written in a Roman hand in Latin, beginning thus, *Dilecte fili, salutem.* I asked what it was? Barker told me it was a letter from the Pope to me, wherewith I was offended, and said, 'A letter to me from the Pope! How cometh this to pass?' Barker excused it, and said that Rodolph had procured it for his own credit."—*Solic.* "The Duke received it and read it, and said, Rodolph hath been at Rome: I perceive there is nothing to be done this year. By this it appeareth that he reproved not Barker for bringing it unto him." Mr. Solicitor having proved his position according to the law and logic then prevailing, thus concluded: "I have also, my Lords, one thing more to say to you from the Queen's Majesty's own mouth. The Lords that be here of the Privy Council do know it very well,—not meet here in open presence to be uttered, because it toucheth others that are not here now to be named but by her Highnesse's order. We pray that your Lordships will impart it unto you more particularly. In Flanders, by the ambassador of a foreign Prince there, the whole plot of this treason was discovered, and by a servant of his brought to her Majesty's intelligence; the minister not meaning to conceal so foul and dishonorable a practice, gave intelligence hither by letters, and hath therein disclosed the whole treason in such form as hath here been proved unto you: whereupon I refer the more particular declaration thereof to the Peers of the Privy Council."

So a capital charge was to be made out by the parol statement, in the absence of the accused, of the Queen's ministers (who had advised the prosecution) of the contents of a dispatch from a foreign minister, giving an account of something he had heard from others abroad respecting a plot to be carried into effect in England;—but no doubt could be entertained either as to the admissiblity or conclusiveness of this evidence, for it was produced by an express order from the Queen's Majesty's own mouth.

After a speech from Wilbraham, the Attorney of the Court of Wards, said to have been the most eloquent that had then ever been heard at the English bar, and some more copies of letters, confessions, and examinations,—without any witness being called, the case for the Crown was closed. The prisoner had asked for the assistance of counsel; but the Chief Justice declared the unanimous opinion of the Judges, that to allow counsel against the Queen was contrary to all precedent and all reason.[1] He was asked whether he had aught else to say? He answered, "he trusted to God and truth." He was then removed, and the Lord High Steward summed up the case to the Lords Triers, and willed them to go together. They withdrew from Westminster Hall into the Court of Chancery, and after a consultation of an hour and a quarter returned with an unanimous verdict of *Guilty*. On the prayer of the Queen's Sergeant, the frightful sentence in cases of high treason was pronounced on the undaunted Norfolk.[2] But this conviction, even in that age, caused such dissatisfaction, that the government did not venture to carry it into execution for several months; nor until the public mind had been alarmed by reports of an insurrection to rescue him from the Tower, and to dethrone the Queen.[3]

Mary was thrown into the deepest grief by the fate of Norfolk. If his manly beauty and elegant accomplish-

[1] Before they are heavily censured for the horror with which they viewed such a proposal, let it be remembered that the bill to allow prisoners the assistance of counsel in cases of felony was strongly condemned by all the Judges of England, except one, in the reign of King William IV.

[2] 1 St. Tr. 978.

[3] I ought not to have any bias in favor of the Duke of Norfolk, for he seems to have thought that all my countrymen were without honor or veracity, and he was ready, in a very peremptory manner, to avow this sentiment. The written examination of Lesley, Bishop of Ross, being given in evidence against him, he considered that it required no other answer than this:—*Duke.* "He is a Scot." The reply was, "A Scot is a Christian;" * but this did not at all satisfy the Duke.

[1] St. Tr. 978.

ments had not made an impression upon her heart, at any rate she was touched by his devoted services, and she considered him a martyr in her cause. It was hoped that while she was in this state of mind she might be induced to make concessions which she had hitherto haughtily refused. Accordingly, Bromley, the Solicitor General, attended by several others, was sent to negotiate with her.

Being admitted by her to an audience, he enumerated the injuries of which the English government complained, —her assuming the arms of England,—her refusing to ratify the treaty of peace between England and Scotland, —her plan of marrying without the Queen's consent,— her stirring up sedition at home,—her attempt to engage the King of Spain in an invasion of England, and her procuring the Pope's bull for the excommunication of Elizabeth. The object was, that she should formally resign the crown of Scotland, and transfer to her son all her rights both in Scotland and in England; after which she could no longer have been considered a rival, and the hopes of the Catholics, from having the presumptive heir to the Crown of their religion, would have been extinguished.

But all Bromley's eloquence and ingenuity were wasted upon her. She either denied the grievances of which the English Queen complained, or threw the blame of them upon others; she said she never would do any thing to hazard the independence of Scotland, or bring dishonor on her race, or compromise the interests of her religion; and she expressed a fixed purpose,—sacrificing none of her rights,—to live and to die a Queen. She again earnestly renewed her supplication that she might be admitted to the presence of Elizabeth, so that all doubts might be cleared up, and lasting harmony might be established between them.[1]

When Bromley reported this answer, instead of the proposed meeting being granted, her existence was considered inconsistent with the public safety, and a determination was formed to bring her to the scaffold. But this could only be carried into effect by great caution, and by waiting for, or contriving, or hastening events, which should soften the atrocity of such an outrage in the eyes of mankind.

[1] Camden, p. 440. Strype, vol. ii. p. 40, 51.

In the meanwhile Bromley performed the routine duties of his office of Solicitor General in a very satisfactory manner, and he was consulted by the Council in matters of a political nature, rather than Sir Gilbert Gerrard, the Attorney General. Of him they were heartily tired, but they did not know how to dispose of him, for he would not give up his lucrative place to be made a puisne Judge, and his long services and respectable character forbade his uncermonious dismissal.

Things proceeded on this footing till the death of Lord Keeper Bacon, when, after the hesitation and struggle I have described, Bromley was put over the head of Gerrard and made Lord Chancellor.

Queen Elizabeth, when she delivered the Great Seal to him, addressed him in a set speech complimenting him on his good qualities, and giving him much wholesome advice as to the manner in which he ought to perform the duties of his new office. He thus replied:

"I do most humblie thanke your Ma^{ie} for this so greate and singuler good opynion which your Highnes hath conceived of me as to thinke me fyt for this greate service and credit under your Ma^{ie}, and I am very sory there is not in me such sufficiency as might satisfie and answere this your Ma^{ies} good opynion. If I had all the wisdome, and all the learninge, and all other good qualities and virtues that God hath given to all men livinge, I should thinke them too fewe and to small to be imploied in your Highnes' service. But when I consider my selfe and fynde my greate wantes and lackes to do your Ma^{ie} such service as appertayneth, I am driven most humbly to beseech your Ma^{ie} to tollerate with me my many and sondry defectes and ymperfections. To this humble petition I am the more forced for two other causes: the first is the greate learninge, wisdome, and judgmente that resteth in your Ma^{ie}, to whome my ignoraunce and rudeness will easily appere: the seconde is, that yf your Highnes shall ympose this greate charge upon me, I shall succede one in whom all good qualities did abounde fyt for the due execution of your Ma^{ies} service in that place, wherby my want and insufficiency shalbe made more manifest. Yet nevertheles, trustinge in the assistaunce of Almightie God, and in the noblenes and bounty of your Ma^{ies} nature, I do, as my duty bindeth me, humblye submyt my selfe to be disposed of as shall stande with your Ma^ies good pleasure. Concerning these good preceptes and admonitions which it hath pleased your Highnes very prudentlie to give unto me, I shall pray ernestlie to Almightie God to give me his grace that I may follow the same, and do my best and uttermost endevor effectually to performe them."[1]

Lord Chancellor Bromley, as an Equity Judge, followed in the footsteps of Lord Keeper Bacon, and gave almost as great satisfaction. Although he had previously practiced principally in the Court of Queen's Bench,—from the time when he was made Solicitor General he had been engaged in all the important cases which occurred in Chancery, and he was well acquainted with the practice of the Court, which had now assumed considerable regularity. The common-law Judges at this time were very distinguished men,—Wray, Anderson, Manwood, Gawdey, Windham, Periam. The Chancellor showed much deference for their opinion, without hesitating to interfere by injunction where he thought that, from the defective or too rigid rules of the common law, justice was likely to be perverted. He professed to hold jurisdiction over "covin, accident, and breach of confidence," according to the rule that "matters cognizable by the common law ought not to be decided in Chancery,"—but by "cognizable" by the common law, he understood where by the common-law

[1] "Egerton Papers," published by Camden Society, p. 82. It is there supposed that Bromley was first made Lord Keeper and afterwards Lord Chancellor, and a speech is given supposed to be spoken by him on the former occasion ; but the Close Roll demonstrates that he was constituted Lord Chancellor when the Great Seal was first delivered to him, and the first speech can only be a MS. sketch with which he was dissatisfied.

The Close Roll takes no notice of these speeches, but describes the melodramatic part of the ceremony with great minuteness. "Quod antedictum Mag. Sig. in binas separatim partes dicta Dna Regina unam in sua manu propria sublimitas tenuit partem et prdus Comes Sussex alteram sua partem tenuit manu Et cum prda Dna Regina in eam paulisper contemplata esset prdm sigillum precepit conjungi et in prdo loculo in coreo insigillat. locari et extempore reponi in sacculum prdum ex purpureo veluto factum et tunc prdm in manu sua propria respiciens sacculum ac ibidem in manibus suis aliquantisper retinens, illud et Mag. Sig. prdm in nobilium et egregiorum virorum Edwardi Comitis Lincoln," &c. "presencia prfto honorabili viro Thome Bromley militi tradidit et deliberavit," &c. Then follows the usual language, that he was constituted Chancellor with all the powers exercised by his predecessors, and that he, gratefully accepting the Seal, carried it off and still retains it.—Rot. Cl. 21 Eliz. See Cary's *Reports*, p. 108.

process truth could be effectually discovered, and right done to all parties interested.[1] He was likewise in the habit of calling in the assistance of common-law Judges when questions of novelty and difficulty arose before him; and in this way the indecent contests which agitated the opposite sides of Westminster Hall in the succeeding reign were avoided.

Bromley is not celebrated as a great jurist, or as being one of those who laid the foundation of our system of Equity; but while he held the Great Seal I find no trace of any complaint against him as a Judge, either on the ground of corruption, or usurpation, or delay; and we may be sure if there had been abuse there would not have been silence, from the shout of discontent set up when a mere courtier was appointed to succeed him. Camden describes him as "Vir jurisprudentia insignis;" and it was said of him that "such was his learning and integrity, that although he succeeded so popular a Judge as Sir Nicholas Bacon, the bar and the public were not sensible of any considerable change."

He had to take his place on the woolsack in the House of Lords on the 16th of January, 1582. The Commons, in great perplexity on account of the death of their Speaker during the recess, sent a deputation to the Lord Chancellor and the Lords to request their aid and advice. The Lord Chancellor, having ordered them to withdraw, informed the House of their petition, and it was resolved to appoint such of the Lords as were of the Privy Council to go along with a select number of the Commons to represent the case to the Queen. A commission thereupon passed the Great Seal authorizing the Chancellor to require the Commons to choose a new Speaker. Popham, the Queen's Solicitor General, was chosen accordingly and approved of. But when he claimed the accustomed privileges of the House, the Chancellor, by the Queen's order, gave him this admonition: "That the House of Commons should not deal or intermeddle with any matters touching her Majesty's person or estate, or Church government."[2]

This injunction was not very strictly observed, especially by the Puritans, who now began to be very troublesome. Therefore, as soon as a subsidy had been voted, the

[1] See 4 Inst. 83, 84.   [2] 1 Parl. Hist. 811.

session was closed, and the Lord Chancellor in his speech took care to exclude from the Queen's thanks " such members of the Commons as had dealt more rashly in some things than was fit for them to do." He soon afterwards dissolved this parliament, which had been continued by prorogations during a period of eleven years.[1]

It is remarkable how few instances of poisoning or assassination occur in the history of England compared with that of France or the States of Italy. The reason may be, that with us a parliament was a more ready and convenient instrument of vengeance than the bowl or the dagger, and the object of the ruling party could always be attained under the forms of law. The captive Queen of Scots, the presumptive heir to the Crown of England, had not only rendered herself odious and dangerous to Elizabeth, but the English ministers who had concurred in all the rigorous measures against her were alarmed by the apprehension that, in case of any accident happening to the reigning Sovereign, she whom they had persecuted might at once be taken from a prison and placed on the throne, the arbitress of their destiny. Leicester repeatedly recommended that she should be taken off by poison, and, with all his profligacy, pretending a great regard for religion, defended the lawfulness of this expedient. The wary Burghley, consulting with the Chancellor, thought it would be much better to proceed by act of parliament and a mock court of justice ;—" thus they would make the burden better borne, and the world abrod better satisfyeed."[2] Accordingly, summonses were issued for a parliament to meet on the 23rd of November, 1585.

Lord Chancellor Bromley opened the session with a speech stating that parliament was called to consider of a new law, which had become necessary for the protection of her Majesty's person against the machinations of her enemies, and for securing the peace of the realm.[3]

It was resolved that Mary should be brought to trial, but a great difficulty arose as to the tribunal before which she should be tried. The House of Peers, or a Lord High Steward's Court consisting of a selection of Peers, would have been very convenient; but although of the blood royal of England, she was not an English peeress.

[1] 1 Parl. Hist. 821. [2] Ellis, iii. 5. [3] 1 Parl. Hist. 821.

A packed jury might easily have been impanneled to convict her; but foreign powers would have exclaimed against a Sovereign Princess being condemned as if she were a common felon. Therefore, a bill was immediately introduced, which speedily passed both Houses, enacting that a Court should be established, consisting of twenty-four at the least, whereof part should be of the Queen's Privy Council, and the rest Peers of the realm, to examine the offenses of such as should make any open invasion or rebellion within the kingdom, or attempt hurt to the Queen's person, or any like offense, by or for any pretending title to the Crown, and that any such offender being convicted shall be disabled to have or pretend title to the Crown, and shall be pursued to death by all the Queen's subjects.[1]

Elizabeth was so much pleased to find her victim now at her mercy, that she would not trust the Lord Chancellor to return thanks, but herself said,—" My Lords, and ye of the Lower House, my silence must not injure the owner so much as to suppose a substitute sufficient to render you the thanks that my heart yieldeth you, not so much for the safe keeping of my life, for which your care appears so manifest, as for the neglecting your private future peril, not regarding other way than my present state. No prince herein, I confess, can be surer tied or faster bound than I am with the link of your good will, and can for that but yield a heart and a head to seek for ever all your best."[2]

The Lord Chancellor now took an active part in the examination and prosecution of Babington and his associates,[3] whose conspiracy had been under the superintendence of the Cabinet, and they being justly convicted and executed, the time had arrived when proceedings might be taken against Mary herself, who was well aware of the plan to liberate her from imprisonment, but (as I firmly believe) by no means of the intention to assassinate Elizabeth. A commission passed the Great Seal, appointing the Chancellor and forty-five others, Peers, Privy Councillors, and Judges, " a Court to inquire into and determine all offenses committed against the recent statute either by Mary, daughter and heiress of James V., late King of Scotland, or by any other person whatsoever."[4]

[1] 27 Eliz. c. 1.   [2] 1 Parl. Hist. 822.   [3] Ellis, iii. 5.   [4] Camden, 456.

Mary had been removed to Fotheringay, in Northamptonshire, the place selected for her trial and death. On the 11th of October, thirty-six of the Commissioners, headed by Bromley, arrived there, and took the command of the Castle from Sir Amias Paulet, who for some time had acted as her jailer. The next day a letter from Elizabeth was delivered to her by a notary, announcing to her that she was to be tried. She said, "Let it be remembered that I am also a Queen, and not amenable to any foreign jurisdiction;" and she referred to the protest she had before made to Sir Thomas Bromley when Solicitor General. Lord President Bromley was much perplexed; for if she had refused to plead before the Commissioners,—although they might have passed sentence upon her as contumacious, the proceeding would have lost all its dignity and effect. He prevailed upon her to meet him and a deputation of the Commissioners in a preliminary interview in the hall of the Castle to discuss the question of jurisdiction. He then pointed out to her that the commission under which they acted was fully authorized by the statute 27 Elizabeth. She maintained that this statute did not bind her; that she was no party to it; that it was contrived by her enemies, and passed for her ruin; and that, as an independent Sovereign, she was not subject to English law. Bromley read to her a passage in Elizabeth's letter, explaining that, "as she lived under the protection of the Queen of England she was bound to respect the law of England." She eagerly and repeatedly asked him what was the meaning of that part of Elizabeth's letter, and whether she was to be considered as *protected* when she was detained in England against her will, and kept in a state of rigorous imprisonment? The Lord President could only give her an evasive answer, saying that "the meaning was obvious enough, and that it was not for him to interpret the letter of his Sovereign, nor had he come there for that purpose." She said that his Sovereign was her equal, not her superior, and that she could not be lawfully tried till they found persons who were her peers. The baffled President urged that "neither her imprisonment nor her prerogative of Royal Majesty could exempt her from answering in this kingdom; with fair words advising her to hear what matters were to be objected against her; otherwise he threatened that by authority of law they both could and would proceed against her, though she were absent." She still answered, that "she was no subject, and rather would she die a thousand deaths than acknowledge herself a subject; nevertheless she was ready to answer to all things in a free and full parliament. She warned them to look to their consciences, and to remember that the theater of the whole world is much wider than the kingdom of England." The wily lawyer asked her "whether she would answer if her protestation were admitted." "I will never," said she, "submit myself to the late law mentioned in the Commission."

Sir Christopher Hatton, one of the deputation, though then a gay young courtier, thought he might succeed better than the grave old Chancellor with all his saws, and begged her Majesty to call to mind that if she refused to plead, the world might put an unfavorable construction upon her conduct,—whereas, her reputation, to the general joy, might now be cleared from all suspicion. But no reasoning of the lawyers, no threat of proceeding against her for contumacy, not even the imputation cast upon her fame, could at that moment shake her resolution. The last consideration, however, so artfully thrown out by Sir Christopher Hatton, on reflection distressed her, and receiving a second letter from Elizabeth saying,—"Act candidly and you may meet with more favor," she sent a message to Lord Chancellor Bromley that "she was willing to vindicate her innocence before the Commissioners,"—and, their jurisdiction being acknowledged, the trial proceeded in due form.

The Court assembled the next day in the Presence Chamber, the Lord Chancellor, as President, being seated on the right hand of a vacant throne, erected under a canopy of estate in honor of Elizabeth, and the other Commissioners on benches at the walls on both sides. The counsel for the Crown were stationed at a table at the lower end, opposite the throne. The Queen of Scots entered and occupied a chair placed for her near the middle of the room.

Silence being proclaimed, the Lord President, turning to her, thus spoke; "The most high and mighty Queen Elizabeth being, not without great grief of mind, advertised that you have conspired the destruction of her and of

England, and the subversion of religion, hath, out of her office and duty, lest she might seem to have neglected God, herself, and her people, and out of no malice at all, appointed these Commissioners to hear the matters that shall be objected unto you, and how you can clear yourself of them and make known your innocency."

Mary, rising up, said that "she came into England to crave aid which had been promised her, and yet was she detained ever since in prison. She protested that she was no subject of Elizabeth, but had been and was a free and absolute Queen, and not to be constrained to appear before the Commissioners or any other Judge whatsoever, for any cause whatsoever, save before God alone, the highest Judge, lest she should prejudice her own royal majesty, the King of Scots her son, her successors, or other absolute princes. But so protesting she now appeared personally to the end to refute the crimes objected against her."

The Lord President answered, "that this protestation was in vain, for that whosoever, of what place or degree soever, should offend against the laws of England, in England, was subject to the laws of England, and by the late act might be examined and tried; the said protestation, therefore, so made in prejudice of the laws and Queen of England, was not to be admitted."

She was about to withdraw, when, to secure the great advantage they had gained by inducing her to plead, the Court ordered as well her protestation as the Lord President's answer to be recorded.

Gawdey, the Queen's Sergeant, then opened the case against her, and adduced his proofs, consisting of copies of letters in cipher between her and Babington, and the alleged confessions and examinations of her secretaries, Nau and Curle, and the confessions of Babington, and Ballard, his associate. She asked that an advocate might be assigned to her to plead her cause, and this prayer being refused, she defended herself with great spirit and presence of mind.

Without formally admitting, she did not struggle against the charge of being privy to the plan for procuring her enlargment, and she contended that even consenting to a foreign invasion for this purpose would not subject her to the pains of treason. All complicity in the plot to assassinate Elizabeth she most solemnly, and earnestly, and with many tears, denied. This charge, resting entirely on certain expressions in the copy of a letter she was supposed to have written in cipher to Babington, and on the private depositions of her secretaries,—she said her letter had been interpolated, and dared them to produce the original,—she urged that if her secretaries had so deposed, it was from compulsion and to save their own lives,—and she repeatedly required that they should be produced as witnesses, so that she might be confronted with them.

Burghley, that he might not appear too conspicuous, had put forward the Chancellor and others as his puppets to move as he guided them, but he was in truth both the adviser and the conductor of the prosecution. Now becoming alarmed lest she should make an impression on some of her Judges, he superseded the Chancellor as well as Gawdey and the Attorney and Solicitor General, and himself undertook to answer her,—attempting to show the regularity of the proceedings, and the sufficiency of the proof against her. Still, not entirely trusting to his artful pleading, he did not venture to call for the verdict in her presence at Fotheringay, and at the end of the second day of the trial, the Court was adjourned to the 25th of October, in the Star Chamber at Westminster.[1]

Then and there, the Chancellor having taken his place as President, Nau and Curle were produced and examined, while the accused was immured in a distant prison, and the Commissioners all agreed in a general verdict of *guilty* against her, with the exception of Lord Zouch, who was for acquitting her on the charge of assassination.[2]

But Elizabeth, though she had resolved that the sentence should be carried into execution, had to prepare the nation for this appalling step, and a few days afterwards parliament assembled. Thinking it not decent to appear in person, she was represented on the first day of the session by the Archbishop of Canterbury, Burghley, and the Earl of Derby. The letters patent appointing them being being read, they left their places, and went to a seat prepared for them on the right side of the throne; and then

---

[1] In the reign of George III. it was justly thought unconstitutional and improper that the Lord Chief Justice of the King's Bench should be a member of the Cabinet, lest he should sit as judge on the trial of a prosecution which, as minister, he had concurred in instituting. Upon the success of this prosecution depended all that Burghley held most valuable in the world, and he was at once judge, jury, and prosecutor.   [2] 1 St. Tr. 1161.

the Lord Chancellor Bromley, after going first to them and conferring with them, addressed the two Houses from his accustomed place to the following effect:—

"That the present parliament was summoned for no usual causes; not for making new laws, whereof her Majesty thought there were more made than executed; nor for subsidies with which, although there was some occasion for them, her Majesty would not burden her faithful subjects at this time, but the cause was rare and extraordinary; of great weight, great peril, and dangerous consequence. He next declared what plots had been contrived of late, and how miraculously the merciful providence of God, by the discovery thereof, beyond all human policy, had preserved her Majesty, the destruction of whose sacred person was most traitorously imagined, and designed to be compassed. He then showed what misery the loss of so noble a Queen would have brought to all estates; that, although some of these traitors had suffered according to their demerits, yet one remained, that, by due course of law, had received her sentence, which was the chief cause of this assembly and wherein her Majesty required their faithful advice." [1]

After the election and confirmation of the Speaker, the Lord Chancellor made another speech to the Lords, "setting forth the foul and indiscreet dealings practiced by the Queen of Scots against her Majesty and the whole realm, notwithstanding the many great benefits and favors which had been bestowed upon her since her arrival in this kingdom." This performance, however, was not at all satisfactory; and the prime minister himself standing up, said: "The whole proceedings of the said Queen of Scots were better known to him from his having had the honor to serve her Majesty from the commencement of her reign;" and he showed, at great length, the justice of the prosecution, and the necessity for carrying the sentence into effect. No one ventured to say a word for the condemned criminal, or even to hint that she had not had a fair trial.

Both Houses agreed upon an address to the Queen, which was delivered by the Lord Chancellor, urging that the sentence against the Queen of Scots might be immediately carried into execution; "because, upon advised

[1] 1 Parl. Hist. 334.

and grave consultation, we can not find that there is any possible means to provide for your Majesty's safety, but by the just and speedy death of the said Queen, the neglecting whereof may procure the heavy displeasure and punishment of Almighty God, as by sundry severe examples of his great justice in that behalf, left us in the sacred Scriptures, doth appear: and if the same be not put in present execution, we, your most loving and dutiful subjects, shall thereby (so far as man's reason can reach) be brought into utter despair of the continuance amongst us of the true religion of Almighty God, and of your Majesty's life, and of the safety of all your subjects, and the good estate of this most flourishing commonwealth."

Elizabeth, in her answer, in justifying the recent statute, and the trial under it, fell foul of the poor Lord Chancellor and the gentlemen of the long robe:—"You lawyers are so curious in scanning the nice points of the law, and proceeding according to forms rather than expounding and interpreting the laws themselves, that if your way were observed, she must have been indicted in Staffordshire, and have holden up her hand at the bar, and have been tried by a jury of twelve men. A proper way, forsooth, of trying a Princess! To avoid, therefore, such absurdities, I thought it better to refer the examination of so weighty a cause to a select number of the noblest personages of the land, and the most learned of my Judges." However, she would not yet give a decisive answer as to the execution of the sentence; but concluded with a prayer to Almighty God, so to illuminate and direct her heart, that she might see clearly what might be best for the good of his Church, and the prosperity of the commonwealth.[1]

This irresolution was affected, in the hope that Mary might be removed by a natural death, or some other means, so as to avoid the odium to be incurred by beheading upon the scaffold a Queen, her guest, her nearest relative, and the heir presumptive to the throne; but she at last signed the warrant for Mary's execution, directed to the Earl of Shrewsbury, as Earl Marshal, and ordered it to be carried to the Great Seal by Davison, her secretary. The Chancellor immediately appended the Great Seal to it; and having informed Burghley that the instrument was now perfect, a Council was called, and they

[1] 1 Parl. Hist. 842.

unanimously resolved that it should be sent off immediately, on the ostensible ground that the Queen had done all the law required on her part, and that to trouble her further was needless, and would be offensive to her feelings. Bromley, being at the head of the administration of justice, incurred the greatest responsibility in taking this step; but he considered himself safe in co-operating with Burghley, who had before settled with Elizabeth that Davison should be the scape-goat.

In two days the warrant was executed, and Mary Stuart, in the last scene of her life, displayed such fortitude, composure, dignity, tenderness, kindness of heart, resignation, and piety, as to throw a shade over the errors she had committed, and to make us disposed to regard her as one less criminal than unfortunate, and more to be pitied than condemned.[1]

Bromley, who presided at her trial, was soon to present himself with her at the bar of that great Judge to whom all secrets are known. He had suffered much anxiety while the prosecution was going on; he was deeply affected when he heard of the catastrophe; and he felt dreadful alarm when he found that the Queen affected indignation and resentment against all who were concerned in it. Suddenly he took to his bed, and parliament meeting by adjournment on the 15th of February, no business could be done on that or the following day on

[1] I am far from being her indiscriminate defender, and I am sorry to acknowledge that the proofs of her being privy to the murder of Darnley are quite overwhelming. Yet her death was not creditable to the English nation. It was a national act. When the judgment of the Commissioners was proclaimed in London by sound of trumpet, the bells told merry peals for twenty-four hours, bonfires blazed in the streets, and the citizens appeared intoxicated with joy, as if a great victory had been obtained over a foreign enemy. These rejoicings were redoubled on the news of her execution. "La nouvelle de cette exécution vint à Londres; furent sonnés les cloches de toutes les églises vingt-quatre heures durant, et sur le soir furent faites feux dejoie par les rues de la vile."—*Bellievre's Despatch.* The sentiments of the upper classes may be learned from the unanimous petition of the two Houses of parliament that the judgment might be immediately carried into execution. —The national character of Scotland was tarnished by the Scottish army delivering up her grandson, on condition that their arrears of pay were discharged; but this was the sordid act of a few leaders,—of which all Scotsmen have since been ashamed,—while the murder of Mary for political expediency has still defenders in England. If I am accused of national prejudice in my strictures on the execution of Mary, Queen of Scots, I will cite the words of Clarendon, a true Englishman, who describes it as a great blemish on Elizabeth's reign, and as "an unparalleled act of blood upon the life of a crowned neighbor, queen, and ally."

account of his sickness, for which no provision had been made. On the 17th, Sir Edmund Anderson, Chief Justice of the Common Pleas, read publicly, in the House of Lords, a commission from the Queen, directed to himself, by which he was authorized, in the absence of the Chancellor, to act in his stead; and on the 23rd of March, by reason of the continued sickness of the Chancellor, the deputy closed the session and dissolved the parliament.[1]

Bromley never rallied, and on the 12th of April following he expired, in the fifty-eighth year of his age. The Close Roll is quite pathetic in giving an account of the transmission of the Great Seal to the Queen on his demise. After stating that he breathed his last at three o'clock in the morning, and that the Queen, being informed of this event, ordered John Fortescue, Master of her Wardrobe, to go and fetch her the Great Seal, observes, that he proceeded to the house of the late Chancellor, and entering it between seven and eight o'clock, found a large number of distinguished persons bewailing the loss of so great a man.[2]

From incidental notices of him by his immediate contemporaries, he appears to have enjoyed considerable reputation in his own time, but afterwards he rather slipped from the recollection of mankind. He had not the good fortune to have his life written by a secretary or relative, and not being a leader of any great political or religious party, he did not gain posthumous fame by being praised like Cranmer, or abused like Gardyner. He was too ready in seconding the measures of Burghley to get rid of a Popish successor to the Crown, who had such reason to be hostile to the ministers of Elizabeth, but he

---

[1] 1 Parl. Hist. 853.

[2] "Eodem die inter horas septimam et octavam ante meridiem ejusdem diei idem Iohannes Fortescue ad domum dicti nuper Cancellarii veniens ac in diversorum generosorum mortem dicti nobilis viri plagentium presencia," &c. It then goes on to narrate how the Great Seal in its leather and velvet bags under three private seals was found locked up in a chest, was delivered to Fortescue, the Queen's messenger, by Henry Bromley, the eldest son of the Chancellor, and how Fortescue arriving with it at the Court at Greenwich, waited with it in the Queen's outer chamber, where he remained for a little time, till her Majesty coming from her inner chamber where she had slept, received it from his hands, and retained it in her own custody. "Idem Iohannes Fortescue exteriorem privatam cameram dicte Dne Regine cum predicto sigillo solus intravit ac ibidem paulisper moram faciens dicta sacra Majestas Regina ab interiore privata camera ubi requiescebat veniens.' &c.—Rot. Cl. 23 Eliz.

does not seem liable to any other censure; and as an Equity Judge he was regretted till the very conclusion of this reign, when Lord Ellesmere was placed in the marble chair, and so much adorned it. On one occasion he very creditably maintained the independence of his office. Having refused, at the solicitation of Knyvet, a groom of the privy chamber, who had slain a man of the Earl of Oxford's in a brawl, to issue a special commission for his trial, Sir Christopher Hatton, in the Queen's name, sent him an order to do so. But he still resisted, showing that the interference was unconstitutional, and that thus to grant special commissions to humor the accused would lead to a failure of justice.[1]

It ought likewise to be mentioned to his honor, that in an intolerant age he was free from religious bigotry, and that while Chancellor he exerted himself to soften the execution of the laws against heretics.[2]

He was buried with great pomp in Westminster Abbey, where a magnificent monument was erected to his memory.

By his wife Elizabeth, daughter of Sir Adrian Fortescue, he left several sons; but his male line failed in the fifth generation, when the heiress of the family was married to John Bromley, of Thornheath Hall, in the county of Cambridge; and their son, Henry, having represented that county in several parliaments, was, in 1734, raised to the peerage by King George II., under the title of Baron Montfort,—being ancestor of the present Henry Bromley, Lord Montfort.[3]

[1] See Sir Harris Nicholas's Memoirs of Sir Christopher Hatton, p. 256.

[2] Of this we have a striking proof in a letter, dated July 1, 1582, addressed by him to the Bishop of Chester in favor of a Lady Egerton of Ridley, who had been sued in the Bishop's Court, and was in great danger, of the flames:—

"I have been acquainted with her longe, and have alwaies known her in other respects to be very well given, and in regard thereof do pitie her the more. I would be glade that by gentle meanes and by conference with some grave and learned men, she might be persuaded and wonne (yf it maie be), whereof I have some good hope. I have therefore thought good to recommend her simplicitie to y^r Lordship, and to pray you to use some further tolleration with her until Candlemas next."—Peck's *Desiderata*, vol. i. p. 122.

[3] See Grandeur of Law, ed. 1843, by Mr. Foss. Nash's History of Worcestershire, p. 594, where there is a full pedigree of the Bromleys.

CHAPTER XLV.

LIFE OF SIR CHRISTOPHER HATTON, LORD CHANCELLOR OF ENGLAND.

ON the death of Lord Chancellor Bromley, Queen Elizabeth retained the Great Seal in her own custody above a fortnight, while she deliberated upon the appointment of his successor. During this interval, she thrice delivered it for the sealing of writs, commissions, and letters patent, to Lord Hudson, Burghley, and others; and they having carried it into the Council Chamber, and sealed all the instruments with it which required immediate dispatch, returned it into her Majesty's hands.[1]

There was now much speculation at Court, in Westminster Hall, and in the City of London, as to who should be the new Chancellor. Easter term was going on without any one to preside in the Chancery or in the Star Chamber, or to superintend the administration of justice. Opinions were divided between Sergeant Puckering, the Speaker of the House of Commons, Sir John Popham, the Attorney General, and Sir Thomas Egerton, the Solicitor General. The first was in the direct line of promotion to high legal dignities, and he had given great satisfaction from the manner in which he had managed the House of Commons, in the delicate affair of the Scottish Queen, and in repressing the motions of the Puritans. Popham, afterwards so much distinguished as Chief Justice, had now a high reputation for profound knowledge of the common law, and Egerton had given earnest of that intimate familiarity with the general principles of jurisprudence, which being fully developed when he became Lord Ellesmere, made him be considered as the earliest founder of our system of Equity.[2]

---

[1] Iidem nobiles viri dictum magnum sigillum secum portabant usque in Cameram Consilii ibidem et permittebant sigillari omnes tales litteras patentes commissiones et brevia antedicta et sigillacione finita sigillum predictum in bagam de coreo albo in qua antea includebatur reponi preceperunt et cum sigillis eorum muniri fecerunt et sic sigillum predictum ad presenciam sue Majestatis in baga de velueto rubeo insigniis sue Majestatis decorata tulebant et in manus sue Majestatis redeliberabant.—R. Cl. 29 Eliz.

[2] Camden says there was a speculation likewise at Court that Edward Earl of Rutland, whom he describes as "juris scientiâ et omni politiori eruditione

But what was the astonishment of courtiers, of lawyers, and of citizens, when, on Saturday, the 29th of April, it was announced that her Majesty had chosen for the Keeper of her conscience,—to preside in the Chancery and the Star Chamber, and the House of Lords,—and to superintend the administration of justice throughout the realm,—a gay young cavalier never called to the bar, and chiefly famed for his handsome person, his taste in dress, and his skill in dancing,—SIR CHRISTOPHER HATTON!!!

In the long reign of Elizabeth, no domestic occurrence seems so strange as this appointment;—but, with the exception of her choice of Burghley for her minister, she was much influenced in the selection of persons for high employment by personal favor; and on the same principle that Leicester was sent to command in the Low Countries and Essex in Ireland, Hatton was placed at the head of the magistracy of the realm,—because he was her lover. Burghley had resisted her propensity on this occasion as far as his own safety would permit; but considering that Hatton could never be dangerous to him as a rival for power, and that this freak would only be injurious to the administration of justice, which ministers often sacrifice to political convenience, he yielded, and joined in the effort to give *éclat* to the installation of the new Chancellor.— We must proceed to trace the origin and history of this minion, that we may account for his extraordinary elevation.

He was born in the year 1539, being the third and youngest son of William Hatton, Esq., of Holdenby, in Northamptonshire, a family originally from Cheshire, of considerable antiquity, but very moderate wealth. His father died when he was a child, and he had soon to lament the loss of his two elder brothers, so that when still very young he inherited the small patrimonial estate. Under the care of his mother he imbibed with difficulty, from a domestic tutor, the first rudiments of knowledge. He is said to have been idle and volatile, but to have been remarkable for good humor and vivacity, as well as for comeliness.

At the age of fifteen he was entered a gentleman com-

---

ornatissimus," would be appointed Chancellor had he not suddenly died; but this seems exceedingly improbable, for he could have had no professional experience, and he was not a personal favorite.—Camden, *Hist. El.*, 1475.

moner at St. Mary Hall, Oxford. While at the university, he was exceedingly popular with his companions; but he spent much more time in fencing and archery than in perusing Aristotle and Aquinas, and from the fear of being *plucked*, he left Oxford without trying for a degree.

Being intended for the bar, he was now transferred to the Inner Temple; but it was said, that "he rather took a bait than made a meal at the inns of court, whilst he studied the laws therein."[1] He was, in truth, a noted roisterer and swash buckler, hearing the chimes at midnight, knowing where the *bona robas* were; and sometimes lying all night in the Windmill, in St. George's Fields.[2] but while he spent much of his time in dicing and gallantry, there were two amusements to which he particularly devoted himself, and which laid the foundation of his future fortune. The first was *dancing*, which he studied under the best masters, and in which he excelled beyond any man of his time. The other was *the stage;* he constantly frequented the theaters, which, although Shakespeare was still a boy at Stratford-on-Avon, were beginning to flourish,—and he himself used to assist in writing masques, and he took a part in performing them. We first hear of his being admired as "Master of the Game" in a splendid masque with which the Inner Temple celebrated Christmas, and in which Lord Robert Dudley, afterwards the Earl of Leicester and his rival in love, held the mimic rank of "Constable and Marshal." He was afterwards one of five students of the Inner Temple who wrote a play entitled "Tancred and Gismund," which was acted by that Society before the Queen.[3]

[1] When he became a great man, his flatterers pretended that he never meant to make the law a profession, and that he was sent to an inn of court merely to finish his education in the mixed society of young men of business and pleasure there to be met with; but there can be no doubt that it was intended that he should earn his bread by "a knowledge of good pleading in actions real and personal."

[2] See Justice Shallow's career at the inns of courts, Second Part Henry IV. act iii. sc. 2.

[3] This piece was not printed till 1592. It then came out thus entitled: "The *Tragedie* of TANCRED and GISMUND, compiled by the gentlemen of the *Inner Temple*, and by them presented before her MAJESTIE. Newly revived, and polished according to the decorum of these daies, by R. W." This edition was by Robert Wilmot, who is often called the author of the tragedy, but there is no doubt that the five students contributed each an act. The future Lord Chancellor's contribution was the fourth act, at the end of which there is this notice, "*Composuit Chr. Hatton.*" This edition is so scarce, and

He did not act in this piece himself; but his fashionable accomplishments and agreeable manners introducing

so much valued by book collectors, that a defective copy of it sells for ten guineas. There is one in the British Museum which belonged to Garrick.

The story which has been the subject of so many poems and dramas is taken from the first novel of the fourth day of the Decameron. I am afraid that Hatton could not read Boccaccio in the original, but he might find this fable in "Paynter's Collection," and in an old ballad printed by Wynkin de Worde in 1532.

Sir Christopher's contribution being as yet the only tragic effort of a Lord Chancellor, I will offer the reader as a specimen the fourth scene of the fourth act, between Tancred and Guiozard, after the King has discovered the guilty loves of the Count and Sigismunda.

"*Tancr.* And durst thou, villain, dare to undermine
Our daughter's chamber? Durst thy shameless face
Be bold to kiss her? th' rest we will conceal,
Wherefore content thee that we are resolv'd
That thy just death, with thine effus'd blood,
Shall cool the heat and choler of our mood."

"*Guioz.* My Lord the King, neither do I mislike
Your sentence, nor do your smoking sighs,
Reach'd from the entrails of your boiling heart,
Disturb the quiet of my calmed thoughts.
Such is the force and endless might of love,
As never shall the dread of carrion death,
That hath envy'd our joys, invade my breast,
But unto her my love exceeds compare:
Then this hath been my fault for which I joy,
That in the greatest lust of all my life
I shall submit for her sake to endure
The pangs of death. Oh, mighty lord of love,
Strengthen thy vassal boldly to receive
Large wounds into this body for her sake;
Then use my life or death, my lord and King,
For your relief to ease your grieved soul:
Knowing by death I shall bewray the truth
Of that fond heart, which living was her own,
And died alive for her that lived mine."

"*Tancr.* Thine, Palurin? What! lives my daughter thine?
Traytor, thou wrong'st me, for she liveth mine.
Rather I wish ten thousand sundry deaths
Than I do live and see my daughter thine."

[*The King hasteth into his palace.*]

"*Guioz. (solus).* O thou, great God, who from thy highest throne
Hast stooped down and felt the force of love,
Bend gentle ears unto the woful moan
Of me, poor wretch, to grant that I require;
Help to persuade the same, great God, that he
So far remit his might, and slack his fire
From my dear lady's kindled heart, that she
May hear my death without her hurt. Let not
Her face, wherein there is as clear a light
As in the rising moon, let not her cheeks

him into the best company, he at last had a part assigned him in a masque at court, which gave him a very favorable opportunity to show off his accomplishments.

The tender heart of Elizabeth was at once touched by his athletic frame, manly beauty and graceful air; and she openly expressed her high admiration of his dancing. An offer was instantly made by her to admit him of the band of gentlemen pensioners. He expressed great willingness to renounce all his prospects in the profession of the law, but informed her that he had incurred debts which were beginning to be troublesome to him. She advanced him money to pay them off—at the same time (*more suo*) taking a bond and statute merchant to repay her when he should be of ability. He little thought he should ever hear of these securities, which afterwards were supposed to have contributed to his death;—and before he had even reached the degree of apprentice or utter barrister, he joyfully transferred himself from his dull chambers in the Temple to a gay apartment assigned him in the Palace, near the Queen's. He was at first only a gentleman pensioner, or private in the body-guard,[1] but being henceforth the reigning favorite, his official promotion was rapid. He was successively made a gentleman of the Queen's privy chamber, captain of the band of gentlemen pensioners, Vice Chamberlain, and a member of the Privy Council, at last receiving the honor of knighthood, which was then considered as great a distinction as a peerage is now.[2] He likewise obtained royal grants of

> As red as is the party-color'd rose,
> Be paled with the news hereof: and so
> I yield myself, my silly soul, and all,
> To him, for her for whom my death shall show
> I liv'd; and as I liv'd I dy'd, her thrall."
>
> Act. iv. sc. 4.

There is a chorus somewhat after the Greek fashion, and the tragedy is a curious illustration of the state of the drama in England in the beginning of Elizabeth's reign; although we shall in vain look in it for such felicity of Queen thought and harmony of numbers as in Dryden's exquisite poem of "Sigismonda and Guiscardo."

[1] There is extant a warrant, dated June 30, 1564, from the Queen to the Master of the Armory, commanding him "to cause to be made one armor complete, fit for the body of our well-beloved servant Chiistopher Hatton, one of our gentlemen pensioners, he paying according to the just value thereof."

[2] The Secretary of State and the Treasurer of the Household were knighted along with him by the Queen at Windsor.

houses in London, and of lands in Pembrokeshire, Dorsetshire, Leicestershire and Yorkshire.

This delight of the Queen to honor and enrich him caused much envy and some scandal. Complaints were uttered, that under the existing government nothing could be obtained by any others than "dancers and carpet knights—such as the Earl of Lincoln and Master Hatton, who were admitted to the Queen's privy chamber."[1] Sir John Perrot, a stout soldier, could not conceal his indignation, when he found himself neglected for one who he was used to say "came into court *by the galliard*, coming thither as a private gentleman of the Inns of Court, in a masque, and for his activity and person, which was tall and proportionable, taken into favor."[2] Elizabeth's undisguised partiality for the new favorite naturally excited the jealousy of Leicester, and in ridicule of the accomplishment which had in this instance excited her admiration, he proposed to introduce to her a dancing master who outdid all that had been before seen in this department of genius: but her Majesty, drawing a proper distinction between the skill of a professional artist and of an amateur, exclaimed "Pish! I will not see your man; it is his *trade!*"

The Vice Chamberlain, on account of his dancing propensity, was particularly obnoxious to the Puritans;—and Burchet, a student of the Middle Temple, one of the leaders of this sect, in a fit of religious enthusiasm resolved to kill him, but by mistake murdered, first, in the public street, Hawkins, an officer, and then Longworth, the keeper of a house in which he was confined.[3]

But Hatton, though so lightly esteemeed by the multitude, began to feel the stings of ambition as well as love; and in spite of his want of book-learning, from his natural shrewdness and mother wit, he had considerable aptitude for business. He was returned to parliament for Higham Ferrars, and with a little practice in speaking, he became a popular and useful debater. Such a position did he acquire that on Cecil's elevation to the peerage, having become member for Northamptonshire, his native county,

---

[1] Murdin, 124–210. Camden, 254.   [2] Naunton.
[3] The unhappy man was evidently insane, but in those days they did not stand on such a nicety as criminal responsibility. He was convicted and executed. Camden, 284.

he was the organ of the government in the Lower House, and with the assistance of the Speaker managed it according to the Queen's directions. When Wentworth the Puritan made his famous speech, which gave such offense to the courtiers, Hatton moved his commitment to the Tower, and afterwards brought down the message from her Majesty, that "whereas a member had uttered divers offensive matters against her for which he had been imprisoned, yet she was pleased to remit her justly occasioned displeasure, and to refer his enlargement to the house;"—whereupon, after an admonition from the Speaker, he was set at liberty.[1]

Our senator, however, continued sedulously to practice the arts by which he first established himself in the royal favor. At court balls he danced with the same spirit as ever, and he particularly distinguished himself as one of the challengers in "a solemn tournay and barriers" before the Queen at Westminster—his colleagues being the Earl of Oxford, Mr. Charles Howard, and Sir Henry Lee, "who did very valiantly."[2] Yearly he presented the Queen with a new-year's gift, such as "a jewel of pizands of gold adorned with rubies and diamonds and flowers set with rubies, with one pearl pendent and another at the top."[3] In return he received a present of silver-gilt plate; and it is remarkable that while the portion of other courtiers never exceeded two hundred ounces, and was seldom more than fifty, his never fell short of four hundred.[4]

These marks of fondness gave rise to malicious whispers about the Court; and among the vulgar the Queen was openly charged with lavishing her favors on the Vice Chamberlain.

One Mather made a traitorous speech before a large assembly of people, in which he said, "The Queen desireth nothing but to feed her own lewd fantasy, and to cut off

---

[1] 1 Parl. Hist. 802.
[2] Nichol's Progresses of Queen Elizabeth. There is a particular description of this passage of arms in the Dispatches of *De la Mothe Fénelon*, the French ambassador at the Court of Elizabeth, lately published by the French Government, under the direction of my friend Mr. Charles Purton Cooper. He says that the combatants fought "à la pique et à l'épée à la barrière." "Le Compte d'Oxford avoit dressé la partie, lequel, avec Sire Charles Havart, Sire Henry Lay, et M. HATTON, ont été les quatre tenans contre aultres vingt sept gentishommes, de bonne mayson, assaillans, et n'y est advenu nul inconvenient."—*Note to 4th Edition.*
[3] New Year's Day, 1572.
[4] See lists of royal presents, Nichol's Progresses, vols. ii. and iii.

such of her nobility as are not perfumed and court-like to
please her delicate eye, and to place such as are for her
turn,—*dancers*, who have more recourse unto her Majesty
in her privy chamber than reason would suffer if she were
so virtuous and well inclined as some noise her."[1] In a
letter written soon after by Archbishop Parker to Burghley,
he gives information that a man examined by the Mayor
of Dover and another magistrate, " uttered most shameful
words against the Queen's Majesty, namely, that the Earl
of Leicester and Mr. Hatton should be such towards her
as the matter is so horrible that they would not write
down the words, but would have uttered them in speech
to your Lordship if ye could have been at leisure."[2]

Hatton, who for a time had triumphed over Leicester,
being himself neglected for eccentric, but young, handsome, and accomplished Earl of Oxford, was thrown into
a state of deep despondency, and imparted to his bosom
friend, Mr. Edward Dyer, a resolution he had formed to
reproach Elizabeth for her inconstancy. He received a
very long letter in answer, containing the following sage
reflections and advice:—

" One that standeth by shall see more in the game than
one that is much more skillful, whose mind is too earnestly
occupied. First of all you must consider with whom you
have to deal, and what we be towards her; who, though
she do descend very much in her sex as a woman, yet we
may not forget her place, and the nature of it as our
Sovereign. Now if a man, of secret cause known to himself, might in common reason challenge it, yet if the
Queen mislike thereof, the world followeth the sway of
her inclination; and never fall they in consideration of
reason, as between private persons they do. And if it be
after that rate for the most part in causes that may be
justified, then much more will it be so in causes not to be
avouched. A thing to be had in regard; for it is not
good for any man straitly to weigh a general disallow-
ance of her doings. That the Queen will mislike of such
a course, this is my reason: she will imagine that you go
about to imprison her fancy, and to warp her grace within
your disposition; and that will breed despite and hatred
in her towards you: and so you may be cast forth to the
malice of every envious person, flatterer, and enemy of

---

[1] Murdin, p. 204.   [2] Strype's Life of Archbishop Parker, ii. 127.

yours; out of which you shall never recover yourself clearly, neither your friends, so long as they show themselves your friends. But the best and soundest way in mine opinion is, to put on another mind; to use your suits towards her Majesty in words, behavior, and deeds; to acknowledge your duty, declaring the reverence which in heart you bear, and never seem deeply to condemn her frailties, but rather joyfully to condemn such things as should be in her, as though they were in her indeed; hating my Lord of Ctm,[1] in the Queen's understanding for affection's sake, and blaming him openly for seeking the Queen's favor. For though in the beginning when her Majesty sought you (after her good manner), she did bear with rugged dealing of yours until she had what she fancied, yet now, after satiety and fulness, it will rather hurt than help you; whereas, behaving yourself, as I said before, your place shall keep you in worship, your presence in favor, your followers will stand to you, at the least you shall have no bold enemies, and you shall dwell in the ways to take all advantages wisely, and honestly to serve your turn at times.

"You may perchance be advised and encouraged to the other way by some kind of friends that will be glad to see whether the Queen will make an apple or a crab of you, which, as they find, will deal accordingly with you; following, if fortune be good; if not, leave, and go to your enemy: for such kind of friends have no commodity by hanging in suspense, but set you a fire to do off or on,—all is one to them; rather liking to have you in any extremity than in any good mean."[2]

Hatton accordingly wrote a long and respectful letter to the Queen, in which he does not allude to the new favorite, but supposes that he has fallen into disfavor for imputed faults of his own,—"unthankfulness, covetousness, and ambition." Against these he proceeds to justify himself:—

"To the first, I speak the truth before God, that I have most entirely loved your person and service; to the which without exception, I have everlastingly vowed my whole life, liberty, and fortune. Even so am I yours, as, whatever God and you should have made me, the same had been your own; than which I could, nor any can, make

---

[1] Oxford.   [2] Harleian MSS. 787, fol. 88.

larger recompense. This I supposed to have been the true remuneration of greatest good turns, because I know it balanceth in weight the greatest good wills. Neither hath the ceremony of thanksgiving any way wanted, as the world will right fully witness with me; and therefore in righteousness I most humbly pray you condemn me not. Spare your poor prostrate servant from this pronounced vengeance."

After showing, at great length, that he had "ever found her largess before his lack, in such plenty as he could wish no more," and that he had "never sought place but to serve her," he goes on to say:—

"Believe not, I humbly beseech you for your wisdom and worthiness, the tale so evil told of your most faithful: be not led by lewdness of others to lose your own, that truly loveth you. These most unkind conceits wonderfully wring me: reserve me most graciously to be bestowed upon some honorable enterprise for you; and so shall I die a most joyful man and eternally bound to you. But would God I might win you to think well according with my true meaning; then should I acquiet my mind, and serve you with joy and further hope of goodness. I pray God bless you for ever.

"Your despairing most wretched bondman,
CH. HATTON."

Nevertheless, the Earl of Oxford was preferred till Hatton fell into a serious illness, which revived the Queen's affection for him.

The Court scandal of that day is recorded in a very lively letter written by Gilbert Talbot to his father, the Earl of Shrewsbury:

"My Lord of Oxford is lately grown into great credit; for the Queen's Majesty delighteth more in his personage, and his dancing and valiantness, than any other. At all these love matters my Lord Treasurer winketh, and will not meddle any way. Hatton is sick still: it is thought he will very hardly recover his disease, for it is doubted it is in his kidneys: the Queen goeth almost every day to see how he doth."

He slowly recovered, and Talbot, in another letter, after stating that the Queen hath postponed a projected progress to Bristol, adds, "Mr. Hatton, by reason of his great sickness, is minded to go to the Spa for the better recovery of his health." Strype says, "Mr. Hatton (not well in health) took this opportunity to get leave to go to the Spa, and Dr. Julio (a great Court physician) with him; whereat the Queen showed herself very pensive, and very unwilling to grant him leave, for he was a favorite."[1]

However, on the 29th of May, an order was made by the Privy Council for allowing Hatton "to pass over the seas for recovery of his health."—and having taken a tender leave of Elizabeth he proceeded on his journey in company with Dr. Julio, on the 3rd of June following.

During their separation, the lovers kept up a constant correspondence. All her letters are unfortunately lost, but the originals of many of his have lately been discovered in the State Paper Office—written in the style of an ardent and successful admirer to his mistress—his passion being rendered more romantic by distance and illness. She had given him the pastoral name of "Lydds," and they had agreed on certain ciphers expressing sentiments of endearment, the exact meaning of which is not disclosed to us. Here is the first, written to her only two days after their separation, showing that he had received several from her in the interval:

"If I could express my feelings of your gracious letters, I should utter unto you matter of strange effect. In reading of them with my tears I blot them. In thinking of them I feel so great comfort, that I find cause, as God knoweth, to thank you on my knees. Death had been much more my advantage than to win health and life by so loathsome a pilgrimage. The time of two days hath drawn me further from you than ten, when I return can lead me towards you. Madam, I find the greatest lack that ever poor wretch sustained. No death, no, not hell,

[1] Strype, ii. 449.

no fear of death shall ever win of me my consent so far to wrong myself again as to be absent from you one day. God grant my return. I will perform this vow. I lack that I live by. The more I find this lack, the further I go from you. Shame whippeth me forward. Shame take them that counselled me to it. The life (as you will remember) is too long that loathsomely lasteth. A true saying, Madam. Believe him that hath proved it. The great wisdom I find in your letters, with your Country counsels, are very notable, but the last word is worth the Bible. Truth, truth, truth. Ever may it dwell in you. I will ever deserve it. My spirit and soul (I feel) agreeth with my body and life, that to serve you is a heaven, but to lack you is more than hell's torment unto them. My heart is full of woe. Pardon (for God's sake) my tedious writing. It doth much diminish (for the time) my great griefs. I will wash away the faults of these letters with the drops from your poor Lydds and so inclose them. Would God I were with you but for one hour. My wits are overwrought with thoughts. I find myself amazed. Bear with me, my most dear, sweet Lady. Passion overcometh me. I can write no more. Love me; for I love you. God, I beseech thee witness the same on the behalf of thy poor servant. Live for ever. Shall I utter this familiar term (farewell)? yea, ten thousand thousand farewells. He speaketh it that most dearly loveth you. I hold you too long. Once again I crave pardon, and so bid your own poor Lidds farewell. 1573, June.

"Your bondman everlastingly tied,
"CH. HATTON."

He wrote her a long letter on his arrival at Antwerp, in which he says,

"This is the twelfth day since I saw the brightness of that Sun that giveth light unto my sense and soul. I wax an amazed creature. Give me leave, Madam, to remove myself out of this irksome shadow, so far as my imagination with these good means may lead me towards you, and let me thus salute you: Live for ever, most excellent creature; and love some man, to show yourself thankful for God's high labor in you. I am too far off to hear your answer to this salutation; I know it would be full of virtue and great wisdom, but I fear for some part thereof I would have but small thanks. Pardon me; I will leave these matters, because I think you mislike them. But, Madam, forget not your Lydds that are so often bathed with tears for your sake. A more wise man may seek you, but a more faithful and worthy can never have you. Pardon me, my most dear, sweet Lady, I will no more write of these matters. I wish you like welfare your presence might give me; it is, I assure you, the best farewell that ever was given you."[1]

From Spa his letters are equally amorous. In one he says,

" It might glad you (I speak without presumption) that you live so dearly loved with all sincerity of heart and singleness of choice. I love yourself. I can not lack you. I am taught to prove it by the wish and desire I find to be with you. Believe it, most gracious Lady, there is on *illud mitius*, you are the true felicity that in this world I know or find. God bless you forever. Pardon me, most humbly on my knees I beseech you. The abundance of my heart carrieth me I know not to what purpose; but guess you (as the common proverb is), and I will grant. I guess by my servant you should not be well, which troubleth me greatly. I humbly pray you that I may know it, for then will I presently come, whatever befal me. Humbly on the knees of my soul, I pray God bless you forever. Your slave and *EveR*[2] your own,

Hatton returned to England in the autumn of the same year, when Elizabeth was so much alarmed by the attempt made upon his life by Burchet, the fanatical Puritan, that she could hardly be prevented from issuing a commission for executing the offender by martial law.

Oxford was now discarded, and she continued steadily attached to Hatton for some years. In the following summer she accomplished her visit to Bristol, accompanied by him, and she issued a mandate to the Bishop of Ely to alienate to him the greatest part of the ground

[1] Autograph in the State Paper Office. No address or superscription.
[2] The *E* and *R* are capitals, and are so written by him in subsequent letters, evidently in allusion to the Queen's initials,—*E*lizabetha *R*egina.
[3] Autograph in the State Paper Office.

in Holborn belonging to that see. The Bishop at first promising to do so, and then pleading scruples of conscience, she sent him this reprimand:

"Proud Prelate! I understand you are backward in complying with your agreement, but I would have you know, that I who made you what you are, can unmake you; and if you do not forthwith fulfill your engagement, by God I will immediately unfrock you.

"Yours, as you demean yourself,
"ELIZABETH."

This menace had the desired effect, and where grew the famous strawberries, so much praised by Richard III. now stands "Hatton Garden."

Notwithstanding these grants, the favorite from his habitual extravagance, being still embarassed, we find soon after a royal mandate to Burghley, requiring him "to apply £50 as he might think most fit for her to part with to the use of Hatton, for that she is content to bestow so much on him presently towards the payment of his debts."[1]

Now he received his appointment as Vice Chamberlain, and being sworn of the Privy Council, he became what we should call a *Cabinet Minister*. The existing distinction, between the "Household" and the "Cabinet," which even requires that the Lord Chamberlain, the Lord Steward, and the Master of the Horse shall withdraw when the Queen's speech is read in the Council for her approval, was then unknown; and all privy councillors were summoned to deliberate on important affairs of state in the presence of the sovereign.

Hatton was chiefly relied upon for making any communication to the Queen of peculiar delicacy. Thus the Prime Minister writes to him, begging him to suggest to her that the only cure for tooth-ache, from which she then suffered, was to have the tooth extracted,—information which her physicians were afraid to communicate to her, *chloroform* being then unknown.

"Mr. Vice Chamberlain, I heard of her Majesty's indisposition by some pain in her head; and then how can any of her poor members, having life by her as our head, be without pain? If my coming thither might either diminish her pain, or be thought convenient, I would not

[1] 12 Dec. 1574. Lansdowne MSS. 18, art. 96.

be absent; although in grief I am present, and do most heartily beseech God to deliver her from all grief, praying you to let me know of her Majesty's amendment; not doubting but you are careful by the physicians to provide the remedy, which is said to be only the withdrawing of some one tooth that is touched with some humorous cause, and, except that be removed, her Majesty's pain shall not be quit. And though her Highness doth not or will not so think, yet I assure you it is said that the physicians do of knowledge affirm it, howsoever they forbear to impart it unto her. Besides my prayer, I can not tell what to yield for her Majesty's ease more than this information; praying you to examine the truth and further truth to her Majesty's service, and to her ease in this point. 21st, April, 1578. Yours assuredly,
"W. BURGHLEY."

The Earl of Leicester writes to him in a strain which shows that, though rivals, they were now friends. The Queen being on a visit at Wanstead, while the gallant host was kept at a distance by illness, he thus addresses the Vice Chamberlain, who was in waiting upon her:

"I humbly thank God to hear of the increase of her Majesty's good health, and am most glad that she took that happy medicine that wrought so well with her, as I perceive by your letter it did. I trust it will help to prolong and perfect that which we all daily pray for. I hope now, ere long, to be with you, to enjoy that blessed sight which I have been so long kept from. A few of these days seem many years, and I think I shall feel a worse grief ere I seek so far a remedy again."

Nay, Leicester soon after, having quarreled with Elizabeth, employs Hatton to soothe the Queen, and to excuse his absence from Court:—

"I do most earnestly desire you to excuse me that I forbear to come, being as I wrote to you this morning troubled and grieved both in heart and mind. I am not unwilling, God knows, to serve her Majesty, wherein I may, to the uttermost of my life, but most unfit at this time to make repair to that place where so many eyes are witnesses of my open and great disgraces delivered from her Majesty's mouth."

Hatton soon after incurred much discredit by taking a very active part in prosecuting what was called "a seditious libel," being a pamphlet showing the dangers which would arise to the state from the Queen's proposed marriage with the Duke of Anjou. Stubbes the author, and Paget the publisher, were condemned to lose their right hands, and to suffer perpetual imprisonment. Camden, who was present, says that "their right hands were cut off with a cleaver, driven through the wrist with the force of a beetle." Stubbes, in hopes of a remission of the rest of the sentence, soon wrote a letter to the Vice Chamberlain, in which he says, "the judgment-seat which gave sentence against my fault, will yet testify my humble and dutiful reverence throughout all my defense and answering for myself. The scaffold of execution can witness my loyal care to give all good example of meet obedience; insomuch as, notwithstanding the bitter pain and doleful loss of my hand immediately before chopped off, I was able, by God's mercy, to say with heart and tongue, before I left the block, these words, 'God save the Queen!'"

Yet Hatton himself, on every account, highly disapproved of the French match, and actually took a prominent part in breaking it off. He is represented as having then assisted Elizabeth to answer the reproaches of her discarded suitor, by a speech which few would have ventured to make in her hearing; for he pointed out the disparity of age between them, and the improbability of her having issue if she were to marry. The Duke declared that "the women of England were as changeable and capricious as the waves which encircled their island."[1]

Yet Sir Christopher himself continued, now and long after, to address her as a lover.

"TO THE QUEEN'S MOST ROYAL MAJESTY.

"I most humbly with all dutiful reverence beseech your sacred Majesty to pardon my presumption in writing to your Highness. Your kingly benefits, together with your most rare regard of your simple and poor slave, hath put this passion into me to imagine that for so exceeding and infinite parts of unspeakable goodness I can use no other means of thankfulness than by bowing the knees of my

[1] Camden, 375.

own heart with all humility to look upon your singular graces with love and faith perdurable.

"I should sin, most gracious Sovereign, against a holy ghost most damnably, if towards your Highness I should be found unthankful. Afford me the favor, therefore, most dear Lady, that your clear and most fair eyes may read and register these my duties, which I beseech our God to requite you for.

"The poor wretch my sick servant receiveth again his life, being as in the physician's opinion more than half-dead, through your most princely love of his poor Master, and holy charitable care, without respect of your own danger, of the poor wretch. We have right Christian devotion to pray for your Highness, which God for His mercy's sake kindle in us for ever to the end of our lives.

"I should not dissemble, my dear Sovereign, if I wrote how unpleasant and froward a countenance is grown in me through my absence from your most amiable and royal presence, but I dare not presume to trouble your Highness with my not estimable griefs, but in my country I dare avow this fashion will full evil become me. I hope your Highness will pardon my unsatisfied humor, that knoweth not how to end such complaints as are in my thoughts ever new to begin; but duty shall do me leave off to cumber your heavenlike eyes with my vain babblings. And, as most nobly your Highness preserveth and royally conserveth your own poor creature and vassal, so shall he live and die in pure and unspotted faith towards you for *EveR*. God bless your Highness with long life, and prosper you to the end in all your kingly affairs. At Bedford, this Wednesday morning, September, 1580. Would God I were worthy to write

"Your bounden slave,
"CHR. HATTON."[1]

Still more strange is the following letter, written in a time of epidemic sickness by him to the confidant of Elizabeth and himself, Sir Thomas Heneage,—evidently intended to be shown to her. I hardly venture to copy it, and have not the courage to comment upon it:

"My good Sir Thomas,—I thank you much for your happy letters, assuring our dear Mistress her present health unto me; pray God continue it for *EveR*. I have

[1] Original in State Paper Office.

one servant yet free of infection, which I trust I may use to deliver my care and duty, to my singular comfort and satisfaction. I have presumed to send him, that I may daily know either by my own or yours the true state of our Mistress, whom through choice I love no less than he that by the greatness of a kingly birth and fortune is most fit to have her. I am likewise bold to commend my most humble duty by this letter and ring, which hath the virtue to expel infectious airs, and is, as is telled to me, to be wearen betwixt the sweet dugs,—the chaste nest of most pure constancy. I trust, Sir, when the virtue is known, it shall not be refused for the value." [1]

In recompense for this *charm*, he received from the Queen a very tender epistle, which revived his romantic passion to its pristine fervor, and he is again her " Lyds" and her " *Sheep*."

"TO THE QUEEN'S MOST ROYAL MAJESTY.

△ △

"The gracious assurance which your Highness's grave letters do most liberally give me of your singular favor and inestimable goodness, I have received on my knees with such reverence as becometh your most obliged bondman; and with like humility, in my most dutiful and grateful manner, I do offer in God's presence myself, my life, and all that I am or is me, to be disposed to the end, and my death to your service, in inviolable faith and sincerity.

"The cunning of your Highness' style of writing, with the conveyance of your rare sentence and matter, is exceedingly to be liked of; but the subject which it hath pleased your Majesty to endite for my particular, exceedeth all the eloquence, yea, all the eloquence of the world. Your words are sweet, your heart is full of rare and royal faith: the writing of your fair hand, directed by your constant and sacred heart, do raise in me joy unspeakable. Would God they did not rather puff up my dejected spirits with too much pride and hope. I most humbly thank God for these admirable gifts in your Majesty; they exceed and abound towards your Highness unequally in

[1] Original in Harleian MSS. 416, f. 200.

the measure of His graces amongst men, so far as, God knoweth, there is not your like. I crave most humbly your gracious favor and pardon for the offense I have made you. Frogs, near the friends where I then was, are much more plentiful, and of less value, than their fish is; and because I knew that poor beast seasonable in your sight, I therefore blindly entered into that presumption, but *Misericordia tua super omnia opera tua.*

"God bless your Highness in all your kingly affairs, and direct them through your wonted wisdom in that course that shall *EveR* succeed to your comfort. I find the gracious sign of your letters of most joyful signification, and the abbreviation of delays will breed a much more delightful hope in that great cause.[1] Against love and ambition your Highness hath holden a long war; they are the violent affections that encumber the hearts of men; but now, my most dear Sovereign, it is more than time to yield, or else this love will leave you in war and disquietness of yourself and estate, and the ambition of the world will be most maliciously bent to encumber your sweet quiet, and the happy peace of this most blessed Realm. I pray God bless your kingly resolutions what-*EveR*. I trust your Highness will pardon this part of my presumption, because your little $ *siphere* hath proffered the occasion. And so your Highness' most humble Lydds, a thousand times more happy in that you vouchsafe them yours, than in that they cover and conserve the poor eyes, most lowly do leave you in your kingly seat in God's most holy protection. Your Majesty's Sheep and most bound vassal,

"CHR. HATTON."[2]

Hatton seems now to have enjoyed a great influence over the Queen, and to have lived very quietly for some years, often receiving letters from Bishops and Archbishops, as well as from lay courtiers, praying him to intercede with her Majesty in their behalf. However, he suffered such ill usage from her again that he withdrew from Court to his house at Holdenby, in Northamptonshire, where he remained in great sorrow and perplexity many days. At last she took compassion upon him, and sent a kind message begging him to return. Thereupon

---
[1] These and other allusions in this letter are very obscure
[2] Autograph in the State Paper Office.

he wrote her the following letter full of humility and contrition, yet showing a deep sense of her arbitrary and capricious demeanor:—

"On the knees of my heart, most dear and dread Sovereign Majesty, I beseech pardon and goodness at your princely hands. I fear I offend you in lack of attendance on your princely presence, wherein, before our God, frowardness and obstinacy of mind are as far from me as love and duty would have them; but that the griefs and sorrows of my soul so oppress me as I can not express unto you, and so entangle my spirits that they turn me out of myself, and thereby making me unfit to be seen of you, is the true cause that I forbear access. I most humbly thank your sacred Majesty for your too late recomfortations. Would God I had deserved your former goodness; for, God knoweth, your good favor hath not been ever, or at any time, evil employed on me, your poor disconsolate wretch. I will leave all former protestations of merit or meanings; only I affirm, in the presence of God, that I have followed and loved the footsteps of your most princely person with all faith and sincerity, with a mind most single, and free from all ambition or any other private respect. And though, towards God and Kings, men can not be free from faults, yet, wilfully or wittingly, He knoweth that made me, I never offended your most sacred Majesty. My negligence towards God, and too high presumptions towards your Majesty, have been sins worthily deserving more punishments than these. But, Madam, towards yourself leave not the causes of my presumptions unremembered; and though you find them as unfit for me as unworthy of you, yet in their nature, of a good mind, they are not hatefully to be despised. I humbly prostrate myself at your gracious feet, and do most heartily recognize that all God's punishments laid on me by your princely censure are taken by me with singular humility; wherein I stand as free from grudging of hearts as I am full of intolerable and vain perplexity. God in Heaven bless your Royal Majesty with a long life, a joyful heart, a prosperous reign, and with Heaven at last. Your Majesty's most lowly subject and most unworthy servant, CH. HATTON."

Hatton was next alarmed by the Queen's growing partiality for Sir Walter Raleigh; but when New Year's

Day came round he sent her a true lover's knot, with bracelets and other presents. Sir Thomas Heneage, who had been the bearer of these tokens, greatly comforted him by stating they had been much prized, and that his new rival was slighted:—

"Sir,—Your bracelets be embraced according to their worth, and the good-will of the sender, which is held of such great price as your true friend tells you, I think in my heart you have great cause to take most comfort in, for seldom in my life have I seen more hearty and noble affection expressed by her Majesty towards you than she showed upon this occasion, which will ask more leisure than is now left me particularly to let you know. The sum is, she thinks you faithfulest and of most worth, and thereafter will regard you: so she saith, so I hope, and so there is just cause. She told me, she thought your absence as long as yourself did, and marvelled that you came not. I let her Majesty know, understanding it by Varney, that you had no place here to rest yourself, which after standing and waiting you much needed; whereupon she grew very much displeased and would not believe that any should be placed in your lodging, but sending Mr. Darcy to understand the matter, found that Sir Wa. R. lay there, wherewith she grew more angry with my L. Chamberlain than I wished she had been, and used bitterness of speech against R., telling me before that she had rather see him hanged than equal him with you, or that the world should think she did so. Messengers bear no blame; and though you give me no thanks, I must tell you, that her Highness saith you are a knave for sending her such a thing and of that price, which you know she will not send back again; that is, the knot[1] she most loves, and she thinks can not be undone; but I keep the best to the last. This enclosed, which it pleased her to read to me, and I must be record of, which if I might see surely performed, I should have one of my greatest desires upon earth; I speak it faithfully."

Hatton's hold of the Queen's heart was, in truth, considerably weakened; but he now gained her good opinion and friendship more than ever, by his exertions to free her from the dread which she entertained of Mary, Queen of Scots. He began with a piece of hypocrisy, which,

[1] "The true love knot."—Marginal note.

considering his notorious profligate life, must have a little shocked the religious feelings of his audience, though no one present ventured to oppose him. Rising in his place in the House of Commons, and detailing the plots which he alleged to be concocted against Elizabeth and the Protestant faith, he moved, "that besides the rendering of our most humble and loyal thanks unto her Highness, we do, being now assembled, forthwith join our hearts and minds together in most humble and earnest prayer unto Almighty God for the long continuance of the most prosperous preservation of her Majesty, with most due and thankful acknowledgement of his infinite benefits and blessings poured upon this whole realm through the mediation of her Highness's ministry under him." This being carried unanimously, the gentleman of her Highness's Privy Chamber, acting the part of Chaplain to the House, pulled a form of supplication from his pocket to the above effect, and all the members present, dropping down on their knees with seeming devotion, joined with him in his litany.[1]

He was very active in passing through the House of Commons the bill under which Mary was to be tried.[2]

He sat on the bench as a commissioner at the preliminary trials of Babington, Savage, Ballard, Abington, Tilney, and the other conspirators. Savage's confession being proved,—with a view to the use to be made of it as evidence against Mary, Lord Commissioner Hatton thus addressed him:—"Savage, I must ask thee one question: Was not all this willingly and voluntarily confessed by thyself without menacing, without torture and without offer of any torture?" The poor wretch, in the vain hope of mercy, eagerly replied, "Yes!"

Although the two Chief Justices, May and Anderson, and Chief Baron Manwood, were present, Hatton took the lead in the conduct of the trial; and when it was getting late in the evening observed, they should hardly be able to finish the business if they sat up all night, and ordered the Court to be adjourned till seven o'clock next morning.[3]

He then strongly urged Ballard to a full confession, saying to him, "O, Ballard, Ballard, what hast thou done? A sort of brave youths, endowed with good gifts, by thy inducements hast thou brought to their utter destruction

[1] 1 Parl. Hist. 828.   [2] 27 Eliz. c. 1.   [3] 1 St. Tr. 1127, 1131.

and confusion." The young man exclaiming, "Howbeit, say what you will, I will say no more!" Hatton added, "Nay, Ballard, you must say more, and shall say more, for you must not commit high treasons and then hurdle them up. But is this thy *Religio Catholica?* Nay, rather it is *Diabolica.*"

He next took in hand Barnewell, another prisoner, administering to him this string of interrogatories. "O, Barnewell, Barnewell, didst not thou come to Richmond, and when her Majesty walked abroad, didst not thou there view her and all her company—what weapons they had, and how they walked along? and didst traverse the ground, and thereupon coming back to London didst make relation to Babington, how it was a most easy matter to kill her Majesty, and what thou hadst seen and done at the Court? Yes, I know thou didst so." Taking all this for confessed, he then, without being sworn, gives some evidence himself: "Nay, I can assure thee, moreover, and it is most true which I say, that her Majesty did know that thou didst come to that end, and she did see and mark thee how thou didst view her and her company; but had it been known to some there as well as unto her, thou hadst never brought news to Babington. Such is the magnanimity of our Sovereign, which God grant be not overmuch in not fearing such traitors as thou art."

The sentence on the prisoner was pronounced by Lord Chief Justice Anderson, but this was prefaced by "an excellent good speech from Sir Christopher Hatton, showing how stirred up by wicked priests, the ministers of the Pope, they had conspired to murder the Queen's Majesty, to deliver the Queen of Scots"—(charges which were proved);—"to sack the city of London; to rob and destroy all the wealthy subjects of the realm; to kill divers of the Privy Council; to set fire to all the Queen's ships, and to clog all the great ordnance"—(charges unsupported by any evidence). He concluded by pointing out the falsehood of a book recently printed at Rome, and made by the Papists, wherein they affirm that "the English Catholics who suffer for religion be lapped in bear-skins and bated to death with dogs."

But although he had very roughly refused a prisoner's request to have a pair of writing tables to set down what was alleged against him,—another, after sentence of death, praying that his debts might be satisfied out of his property, praying that his debts might be satisfied out of his property, the Vice Chamberlain good naturedly asked the amount· and being told that six angels would be sufficient, he said, "Then I promise thee it shall be paid."

He was next engaged in the very delicate task of interrogating Nau and Curle, Mary's secretaries, whose examinations were to be used as the chief evidence against their mistress. He was prepared for this by a letter from Burghley, saying "they wold yeld soewhat to confirm ther mystriss, if they war persuaded that themselves might scape, and the blow fall upon ther M^n. betwixt hir head and shoulders."[1] Most strangely, the original letter, supposed to establish Mary's complicity, was not shown to them, and "an abstract of the principal points of it" being read, they were required to say, upon oath, whether they could not recall these points to their recollection as having been contained in it.[2]

Hatton was named as one of the Judges for the trial of the unhappy Mary. While the proceedings against her were pushed forward at Fotheringay, he slept every night at Apthorpe, the seat of Sir Walter Mildmay, about five miles off. Here he carried on a private epistolary correspondence with Elizabeth, and it is curious to observe that on such a solemn occasion he still addressed her as a lover.

I suspect that when the Court rose on the morning of the 12th of October, he had sent off an express to inform Elizabeth that Mary had hitherto resolutely refused to recognize the authority of the tribunal, and that Elizabeth had returned an answer which had reached him early next morning, reproaching him and the other Judges with their ill success. In the State Paper Office, at Westminster, there is extant the following reply in the handwriting of Sir Christopher Hatton:—

"MAY IT PLEASE YOUR SACRED MAJESTY, Your princely goodness towards me is so infinite, as in my poor wit I am

[1] Burghley to Hatton, Sept. 4, 1586,—a sportive anticipation of Mary's fate, probably written to be shown to Elizabeth. [2] Ellis, iii. 5.

not able to comprehend the least part thereof. I must therefore fail in duty of thankfulness as your Mutton, and lay all upon God, with my humble prayers to requite you in Heaven and Earth in the most sincere and devout manner, that, through God's grace, I may possibly devise. Your Majesty's good servant, Mr. Conway, hath taken a wonderful sore journey. He hath from your Majesty a little daunted me. I most humbly crave your Majesty's pardon. God and your Majesty be praised I have recovered my perfect health; and if now for my ease or pleasure I should be found negligent in your service, I were much unworthy of that life which many a time your Royal Majesty hath given me. I might likewise sustain some obloquy, whereof I have heard somewhat; but my will and wit, and whatever is in me, shall be found assuredly yours, whether I be sick or whole, or what *EveR* become of me deem they what pleaseth them. God in Heaven bless your Majesty, and grant me no longer life than that my faith and love may *EveR* be found inviolable and spotless to so royal and peerless a Princess. At Apthorpe, this 13th of October, 1586. Your Royal Majesty's most bounden poor slave,

"CHR. HATTON."

Conway, charged with this missive, having started on "a wonderful sore journey" back again to Westminster, Hatton had hastened to Fotheringay, resolved to show that his *will* and his *wit* were wholly devoted to his mistress, let others deem of him what they pleased. And now he did good service, for it was entirely by his artful persuasion that Mary was this day induced "to lay aside the bootless privilege of royal dignity, to appear in judgment and to show her innocency, lest by avoiding trial she might draw upon herself suspicion, and lay upon her reputation an eternal blot and aspersion."[1]

The trial now proceeding, he left the conduct of it to Burghley and the other counsel for the Crown, silently enjoying the effect of the confessions and examinations which he had so dexterously prepared.

But when judgment had been given he delivered a violent speech in the House of Commons, urging the House to petition that it might immediately be carried into execution. "He explained, at great length, the

[1] 1 St. Tr. 1171. Camden, b. iii. p. 37. Ante, p. 264.

practices and attempts caused and procured by the Queen of Scots, tending to the overthrow of the true and sincere religion established in this realm; yea, and withal (which his heart quaked and trembled to utter and think on), the death and destruction of the Queen's most sacred person, to the utter desolation of this most noble realm of England. He therefore thought it good for his part, that speedy consultation be had by this House for the cutting off this great delinquent by due course of justice; concluding with these words of Scripture—*Ne pereat Israel, pereat Absolon.*"

Hatton afterwards brought down a message, "that her Highness, moved by some commiseration for the Scottish Queen in respect of her former dignity and great fortunes in her younger years, her nearness of kindred to her Majesty, and also of her sex, could be well pleased to forbear taking of her blood, if by any other means, to be devised by the great Council of the realm, the safety of her Majesty's person and government might otherwise be preserved. But herein she left them, nevertheless, to their own free liberty and disposition." He concluded his speech by moving a resolution, which was carried unanimously, " That no other way, device, or means whatsoever could or can possibly be found or imagined, that such safety can in anywise be had, so long as the said Queen of Scots doth or shall live."[1]

The zealous Vice Chamberlain was subsequently instrumental in causing the death-warrant to be sent off to be executed. Being informed by Secretary Davison that the Great Seal was appended to it, and that the Queen had pretended to chide him for his precipitancy, he immediately went to Burghley, and they called the meeting of the Council, at which it was resolved that, the forms of law having been all duly observed, it was their duty, without giving further needless trouble to her Majesty, to take all the remaining responsibility on themselves.

When the news arrived of the close of Mary's sufferings at Fotheringay, Hatton was, of course, a marked object of Elizabeth's assumed indignation, and he was ordered, with the other Councillors who had concurred with him, to answer for their misconduct in the Star Chamber; but Secretary Davison, according to the pre-

[1] 1 Parl. Hist. 844.

concerted plan being made, the only victim, all the others were speedily pardoned, and the Vice Chamberlain, for his recent services, was in higher favor than ever. Balls and masques were resumed; and still the handsomest man, and the best dressed, and the most gallant, and the most graceful dancer at Court,—he gained new consequence, being hailed as a successful orator and statesman.

It was at this conjuncture that Lord Chancellor Bromley died, and the Great Seal was to be disposed of. Love and gratitude filled the mind of Elizabeth, and after some misgivings,—whether he who would have made a most excellent Lord Chamberlain was exactly fitted for the duties of Lord Chancellor,—she resolved at all hazards to appoint him. The intention, however, was kept a profound secret from all except Burghley, till the time when the deed was done. The Court then lay at the Archbishop of Canterbury's Palace at Croydon, and there, in a walk near her private chamber, the Queen, in the midst of a numerous circle of nobles and courtiers, taking the Seal in its velvet bag, delivered it to her Vice Chamberlain, ordered him before the assembled company to seal a writ of subpœna with it, and then declared that he was to hold it as Lord Chancellor of England.[1]

Some of the courtiers at first thought that this ceremony was a piece of wicked pleasantry on the part of the Queen; but when it was seen that she was serious, all joined in congratulating the new Lord Chancellor, and expressing satisfaction that her Majesty had been emancipated from the prejudice that a musty old lawyer only

[1] "Memdum qd die Sabbati, &c. (April 29. 29 Eliz.) Mag. Sigill. in custodia Dne Regine existens apud Croydon in Com. Sarr. sua serenissima Majestas ibidem residens ad benepltum suum in Palacio Reverendissimi in Xto Patris Johannis Cantuar, &c. ac ibidem similiter in privato ambulatorio juxta privatam cameram sue Majestatis sua serenissima Majestas essend. presens circa horam quartam post meridiem ejusdem diei ac in presencia dicti reverendissimi Patris, &c. &c. Sigill. Mag. prdm jacens in fenestra in fine dicti ambulatorii in baga de velueto rubeo incluso sua serenissima Majestas accepit in manibus suis et tulebat secum ad medium ejusdem ambulatorii ac ibidem in presencia prda dicto Egregio Viro Xtofero Hatton militi tradidit et iterum immediate e manibus dicti egregii viri recipiebat et extrahi jubebat et nudari." Then comes the sealing of the subpœna, with the restoration of the Seal to the bag. "Et sigill. prdm in bagam predictam de velueto rubeo impositum dicta sacra Majestas regia dicto nobili viro Xtofero Hatton militi in presencia prda redeliberabat Ipsaque Xtoferum Hatton militem Dnm Cancellarium Anglie adtunc et ibidem fecit ordinavit et constituit Habendam," &c. &c.—Rot. Cl. 29 Eliz. p. 24.

was fit to preside in the Chancery, whereas that Court being governed not by the strict rules of law, but by natural equity, justice would be much better administered there by a gentleman of plain good sense and knowledge of the world.

Very different was the reasonings in Westminster Hall and the Inns of Court when the news of Hatton's appointment arrived from Croydon. "The gownsmen grudging hereat, conceived his advancement their injury, that one not thoroughly bred to the laws should be preferred to the place. They said, how could he cure diseases unacquainted with their causes, who might easily mistake the justice of the common law for rigor—not knowing the true reason thereof?"[1]

Considering that the Great Seal had now been held for thirty years successively by eminent lawyers who had established a procedure, and laid down rules which were well understood, and had been steadily adhered to, the prospect must have been very alarming of practicing before a Chancellor who, when he was appointed, could hardly know the distinction between a subpœna and a latitat; for surely no greater misfortune can befall an advocate than to lose a consummate Judge whose decisions might have been confidently anticipated by the initiated, and to be obliged to practice under an incompetent successor, before whom no case is safe and no case is desperate.

Meetings of the bar were held, and it was resolved by many Sergeants and Apprentices that they would not plead before the new Chancellor; but a few who looked eagerly forward to advancement dissented. The Chancellor himself was determined to brave the storm, and Elizabeth and all her ministers expressed a determination to stand by him.

The 3rd of May was the first day of Trinity term, and the great officers of state, and the heads of the law, were entertained at breakfast at the Chancellor's mansion in

---

[1] Naunton. Camden's account of the grumbling of the leaders of the bar is likewise very striking. "Christopherus vero Hattonus, florentissima apud Principem gratia, suffectus erat ex aula Cancellarius, *quod juris Anglici consultissimi permolestè tulerunt.* Illi enim ex quo Ecclesiastici de gradu dejecti, hunc magistratum, summum togatæ dignitatis culmen, viris ecclesiasticis et nobilibus plerunque olim delatum, magna cum æquitatis et prudentiæ laude gesserant"—Camd. Eliz. vol. i. p. 475.

Ely Place, Holborn. Thence there was a procession to Westminster Hall, exceeding in magnificence any thing seen on a similar occasion since the time of Cardinal Wolsey, whose crosses, pillars, and pole-axes some old men could still remember. First went forty gentlemen of the Chancellor's household, all in the same livery, with chains of gold about their necks. They were followed by divers pensioners and gentlemen of the Queen's Court, upon splendid foote clothes; then came the Masters in Chancery and the officers of the Court; next rode the Lord Chancellor on a palfrey richly caparisoned, having on his right hand Burghley, the Lord Treasurer, and on his left the Earl of Leicester; after whom came many of the nobility, riding two and two; and then all the Judges in their robes and coifs, with Sergeants and Apprentices; and last of all, many Knights and a great troop of their retinue.[1]

This was a much more gallant show than the line of close carriages now to be seen moving from the Chancellor's levee on the first day of term; though our predecessors must have been in an uncomfortable plight when it rained during their march along the Strand to Charing, and thence to Westminster,—and though there were many traditionary stories of the misfortunes which had befallen the Judges on their march, notwithstanding the skill in horsemanship which they acquired from riding their circuits.[2]

It is said that Hatton was received in the Court of Chancery with cold and silent disdain. Nevertheless there was, from the first, some little business brought on before him. The Attorney and Solicitor General, lest they should themselves be dismissed, were obliged, however discontented they might be, to appear to countenance him. He made no public complaint of his reception, and gradually gained ground by his great courtesy and sweetness,—to say nothing of the good dinners and excellent sack for which he was soon famous.

It would appear that there was much public curiosity to see " the dancing Chancellor " seated upon his tribunal,

---

[1] Stow, Eliz. 741.
[2] The last which has reached us is that of Mr. Justice Twisden, who was thrown from his horse near Charing Cross, while attending Lord Chancellor Shaftesbury.

and the crowd of strangers in the Court of Chancery was so great that there came out an order "by the Right Honorable Sir Christopher Hatton, Knight of the most noble Order of the Garter, and Lord Chancellor of England," in these words:—"For the avoydinge of suche great numbers of suitors and others as doe daylye pester the Courte in the tyme of sittinge, by reason whereof heretofore yt hath manye tymes happened that the due reverence and sylence which ought to be kepte and observed in that honourable courte hathe bene undeutifully neglected, and contrayewise muche unmannerlye and unseemlye behavyour and noise hath bene there used to the hinderaunce of the due hearinge of such matters and causes as were there to be handled, and to the great derogacion of the honour of this courte and due reverence belonging to the same—." Then follow regulations by which none were to come into court but counsel, attorneys, officers and their clerks, and parties—who were "to continue soe longe as the cause shal be in hearinge and no longer, and all other suytors whatsoever (excepte noblemen and suche as be of her Majesties Privy Counsell) were to stand without the courte, and not suffered to come in without special licens."[1]

He was quite at home when presiding in the Star Chamber, where he had before been accustomed to sit as a Privy Councillor, and he had the Chiefs of the common law to assist him. To this Court, according to usage, he dedicated Wednesdays and Fridays. On other days he sat for equity business in the Court of Chancery,—in Westminster Hall in the mornings, and in his own house in the afternoons.[2] He made an order that four Masters in Chancery should always attend and sit on the bench with him in Court, and two in his own house.[3]

[1] Reg. Lib. B. 31 & 32 (Eliz. 1589, p. 498). I once saw the Court of Chancery crowded and overflowing, like Drury Lane when Mrs. Siddons appeared as Lady Macbeth; but it was to hear Sheridan address Lord Eldon. This was shortly before the death of Thurlow: he said, "I have been told that Jack Scott has been acting plays in Lincoln's-Inn-Hall."

[2] Morning seems to have been from eight to eleven, and afternoon from two to five; the intermediate space being allowed for dinner and recreation.

[3] Ordo Curiæ. Decimo viij°. die Aprilis Anno Regni Elizabeth Regine xxx₀.

"The R^t. Ho. Sir Christopher Hatton, Knight, Lo. Chauncelor of England, having been enformed that of late yeres the Courte of Chauncery hathe bene for the most parte unfurnished of such Masters of the Chauncery as are

He was exceedingly cautious, "not venturing to wade beyond the shallow margin of equity, where he could distinctly see the bottom." He always took time to consider in cases of any difficulty; and in these he was guided by the advice of one Sir Richard Swale, described as his "servant-friend," who was a Doctor of the Civil Law, a Master in Chancery, and well skilled in all the practice and doctrines of the Court.

By these means Lord Chancellor Hatton contrived to get on marvelously well; and though suitors might grumble, as well as their counsel, the public took part with him, and talked with contempt of "the sullen sergeants," who at first refused to plead before him. All were dazzled with the splendor of his establishment; and it was said that he made up for his want of law by his constant desire to do what was just.[1] But the more judicious grieved; and, in spite of all his caution and good intentions, he committed absurd blunders, and sometimes did injustice.[2]

The attention of the nation was soon taken from all

in ordynary and have her Maties fee to attende there, whereby the dignitye of that honorable courte hath bene in some sort blemished, and the same destitute of such assistauntes and advice of theirs as were meete and necessary. For remedy thereof the said Lo. Chauncelor dothe order that fower of the said ordynary Masters of Chauncery shall dayly in their course attende at or in the said Courte of Chauncery upon the benche there, unles some speciall cause shall draw them from thence, and then he or they whose course it shalbe,* to procure some other of the ordynary Masters of this Courte to supply their places in their absence. And also the Lo. Chauncelor dothe also farther order that two of the said Masters being in ordynary, shall lykewise daylye attende on every Monday, Tuysday, and Thursday, in the afternoones, at the said Lo. Chauncelor's howse, to assist his Lop. in such causes as there shalbe opened and heard before him in every terme." The order then makes some regulations about fees, "secluding all Extraordinary Masters within three myles compasse of the Citty of London, and suburbs of the same, and in all other places where the said ordynary Masters shalbe from doinge any manner of actes or exercisinge any authoryty belonging to the offyce and cleeve to the same."

[1] Splendidissime omnium quos vidimus gessit et quod ex juris scientiâ defuit, æquitate supplere studuit."—Camden.

[2] There was one ceremony which he must have performed with peculiar grace,—installing a Master, May 16, 1587. "This present day Richard Swale, gentleman, Doctor of the Civil Law, was placed as a Master of the Chancery in ordinary in the room of Mr. Doctor Barkeley deceased, by the Right Honorable Sir Christopher Hatton, Knight, Lord Chancellor of England: *and his lordship did put on the said Mr. Swale's cap*," &c.—Reg. Lib. B. p. 492. A hat being substituted for the cap, the ceremony remained down to Lord Brougham's time.

* It was not yet settled what particles and parts of the auxiliary verbs should be used as separate words.

such matters by the danger which threatened the religion and liberties of the country. The INVINCIBLE ARMADA was now afloat; and Elizabeth was reviewing her army at Tilbury. The Chancellor attended her; and, if the Spaniards had landed, was ready to have fought valiantly by her side.[1]

English bravery, assisted by the elements, having swept from the seas the armament which was to overpower and to subjugate England, a parliament was called; and, on the first day of the session, the Queen being on the throne, Lord Chancellor Hatton eloquently opened to the two Houses the cause of the summons: he told them "that her Majesty had made it her constant study, from the very beginning of her reign to this time, to preserve peace, not only at home, but also abroad. That she had given no occasion to the many princes about her to invade her dominions, nor had taken arms to revenge the many injuries which others had inflicted upon her. Neither the infant state of Scotland, nor the treachery of France, nor the divisions of her enemies, nor the frequent solicitations of the Dutch, nor all these things combined, could move her to war. And when she heard that mighty preparations were making against her and her kingdom, she chose rather to propose peace than to cast all hopes of it aside; for she sent a set of grave, prudent, and noble persons as her ambassadors to treat of it. Which, while they were laboring to effect, behold a vast navy of Spanish ships were seen on our English coasts; such a navy, that, for numbers and greatness of the ships, for quantity of arms and military forces, and for all kinds of necessary stores, were never

---

[1] It is upon this occasion that the famous dialogue is supposed to have passed between him and Sir Walter Raleigh :—

" *Sir Christ. Hat.* True, gallant Raleigh ;
But O, thou champion of thy country's fame,
There is a question which I still must ask,
A question which I never ask'd before,
What mean these mighty armaments,
This general muster and this throng of chiefs?

" *Sir Walter R.* O most accomplish'd Christopher, I find
Thy stanch sagacity still tracks the future
In the fresh print of the o'er taken past,
You know, my friend, scarce two revolving suns
And three revolving moons have clos'd their course,
Since haughty Philip in despite of peace.
With hostile hand has struck at England's trade."   *Critic.*

seen to float on the ocean before. But God Almighty, her Majesty's hope, defender, and preserver, rendered this vast armada of her enemies vain and useless. For the British navy, by far inferior in numbers and strength, happily attacked once and again those huge raised-up rocks and mountains of ships, and, at the third conflict, so dispersed, shattered, and disabled them, that, never thinking to renew the fight, they fled for it and took a long course hitherto unheard of; for they steered round Scotland, Ireland, and the most northern regions, and by those means hoped to regain the Spanish coasts. But what shipwrecks they suffered,—what hardships they bore,—how many ships, soldiers, and seamen they lost, neither can they yet know, nor we for certain learn. But do you not imagine that they are ardently studious of revenge? and that they will employ the power and riches of Spain to accomplish it? Know you not the pride, fury, and bitterness of the Spaniard against you? Yes: behold the great cause of summoning this parliament, that, in this full assembly of the wisest and most prudent persons of this kingdom, a diligent preparation may be made, that forces, arms and money may be in readiness, and that our navy, our greatest bulwark, may be repaired, manned, and fitted out for our protection and safeguard."[1]

Although not a peer himself, he was anxious for the honor of the House over which he presided as Speaker, and he mentions in a letter a vain attempt he had made to remove a complaint which for centuries had been uttered there: "The use of the higher House is not to meddle with any bill until there be some presented from the Commons; and so, by reason thereof, the first part of the sitting should be spent idly, or to small purpose, I thought it fit to inform myself what bills there were remaining since the last parliament, of which the Lords had good liking, but could not be passed by reason of want of time, and those I meant to offer to their Lordships till such time as there came some from the Lower House."[2]

Sir Christopher was now installed Knight of the Garter, (being the third Chancellor on whom this honor was con-

---

[1] Taken from Lord's Journals. See 1 Parl. Hist. 353. I must say that this speech of "the dancing Chancellor" is in better taste than any performance of his predecessors either ecclesiastical or legal.
[2] Harl. MSS. 6994, f. 148.

ferred,) and he was at the height of his greatness. But although he was never turned out of office, he met with much mortification before his death. Camden represents that his appointment was maliciously suggested to the Queen by his rivals in her good graces, that by his absence from Court, and the troublesome discharge of so great a place, which they thought him not able to undergo, his favor with the Queen might flag. They were mistaken if they supposed that he would be utterly disgraced by the incompetent manner in which he must discharge his judicial duties; but they calculated rightly in anticipating that, prevented from showing her the devoted attention with which he had hitherto ever cultivated her as an admirer of her person as well as a member of her government, he would gradually lose his interest in her affections. The Earl of Leicester, who had occasionally been superseded by Hatton, now completely regained his ascendency, and he prevailed upon her to create for him the new office of "Lord Lieutenant of England and Ireland," which would have conferred upon him almost royal authority throughout the empire. A warrant had been made out for his appointment; but the Chancellor, on constitutional and personal grounds, highly disapproved of it. He ventured to remonstrate against it, and he induced Burghley to join with him in trying to convince the Queen of the impolicy of the measure. Without any open rupture with the Queen, the Chancellor contrived still to withhold the Great Seal from the patent,—when the man who had so long swayed her inclinations and had compromised her reputation, was opportunely seized with a violent disorder which, whether it arose from natural causes, or from the anguish of disappointed ambition, or from poison administered by his wife and her paramour, quickly terminated his existence.

The Queen's extravagant purpose was thus concealed from the public, and after a plentiful effusion of tears in memory of her worthless favorite, tranquility was restored to the Court. Had Hatton been still Vice Chamberlain and Gentleman of the Privy Chamber,—at leisure to masque it as in former days, he probably would now have filled, without dispute, the vacancy which Leicester's death created; but while he was sitting in the Star Chamber and in the Court of Chancery, and listening to applications at his private house for injunctions in cases of great emergency, and consulting anxiously with Dr. Swale how he should dispose of petitions, and what decrees were to be pronounced in the causes which he had heard, (besides, that he was now somewhat declining into the vale of years),—the young Earl of Essex, not yet twenty-one, was sighing at her feet, and by his songs and his tilting, by his spirit and address, by his flowing locks and unrazored lip, had captivated her affections, and had been rapidly promoted to be Master of the Horse, Captain General of the cavalry, a Knight of the Garter, and Prime Favorite. The spoiled school-boy, tired of the fondness of "the old woman," as he called her, had fled the Court and clandestinely joined the expedition fitted out under Sir Francis Drake, for the coast of Spain, to avenge on Philip the insults of the Armada. Still Hatton was too much occupied to avail himself of this conjuncture, and he had the deep mortification of finding himself, on his occasional visits to Whitehall or St. James's, to Richmond or Greenwich, entirely neglected and slighted for younger men.

The handsome youth from Devonshire who had thrown his brave silken cloak into the mire for a foot-cloth to the Queen had been appointed to the post which he himself had once held, and which he would now have been delighted to exchange for the Great Seal: Sir Walter Raleigh was intrusted with the special care of her person as "Captain of her band of Gentlemen Pensioners."

Once, while Hatton was holding the Great Seal in its red velvet bag, at a tilting match to which he had been invited during the vacation, he was present when the Queen singled out Charles Blount, the second son of Lord Mountjoy, then a student in the Inner Temple, expressed her approbation of his looks and agility, presented her hand for him to kiss, and sent him a chess queen of gold as a token which he openly bound to his arm with a crimson ribbon.[1]

These youths could not have any serious apprehensions from the rivalry of the Chancellor, but they com-

---

[1] This incident afterwards gave rise to a duel between Blount and the Earl of Essex, to the great delight of the Queen, who said "that her beauty had been the object of the quarrel." Had the Chancellor been the challenger, he might have recovered his lost ground.

bined with other more experienced courtiers, who marked his declining favor, to set the Queen against him, and there was a general disposition at Court to vex and annoy him. We may remember that the Queen had lent a sum of money to free him from the embarrassments occasioned by his youthful extravagance, and he had since become farther indebted to her in respect of certain crown rents he had received, for which he was liable to account. Perhaps, without any prompting (for she was always very mean in money concerns), she now desired that all these debts should be discharged, and she represented to him that as he had been for two or three years in possession of the most lucrative office in her gift, he could no longer plead poverty. He acknowledged the debt and her Majesty's forbearance, but represented his total inability yet to discharge it on account of the great charges brought upon him by the manner in which his installation had been conducted for her Majesty's honor, and by reason of his having confined himself strictly to the ancient fees, which, from the increased expense of living, had become very inadequate. He did not ask her to forgive him the debt, but he earnestly implored that further time might be allowed him for its payment. She was inexorable, and believing that this excuse was a mere pretense for cheating her, she directed her Attorney and Solicitor General to institute legal proceedings against him on his bond and statute merchant, under which the whole of his goods and lands might have been seized, and his person would have been liable to imprisonment.

All contemporary accounts agree that the Queen's neglect and cruelty had such an effect upon Lord Chancellor Hatton's spirits that he died of a broken heart. In Trinity term, 1591, it was publicly observed that he had lost his gayety and good looks. He did not rally during the long vacation, and when Michaelmas term came round he was confined to his bed. His sad condition being related to Elizabeth, all her former fondness for him revived, and she herself hurried to his house in Ely Place with cordial broths, in the hope of restoring him. These she warmed and offered him with her own hand, while he lay in bed,—adding many soothing expressions, and bidding him *live for her sake*. "But," he said, " all will not do: no pulleys will draw up a heart once cast down, though a Queen herself should set her hand thereunto." He died in the evening of Friday, the 21st of November, in the 52nd year of his age.[1]

He was immediately compared to Jonah's gourd, and described as "a mere vegetable of the Court, that sprung at night and sunk again at noon."[2]

He had, however, a most splendid funeral; and now that he was gone, the Queen, to divert her grief, did all that lay in her power to honor his memory. On the 16th of December, his remains were interred in St. Paul's Cathedral, more than 300 Lords of the Council, nobles, and knights, attending by her order, and her band of gentlemen pensioners, which he had commanded, guarding the procession. A sumptuous monument was raised to him, which perished in the fire of London.

Looking only to the frivolous accomplishments to which chiefly he owed his elevation, we must not forget the merits which really belonged to him. Although he possessed a very slender portion of book-learning, he had a very ready wit, and was well versed in the study of mankind. "He was a person," says Naunton, "that besides the graces of his person and dancing, had also the adjectiments of a strong and subtle capacity,—one that could soon learn the discipline and garb both of the times and the Court."

He is said to have shown great industry when he was made Lord Chancellor, and to have made himself tolerably well acquainted with the practice of the Court of Chancery; but with a mind wholly unimbued with legal principles, his knowledge of it must have been superficial. He issued several new orders to improve it, which were much applauded. With respect to these he could only have had the merit, so useful to Chancellors, of availing himself of the experience and talents of others. Again, it is said that none of his decrees were reversed; but if Dr. Swale

[1] Camden, without descending into particulars which he considered inconsistent with the dignity of history, and although showing his usual tenderness for the reputation of Elizabeth, confirms the general account we have of the death of Hatton. Speaking of the severe proclamation against Catholics which it was supposed that the Chancellor condemned, he says, "Verum obierat Hattonus pridie quam hoc edictum publicatum ex diabete et animi mœrore, quod Regina ingentem pecuniam ex decimis et primitiis quibus præfuit, collectam paulo acerbius exagerat quam pro ea qua apud ipsam floruit gratia condonandam sperarat. Nec hominem verbo dejectum relevare poterat quamvis inviscret et consolatione dimulceret."   [2] Naunton.

and he had erred ever so much, there was hardly any means of correcting them; for there was no appeal to the House of Lords in Equity suits till the reign of Charles II., and there was no chance of bringing, with any effect, before the Council the decree of a Chancellor still in power. To give the public a notion that he had attended to the study of the law, he composed a "Treatise concerning Acts of Parliament, and the Exposition thereof;" but it was a very poor production.

When presiding in the Court of Chancery, he disarmed his censurers by courtesy and good humor, and he occasionally ventured on a joke. At one time, when there was a case before him respecting the boundaries of an estate, a plan being produced, the counsel on one part said, "We lie on this side, my Lord;" and the counsel on the other part said, "And we lie on this side, my Lord;" whereupon the Lord Chancellor Hatton stood up and said, "If you lie on both sides, whom will you have me to believe?"[1]

Although none of his decisions in Chancery have come down to us, we have a full account of a trial before him in the Star Chamber for a libel,—when he presided with great gravity,—and with many apologies for the leniency of the sentence, he fined the defendant £2,000, and directed the Judges to testify this punishment on their circuits, to the end the whole realm might have knowledge of it, and the people no longer be seduced with these lewd libelers.[2]

His most elaborate effort while he held the Great Seal was his address "on the elevation of Mr. Clerke to the dignity of a Sergeant." After some preliminary observations on the gratitude due to her Majesty for such a distinction, he thus continued:—"No man can live without lawe. Therefore I do exhort you that you have good care of your dutie in the calling, and that you be a father to the poore. That you be carefull to relieve all men afflicted. You ought to be an arm to helpe them, and a hande to succoure them. Use uprightness and followe truthe. Be free from cawtell. Mix with the exercise of the lawe no manner of decepte. Let these thinges be farre from your harte. Be of an undoubted resolution. Be of good cour-

---

[1] Recorded by Lord Bacon in his Apophthegms, or Jest Book.
[2] Regina v. Knightley, 1 St. Tr. 1270.

age, and feare not to be carried away withe the authoritie, power or threatenings of anye other. Maynteyne your clientes cause in all right. Be not put to sylence. As it is alleged out of the booke of Wisdome, '*Noli quærere fieri Judex, ni forte extimescas faciem potentis, et ponas scandalam in agilitate tua.*"[1] Know no man's face. Go on withe fortitude. Do it in uprightnes. '*Redde cuique quod suum.*' Be not parciall to yourself. Abuse not the highest guift of God which no doubt is great in equity. Theis thinges be the actions of nobilitie. He that doth theis thinges dewlie deserves high honour, and is worthy in the world to rule. Let truthe be famyllier with you. Regard neither friende nor enemye. Proceede in the good worke layed upon you. And the laste point that I am to saye to you— Use diligence and carefulnes. And althoughe I have not been acquainted withe the course of the lawe, albeit in my youthe I spent some time in the studye thereof, yet I find by daily experience that diligence bringes to pas greate thinges in the course and proceedinge of the lawe, and, contrarilie, negligence overthrowes many good cawses. Let not the dignitie of the lawe be geven to men unmeete. And I do exhorte you all that are heare present not to call men to the barre or the benche that are so unmeete. I finde that there are now more at the barre in one house than there was in all the Innes of Courte when I was a younge man." He concludes by an exhortation to avoid Chancery, and to settle disputes in the Courts of Law. "We sit heare to helpe the rigor and extremities of the lawe. The holy conscience of the Queene for matters of equitie in some sorte is by her Majesties goodness committed to mee, when *summum jus* doth minister *summam injuriam*. But the lawe is the inheritance of all men. And I praye God blesse you and send you as much worshipp as ever had anie in your cawlinge."[2]

The only very serious suspicion ever thrown upon Hatton's conduct arose out of his connection with the death of Henry Percy, Earl of Northumberland. After this nobleman had been long confined in the Tower, without being brought to trial, the Lieutenant received an order to remove the Earl's keeper, and to substitute for him a

---

[1] Ecclesias. cap, 7, v. 6. This is the Vulgate still always quoted. In the margin "Æquitate" is proposed for Agilitate. In the Septuagint the word is $εὐθυτητί$.   [2] Reg. Lib. B. 1586, f. 661.

servant of Sir Christopher Hatton. The same night the prisoner was found dead in his bed, having been shot through the heart with three slugs. A verdict of *felo de se* being returned by the coroner's jury, the subject was taken up in the Star Chamber, and there Sir Christopher and other members of the Court delivered harangues to prove that the deceased had been guilty of treason, and that to escape a public trial and conviction, with the forfeiture of his houses and estate, he had put an end to his existence.[1] Sinister inferences were drawn by the multitude from the change of his keeper, the difficulty of conveying fire-arms to a prisoner in the Tower, and the eagerness of the government to have him found guilty of suicide; but there is no ground for imputing such a crime to one to whose disposition and habits it must have been most repugnant.

Even while holding the Great Seal his highest delight continued to be in dancing, and, as often as he had an opportunity, he abandoned himself to this amusement. Attending the marriage of his nephew and heir with a Judge's daughter, he was decked, according to the custom of the age, in his official robes; and it is recorded, that when the music struck up, he doffed them, threw them down on the floor, and saying, "Lie there, Mr. Chancellor!" danced the measures at the nuptial festivity.[2]

He affected to be a protector of learned men, and Spenser presented to him a copy of his immortal poem, "The Faery Queen," accompanied by the following sonnet:—

> *To the R. H. Sir C. Hatton, Lord High Chancellor of England.*
> Those prudent heads, that with their counsels wise,
>   Whilom the pillars of th' earth did sustain;
> And taught ambitious Rome to tyrannize,
>   And in the neck of all the world to reign,
> Oft from those grave affairs were wont t' abstain,
>   With the sweet lady-muses for to play.
> So Ennius, the elder Africain;
>   So Maro oft did Cæsar's cares allay.
> So you, great Lord! that with your counsel sway
>   The burden of this kingdom mightily;
> With like delights sometimes may eke delay
>   The rugged brow of careful policy;
> And to these idle rhymes lend little space,
>   Which, *for their title's sake*,[3] may find more grace.

---

[1] See Stow's Annals, p. 706. Camden, B. iv. 50. Somers' Tracts, **i. 223.**
[2] Captain Allen's Lett. in Birch, vol. i. p. 56.
[3] "The Faery Queen," representing Queen Elizabeth.

Thus was he celebrated by Ockland, in his character of Queen Elizabeth's ministers:—

> "Splendidus Hatton,
> Ille Satelitii regalis ductor, ovanti
> Pectore, Mæcenas studiosis, maximus altor
> Et fautor veræ virtutis, munificusque."

Much erudition and great acquirements were now found to belong to the scapegrace student of the Temple,—and the University of Oxford elected for their Chancellor him to whom they would not grant a degree.

He was celebrated, or rather censured, in the intolerant age in which he lived, for trying to screen from persecution both Papists and Puritans.[1]

The nature of his intimacy with Elizabeth, it is to be hoped, was not such as to deprive her of the right to the title that she so often boasted of in public, and much allowance ought to be made for the manners of the age;—but, notwithstanding the warmth of language and the freedoms between the sexes then supposed to be consistent with innocence, this intimacy certainly caused much scandal in their own time.

Lord Chancellor Hatton was never married, which, if we may trust the representation upon this subject in Mary's celebrated letter respecting the private life of Elizabeth, arose from the jealousy of his royal mistress, who even broke off a match between him and a daughter of the Earl of Shrewsbury, afterwards married to the Earl of Lennox.[2]

---

[1] "Qui in religionis causa non urendum non secandum censuit."—Camden.

[2] The most striking proof of the prevalent suspicion is to be found in this letter of Mary to Elizabeth, relating the stories circulated by the Countess of Shrewsbury,—which a regard to historical truth requires me to insert,—cautioning my female readers against perusing it, though written by a Queen to a Queen. After some prefatory remarks, she says, "J'apelle mon Dieu à tesmoing que la Comptesse de Schreusbury madit de vous ce qui suit au plus près de ces termes. . . . . Premièrement, qu'un auquel elle disoit que vous aviez faict promesse de mariage devant une Dame de vostre chambre, avoit cousche infinies foys auvesque Vous avec toute la licence et privaulte qui se peut user entre mari et famme; Mays qu'indubitablement Vous nestiez pas comme les aultres fammes, et pour ce respect cestoit follie à touz ceulx qui affectoient vostre Mariage avec Monsieur le Duc d'Anjou, d'aultant qu'il ne ce pourroit accomplir; et que Vous ne vouldriez jamays perdu la liberte de Vous fayre fayre l'amour et auvoir vostre plesir tousjours auveques nouveaulx amoureulx, *regretant ce*, disoit elle, *que vous ne vous contentiez de Maister Haton*, et un aultre de ce Royaulme; mays que pour l'honneur du pays il luy faschoit le plus, que vous aviez non seullement engagé vostre honneur auveques un estrangier Nommé Simier, l'alant

Notwithstanding these tender sentiments, Elizabeth did not distinguish him from her other courtiers, by abstaining from the public manifestation of her resentment when he offended her; for as she gave a box on the ear to the Earl Marshal, and spat at Sir Matthew Arundel, on one occasion she collared Hatton before the whole Court.[1] By this missive he tried to appease her:—" If the woundes of the thought wear not most dangerous of all wthout speedy dressing, I shold not now troble yor Ma^{ty} wth the lynes of my co'playnt; and if whatsoever came from you wear not ether very gracious or greevous to me, what you sayd wold not synke so deepely in my bosome. My profession hath been, is, and ever shalbe, to your Ma^{ty} all duty wthin order, all reverent love wthout mesure, and all trothe wthout blame; insomuch as when I shall not be fownde soche as to yor Highnes Cæsar sought to have hys wife to himselfe, not only wthout synne, but also not to be suspected, I wish my spright devyded from my body as his spouse was from his bedde; and there-

trouver de nuit en la chambre d'une dame, que la dicte Comptesse blasmoit forte a ceste occasion la, ou Vous le baisiez et usiez auvec luy de diverses privaultes deshonnestes; mays aussi luy revelliez les segretz du Royaulme, trahisant vos propres Counseillers avvesques luy: Que Vous vous estiez desportée de la mesme dissolution avec le Duc son Maystre, qui vous avoit este trouver une nuit à la porte de vostre chambre, ou vous laviez rancontre auvec vostre seulle chemise et manteau de nuit, et que par apres vous laviez laisse entrer, et qu'il demeura avveques Vous pres de troys heures. *Quant au dict Haton, que vous le cou$_1$iez a force, faysant si publiquement paroitre l'amour que luy portiez, qui luy mesmes estoit contreint de s'en retiere, et que Vous donnastes un soufflet a Kiligreu pour ne vous avoir ramene le dict Haton, que vous avviez envoiay rappeller par luy, s'etant desparti en chollere d'auveques vous pour quelques injures que luy avviez dittes pour certiens boutons dor qu'il auvoit sur son habit. Qu'elle auvait travaille de fayre espouser au dit Haton, la feu Comtesse de Lenox sa fille, mays que de creinte de Vous, il ne osoit entendre;* que mesme le Comte d'Oxfort nosoit ce rappointer auveques sa famme de peur de perdre la faveur qu'il esperoit recepvoir par vous fayre l'amour: Que vouz estiez prodigue envers toutes telles gens et ceulx qui ce mesloient de telles mesnees, comme a un de Vostre Chambre Gorge, auquel Vous avviez donne troys centz ponds de rante *pour vous avoir apporte les nouvelles du retour de Haton:* Qu'a toutz aultres Vous estiez fort ingrate chische, et qu'il ni avoit que troys ou quatre en vostre Royaulme a qui Vous ayes jamays faict bien: Me conseillant, en riant extresmement, mettre mon filz sur les rancs pour vous fayre l'amours, comme chose qui me serviroit grandement et metroit Monsieur le Duc hors de quartier." She then gives various other disgusting particulars respecting Elizabeth's person and her habits, which, as they do not affect my hero, I am glad that I am at liberty to pass over. This letter, written by Mary very indiscreetly a short time before her trial, must have cut off from her all chance of mercy. See it at full length as copied from Lord Salisbury's Papers.—1 St. Tr. 1202. [1] Nugæ Ant. 167, 176.

fore, upon yesternight's wordes, I am driven to say to yo' Ma'^ty, either to satisfye wronge conceyts or to answer false reports, that if the speech you used of yo' Turke did ever passe my pen or lippes to any creature owt of yo' Highnes' hearing, but to my L. of Burghley, wth whom I have talked bothe of the man and the matter, I desyre no less condemnation then as a traytor, and no more pardon then hys ponyshment; and, further, if ever I ether spake or sent to the embassad. of France, Spayne, or Scotland, or have accompanied, to my knowledge, any that conferres wth them, I doe renownce all good from your Ma^ty in erthe, and all grace from God in heaven; wch assurans if yo' H. think not sufficyent, upon the knees of my harte I hu'bly crave at yo' Ma^tys handes, not so much for my satisfaction as yo' own suerty, make the perfitest triaall hereof; for if upon such occasions it shall please yo' Ma^ty to syfte the chaffe from the wheate, the corne of yo' co'monwealth wolde be more pure, and myxt granes wold lesse infect the synnowes of yo' suerty wch God must strengthen, to yo' Ma^tys best and longest preservation."[1]

The following letter, addressed to the young Earl of Essex while commanding the English forces at the siege of Rouen, where his younger brother, Walter had fallen, was written by Hatton a few months before his death (as is supposed) by the command of the Queen, who had become alarmed for the safety of her new favorite; and it must have been a cruel task to impose upon the old Chancellor to pretend to take such an interest in the youth who had supplanted him:—"My good Lord, lett me be bolde to warne you of a matter that many of yo' frendes here gretely feare, namely, that the late accident of yo' noble brother, who hathe so valiantly and honorably spent his lyfe in his Prince's and countrey's service, draw you not, through griefe or passion, to hasard yo' selfe over venturously. Yo' Lo^p best knoweth that true valour consisteth rather in constant performenge of that wh^ch hath been advisedly forethought than in aptnes or readiness of thrusting yo' person indifferently into every danger. You have many waies and many tymes made sufficient proof of yo' valientnes. No man doubteth but that you have enough, if you have not overmuche; and therefore, both in regard of the services her Ma^ty ex-

[1] Lodge, Hist. Ill.

pecteth to receive from you, and in respect of the griefe that would growe to the whole realme by the losse of one of that honorable birth, and that worthe wch is sufficiently known (as greater hathe not been for any that hathe been borne therin these many and many yeeres), I must even, before Almighty God, praye and require yor Lo^p to have that circumspectnes of yor selfe wch is fitt for a generall of yor sorte." [1]

Of his magnificent style of living, even when his means were slender, we have a striking account in an intercepted letter of M. de Champanaye, who was ambassador to Elizabeth from the Low Countries: " I was one day by Sir Christopher Hatton, captain of her Majesty's guard, invited to Eltham, a house of the Queen's whereof he was the guardian, at which time I heard and saw three things that in all my travel in France, Italy, and Spain, I never heard or saw the like. The first was a concert of music so excellent and sweet it can not be expressed; the second a course at a buck with the best and most beautiful greyhounds that ever I did behold ; and the third a man of arms, excellently mounted, richly armed, and, indeed, the most accomplished cavaliero I had ever seen." [2]

In 1576 the Queen dined with Sir Christopher at Eltham, and he provided hunting, music, and a passage of arms for her amusement.[3]

At Stoke Pogis, in Buckinghamshire, he had a country house constructed in the true Elizabethan taste. Here, when he was Lord Chancellor, he several times had the honor to entertain her Majesty, and showed that the agility and grace which had won her heart when he was a student in the Inner Temple remained little abated:

> To raise the ceiling's fretted height,
>   Each panel in achievements clothing,
> Rich windows that exclude the light,
>   And passages that lead to nothing.
> Full oft within the spacious walls,
>   When he had fifty winters o'er him.

[1] Lodge Hist. Ill. 649.

[2] Segar's Tournaments, in Walpole's "Miscellaneous Antiquities."

[3] It would appear likewise that he was very kind to his poorer neighbors. In the churchwardens' accounts of the parish of Eltham for the year 1573, there is the following item:—

"Paid at the eating of the buck which Mr. Hatton gave to ye parishe, xxxvij$s$. vj$d$. ;"—no doubt for washing down the buck, as good eating requires good drinking.—*Communicated to me by Geo. R. Corner, Esq., of Eltham.*

> My grave Lord Keeper[1] led the brawls,
> The Seal and maces danc'd before him.
> His bushy beard and shoe-strings green,
> His high-crowned hat and satin doublet,
> Mov'd the stout heart of England's Queen,
> Though Pope and Spaniard could not trouble it.

Sir Christopher Hatton left considerable estates to the son of his sister by Sir William Newport. This nephew took the name of Hatton, and married the daughter of the first Lord Exeter, the granddaughter of Lord Treasurer Burghley, and afterwards famous as "the Lady Hatton,"—a beauty at the Court of James I., courted in second marriage by Sir Francis Bacon and Sir Edward Coke. She having the bad taste to prefer the Chief Justice, he got possession of a great part of Chancellor Hatton's property, along with a companion who kept him in trouble for the rest of his days.

The heir male of the Lord Chancellor, sprung from a collateral branch of the family, was ennobled in the reign of Charles I., by the title of Baron Hatton, of Kirby, in the county of Northampton; and his son, in the year 1682, was created a Viscount by the title of Viscount Hatton, of Gretton. The family in the male line is now extinct, but is represented through a female by the present Earl of Winchelsea and Nottingham[2]

CHAPTER XLVI.

LIFE OF SIR JOHN PUCKERING, LORD KEEPER OF THE GREAT SEAL.

THE Queen heard of the death of Sir Christopher Hatton in the evening of the 20th of November, but, from ancient recollections and a little remorse, she was too much affected to give any directions respecting the Great Seal till the next morning. She then ordered two Knights of the Garter, Lord Cobham and

---
[1] By a pardonable contraction, Gray might have allowed Sir Christopher to retain his just rank of Lord Chancellor, instead of reducing him to "Lord Keeper."

[2] Grandeur of Law, ed. 1684, p. 16. Sir Harris Nicolas's Memoirs of Sir Christopher Hatton.

Lord Buckhurst, to bring it to her. They found it locked up in an iron chest,[1] in the house of the late Chancellor in Holborn, and forthwith delivered it to her Majesty in the palace at Westminster. She was still more perplexed than she had ever been before as to the disposal of it.

Although the last experiment had turned out better than could have been reasonably expected, such heavy complaints had reached her ears against the appointment, that she would not venture again to select a Lord Chancellor or Lord Keeper merely from his good looks and fashionable accomplishments. Her court consisted of two orders,—favorites and men of business. She now felt that it was among the latter she was bound to look for the first Judge of the land. But Puckering, her Prime Sergeant, who was next in succession to the office,—a profound Jurisconsult it is true,—was in manners and appearance such a contrast to his gay and gallant predecessor;—he was so dull, heavy, and awkward;—his whole deportment was so "lawyer-like and ungenteel,"—that she for a long time could not summon resolution to consent to his appointment. Meanwhile an expedient was resorted to which, I believe, was quite new, and has never since been followed,—of having two Commissions for doing the duties of the Great Seal. Lord Burghley, Lord Hunsdon, Lord Cobham, and Lord Buckhurst were appointed to seal writs, patents, and decrees; and Sir Gilbert Gerrard, the Master of the Rolls, and others, were authorized to hear and decide causes in the Court of Chancery.[2]

Things went on according to this plan for seven months, but not very satisfactorily; for there were disputes between the two sets of Commissioners respecting jurisdiction and fees; and Gerrard's colleagues not deferring, as he expected they would, to his experience and rank,—from their division of opinion the decrees pronounced by them had less weight.

Prime Sergeant Puckering had about this time pleased her Majesty by the able manner in which he had conducted the trial of Sir John Perrot, the Lord Deputy of

[1] "In cista de ferro coloris rubei sub clavi nuper Cancellarii reclusa."—R. Cl. 34 Eliz.
[2] "Eodem die altera Commissio directa Gilberto Gerrarde, militi, Magro Rot. et aliis pro audiendo et terminando causas in honorabili curia Cancell. sigillata fuit.'—R. Cl. 34 Eliz.

Ireland, before the Star Chamber, and at last she consented to his having the Great Seal, with the lower rank of Lord Keeper.

JOHN PUCKERING is an instance of a man, without possessing brilliant parts or committing any dishonorable action,—by industry, perseverance, and good luck, raising himself from obscurity to the highest civil office in the state.

He was the younger son of a gentleman of very small fortune, residing near Flamborough Head, in the county of York, who had great difficulty in giving him a decent education, and could give him nothing more.

It is doubtful whether the future Lord Keeper ever had the advantage of being at a University. He studied law with great assiduity in Lincoln's Inn, and in the mootings in which he engaged he displayed much familiarity with the *Year Books*, which he pored over day and night. As an apprentice, or utter barrister, he had not much practice in common matters; but he had a high reputation for learning, and he was consulted in cases of weight and difficulty. He was called to the degree of Sergeant at Law in the twenty-second of Elizabeth, along with Clench, Walmesley, Fleetwood, Periam, and other distinguished lawyers; and now being entitled to practice in the Court of Common Pleas, his extraordinary knowledge of the law of real actions, exclusively tried there, gave him such an advantge, that he at once rose to eminence.

He next became a member of the House of Commons, where he gained considerable authority on questions respecting regularity of proceeding and privilege, in the two last sessions of the parliament which, after continuing on foot for eleven years, was dissolved in the beginning of the year 1583.

When a new parliament was assembled, in November, 1585, Puckering was elected Speaker, and filled the chair efficiently, if not gracefully. During the session the Queen sent for him, and reprimanded him for allowing a bill to be introduced for a further reform of the Church. He communicated her displeasure to the House, and the bill was allowed to drop. At the prorogation he delivered an address to the Queen, most insufferably long, perplexed and tedious. Alluding to the Queen's complaint of their debates, he said, "I can assure your Majesty, that in this assembly there was never found in any speech, private or public, any argument or token of the mind of any person that showed any intention to be offensive to your Majesty. And for proof hereof, when it pleased your Majesty to direct me to declare your pleasure to the Commons' House in what sort you would they should stay any further debating of the manner of reformation of such things as they thought might be reformed in that Church, I found them all ready to obey your Majesty's pleasure therein." He concluded by asking her to give her royal assent to the bills they had passed,—exhibiting a specimen of the performance of a Sergeant at law trying to be eloquent: "Lastly, I am, in their names, to exhibit our most humble and earnest petitions to your Majesty to give life to the works, not of our hands, but of our minds, cogitations, and hearts; which, otherwise than being lightened by the beams of your favor, shall be but vain, dumb, and dead."[1]

At this time it was usual for a lawyer filling the chair of the House of Commons to continue to practice at the bar, and Puckering was employed as counsel for the Crown in the state trials, arising out of the plot to rescue the Queen of Scots. The prosecution of Babington and Tilney, two of the principal conspirators, was chiefly conducted by him, and he made speeches against them, read confessions, put questions to the accused, and, at a pinch, gave a little evidence himself, after the manner of the times.

When a new parliament was called, with the view of carrying into execution the sentence pronounced against Mary, Puckering was again chosen Speaker, and was approved of by "the Lords Lieutenants," who represented the Queen. There was a special order from her, which was implicitly obeyed, "that no laws should be made at all in this session." And the only business stirred was the execution of the sentence upon Mary.[2]

When the preliminary forms had been gone through, the Speaker reminded the House of going upon the "Great Cause," as they termed it, and was unanimously directed to wait upon the Queen, and to urge her to comply with their wishes. Puckering was received by her at Richmond, and stated five reasons why the Queen of

[1] 1 Parl. Hist. 830. [2] 1 Parl. Hist. 835.

Scots should be put to death. "1st. She and her favorers think she has not only a right to succeed to your Crown, but to enjoy it in possession. 2ndly. She is obdurate in malice against your royal person, and there is no place for mercy, since there is no hope that she will desist from most wicked attempts. 3rdly. She boldly and openly professes it lawful for her to move invasion upon you. 4thly. She thinks it not only lawful, but honorable and meritorious, to take your life, as being already deprived of your Crown by the Pope's excommunication. 5thly. She is greedy for your Majesty's death, and prefers it before her own life and safety; for in her directions to one of her late accomplices, she advised, under covert terms, that whatever should become of her, tragical execution should be performed upon you."

Elizabeth delivered an extempore harangue in answer, saying, that "if, instead of Queens, they were but as two milkmaids with pails upon their arms, and if her own life only were in danger, and not the whole estate of their religion and well-doing, she would most willingly pardon the offense committed against her; but that she would, for the good of her subjects, take the matter into consideration, and send them her resolution with all conveniency." The ungainly Puckering was attended on this occasion, and prompted by, that accomplished courtier, Hatton, the Queen's Vice Chamberlain, who pleased her much more than the Sergeant, and, without any one suspecting it, was now so near to greatness.

The fears of Elizabeth and the English nation being quieted by the death of Mary, for which they were all so eager,—Puckering's next appearance was as counsel to prosecute Secretary Davison, in the Star Chamber, for his presumption in sending off the warrant for execution without due authority. The account says, that "he aggravated Davison's offense, and was forward to accuse, and yet seemed more *pro forma tantum* than of any matter he had to charge him withal.'" And certainly those who were then assembled must have had more gravity than the Roman Augurs meeting each other, if they were able to keep their countenance while they were playing their parts in this farce; although it turned out a serious matter for the poor Secretary, who had a heavy fine im

[1] 1 St. Tr. 1233.

posed upon him, and was permanently deprived of his office.

For these services, Puckering was now made Queen's Sergeant, and thereby put over the Attorney and Solicitor General.[1]

He was soon after leading counsel for the Crown in the celebrated prosecution of Knightley for a libel before the Star Chamber,[2] and the important trial of the Earl of Arundel for high treason, before the Court of the Lord High Steward.[3]

On this last occasion he had rather a curious dialogue with the noble prisoner, who desired to know how he was a traitor? *Puckering, Serg.* "The traitors have a good conceit of my Lord of Arundel, knowing him to be affected to the Catholic cause. It is defined, that the Catholic cause is mere treason. Petro Paulo Rosetto came over to sound noblemen and gentlemen in England."[4] There was a picture produced, found in my Lord's trunk, wherein was painted a hand bitten with a serpent, shaking the serpent into the fire,—about which was written this posy, *Quis contra nos?*—on the other side a lion rampant, with his chops all bloody, and this posy, *Tamen Leo*. The noble prisoner in vain said "he had received it innocently as a new year's gift." He was found guilty by his Peers; but being respited, he died a natural death in the Tower.[5]

Puckering's last appearance at the bar was on the trial of Sir John Perrot, late Lord Deputy of Ireland, for high treason. This rough soldier had always been very loyal to the Queen; but, when in a passion, had been in the habit of speaking of her very disrespectfully; and being recalled in disgrace, his enemies, taking advantage of his hasty expressions, were resolved to bring him to the scaffold.

Puckering, in opening the case to the Jury, gravely contended, that words were sufficient to establish the charge against the prisoner, for "the original of his treasons proceeded from the imagination of his heart, which imagination was in itself high treason, albeit the same proceeded not to any overt act; and the heart being possessed with

---

[1] Or. Jur. 97. [2] 1 St. Tr. 1263.
[3] "PUCKERINGUS, Regius ad legem serviens, exorsus primam accusationis partem *fusius* explicavit."—Camd. Eliz. vol. ii. 4.
[4] 1 St. Tr. 1253. [5] Ib. 1263.

the abundance of his traitorous imagination, and not being able to contain itself, burst forth in vile and traitorous speeches, for *Ex abundantia cordis os loquitur*."[1]

Evidence was then given that the prisoner, when Lord Deputy, had said at the Council table, " Stick not so much on the Queen's letters of commandment, for she may command what she will, but we will do what we list." " Nay, God's wounds ! I think it strange she should use me thus." " This fiddling woman troubles me out of measure." " It is not safe for her Majesty to break such sour bread to her servants ;" and that he had used other such uncourtly expressions. A feeble attempt was likewise made to show that he had been engaged in a treasonable correspondence with the Prince of Parma.

Puckering, as leading counsel for the Crown, then summed up, and (seemingly without any speech from the prisoner, or direction from the bench) "prayed the jury to consider well of that which had been said, and willed them to go together." Perrot, however, burst out in a passion, desiring them to have a conscience in the matter, and to remember "that his blood would be required at their hands." The jury departed from the bar, and in three quarters of an hour returned with a verdict of *Guilty*.[2]

The Queen was much pleased with the report brought to her of Sergeant Puckering's zeal on this occasion, and she forthwith rewarded him for it; but it should be remembered to her honor, that when she afterwards read an account of the trial, she refused to allow the sentence to be carried into execution,—repeating with applause the rescript of Theodosius: "If any person speak ill of the Emperor through a foolish rashness or inadvertency, it is to be despised ; if out of madness, it deserves pity ; if from malice, it calls for mercy."

Puckering's honors were showered upon him at Greenwich in the evening of Sunday, the 28th of May, 1592. First he was conducted into the Queen's closet and there knighted.[3] He was next admitted of the Privy Council, and having taken the oaths, he was led into the Council Chamber, placed at the lower end of the Council table, and made to sign a paper as Privy Councillor. He was

[1] 1 St. Tr. 1318. [2] Ib. 1326.
[3] " Per semetipsam Dnam Reginam in privata camera sua in Equestrem dignitetem receptus fuit et ornatus."

then conducted back to the Queen's closet, where her Majesty having addressed to him an eloquent discourse upon the duties of the office she was about to bestow upon him, and exhorted him to strive to please God and to do justice to all who should come before him as suitors,[1] delivered into his hands the Great Seal, with the title of "Lord Keeper." He then, with the other Councillors, returned to the Council Chamber, and took his place at the upper end of the table according to his new rank.

Other memorable legal promotions took place at the same time,—Sir John Popham being made Chief Justice of the Queen's Bench,—Sir Thomas Egerton, Attorney General,—and Sir Edward Coke, Solicitor General.

On the 4th of June, the Lord Keeper rode in great state from York House, near Charing Cross, which became the official residence of several successive Lord Keepers and Lord Chancellors, to Westminster Hall, attended by a long retinue of Lords, Knights, Judges, and lawyers,—and publicly took the oaths in the Court of Chancery. Four days afterwards he sat the first time in the Star Chamber.

Puckering held the Great Seal as Lord Keeper till his death,—a period of four years,—with the character of judicial ability and personal integrity.—But although profoundly versed in all the mysteries of the common law, he was nothing of a civilian, and his mind was not much imbued with the general principles of jurisprudence. His practice had been confined almost entirely to the Common Pleas, till, in his capacity of Queen's Sergeant, he was obliged to conduct Government prosecutions. He had occasionally of late gone into the Court of Chancery; but from Lord Chancellor Hatton his knowledge as an Equity lawyer did not much improve. He was thought, therefore, to take too narrow and technical a view of the questions which came before him, and he left the field of equity almost virgin ground to his successor, Lord Ellesmere, by whom it was cultivated so successfully.

There being a call of Sergeants soon after his installation, he gave his brethren these admonitions, some of

---

[1] "Quoad tam placitandum Deo, qm ut ppli sui omnes coram ipso causas ad agendum bentes, bono moderamine tractarent et recte ab eo in omnibus satisfierent."—Rot. Cl. 34 Eliz.

which would be very serviceable to the bar at the present day:—

"If you find the cause to be unconscionable, cruel, unmerciful, or grounded upon malice or for vexation, reject it and deal not therein. Dissuade your client from it, which if you can not do, leave him in his madness and phrensy. In all your pleadings seek not advantages to trip one of you the other by covin or niceness; and as you are of one profession, so lovingly and brotherly warn the one the other of anything mistaken or misconceived in pleading. *I am to exhort you also not to embrace multitude of causes, or undertake more places of hearing causes than you are well able to consider of or perform, lest thereby you either disappoint your clients when their causes be heard, or come unprovided, or depart when their causes be in hearing. For it is all one not to come, as either to come unprovided, or depart before it be ended.*"[1]

A new parliament was called in the beginning of the year 1593, and Lord Keeper Puckering, in the presence of the Queen, delivered the initiatory harangue to the two Houses. With all the prolixity and tediousness of Sergeants in old times, he dilated upon the relations of England with Spain, France, the Empire, the Low Countries, and Scotland: He drew a piteous picture of her Highness's necessities, "which had actually caused her to sell part of her Highness's Crown:" He warned them that the calling of this parliament was "not for the making of any more new laws, for there were already so many that, rather than burden the subjects with more, it were fitting that an abridgement were made of those there were already; and," said he, "whereas, heretofore, it hath been used that many have delighted themselves in long orations, full of verbosity and of vain ostentations, the time that is precious should not be so spent."[2]

The Speaker elected was the famous Edward Coke, lately made Solicitor General, who, when presented at the bar of the House of Lords, disqualified himself to the Queen in quaint phrase, saying, among other things, "as in the heavens a star is but *opacum corpus* until it have received light from the sun, so stand I *corpus opacum*, a mute body, until your Highness's bright, shining wisdom hath looked upon me and allumed me. How unable I

[1] Reg. Lib. A. 1580, f. 189.   [2] 1 Parl. Hist. 858.

am to do this office my present speech doth tell: of this House I am most unfit; for amongst them there are many grave, many learned, many deep wise men, and those of ripe judgments; but I am untimely fruit, not yet ripe, a bud scarcely blossomed. So, as I fear me, your Majesty will say, *Neglecta frugi, eliguntur folia,*—amongst so many fair fruit ye have plucked a shaken leaf."[1]

The Lord Keeper, by the Queen's command, thus addressed him:—

"Mr. Solicitor, her Grace's most excellent Majesty hath willed me to signify unto you, that she hath ever well conceived of you since she first heard of you, which will appear when her Highness elected you from others to serve herself. By this, your modest, wise, and well-composed speech, you give her Majesty further occasion to conceive of you above that which ever she thought was in you. By endeavoring to deject and abase yourself and your desert, you have discovered and made known your worthliness and sufficiency to discharge the place you are called to. And whereas you account yourself *corpus opacum*, her Majesty, by the influence of her virtue and wisdom, doth enlighten you, and not only alloweth and approveth you, but much thanketh the Lower House, and commendeth their discretion in making so good a choice, and selecting so fit a man."

Speaker Coke then delivered another florid oration in her Majesty's praise, concluding with the triple prayer in the name of the Commons, for freedom of speech, freedom from arrest, and access to her royal person.

Lord Keeper Puckering.—" Liberty of speech is granted you; but you must know what privilege you have;—not to speak every one what he listeth, or what cometh in his brain to utter—but your privilege is *Aye!* or *No!* Wherefore, Mr. Speaker, her Majesty's pleasure is, that if you perceive any idle heads which will not stick to hazard their own estates, which will meddle with reforming the Church, and transposing the Commonwealth, and do exhibit any bills to that purpose, that you receive them not until they be viewed and considered by those who it is fitter should consider of such things, and can better judge of them."[2]

The famous Peter Wentworth, the Puritan, and three

[1] 1 Parl. Hist. 861. [2] Ib. 862.

other members, thought to evade this injunction by presenting a petition to the Lord Keeper, instead of making a motion in the House, that the Lords will join in supplicating her Majesty that she would agree to settle the succession to the Crown, for which they had a bill ready drawn. But they were immediately called before the Council, and the Lord Keeper telling them that the Queen was highly displeased at their presumption, they were all committed to prison. A motion was made for their release; but it was answered that her Majesty had committed them for causes best known to herself, and that she would release them whenever she thought proper, and would be better pleased to do it of her own proper motion than from their suggestion.[1]

At the close of the session Speaker Coke, having delivered an oration comparing her Majesty to the queen bee, *sine aculeo*, Lord Keeper Puckering was not very complimentary to the Commons, saying that "her Majesty thought that, in some things, they had spent more time than they needed. She misliked also that such irreverence was shown to Privy Councilors, who were not to be accounted as common knights and burgesses of the House, who are councillors only during the parliament; whereas the others are standing councillors, and for their wisdom and great service are called to the service of the State."—So was privilege dealt with by these great lawyers, Puckering and Coke, who were probably applauded by many for assisting in restraining the usurpation of the Commons!

During Puckering's time parliament did not again meet, and no other public event occurred in which he was concerned, entire tranquillity prevailing at home, and the attention of the nation being absorbed by the expeditions fitted out against Spain.

He died of an apoplexy, at York House, on the 30th of April, 1596, and was buried in Westminster Abbey, where there is a monument erected to his memory.

Lord Keeper Puckering was a mere lawyer, having no intercourse with scholars or men of fashion, and mixing with statesmen only when, in the discharge of his official duties, he was drawn among them from the society of Judges, Benchers, and Readers, in which he delighted.

[1] D'Ewes, p. 407.

No sonnet was ever addressed to him. He probably never read the "Faery Queen," or heard of WILLIAM SHAKESPEARE, who was now rising into fame. Hence no personal anecdotes of him have descended to us, and for his history we are obliged chiefly to resort to musty rolls and records. Nevertheless, there can be no doubt that he was much respected, and looked up to in his own time.[1]

The only charge ever brought against him was, that he sold his church patronage; and this was supposed to have arisen from the corrupt practices of some of his officers, which never came to his knowledge.[2]

Lord Keeper Puckering was the last of four individuals who successively died in the reign of Elizabeth holding the Great Seal. In spite of the foibles imputable to her, it is impossible not greatly to admire her enlightened and steady administration of the state. In the preceding and succeeding reigns we find frequent changes in the high offices under the Crown from the personal caprice of the Sovereign, or the uncontrolled struggles of opposing factions; but she had the same prime minister for forty

---

[1] Law books were dedicated to him in flattering phrase. CROMPTON, the author of "L'Authoritie et Jurisdiction des Courts de la Majestie de la Roygne," thus addresses him:—

A Monseigneur,
   Monseigneur Jehan Puckering, Chiv.
     Gardien du Grand Sceau Dangleterre,
       Et Conseillier d'estate a Sa Majesté.
    Monseigneur . .

M'estant retire aux champs et en ma maison, pour le soulagement de ma veeillesse, et aiant employé jòurnellement quelque heure de loisir a composer ce petit recueil pour aider a l'industrie de ceux qui sans telles collections seroient aulcunes fois, peult estre, empeschés a passer de l'oeil tant et de si gros volumes, Jay trouves bon, me confiant en vostre naifue bonte et courtoisie, de vous dedier treshumblement ce mien petit ouvrage. Et cela dautant plus hardement, que Je sache ny estre contenue aulcune chose qui soit de ma propre invention, ou qui puisse pur sa noueaulte estre desagreable ny a sa Majesté ni a vostre Seigneurie, que tant Je honore et au quel Je souhaite le comble de tout honeur et felicité.

De vostre Seigneurie
Le tres humble et affectioné Serviteur
RICHARD CROMPTON.

This is a curious specimen of the dialect which English lawyers then used in their writings, and continued to use till the 18th century.

[2] "Intra hunc annum (MDXCVI) nounnulli insignioris notæ et nobilitatis ex hujus vitæ statione evocati fuerunt; e quibus inprimis memorandus Joannes Puckeringus, Magni Angliæ Sigilli Custos, qui ob famulorum sordes et corruptelas in ecclesiasticis beneficiis nundinandis, ipse vir integer apud ecclesiasticos haud bene audivit."—Camden, vol. ii. p. 128.

years, and she never took the Great Seal from any Keeper or Chancellor to whom she had entrusted it.

Puckering left behind him a large estate, acquired by his industry, without such royal grants as had swelled the possessions of his predecessors. In the reign of Charles II. his family ended in a female.[1]

CHAPTER XLVII.

LIFE OF LORD ELLESMERE FROM HIS BIRTH TILL THE EXECUTION OF THE EARL OF ESSEX.

ON the death of Sir John Puckering, Queen Elizabeth, according to her usual practice, was herself Chancellor; but on this occasion only for a very short time, having speedily made up her mind as to the mode in which the office was to be disposed of. On Saturday, the first of May, she sent Sir John Fortescue to York House for the "Clavis Regni," and he, having received it from the officers of the late Lord Keeper, brought it to her at Greenwich. At the palace there a sealing took place on the 3rd of May, when Lord Cobham and Lord Buckhurst, by her orders, and in her presence, and in her name, sealed all writs and processes ready to be issued, restoring the Seal to its silken purse, and leaving it with her Majesty, who kept it in her bed-chamber.[2]

Three days afterwards she delivered it, with the applause of the whole nation, to Sir THOMAS EGERTON, and he held it uninterruptedly for a period of twenty-one years.

It is refreshing now to have to contemplate the life of

[1] This Lady whose name was Jane Puckering, when only sixteen years of age, while walking in Greenwich Park, on the 26th of September, 1649, was seized by several armed men, who put her on horseback and carried her to Erith. There she was introduced to one James Welsh, who pretended to have been long in love with her. Forcing her into a cutter he set sail for Flanders, and confined her many months in a nunnery there,—till at last she was induced through fear to marry him. As soon as she recovered her liberty she fled to England, and took legal means to invalidate the marriage. It was accordingly declared null by Chief Justice Rolle and other commissioners appointed by the parliament to adjudicate upon it. She afterwards intermarried with Sir John Bate of Carlton, in the county of Leicester, but died without issue.—*Siem. in Coll. Arm. Clutterbuck's History of Herts.*

[2] Rot. Cl. 38 Eliz. p. 14.

a man remarkable alike for talent, learning, and probity, who raised himself from obscurity by his own exertions, and who reached the highest honors without affixing any stain on his character, and with merit so acknowledged that he did not even excite the envy of rivals.

He was the natural son of Sir Richard Egerton, of an old knightly race in Cheshire, and was born in the parish of Doddlestone, in that county, in the year 1540. His mother's name was Sparks, from whom he is said to have inherited great beauty of countenance.[1] The tradition of the country is that he was nursed by a farmer's wife at Lower Kinnerton, in the neighborhood,—and that being carried, while a child, to Doddlestone Hall, which he afterwards purchased when Chancellor, he expressed an eager desire to rise in the world, and to become the owner of it.—He appears to have been very tenderly and carefully reared, and to have been acknowledged and cherished by his father's family. From their kindness he had the advantage of a regular education. Everything else he achieved for himself.

Having been well grounded in Latin and Greek under private tuition, in his sixteenth year he was entered of Brasen Nose College, Oxford. Here he remained three years, to the great contentment of his teachers; and, besides extending his knowledge of the classics, he particularly distinguished himself by his proficiency in the logic of Aristotle, which then constituted, and still constitutes, so important a branch of the studies of that University. He was destined to the profession of the law, for which it was well judged that, by his habits and turn of mind, he was apt; and having taken his bachelor's degree, he was removed to Lincoln's Inn. He now not only gave himself to the perusal of Bracton and Fleta, but he diligently attended the lectures of the "Readers," and the "Mootings," to which students were admitted in his Inn; and he was present at all remarkable pleadings and trials which took place at Westminster. It is related that he first gave earnest of his future eminence by interposing as *Amicus Curiæ*, while yet a student, when a verdict was about to be pronounced which would have ruined a worthy old lady who kept a house of public entertainment in Smith-

[1] The place where his parents met is still pointed out to travelers under the name of "Gallantry Banke."

field. Three graziers had deposited a sum of money with her, to be returned to them on their joint application. One of them, fraudulently pretending that he had authority to receive it, induced her to give him the whole of the money, and absconded with it. The other two brought their action against her; and (as the story goes) were about to recover, when young Egerton begged permission to befriend the Court by pointing out a fatal objection which had escaped her Counsel as well as my Lord Judge. Said he: "This money, by the contract, was to be returned to *three*, but *two* only sue;—where is the *third?* let him appear with the others; till then the money can not be demanded from her." This turned the fortune of the day; the plaintiffs were nonsuited, and our young student was from that day considered to be of great mark and likelihood.[1]

He by no means confined himself, like Sergeant Puckering, to the learning of real actions, but made himself a general jurist; and although there was not then such a custom as has been established within the last forty years, for young gentlemen to prepare themselves for the Court of Chancery exclusively, by spending their whole time, while they are keeping terms, in drawing bills and answers, —he paid more attention than perhaps any one before him had done to the nature, extent, and history of the equitable jurisdiction of the Lord Chancellor; and he now laid the foundation of that knowledge which he afterwards displayed in his writings on this subject, and in his decrees when he himself held the Great Seal.[2]

[1] This "traditionary story," although the law of it be unexceptionable, I consider an invention, as much as Miss Edgeworth's anecdote of the young barrister, who, being junior in a case at *nisi prius* to try the validity of a will of *personal* property,—*when it came to his turn to address the jury* made his fortune by bringing out an objection *which he had carefully concealed from his leader.* But the fair writer had an undoubted right to dispense both with the forms of legal process, and with professional etiquette.

I take my anecdote from the Reverend Francis Egerton's "Life of Lord Ellesmere," the worst piece of biography I have ever had the misfortune to be condemned to read.

[2] On an examination of the books of the Society of Lincoln's Inn, the only entries respecting him are one of 22 Eliz., when it was resolved that "Mr. Egerton should be called to the bench next moot, and that he should have ancientie of Mr. Clerke and Mr. Owen;" and one of 29 Eliz., when, being Solicitor General, he was appointed Treasurer. He appears to have attended Councils regularly till 27th May, 35 Eliz., after which his name is not to be found in the list of benchers present.[1]

Being called to the bar, he soon got into respectable practice, which steadily increased. In a few years, although he never took the degree of the coif, and therefore could not practice in the Court of Common Pleas, there were few cases of importance in the Court of Queen's Bench, in the Chancery, or the Exchequer, in which he was not counsel.

It is well known that Queen Elizabeth took a lively interest in all suits in which her revenue, or any of her rights, were concerned, and personally exercised a superintendence over the manner in which they were conducted. It is related, that happening to be in court when Mr. Egerton was pleading in a cause against the Crown, her Majesty exclaimed: "On my troth, he shall never plead against me again!" and immediately made him one of her counsel; whereby he was entitled to wear a silk gown, and to have precedence over other barristers. But he continued not only to argue the cases of his clients in Court, but most laboriously to assist in advising upon the witnesses to be called and the evidence to be adduced;—rather mixing what we consider the distinct functions of the attorney and the counsel.[1]

---

[1] I give as a specimen a letter from him to a country client, respecting the progress of a suit in Chancery. There can be little doubt of his perfect sincerity respecting the evidence of the entry to avoid the fine, but his language reminds me of an anecdote I have heard of the manner in which a similar difficulty was obviated in a case tried on the Oxford circuit. At a consultation the night before the trial, the plaintiff's attorney, whose name was Timothy Tickler, intimated that the defendant had discovered that there had been a fine levied, which was to be given in evidence next day.—*Counsel.* "That will be fatal, unless there has been an entry to avoid the fine."—*Tickler.* "What is the meaning of an entry to avoid a fine?" "*Counsel.* "The party who claims the land, after the fine is levied goes upon the land and says, *I enter to avoid all fines.*" The consultation broke up without a ray of hope. But next morning a supplemental brief was delivered,—" to prove that after the fine levied in this case, an entry was duly made by the plaintiff to avoid it,—call—TIMOTHY TICKLER."

"The right worshipp.ll Richard Brereton, esqr., thes be delivered at Worsley."

"Your cause touchinge Pendleton Heye hath bene twyse hearde, upon Thursdaye last, and this Saterdaye, beinge the xvth of this October, and hath houlden the Court both the same dayes without dealinge in any other matter. Yt hath sythens fallen out very well, and this daye, when I expected an order for you, M^r. Sherington dyd stand upon a relesse, which he supposeth to have bene made by your grandmother to M^r. Tyldesleye, and a fine with proclam. levyed by M^r. Tyldeselye to M$_r$. Sherington, beyen selfe in the viijth yere of the quene's Ma^{ty} raigne; which fyne as yet came unloked for, and for my parte was never hearde of before, so I affiyrmed that you had made severall entries to avoyde the same and all such lyke incombrances; which yf you can prove, the opynyon of the Court semeth to waye fullye with you,

In the year 1581, there was a move in the law on the death of Sir William Cordwell, the Master of the Rolls, when Gerrard, the Attorney General, succeeded him; Pop- and so all your counsell thynke. The Courte, therefore, is desyrous to be satysfyed by some prooffe to be made by you touchinge that poynt; twoo wytnesses alone will suffyse. You maye at your choyse eyther send them by thes, or else have a commyssion returnable the next terme, wherein M^r. Sherington must then joyne with you. Wherfore, in myne opynyon, the bet- ter waye bothe for spedye procedinge and ease of charge, is to sende upp twoo by thes so soone as you can. I woulde you shoulde make choyse of twoo such as are of good credyte and understandinge, which can depose the fyrst entree which you made into Pelton Heye after your grandmother's death, which (as I thynke) was before you came to your full age; yf the same can also testyfye the other entrees which you made synce, it will be the better. I thynke M^r. Wyll. Leycester and James Russell have bene with you at all the entrees you have made. Such as you sende may bring the notes which you dyd sette downe of the tyme and manner of your entry into Pelton Heye, and also a copye of the offyce roule after the death of youre grandmother, by which it may appere what daye and yere she died. I doe think that this course will be lesse charge than to have a commission, besides the delaye, and as yet nothing is saved of the fyne which was levyed for the assuring of your Aunt Dorothye's annuyte, which I feare more than all the rest, and which, by longe delaye, maye happelye come to lyght. Yf that fyne be not objected, I doubt not but before thende of this terme, upon prooffe of your entree, you shall have such an order for Pelton Heye as you shall have no cause to myslyke.

"For Swynton Moore this daye, at rysinge of the Court, the matter was a little entred into, but for want of tyme deferred untyll Thursdaye next, and is then to receyve order, for that I suspecte (as I have done always) that you are lyke to be dismissed to the common lawe; but what may be done shall, for now I begynne to learne to playe the Solycytor, pretylye. Your wytnesses are all charged with perjurye by M^r. Sherington, for it semeth he is perswaded that no man can speake truth. Yf you should deal with his wytnesses in lyke sort, I thynke you shoulde but requyte hym as he deserveth, but of that you maye consyder, and let me knowe youre minde before thende of the terme.

"Thus, in hast, I take my leave, with my hartye commendations to you and your wyffe, and M^r. Wyll. Leycester, and all other my frendes. Lyncolne's Inne, this Saterdaye, 15º Octobris, 1580. Your's assured, in all I can,
"Tho. Egerton."

"After I had wrytten thus much, and so had fynyshed my letter, I had un- derstandinge that M^r. Sherington meant to stande upon the former oulde tytle of Worseley of Brothes, and that you were not the right heyre, and so to call in question your tytle, and the old poynt of the bastardye agayne. For doubt of this you shall doe well to sende uppe the Pope's bull touching that mariage, and the copye of the recorde in the seconde yeare of Kinge Henrye the Fourthe's tyme, by which your auncestor recovered in the assyse agaynst Wors- eley of Brothes. Yf you sende uppe also the copye of the receverye at Lan- caster, and the copye of the indenture inrolled at Chester, and dedes of refeffment made aº 9 H. 8, you shall doe well. You have all but the dede of refeffment layed togyther to have used the same at Lancaster agaynst Tho. Brereton, and the dede of refeffment I thought good to suppresse and not to shewe in that matter, but now, for the better answering of all thes and such lyke quarrellinge objections, I would have you to send all uppe to me, and then they maye be used as occasyon shall requyre, And so I bid you agayne fare well. 16 Octobris, 1580. Your's all I can, Tho. Egerton."

From Lord Francis Egerton's MSS.

ham, the Solicitor General, was made Attorney; and Egerton, who, on account of his unrivaled eminence, had been long destined to the honors of the law, both by the Queen and the voice of his profession, was the new Solicitor General. He held this office near twelve years, during which time he took a very prominent part in conducting state prosecutions, and all the business of the Crown; for, though inferior in rank, he was superior in eloquence and address to the Queen's Sergeants and the Attorney General. Conforming to the practice of the times,—when prosecuting for high treason, he put questions to the prisoner, and stated facts of which he offered no proof beyond his own assertion. For example, on the trial of Tilney, charged with being concerned in a conspiracy along with Babington and Ballard to assassinate the Queen, the prisoner having answered, "As for Ballard's coming to me, I do confess it; but it was in such public manner as no man in the world could judge his coming for any such intent as treason: he came openly in the day-time, and undisguised;"—this retort is made by the Solicitor General:—" Tilney, you say true; he came not disguised, but I will tell you how he came; being a popish priest, he came in a grey cloak, laid on with gold lace, in velvet hose, a cut satin doublet, a fair hat of the newest fashion, the band being set with silver buttons." [1]

When the unfortunate Mary was to be tried before her prosecutors, Egerton was particularly consulted as to the designation by which she ought to be indicted. There was a great scruple about calling her "Queen of Scots," because many thought a Sovereign Prince could not lawfully be tried before any earthly tribunal; therefore he recommended that she should be named "Maria filia et hæres Jacobi Quinti, nuper Regis Scotorum, communiter vocata Regina Scotorum, et Dotaria Franciæ." The indictment being framed, he went special with Gawdey and Popham, to Fotheringay, to conduct the prosecution. He summed up at the conclusion of the second day, putting the Commissioners in mind what would become of them, their honors, estates, and posterity, if the kingdom were to be transferred from her present Majesty to a Popish successor.[2] The Lord Treasurer, through the direct-

[1] St. Tr. 1150.
[2] "Solicitator Delegatos submonuit quid de illis et eorum honoribus fortunis

ing Judge, followed on the same side before he asked the royal prisoner for her defense;—when she begged to be admitted to the presence of Elizabeth, and to be heard before a full parliament.

Mr. Solicitor was particularly severe as Counsel against the Earl of Arundel, arguing that, because it was proved he had said he would be ruled by Cardinal Allen in any thing that should concern the Catholic cause, " My Lord must needs be culpable for all the treasons Allen hath practiced or procured. When the Spanish fleet was upon our coast, and news was brought to the Tower, (where he was confined) that the Spaniards sped well, then the Earl would be merry; and when news came that the English fleet sped well, the Earl would be sorry. When the Spanish fleet was upon the coast of Kent, my Lord said, It is a great wood, and a puissant fleet; we shall have lusty play shortly, and I hope we shall plague them that have plagued us."[1] On such overt acts of treason, so proved, was the head of the house of Norfolk convicted; but Elizabeth wished only to daunt him and his adherents, and she suspended the execution of his sentence till, after a long imprisonment, he died a natural death.

On the 2nd of June, 1592, Egerton succeeded Popham as Attorney General, and had for his new colleague, as Solicitor, the famous Sir Edward Coke, who had already fixed the attention of the public by his extraordinary vigor of intellect, his profound knowledge of the common law, and his unexampled arrogance.

The only official act of Mr. Attorney General Egerton which has come down to us is his praying for judgment against Sir John Perrot, late Lord Deputy of Ireland, who had been previously convicted of treason for using some discourteous language respecting the Queen. Mr. Attorney now complained much that " Sir John protested his innocency to seduce and deceive the audience to think him innocent, whereas it was most manifest that he was most justly condemned of most heinous treason, and that in his trial he received most favorable hearing." Whereunto Sir John Perrot replied, and said, " Mr. Attorney,

---

et posteris fieret si regnum ita transferretur."—Camd. Eliz. vol. i. p. 430. See 1 St. Tr. 1188.

[1] Camden's account of this proceeding agrees substantially with that in the

you do me wrong now, as you did me before." "I never did you wrong," said Mr. Attorney. "You did me wrong," said Sir John. "Instance wherein I did you wrong," said Mr. Attorney. "You did me wrong," said Sir John. "I never did you wrong," said Mr. Attorney. All these speeches were spoken with great vehemency, each to the other.[1] But notwithstanding this unseemly altercation, Egerton was a man of mild demeanor, and was never known to be betrayed into such invective and vituperation as his successor indulged in upon the trials of the Earl of Essex and Sir Walter Raleigh.

He now reached the honor of knighthood, which was in that age highly esteemed, and conferred only as a reward of long service.[2]

While Attorney General he was appointed Chamberlain of the County Palatine of Chester, an office of considerable power and dignity.[3]

On the 10th of April, 1594, he was made Master of the Rolls, as successor to Sir Gilbert Gerrard. In his new office, ably disposing of certain suits which were referred to him, and occasionally assisting the Lord Keeper, he speedily showed the highest qualifications as an Equity Judge,—and the Great Seal was considered his on the next vacancy.

During this interval, having comparative leisure, he exercised his pen, and, amongst other things wrote a little treatise, which we should have found a great curiosity if it had been preserved to us, "On the Duties of the Office of Solicitor General." This was dedicated to young Francis Bacon, who was then impatiently expecting the office, whom he always patronized, and whose claims he thought he might thus strengthen.[4]

State Trials. "Egertonus Solicitator, sive procurator secundarius, his summatim repetitis, Majestatem læsisse arguit ex triplice temporis distinctione, silicet priusquam classis Hispanica adveneret, cum advenerit, cum fugeret," &c.—Camd. Eliz. vol. ii. p. 6.   1 St. Tr. 1249.

[1] 1 St. Tr. 1329.
[2] I have observed various instances during the Tudor reigns of men being knighted after having been long in the office of Attorney or Solicitor General, Chancellor of the Exchequer, or Speaker of the House of Commons.
[3] Eg. Pap. 192.
[4] Sir Robert Cecil thanked Egerton in a letter, in which he says, "I have understood, by my cousin Bacon, what a friendly and kind offer you have made him, the better to arm him with your observations (for the exercise of solicitorship), which otherwise may be got with time. I will study to let you know how great an obligation any man's kindness to him doth throw upon

On the sudden death of Lord Keeper Puckering, Egerton was immediately hailed as his successor. The Queen having made up her mind in his favor, he was sent for to the Court at Greenwich. On the landing at the top of the stair, Lords Cobham and Buckhurst and Sir Robert Cecil were ready to receive him. They conducted him into the Queen's outer private room, where her Majesty was standing upon a piece of embroidered carpet,—Lord Burghley, the Lord Treasurer, attending her. Him, alone, on account of his age and infirmity, she desired to be seated, and she begged him to lean his back against the tapestry.[1] Egerton having then knelt down on his right knee, the Queen made a speech magnifying his fame and fitness for high judicial dignity ; and, taking the Great Seal with both her hands, she delivered it into his keeping. He, remaining on his knees, made a suitable reply, acknowledging his insufficiency, and comparing himself disparagingly with his predecessors. Her Majesty placed both her hands on his shoulders, and offered to raise him from the ground.[2] He was then sworn of the Privy Council ; and, having sealed a writ, and gone through the usual forms, he gave the Seal to his purse-bearer, to be borne before him. After which it pleased her Majesty to hold a private conversation with him for near half an hour, and then very graciously to permit him to walk off with the Great Seal.[3]

As a special mark of her Majesty's favor, Egerton still continued Master of the Rolls; and he held this office, along with the Great Seal, during the remainder of the present reign. He was so familiarly acquainted with the practice of the Court, and so devoted to the discharge

me." But as we shall see hereafter, the Cecils were jealous of their kinsman, and tried to depress him.

[1] The Close Roll, after stating that Egerton was sent for to Greenwich, thus proceeds: " Et eo ubi ventum est inter horas quintam et sextam ejusdem diei in mesaula juxta cacumen gradus honoratissimi Dns Cobham Dns Buckhurste et Robertus Cecil miles aderant quando omnes tres dem Thomam Egerton militem Serenissime Dne Regine presentabant que adtunc in exteriore privata camera insimul aderat ibique stetit super polymitam Phrigiam infra peristromæ Regale honoratissimo Dno Burghley Magno Thesaurario Anglie illam attenden. quem ob ætatem inferm et imbecillem Regina sedere jussit et dorsum suum ad aulea attalica declinare."

[2] " Dna Regina utrisque suis manibus super humeros ejus impositis modo quodam illam ab humo quasi obtulit sublevare."

[3] " Serenitati sue visum est secum per dimidiatam fere horam colloqui et tunc cum magno sigill. graciosissime abire permisit."—Cl. R. 38 Eliz.

of his judicial duties, that he could easily get through the business of Chancery without any assistance, and the suitors never had such cause to be satisfied since the time of Sir Thomas More, although there had been at the same time both a Lord Chancellor or Lord Keeper and a Master of the Rolls to act as his assistant or deputy.

His appointment to the Great Seal seems to have given universal satisfaction. "The Master of the Rolls," says Reynolds, in a letter to the Earl of Essex, " has changed his style, and is made Lord Keeper—only by her Majesty's gracious favor and her own choice. I think no man ever came to this dignity with more applause than this worthy gentleman."[1]

So Anthony Bacon, the elder brother of Francis, writing at this time to a friend at Venice, after mentioning the death of Lord Keeper Puckering, thus proceeds,—" into whose place, with an extraordinary speed, her Majesty hath *ex proprio motu et speciali gratia*, advanced Sir Thomas Egerton, with a general applause both of court, city, and country, for the reputation he hath of integrity, law, knowledge, and courage. It was his good hap to come to the place freely, without competition or mediator."[2] Camden's testimony, though more moderate, is more valuable. " Successit Thomas Egertonus, primarius Regis Procurator, magna expectatione et integritatis opinione."[3]

High as the expectations of the public were of the new Lord Keeper, they were by no means disappointed. Having taken his seat in the Court of Chancery in Easter Term with as little parade as possible, he immediately proceeded to the dispatch of business, and from the beginning he afforded the example of a consummate Judge. He was not only courteous in his manner, but quiet, patient, and attentive—waiting to be instructed as to the facts and law of the case by the counsel who had been studying them—never interrupting to show quickness of perception or to anticipate authorities likely to be cited, or to blurt out a jest—yet venturing to put a question for the right understanding of the points to be decided, and gently checking wandering and prolixity by a look or a hint. He listened with undivided attention to the evi-

---

[1] Birch's Memoirs of Queen Elizabeth.   [2] Ibid.
[3] Cam. Eliz. vol. ii. 128.

dence, and did not prepare a speech in parliament or write letters to his correspondents under pretense of taking notes of the arguments addressed to him. Nor did he affect the reputation of great dispatch by deciding before he had heard both parties, or by referring facts and law to the Master which it was his own duty to ascertain and determine. When the case admitted of no reasonable doubt, he disposed of it as soon as the hearing was finished. Otherwise, he carried home the papers with him,—not throwing them aside to moulder in a trunk, till, driven by the importunity of counsel asking for judgment, he again looked at them, long after the arguments he had heard were entirely forgotten and he could scarcely make out from his "breviate book" the points that had been raised for his decision—but within a short time spontaneously giving judgment in a manner to show that he was complete master of the case, and never aggravating the anguish of the losing party by the belief that if the Judge had taken more pains, the result would have been different. Being himself Master of the Rolls, and there being no Vice Chancellors—he was tried as a Judge of appeal only in hearing exceptions to the Master's reports; but on such occasions he did not grudge the necessary trouble to understand the matters submitted to him, nor shrink from the responsibility of reversing what he considered to be erroneous.

Although a few of his judgments are mentioned in Tothill and other compilers, none of them have come down in a shape to enable us to form an adequate opinion of their merits; but they are said to have been distinguished for sound learning, lucid arrangement, and great precision of doctrine.

The only persons by whom he was not entirely approved were the Common-law Judges. He had the boldness to question and correct their pedantic rules more freely than Lord Keeper Puckering, Lord Keeper Bacon, or any of his predecessors had done, and after judgment in actions at law he not unfrequently granted injunctions against execution, on the ground of fraud in the plaintiff, or some defect of procedure by which justice had been defeated. He thus not only hurt the pride of these venerable magistrates, but he interfered with their profits, which depended mainly upon the number of suits brought before them, and the reputation of their respective Courts. These jealousies, which began soon after his appointment, went on constantly increasing, till at last, as we shall see, they produced an explosion which shook Westminster Hall to its center.

In this struggle he finally triumphed over the Common-law Judges; but they entirely defeated him in an attempt which he made to strengthen the jurisdiction of his Court by the imposition of fines. It had always been held, as it now is, that a decree in Chancery does not directly bind the land like a judgment of the Court of Common Pleas, and that it can only be enforced by imprisonment of the person. Egerton imposed a fine upon Sir Thomas Thomilthorp for not performing his decree in Chancery concerning lands of inheritance, and estreated it into the Exchequer, with a view of its being there levied by Crown process. The party pleaded that the fine was illegal, "and upon debate of the question in Court and good advisement taken, it was adjudged that the Lord Chancellor had no power to assess any such fine, for then, by a mean, he might bind the interest of the land where he had no power, but of the person only, and thereupon the said Sir Thomas Thomilthorp was discharged of the said fine."[1]

Not satisfied with this, Egerton made another experiment with the like view and the like success. For nonperformance of a decree against one Waller he fined him, and upon process of extent out of Chancery seized his lands in Middlesex, " whereupon Waller brought his assize in the Court of Common Pleas, where the opinion of the whole Court agreed *in omnibus* with the Court of Exchequer."[2]

. We have on record a very striking instance of the vigor with which he strove to correct the prolixity of the written pleadings in his Court. In a case of Mylward *v.* Weldon, there being a complaint of the length of the Replication, and the Lord Chancellor being satisfied that "whereas it extended to six score sheets, all the matter thereof which was pertinent might have been well contained in sixteen," an order was made in these words :—" It appearing to his Lordship, by the confession of Richard Mylward, the plaintiff's son, that he did devise, draw, and engross the

[1] Sir Thomas Thomilthorp's case, 4 Inst. 84.
[2] Waller's case, 4 Inst. 84.

said Replication, and because his Lordship is of opinion that such an abuse is not in any sort to be tolerated—proceeding of a malicious purpose to increase the defendant's charge, and being fraught with much impertinent matter not fit for this Court, it is therefore ordered that the Warden of the Fleet shall take the said Richard Mylward into his custody, and shall bring him into Westminster Hall on Saturday about 10 of the clock in the forenoon, and then and there shall cut a hole in the myddest of the same engrossed Replication, which is delivered unto him for that purpose, and put the said Richard's head through the same hole, and so let the same Replication hang about his shoulders with the written side outward, and then, the same so hanging, shall lead the same Richard, bareheaded and barefaced, round about Westminster Hall whilst the Courts are sitting, and show him at the bar of every of the three Courts within the Hall, and then shall take him back again to the Fleet and keep him prisoner until he shall have paid £10 to her Majesty for a fine, and 20 nobles to the defendant for his costs in respect of the aforesaid abuse, which fine and costs are now adjudged and imposed upon him by this Court for the abuse aforesaid."[1] The order should have gone on to require that a print of the unlucky Richard, with his head peeping through the volumes of sheep skin, should *in terrorem*, be hung up in the chambers of every equity draughtsman.

During a year and a half, Lord Keeper Egerton had few distractions from the discharge of his judicial duties; but in the end of 1597, the exhausted state of the Exchequer, from the great charges of the Spanish war, compelled Elizabeth reluctantly to call a parliament. On the first day of meeting, the Queen being seated on the throne, he, by her command, declared to the two Houses the cause of the summons. After confessing that the royal presence of her Majesty, the view of such an honorable assembly, the weightiness of the service, and his own weakness, appalled him much, he gives a florid description of the prosperity of the kingdom, with a compliment to the Queen's extraordinary modesty. "This *Her Majesty is pleased to ascribe* to the great power and infinite mercy of the Almighty; and *therefore* it shall well become us all most thankfully, on the knees of our hearts, to acknowledge no

[1] Reg. Lib. A. 1596, f. 672.

less unto his holy name." Next comes a most excellent passage on Law Reform, very applicable to the present time. "And whereas the number of the laws already made are very great, some also of them being obsolete and worn out of use; others idle and vain, serving to no purpose; some again over heavy and too severe for the offense; others too loose and slack for the faults they are to punish, and many of them so full of difficulties to be understood that they cause many controversies; you are therefore to enter into a due consideration of the said laws, and where you find superfluity to prune, where defect to supply, and where ambiguity to explain, that they be not burthensome, but profitable to the commonwealth." He then strongly presses for a supply,—thus concluding, "*Quod justum est necessarium est;* nothing can be more just than this war; nothing ought to be more necessary than carefully to provide due maintenance for the same."

Sergeant Yelverton being presented at the bar as Speaker-elect, the Lord Keeper, in the Queen's name, overruled his disqualification,[1] and gave her assent to his prayer for the ancient liberties and privileges of the Commons, "with admonition, however, that the said liberties and privileges should be discreetly and wisely used, as was meet."[2]

The Lord Keeper not yet being a Peer, during the session he had only to put the question in the House of Lords, without taking any share in the debates; but he was once asked his opinion on a question of precedence. Thomas Howard, second son of the Duke of Norfolk, being created Baron Howard de Walden, claimed to take place next after Earls, because the younger son of a Duke

[1] We have not the particulars of Yelveton's disqualifying speech at the bar of the House of Lords, but it was probably a repetition of that in the Commons, where he expressed wonder how he came to be chosen, "as it could not be for his estate, his father dying having left him only a small annuity." "Then," said he, "growing to man's estate and some small practice of the law, I took a wife, by whom I have had many children, the keeping of us all being a great impoverishment to my estate, and the daily living of us all nothing but my daily industry. Neither from my person nor nature doth this choice proceed; for he that supplieth this place ought to be a man big and comely, stately and well spoken, his voice great, his courage majestical, his nature haughty, and his purse heavy; but contrarily, the stature of my body is small, myself not so well-spoken, my voice low, my carriage lawyer-like and of the common fashion, my nature soft and bashful, my purse thin, light, and never yet plentiful."—1 Parl. Hist. 898.   [2] Ib. 895.

is considered by the heralds of higher rank than a Viscount; but, by the advice of the Lord Keeper, he was placed below all Barons, without prejudice to his precedence elsewhere.

A subsidy being granted, the attempts in the Commons at reform became very distasteful to the Queen;—particularly a bill to put down the nuisance of monopolies, which now caused deep and universal discontent;—and she brought the session to a speedy close. The Lord Keeper then, by her order, rebuked the Commons for their presumption: "Touching the monopolies, her Majesty hoped that her dutiful and loving subjects would not take away her prerogative, which is the chiefest flower in her garden, and the principal and head pearl in her crown and diadem, but that they would rather leave that to her disposition."[1]

After the death of the great Lord Burghley, although his son, Sir Robert Cecil, was the Queen's chief Councillor, she never was under the sway of any one minister, and Egerton enjoyed a considerable share of her confidence. He was accordingly named chief Commissioner to negotiate in London a treaty with the Dutch, and after long conferences with their ambassadors, an advantageous treaty was signed—by which the Queen was eased of an annual charge of £120,000, the payment of the debt due to her was secured, and a large subsidiary force was stipulated for in case of a Spanish invasion.

In 1601, the Lord Keeper was again employed as a diplomatist in concluding a treaty with Denmark, whereby an important ally was secured, and the Protestant interest in Europe was materially strengthened.

He nowhere appears to greater advantage than in his conduct to the Queen's favorite, the Earl of Essex. This young nobleman had high and generous qualities along with great faults. Egerton, did not, like others, flatter his vices during his prosperity, nor abandon him when his imprudence had involved him in difficulties, and ruin was impending over him. Although unequal in age, and of very dissimilar characters and pursuits, a strict intimacy had subsisted between them almost from the time of Essex's first appearance at Court; and now that Sir Thomas was in the dignified position of Lord Keeper, he exercised

[1] 1 Parl. Hist. 906.

all his influence and authority to correct the irregularities of his youthful friend, and to rescue him from the consequences of his imprudence.[1]

Queen Elizabeth, in a fit of anger, having given her favorite a box on the ear, accompanied with the words "Begone and be hanged," he thought that, though the insult came from a woman, as she was his Sovereign it ought to be resented, and clapping his hand to his sword, he swore "he would not bear such usage were it from Henry VIII. himself." In a great passion he withdrew from Court. The Lord Keeper immediately gave him salutary advice in a long and most excellent letter, of which I will give a passage :—

"It is often seen, that he that is a stander by seeth more than he that played the game, and for the most part any man in his own cause standeth in his own light. You are not so far gone but you may well return. The return is safe, but the progress dangerous and desperate. If you have any enemies, you do that for them which they could never do for themselves, whilst you leave your friends to open shame and contempt, forsake yourself, overthrow your fortunes, and ruin your honor and reputation. My good Lord, I want wisdom to advise you, but I will never want an honest and true heart to wish you well; nor, being warranted by a true conscience, to forbear to speak what I think. I have begun plainly. I hope your Lordship will not be offended if I proceed still after the same fashion. *Bene cedit qui tempori cedit.* And Seneca saith, *Lex si nocentem punit, cedendum est justitiæ ; si innocentem, cedendum est fortunæ.* The best remedy is not to contend and strive, but humbly to submit. Have you given cause, and take scandal to yourself? Why then all you can do is too little to make satisfaction. Is cause of scandal given to you? Yet policy, duty, and religion enforce you to sue, yield, and submit to your Sovereign, between whom and you there can be no proportion of duty."[2]

Essex, unsubdued, thus replied :

---

[1] "They live and join very honorably together—out of which correspondency and noble conjunction betwixt Mars and Pallas, betwixt justice and valor,—I mean betwixt so admirable a nobleman as the Earl, and so worthy a justice as the Lord Keeper, I doubt not but very famous effects will daily spring to her Majesty's honor, the good of the state, and the comfort of both their Lordships' particular true friends."—Birch's *Memoirs of Queen Elizabeth. Letter of Anthony Bacon.*   [2] Birch, Mem. Eliz. vol. ii. 384.

"Although there is not that man this day living whom I should sooner make a judge of any question that did concern me than yourself, yet must you give me leave to tell you, that, in such a case, I must appeal from all earthly judges, and if in any, then surely in this, where the highest Judge on earth hath imposed upon me, without trial or hearing, the most heavy judgment that ever hath been known. When the vilest of all indignities is done unto me, doth religion enforce me to sue, or doth God require it? Is it impiety not to do it? Why, can not Princes err? Can not subjects receive wrong? Is an earthly power infinite? Pardon me, my Lord, I can never subscribe to these principles. Let Solomon's fool laugh when he is stricken; let those who mean to make their profit of Princes show no sense of Prince's injuries. As for me, I have received wrong, I feel it; my cause is good, I know it; and whatsoever happens, all the powers on earth can never exert more strength and constancy in oppressing than I can show in suffering every thing that can or shall be imposed upon me. Your Lordship, in the beginning of your letter, makes me a player and yourself a looker-on, and me a player of my own game, so you see more than I: but give me leave to tell you that, since you do but see and I do suffer, I must of necessity feel more than you."

This correspondence, when circulated and brought to the notice of the Queen, incensed her for a time still more against Essex; but he was at last induced, by the verbal advice of the Lord Keeper, to apologize, and never having lost his place in her heart, he soon regained his ascendency in her Councils, and after the death of Burghley, who always strove to depress him, he was for a time considered her chief Councillor, till he imprudently took upon himself the office of Lord Deputy of Ireland to quell the rebellion in that country,—whereby he exposed himself to the hazards of a very disagreeable service, and left the field at home open to the intrigues of his enemies.

During Essex's absence in Ireland, the Lord Keeper did what was possible with the Queen to place his actions in the most favorable point of view, but she was so much disappointed by his want of success against Tyrone, and so much provoked by his presumption and obstinacy, and so much exasperated by the representations of the Cecils, who turned every incident to account in their struggle for undivided power,—that he thought his only chance was to try the effect of his personal presence,—an experiment that had once succeeded with Leicester, her former favorite. He presented himself in her bed-room at Nonsuch, while she was still at her toilette, and her hair was scattered over her face. Thus surprised, she at first gave him rather an affectionate welcome; but when she had leisure to reflect upon his conduct she was very much dissatisfied, and (according to English fashion) would have brought him to trial for high treason,—had it not been that, by an extraordinary effort of courage, the Judges and law officers reported that disobedience of orders and return without permission did not exactly amount to that offense.

Nevertheless, he was examined before the Privy Council, suspended from all his employments, and committed to the custody of the Lord Keeper, to be kept in ward at York House. It seems strange to find a great noble, or an officer of state, turned into a gaoler; but this was by no means an unprecedented course where a milder and more honorable imprisonment was to be inflicted; and the Queen of Scots had been for many years in the custody of the Earl of Shrewsbury.

The Lord Keeper now rendered to his prisoner all those kind offices that humanity the most sensible, and politeness the most delicate, could suggest; and, when he had to sit judicially upon his case, tempered justice with compassion, preserving a proper medium between the duty of the magistrate and the generosity of the friend. There is preserved a warm-hearted effusion of his in the shape of a letter from the Court at Richmond by way of consolation and advice to his prisoner:

"Her Majesty is gracious towards you, and you want not friends to remember and commend your former services. Of these particulars you shall know more when we meet. In the meantime, by way of caution, take this from me: there are sharp eyes upon you; your actions, public and private, are observed; it behoveth you, therefore, to carry yourself with all integrity and sincerity both of hands and heart, lest you overthrow your own fortunes and discredit your friends, that are tender and careful of reputation and well-doing.

"So in haste I commit you to God with my hearty commendations,
               "And rest
          "Your assured loving friend,
               "THOMAS EGERTON, C. S.
"*At the Court at Richmond,
     October* 21, 1599."

The first public proceeding against Essex was in the Star Chamber, and a sketch of it may be interesting, as showing how this tribunal was then used, not only to punish obnoxious individuals, but as an instrument to lead public opinion in the absence of government newspapers and parliamentary reports. On the day after Michaelmas term, the Lord Keeper, the Lord Treasurer, the Lord Admiral, the Lord Chamberlain, most of the other ministers, and nearly all the Judges assembled in the usual place of meeting at Westminster, and an immense crowd from the City of London attended. The object was to check " the dangerous libels cast abroad in court, city, and country, as also by table and alehouse talk, both in city and country, to the great scandal of her Majesty and her Council."

The Lord Keeper opened with a long speech. He first declared it to be her Majesty's pleasure and express command, that all justices of the peace should forthwith repair to the country, there to exercise hospitality and to preserve the public tranquility. He lamented that, at this time, there were very many seditious people breeding rebellion by vomiting abroad many false and slanderous speeches against her Majesty and Council concerning the affairs of Ireland, and publishing many scandalous libels, " which kind of people he did censure to be no better than traitors." " Therefore, in her Majesty's name, he commanded all Judges, Justices, and other officers to proceed diligently against all such talkers of sedition and makers of such libels, and all who kept company with them, that the authors thereof might be the better bolted out and known, and those who, by the ancient laws of this realm, were traitors might receive due punishment." He added, "to stop the mouths of all seditious discoursers and traitorous libelers, and to satisfy all that have true and faithful hearts to judge, and any common sense to discern, it shall not be amiss, in a matter so manifest, to remember some particularities, to the end that it may demonstratively appear that there was never Prince did, with greater care and more royal means, provide to suppress rebellious subjects, and to preserve a torn and declining kingdom, than her Majesty hath done for this accommodation of Ireland."—The Lord Keeper proceeds with a narrative of the formidable preparations for putting down Tyrone's rebellion, of the great military force and resources intrusted to Essex, and the wise instructions he had received. He then complains of the General's inaction, and still more of his conference and composition with the arch-rebel, and his unwarranted return from Ireland. "In this dangerous and miserable state he presumed to leave that realm, and to come over hither under pretext to present unto her Majesty this dishonorable and deceitful composition, with no better assurance than the rebel's own word for temporary cessation of arms. These things being thus, what malicious and traitorous hearts can bear these insolent and wicked persons, that dare intrude into the counsels of a Prince, and take upon them to censure their Sovereign for that which either she hath done or which God shall direct her heart to do in a matter of so high and weighty importance?"

The Lord Treasurer Buckhurst, the Earl of Nottingham, High Admiral, Mr. Secretary Cecil, and others of the Council, severally addressed the assembled multitude to the same effect, and then the Court adjourned,—the ministers having had the advantage of publicly praising their own measures, and inveighing against all opposition to them, without any danger of a reply or a division.[1]

Essex remained in the custody of the Lord Keeper above six months without being brought to trial, the Queen saying that she wished "to correct, not to ruin him." During this time he fell, or pretended to fall,

---

[1] The reporter, Francis Woodward, in a letter to Sir Robert Sydney after giving the first three speeches at great length, says "the rest did speak so softly, and the thronge did presse so mightie, that I was driven so far back that I could not hear what they said. I came not in time to take a place where I might convenientlie hear all such matters as were there declared,"— *Sydney State Papers*, vol. ii. p. 146. This reminds one of the abrupt termination to the report of the famous case of STRADLING v. STYLES, in which the question was, whether, under a bequest of all the testator's *black and white horses*, PYEBALLED HORSES passed,—as reported by Martinus Scriblerus: "Le reste del argument Ieo ne pouvois oyer car Ieo fui disturb en mon place."— Pope's *Miscell*. vol. 5. p. 210.

dangerously ill. She ordered eight physicians, of the best reputation, to visit him; and being informed that the issue was much to be apprehended, she sent him some broth, with a message that if she thought such a step consistent with her honor she would herself pay him a visit. He recovered; but a suspicion being instilled into Elizabeth that his distemper had been counterfeit in order to move her compassion, she relapsed into her former rigor against him. She was, however, so far softened by his protestations, that she released him from his imprisonment under the Lord Keeper, and allowed him to reside in his own house in the Strand, and he probably would have escaped with entire impunity had not the complaints of his family and friends raised such a public clamor against the harsh treatment of the individual, who had the rare fortune to be much beloved by the people as well as by the Sovereign. She at last ordered him to be tried—not before the Star Chamber, or any recognized tribunal, but before eighteen Commissioners, consisting of the Lord Treasurer, the Lord Admiral, most of the great officers of state, and five of the Judges. They assembled in the hall of York House, and sat in chairs at a long table for eleven hours, from eight in the morning till seven at night.

His treatment gives us a strange notion of the manners of the time. At his entrance the Commissioners all remained covered, and gave no sign of salutation or courtesy. He knelt at the upper end of the table, and for a good while without a cushion. He was at last supplied with one on the motion of the Archbishop of Canterbury; but he was suffered to kneel till after the Lord Keeper had expounded the nature of the Commission, and till the end of the speech of the Queen's Sergeant, who opened the case for the Crown. He was then allowed to stand up, and by-and-by, through the interference of the Archbishop, he was indulged with liberty to sit on a stool.

He opened his defense by offering thanks to God for his mercy, and to the Queen for her clemency towards him, and was proceeding to justify his conduct, when the Lord Keeper (probably from a friendly motive) interrupted him, telling him "this was not the course that was likely to do him good; that he began well by submitting himself to her Majesty's mercy and pardon, which himself and the rest of the Lords were glad to hear, and no doubt her princely and gracious nature was by that way most likely to be inclined to favor; that all extenuation of his offense was but the lessening of her Majesty's mercy in pardoning; that he, with all the other Lords, would clear him of all suspicion of disloyalty, and that therefore he might do well to spare the rest of his speech, and save time, and commit himself to her Majesty's mercy."

Essex replying "that he spoke nothing but only to clear himself from a malicious, corrupt affection,"—the Lord Keeper told him, "that if he meant the crime of disloyalty, it was that which he needed not to fear, all that was now laid to him being contempt and disobedience, and that it was absurd to cover direct disobedience by a pretended intention to obey. If the Earl of Leicester did evil in coming over contrary to the Queen's commandment, the Earl of Essex did more in imitating the Earl of Leicester, and was so much the more to be punished for it." After a warm panegyric on the Queen and her Irish Government, he then proceeded to pronounce sentence, which, he said, "in the Star Chamber must have been the heaviest fine ever yet imposed, and perpetual imprisonment in the Tower; but in this mode of proceeding the Court, out of favor to him, merely ordered that he should not execute the office of Privy Councillor, nor of Earl Marshal of England, nor Master of the Ordnance; and that he should return to his own house, there to remain a prisoner during the Queen's pleasure."

The sentence, or "censure," as it was called, so pronounced by the Lord Keeper, was dictated by the Queen, who, to bring him again near her person, had directed that the office of "Master of the Horse" should not be included among those for which he was disqualified; and the Court may be absolved from any great violation of the constitution on this occasion, as the whole of the punishment might have been inflicted lawfully by her own authority—with the exception of the imprisonment— which she immediately remitted.

But Egerton had still to pass through extraordinary scenes in connection with Essex, to whom Elizabeth now behaved with a mixture of fondness and severity, which drove him to destruction. He for some time seemed completely restored to her favor, and then she refused to renew his monopoly of Sweet Wines, saying that "an ungovernable beast must be stinted in his provender." He thought that she had completely surrendered herself to the Cecils and Sir Walter Raleigh, and he entered into the conspiracy to raise the City of London, where he was so popular, and by force to get her person into his power, and to rid himself of his enemies.

On the memorable Sunday, the 8th of February, 1601, when he had collected a large force in Essex House, in the Strand, and was about to execute his project with the assistance of the Earls of Southampton and Rutland,— the Queen being informed of these designs, and having ordered the Lord Mayor and Aldermen to take measures to secure the peace of the city, she directed the Lord Keeper, with Chief Justice Popham, the Earl of Worcester, and Sir William Knollys, controller of the household, to repair to Essex House, and demanding admittance, to require in her name that the disturbers of the public peace should disperse and that the law should be obeyed.

This was a service by no means free from danger, for it was well known that Essex had for some weeks been collecting under his roof many desperate characters, who had returned from the wars in Ireland and in the Low Countries, and who were likely to pay very little respect to civil magistrates, however exalted their station. The Lord Keeper proceeded on his mission with becoming firmness, being preceded by his purse-bearer carrying the Great Seal, and followed only by the ordinary attendants of himself, the Chief Justice, and his other companions.

Arriving at the gate of Essex House, a little before ten in the forenoon, they were refused admittance. They desired that it might be intimated to the Earl that they came thither by the express command of her Majesty. He gave orders that they should be introduced through the wicket, but that all their attendants, with the exception of the purse-bearer, should be excluded. On entering, they found the court-yard filled with armed men. The Lord Keeper demanded in the Queen's name the cause of this tumultuary meeting. Essex answered, "There is a plot laid for my life; letters have been counterfeited in my name, and assassins have been appointed to murder me in bed. We are met to defend our lives, since my enemies can not be satisfied unless they suck my blood." The Chief Justice said, "the Queen would do impartial justice;" and the Lord Keeper desired Essex to explain his grievances in private,—when several voices exclaimed, "They abuse you, my Lord ; they are undoing you. You lose your time." The Lord Keeper, undaunted, turned round, and putting on his hat, in a calm and solemn tone as if he had been issuing an order from his tribunal,—commanded them in the Queen's name upon their allegiance to lay down their arms and to depart. Essex entered the house, and the multitude, resolved to offer violence to these venerable magistrates, but divided as to the mode of doing so, shouted out, " Kill them, keep them for pledges, throw the Great Seal out of the window." A guard of musketeers surrounded them, and conducting them through several apartments filled with insurgents, introduced them to a small back room where the found the Earl, who was about to sally forth in military array to join his friends at Paul's Cross. He requested that they would remain there patiently for half an hour, and himself withdrawing, ordered the door to be bolted, and left them as prisoners in the care of Sir John Davis and Sir Gilly Merrick, guarded by sentinels bearing muskets primed and cocked. Here they remained for some hours listening to the shouts of the insurgents and the distant discharge of fire-arms. They frequently required Sir John Davis to allow them to depart, or at least to permit some one of them to go to the Queen to inform her where they were; but the answer was, " My Lord has commanded that ye depart not before his return, which will be very shortly."

They were at last released by the intervention of Sir Ferdinando Gorges. He had accompanied the assailants into the city,—but there being no assemblage of citizens at Paul's Cross as had been promised,—the Sheriff, on whose aid much reliance was placed, having refused to join them,—Lord Burghley and the Lord Admiral having arrived with a considerable force from Westminster,—and a herald having proclaimed the leader of the insurrection a traitor,—Gorges saw that the enterprise was desperate, and he thought only of his own safety. With this view he asked authority from Essex to go and release the Lord Keeper and the other prisoners, representing that for their liberty they would undertake to procure the Queen's pardon for all that had happened. Essex consented to the release of Chief Justice Popham upon his entering into such an undertaking, but positively required that the others should be detained as hostages. Gorges hastening to Essex House reached it about four in the afternoon. Being admitted to the presence of the prisoners, he offered Popham his liberty on condition of his intercession and good offices; but the Chief Justice magnanimously refused the offer unless the Lord Keeper should be permitted to acccompany him.[1] After some consultation Gorges concluded that the best plan for himself would be that he should forthwith release all the four, and, accompanying them to the Court, leave Essex to his fate. Accordingly, pretending that he had authority to that effect, he conducted them by a back staircase into the garden on the bank of the river Thames. Here they found a boat which they immediately entered, and by a favorable tide they were quickly conducted to the Queen's palace at Whitehall. They had hardly got clear from their imprisonment when Essex himself arrived at the spot where they embarked, having returned by water from Queen Hithe, after all his friends in the city had deserted him. His rage was excessive when he found that his prisoners had escaped; and now despairing of success or mercy, he resorted to the vain attempt of fortifying his house, and resisting the ordnance brought from the Tower to batter it down.

The Lord Keeper remained at Whitehall with the Queen till the news was brought of the surrender of Essex, and then he sorrowfully took leave of her. She had behaved with the greatest composure and courage while danger existed, but she could not without emotion give directions for bringing to trial for high treason the unhappy young nobleman, who, notwithstanding all his faults, had still a strong hold of her affections.

The trial speedily took place in the Court of the Lord High Steward in Westminster Hall. The Lord Keeper, not being a peer, was spared the pain of joining in the sentence of condemnation; but he was summoned as a

[1] Some accounts are silent as to the magnanimity of Popham; but Camden's contemporary testimony can leave no doubt upon the subject; "Comes annuit ut solus Pophamus Justitiarius liberetur, qui cum liberari nollet, nisi Custos Sigilli una liberatur, Gorgius liberavit singulos, et cum illis per flumen ad Regiam se contulit."—Camd. Eliz. vol. ii. p. 225.

witness. Trials for treason were at this era in a sort of transition state. The great bulk of the evidence against the Earl of Essex and the Earl of Southampton, who was tried along with him, consisted of written examinations, and among them was "the declaration of the Lord Keeper, the Earl of Worcester, and the Lord Chief Justice of England," containing a narrative of their imprisonment, and signed by the three. They were likewise called as witnesses, and "proved in Court *upon their honors*,[1] that they heard the words 'Kill them, kill them;' but they would not charge my Lord of Essex, that they were spoken either by his privity or command."[2] They were much more forbearing than the counsel for the Crown, Coke and Bacon, who, to the disgrace of both, showed very unnecessary zeal in procuring a conviction,— for the Judges declared, according to what has ever since been held for law, "that in case where a subject attempeth to put himself into such strength as the King shall not be able to resist him, and to force the King to govern otherwise than according to his own royal authority and discretion, it is manifest rebellion, and in every rebellion the law intendeth as a consequent the compassing the death of the King, as foreseeing that the rebel will never suffer the King to live or reign who might punish or take revenge of his treason and rebellion." The prisoners did not deny that they intended forcibly to seize the Queen's person, although they insisted that they loved and honored her, and only wished to rid her of evil councillors.

After his conviction, Essex, at his own request, had an interview in the Tower with the Lord Keeper and other ministers of the Queen, and asking pardon of him for having imprisoned him, took a tender leave of him, and thanked him for all his kindness. The unhappy youth might still have been saved by the good offices of Egerton and other friends, and the inextinguishable regard which lurked in the royal bosom, if the Queen had not waited in vain for the token of his true repentance

---

[1] Nevertheless they appear to have been sworn. Camden says, "Summus Anglie Justitiarius Pophamus rogatus et *juratus* quam indigne Consiliarii habiti fuerunt."—Camd. Eliz. vol. ii. p. 231.

[2] 1 St. Tr. 1340. The prisoner spoke of them with great respect. "Essexius respondet se in honoratissimos illos viros nihil mali cogitasse at summo cum honore observasse."—Camd. Eliz. vol. ii. p. 231.

which he had intrusted to the false Countess of Nottingham, and which being at last produced gave such agony to the last hours of Elizabeth.

In the meanwhile her grief was somewhat assuaged by appointing the Lord Keeper, under a Commission, to summon all who had been implicated in Essex's plot, in order to treat and compound with them for the redemption of their estates, and the Exchequer was filled by the fines imposed upon them as the condition of their pardon.[1]

We must now look back to the events which were happening to the Lord Keeper in domestic life. In January, 1599, he had the misfortune to lose Lady Egerton, his second wife, to whom he was most affectionately attached;[2] and when he was beginning to recover his composure, he received the sad news of the death of his eldest son in Ireland, a very fine young man, who had been struck with a passion for military glory, and was serving under the Earl of Essex.[3]

However, in the following year, he comforted himself by marrying his third wife, the Countess Dowager of Derby, celebrated in youth by Spenser, under the name of Amaryllis, and afterwards the patroness of the early genius of Milton, who wrote his Arcades for her amusement.

[1] Rym. F. tom. xvi. 421.

[2] "My Lady Egerton died upon Monday morning: the Lord Keeper doth sorrow more than the wisdome of soe greate a man ought to doe. He keapes privat, hath desired Judge Gawdey to sit in Chancery, and it is thought that he will not come abroade this terme."—Letter from Rowland Whyte, Esq., to Sir Robert Sidney, 24th January, 1599. *Sydney Papers*, vol. ii. p. 164.

[3] His father had wished to breed him to the law, but consented at last to his becoming a soldier.

"I wysh my sonne woulde have gyven hym selfe to have attended these things; but his mynde draweth hym an other course to followe the warre, and to attende My L. of Essex into Irelande, and in this he is so farre engaged that I cannot staye him, but must leave hym to his wille, and praye to God to guide and blesse him."—Letter of Lord Keeper to his brother-in-law, dated 6th March, 1598. Ellesmere MS.

Letters of condolence on his son's death poured in from all quarters. I give as a specimen one from George More of Losley:—"Y't was the providens of God that your sonne was borne; so was it that he died; he was your's but for a terme of his life, whereof the thred once spunne cold not be lengthned, and the dayes nombered one day cold not be added by all the worldes power. In his byrth as in his death was the hand of the Lord God; in the one for your comfort; in the other for your tryall; in bothe for your good, if in bothe you glorifie God. What comfort greater can be than to have a sonne brought up in the feare of God, to spend the first and to end the last of his strength in the favour and service of his Prince?"—Ellesmere MS.

CHAPTER XLVIII.

CONTINUATION OF THE LIFE OF LORD ELLESMERE TILL THE END OF THE REIGN OF ELIZABETH.

WE have seen that when Egerton was intrusted with the custody of the Great Seal, he still retained his former office in the Court of Chancery. In the first instance, it was intended that this arrangement should only be temporary; and there were as might be expected, several aspirants to the Rolls. Among these, the most pushing and importunate was Sergeant Heele, a lawyer of considerable vigor and capacity, who had raised himself to extensive practice, and amassed great wealth by very doubtful means. His promotion would have been exceedingly disagreeable to the Lord Keeper, who therefore wrote the following memorial that it might be submitted to the Queen.

" The name and office of a delator ys odeous unto me; I abhor yt in nature, and besydes yt fytteth not my place and condition: yet my duetye to my gracious Sovereign & countrye informeth me speciallye being commanded to set down what I have hearde S. H. charged with,—that thereupon her Matie may make judgment how unfytt & unworthye this man ys for so worthye a place as he seketh.

" 1. He is charged to have bene longe a grypinge and excessive usurer. Agaynst such persons the Chancerye doeth gyve remedye, which yt is not lykelye he will doe, beinge hym self so great & so common an offender in the same kynde.

" 2. He is charged to have bene longe a most gredye & insatiable taker of excessive fees, and (which is moost odious) a notorious & common ambodexter, takinge fee on both sydes, to the great scandale of his place and profession.[1]

" 3. By these wycked vyle meanes he is growne to great wealthe & lyely-hood, and therby puffed uppe to such ex-

[1] In the middle of the last century such practices at the bar were still suspected, there being on the stage " Mr. Sergeant Eitherside," and in Westminster Hall " Sir Bullface Doublefee."

treme heygthe of pride that he is insociable, and so insolent & outrageous in his words & behaviour towards such as he hath to deale with (though men much better then hym selfe) as too offensive & intollerable. As, namelye, against the Byshoppe of Excester, Sir Richard Champeron, Sir Edmunde Morgan, Mr. Benjamin Tychbourne, and many others.

"4. He is noted to be a great drunkarde, and in his drunkennesse not onlye to have commonly used quarrelynge and brawlenge words, but sometyme blowes also; and that at a common ordynarye, a vice ille beseeminge a Sergeant, but in a Judge or publicke Magistrate intollerable."[1]

The Sergeant persisting in his suit, the Lord Keeper outwardly kept on good terms with him, found it convenient to pretend to support him, and strange to say, was all the while indebted to the "gryping usurer, ambodexter, drunkarde, and brawler" in the sum of £400 for money lent. At last the Sergeant, finding that he was effectually thwarted by the superior influence of the Lord Keeper, wrote him the following curious epistle :—

"To the Right ho. the Lo. Keeper of the Greate Seale of England, &c.

"It hath byne my spetiall desyre to have your Lo. holde a good opynion of me. I have dealte as became me in all things : what the cause of your sudden mislike with me is I can not gesse, for sure I am I have ever respected and dealte with you as it became me. You know how I came fyrste to entertaine the hope of the Rolles, and have followed your own directions.

"I fynde now that my hope, through your hard conceite against me, is desperate. I shall therefore praie your

---

[1] Among Lord Ellesmere's papers there is a draught of this memorial in his own handwriting, with the following introduction, which, upon consideration, he had omitted: "I see myne error in presumynge that my services had deserved this favour to have a socyable person placed so neare me, yf there were none other respecte. But sythence I must open the gate to lett in another, I never suspected that I shoulde be constrayned to lett in anye agaynst my lykinge and opinion.

"I accuse and bewayle myne own mishappe, that my 20 yeares services waye so light that Serg. H. and his purse should be put in balance agaynst me —a man of so insolent behaviour and indiscrete carriage, and of so little worthe, and taxed with so manye enormyous crymes and disorders in the course of his lyfe, as none of his profession hath these many yeres bene noted of the lyke."

Lo. to delyver to this Bearer my Bandes, and, at your Lo. pleasure, to sende me the £400 you owe me. I shall humblee entreate your Lo. to use me as you doe the meanest of my Brothers. Thus resting humblie your's: from Sergeants Inne, the 14th of November, 1600.

"Your Lp's in all humbleness,
"JOHN HELE."[1]

Sergeant Heele then thought that he might undermine the Lord Keeper, and perhaps clutch the Great Seal instead of the Rolls—by getting into parliament, and slavishly outbidding the whole profession of the law for the Queen's favor. There being a strong opposition to the subsidy demanded by the Court, thus spoke the legal aspirant, now a representative of the people:—"Mr. Speaker, I marvel much that the House will stand upon granting of a subsidy when all we have is her Majesty's, and she may lawfully, at her pleasure, take it from us:

---

[1] There is among Lord Ellesmere's papers a letter to him from Sir Edward Coke, indorsed, "Ser. Hele, Mr. Attorney," indicating that it originated from some intrigue between these parties.

"Right honourable my singular good Lord,—Secrete inquirie have bene made whether your Lo. having not a patent (as all your predecessors had, Cardinall Woolsey excepted, who therefore (as they saye) ranne into a premunire), of the custody of the Greate Seale, be Lord Keeper or no. Howe rediculous this is, and yet how maliceous; your Lo. knowes, and yet thoughe it be to noe purpose, yet my purpose is thereby to signifie a litle parte of that greate dutie I owe unto your Lo., and that in your wisdom you may make some use of it. And so resting ever to doe your Lo. any service with all thankfull readines, I humblie take my leave this 25 of Jan.

"Your Lo. humblie at commandment,
"ED. COKE."

From the Egerton Papers* published by the Camden Society, and very ably edited by Mr. Payne Collier, it appears that this Sergeant Heele afterwards had a suit before the Lord Keeper respecting a sum of money claimed by him from the executors of Lord Cobham, which, notwithstanding an attempt to make the King interfere in his favor, was determined against him, and that he thereupon wrote the following letter.—

"To the right honorable my very good Lo. the Lo. Ellesmere, Lo. Chancellor of England.

"Right Honorable,

"I proteste unto God that ever synce I knewe you, I did truelie desyre your Lo. fryndshipp and favor. The contrary conceite hath disquieted me more than the order againste me. If your Lo. wilbe pleased to remove that opynion, I will acknowledge myselfe moste bounde unto you. Thus with remembrance of my humble duetye,

"Your Lo. in all service,
"JOHN HELE.

"Sergeants' Inn, 5 Januarij, 1604."†

* P. 391. † Egerton Papers, p. 399.

yea, she hath as much right to all our lands and goods as to any revenue of her Crown."[1] But, to the honor of the House, he was speedily coughed down,[2] and he confined himself to usury for the rest of his days.

This scene took place in Queen Elizabeth's last parliament. The opening of it was rather inauspicious. The Queen, though she still allowed herself to be flattered for her beauty, was conscious of increasing infirmities, and had taken unusual pains to conceal them from the public gaze; but, after being seated on the throne, her enfeebled frame was unable to support the weight of the royal robes, and she was sinking to the ground, when the nobleman bearing the sword of state caught her in his arms, and supported her. The Commons were then approaching; but, in the confusion, the door by which they were to enter was shut, and they were all excluded.

The Lord Keeper, however, that Elizabeth might as soon as possible get back into the open air, proceeded with his oration, explaining the causes of the summons. He inveighed bitterly against the Pope and the King of Spain, whom he denounced as enemies to God, the Queen, and the peace of this kingdom, and engaged in a conspiracy to overthrow religion, and to reduce us to a tyrannical servitude. He charged them with attempts to poison the Queen. "I have seen her Majesty," said he, "wear at her girdle the price of her blood: I mean jewels which have been given to her physicians to have that done unto her which I hope God will ever keep from her." He advised that no new laws should be made; but he exhorted them to make provision for our own defense and safety, seeing the King of Spain means to make England miserable, by beginning with Ireland and the territory of the Queen

---

[1] 1 Parl. Hist. 921.

[2] It distinctly appears that this wholesome parliamentary usage was then established. D'Ewes, after giving an account of the Sergeant's speech, thus describes the scene which followed: "At which all the House *hemmed* and laughed and talked. '*Well*,' quoth Serg. Hele, '*all your hemming shall not put me out of countenance.*' So Mr. Speaker stood up and said, '*It is a great disorder that this should be used, for it is the ancient use of every man to be silent when any one speaketh; and he that is speaking should be suffered to deliver his mind without interruption.*' So the Sergeant proceeded, and when he had spoken a little while, saying he could prove his former position by precedent in the times of Hen. III., King John and King Stephen, the House hemmed againe, and so he sat down."—1 Parl. Hist. p. 922. King James seems to have taken his law from the Sergeant in his famous conversation with the Bishops.

herself. He showed that treasure must be our means, as treasure is the sinews of war.¹

Three days after, the Queen again appeared in the House of Lords, and the Commons presented as their Speaker, Crook, Recorder of London,² who, when his disqualification had been overruled by the Lord Keeper, delivered a florid harangue on the peace and prosperous state of the kingdom, which he said had been defended by the mighty arm of our dread and sacred Queen,—when she interrupted him piously and gracefully with these impressive words, "NO, MR. SPEAKER, BUT BY THE MIGHTY HAND OF GOD!"

When he prayed for freedom of speech, the Lord Keeper said, "Her Majesty willingly consenteth thereto with this caution, that the time be not spent in idle and vain matter, with froth and volubility of words, whereby the speakers may seem to gain some reputed credit by emboldening themselves to contradiction, and by troubling the House of purpose with long and vain orations to hinder the proceeding in matters of greater and more weighty importance."

The first act of the Commons after the choice of a Speaker was to complain bitterly of breach of privilege, in being shut out from the House of Lords the first day of the session,—saying they were yet in ignorance of the causes of calling the parliament. Mr. Secretary Cecil having excused the Lord Keeper,—repeated to them the heads of his speech, and they were appeased.

Notwithstanding the exhortation against any new legislation, there was passed in this session the famous Poor Law of forty-third Elizabeth, with several other important statutes still in force,—and a liberal subsidy being granted in return for the abolition of monopolies, the Queen being seated on the throne in the House of Lords, the Lord Keeper, "with what bevity he might—not to be tedious to his most gracious Sovereign," returned thanks in her name, and said, "We all know she never was a greedy grasper, nor straight-handed keeper, and therefore she commanded me to tell you that you that you have done (and so she taketh it) dutifully, plentifully and thankfully."³ He then dissolved the parliament, and Elizabeth

¹ 1 Parl. Hist. 906. ² Ibid. 907. ³ Ibid 908.

was never again seen by the public with the Crown on her head.

In the following year, however, she paid the Lord Keeper a visit of three days at Harefield, his country house, in Middlesex, near Uxbridge. This delightful place, with the river Colne running through the grounds was first made by a distinguished lawyer, Lord Chief Justice Anderson, from whom it was purchased by the Lord Keeper, and it afterwards gained higher celebrity than could be conferred upon it by a royal visit. Horton, the country-house of Milton's father, where the divine poet wrote some of his most exquisite pieces, was in the neighborhood, a little lower down the stream,[1]—and hence the connection between him and the Egerton family, which led to the composition of the ARCADES and of COMUS. The former masque, in which the widow of the Lord Keeper is so much complimented,[2] was written to be performed here.

At this visit of Queen Elizabeth to Harefield, Milton was yet unborn, and no inspired bard wrote a piece for the occasion; but the Lord Keeper did his utmost in all respects for the entertainment of his royal guest, although the weather was most unpropitious, and the hunting and falconry which had been projected were impracticable. A constant succession of in-door amusements made the three days pass off very agreeably. Shakespeare had lately brought out his immortal tragedy of OTHELLO, and the Queen had not seen it played. Accordingly, Burbidge's company were sent for, and a theater being fitted up in the hall, for which little scenery was then required, the piece was admirably performed by the original actors, whose rehearsal of their parts had been superintended by the author. Succeeding so much better as a writer than as an actor, he himself had now almost entirely withdrawn from the stage, and if he was present it was probably only to assist Burbidge in the management of the entertainments.[3]

---

[1] Milton describes this scenery in the Epitaph. Damon.
"Imus? et arguta paulum recubamus in umbra,
Aut ad aquas *Colni*," &c.

[2]
"Here you shall have greater grace
To serve the Lady of this place;
Such a rural Queen,
All Arcadia hath not seen."

[3] Some critics have supposed that Othello was not produced till 1604, and

The less intellectual shows of dancing and vaulting were likewise exhibited for her Majesty's amusement, and a LOTTERY was drawn,—with quaint devices, perhaps composed by Ben Jonson, who was the great deviser of amusements for the Court in this and the following reign. I give a sample of the Prizes and Blanks.

"A MASKE.
"Want you a maske? Here, Fortune gives you one;
Yet nature gives the Rose and Lilly none."

"*A Looking-Glasse.*
" Blinde Fortune doth not see how fare you be,
But gives a Glasse that you yourselfe may see."

"*A Hand-kerchiefe.*
" Whether you seem to weepe, or weepe indeede,
This hand-kerchiefe will stand you well in steed."

"*A Paire of Garters.*
" Though you have Fortune's garters, you must be
More staid and constant in her steps than she."

"*Blanke.*
"*Nothing's* your lot; that's more than can be told,
For *nothing* is more precious than gold." [1]

At her Majesty's departure there was a somewhat clumsy pageant, which I think must have been the invention of the Lord Keeper himself. HAREFIELD was per-

Dr. Warburton postpones it to 1611; but there can be no doubt that it came out in 1602, and that it was acted before Elizabeth at Harefield. In the Egerton Papers, published by the Camden Society, are to be found the accounts of the Lord Keeper's disbursements for this visit, containing the following items:

"Rewardes to the vaulters, players, and dauncers. Of this, xl. to BURBIDGE'S players: for OTHELLO, lxiij^l. xviij^s. x^d. Rewarde to Mr. Lillye's man, which brought the lotterye boxe to Harefield, xl."

These accounts are exceedingly interesting, and give great insight into the manners of the times. In the same collection there is an equally curious account of the presents of "oxen, muttons, bucks, swans, capons, fish, game cheeses, fruit and sweetmeats," which the Lord Keeper received on this occasion from the Lord Treasurer, the Lord Mayor of London, and near a hundred other friends. Among the contributions is a buck from Sir Thomas Lucy, son of the Sir Thomas who had prosecuted Shakespeare for deer-stealing. Sir George Moor sends, "stagge, 1; lobsters, 17; prawns, 200; trouts, 19; breames, 5; pheasantes, 12; partridges, 14; quailes, 2½ dozen; swannes, 4; Salsie cockles, 8 cwt.; puettas, 2 doz.; gulles, 6; pullets, 2 dozen; pygeons, 2 dozen;" the whole valued only at 20^s. The Lord Mayor was very liberal with his "sacke, sturgeon, herons, gulls, peralles, parterages, semondes and phesantes " Lord Norres, besides bucks, sends 2 oxen. The quantity of " preserved apricox, preserved siterons, marmallet, sugirloves and Bambvry cakes," is quite enormous.

[1] Nich. Prog. vol. iii.

sonified, and, attired as a disconsolate widow in sables, thus bade the Queen farewell:

"Sweet Majestie!

"Be pleased to looke upon a poore widdowe, mourning before Your Grace. I am this place which at your coming was full of joye, but nowe at your departure am as full of sorrowe; as I was then, for my comforte, accompanyed with the present cheerful Tyme, but nowe he must depart with You, and blessed as he is must ever flye before you. But alasse! I have no wings as Tyme hath, my heaviness is suche as I must staye, still amazed to see so greate happiness to some, bereft me. O that I could remove with you as other circumstances can! Tyme can goe with You; Persons can goe with You; they can move like Heaven; but I like dull earthe, as I am, indeed, must staye immoveable. I could wish my selfe like the inchanted castle of love, to hould you here forever, but Your vertues would dissolve all my enchantments. Then what remedie? as it is against the nature of an angell to be circumscribed in place, so it is against the nature of place to have the motion of an angell. I must staye forsaken and desolate; You may goe, with Majestic joye and glorie. My onely suite before you goe, is that You will pardon the close imprisonment which you have suffered ever since your comming; imputing it not to me, but to St. Swithen, whoe of late hath raised so many stormes as I was faine to provide this anchor for You *(presenting the Queen with an anchor jewel)* when I understoode You would put into this creeke; but nowe since I perceave the harbour is too little for you, and that you will hoiste saile and begon, I beseech You take this anchor with You, and I praye to Him that made both tyme and place, that in all places wherever You shall arrive, You may anchor as safely as You doe and ever shall doe, in the harts of my Owners."[1]

The Lord Keeper had now the merit of introducing a practical mitigation of the extreme severity of the penal code. Robbery and theft where clergy could not be effectually prayed, as in the case of illiterate persons and of the female sex, were actually capital crimes, and after

---

[1] Talbot Papers, vol. iv. 43. In a petition to the Crown for a grant of lands in the next reign, he estimated the expense to which he was put by this visit, at £2,000.

conviction the law was invariably allowed to take its course, notwithstanding any circumstances of mitigation. The consequence was, that in the reign of Henry VIII. there were 72,000 executions; and notwithstanding the improvement in police and manners, in the end of the reign of Elizabeth forty felons a year were hanged in the single county of Somerset. A commission was now issued, with the Lord Keeper at the head of it, authorizing the Commissioners to reprieve all such persons convicted of felony as they should think convenient, and to send them to serve for a certain time in the Queen's galleys as a commutation of their sentence. Transportation to the colonies was the improvement of a succeeding reign.

Another commission was issued which had the aspect of severity. By this the Lord Keeper and others were required to summon before them all Jesuits and Seminary Priests, whether they were in prison or at large, and, without observing any of the usual forms of trial, to send them into banishment, under such conditions and limitations as might be thought convenient.[1] The object, however, was to draw the execution of the laws against the Catholic religion from the ordinary tribunals, where they were enforced with relentless rigor,—and these novel proceedings, though they seemed to be dictated by a spirit of persecution, were hailed by many as a new era of toleration. The prospect of a popish successor, and the dread of the introduction of the Inquisition by Spanish subjugation, had reconciled the nation to measures of cruelty of which they were beginning to be ashamed,—since the succession of the Protestant James was considered to be certain, and Spain, effectually humbled, had been compelled to sue for peace.

The Catholics prepared an address of thanks to the Queen, who had been driven to persecute them from policy rather than any violent horror of their faith,—to which she had once conformed, and which she still greatly preferred to puritanism;—but before it could be presented she was beyond the reach of human censure or praise.

During her last illness, the Lord Keeper, with the Lord Admiral and Secretary Cecil, remained at Richmond to watch the hour of her dissolution, while the other Councillors were stationed at Whitehall to preserve the public

[1] Rym. F. xiv. 473, 476, 489.

tranquility, and to prepare measures for the peaceable accession of the new Sovereign. When she had lain ten days and nights upon the carpet, leaning on cushions, and her end was visibly approaching, the Lord Keeper, accompanied by the Lord Admiral and the Secretary of State, presented himself before her, concluding that she had no longer any motive for reserve upon the subject of which she had made so mysterious during the whole course of her reign, and that her recognition of the true heir to the throne would strengthen his title with the multitude. Kneeling down, he said "they had come to know her will with regard to her successor." She answered with a faint voice that, "as she had held a regal sceptre, she desired no other than a royal successor." Cecil requesting that she would graciously condescend to explain herself more particularly, she subjoined "that see would have a King to succeed her, and who should that be but her nearest kinsman, the King of Scots?"[1] They then withdrew, leaving the Archbishop of Canterbury with her to administer to her the consolations of religion. She expired at three in the morning of the 24th of March, and by six the Lord Keeper joined the other ministers in London, and concurred in the order for the proclamation of King James.

It will now be proper to take a brief general retrospect of the proceedings in Chancery during this reign. The equitable jurisdiction of the Court was greatly and beneficially extended, and by the appointment of men to preside in it who had been regularly bred to the profession of the law, it acquired the confidence and good will of the public. We no more have bills in the House of Commons for restraining it, and the attempts to prevent injunctions against fraudulent judgment in the courts of common law originated from the jealousy of the common-law Judges, and their regard for their own power and profit. The statute 27 Ed. III. st. 1, c. 1, forbidding an

[1] A somewhat different account of this conference is given by a Maid of Honor who was present; but, even according to her, the designation of James must be considered genuine, and not the invention of the ministers; for if, on the mention of the name of Lord Beauchamp, the representative of the house of Suffolk, claiming under the will of Henry VIII., she exclaimed, "I will have no rascal's son in my seat," this was a clear expression of preference for the Scottish line.—Lady Southwell's MS. She is partly corroborated by Camden, who thus translates the expression "Nolim vilis mihi succedat." —Cam. Eliz. vol. ii. 285.

application to other jurisdictions to impeach the execution of judgment in the King's Courts, which was unfairly resorted to in this dispute, had been passed merely with a view to prevent appeals to Rome. In the 31 Elizabeth there was an indictment on this statute against a barrister for signing a bill filed in the Court of Chancery, praying an injunction against execution on a common-law judgment;[1] but it was not brought to trial, and a truce was established, which was observed till the famous battle between Lord Coke and Lord Ellesmere.

The process of the Court to enforce appearance, and the performance of decrees, was materially strengthened and improved by the introduction of the commission of rebellion and sequestrations,—whereby, substantially, property and person were rendered subject to equitable as well as legal execution.[2]

Full power was now assumed of granting costs in all cases,—which gradually superseded the practice introduced by 17 Richard II. c. 6, and 15 Henry IV., c. 4, of requiring before issuing the subpœna, security to pay damages to the plaintiff, if the suggestions of the bill should turn out to be false; and the scruple was at last got over of allowing costs to the defendant on a demurrer to the bill for want of equity, although the suggestions contained in it were thereby admitted to be true.

The statute 5 Eliz. c. 18, respecting the office of Lord Keeper, prevented the recurrence to the ancient practice of having the aid of a deputy, under the name of Keeper of the Seal or Vice-Chancellor; but the Master of the Rolls, from being the first clerk in the Chancery, was now described in books of authority as "Assistant to the Chancellor in matters of common law, with authority, in his absence, to hear causes and make orders."[3] The practice was likewise established, which continued down to the time of Lord Thurlow, of the Chancellor deputing a puisne Judge to sit for him in case of sickness or political avocations. Common-law Judges were likewise called in as assessors in cases of difficulty. Questions of law arising incidentally were sent to be determined by a court

[1] Crompton on Courts, 57, 58.
[2] Sequestration was long resisted by the common-law Judges, who said, if a sequestrator were killed in an attempt to enter a house, instead of murder, it would be justifiable homicide, *se defendendo*.—See 5 Rene, H. of L. 160.
[3] Crompon, tit. " Chancery."

of common law, and if the certificate returned was not satisfactory to the Chancellor, he sent the question for the consideration of all the twelve Judges in the Exchequer Chamber.[1]

The Clerks, or Masters, in Chancery being freed from all trouble in superintending the issuing of writs, had abundant leisure, and were of great service in working out the details of decretal order. But the complaint already began, that the Equity Judge, to save himself trouble, and to acquire a character for dispatch which he did not merit, instead of patiently examining the facts and the equity of the case, as he might and ought to have done himself, hastily referred every thing to a Master, who was sometimes found listless or incompetent; and if (as it might happen) he possessed more knowledge as well as industry than his superior, still the suitor was vexed with undue delay and expense.[2]

Bills of discovery and bills to perpetuate testimony became common. The old practice of requiring sureties of the peace in Chancery was still preserved; and we find one instance of a criminal jurisdiction being directly assumed upon a bill filed to punish a party for corrupt perjury, where there was not sufficient evidence to convict him at common law. He demurred, but was compelled to answer.[3] The practice of granting protections, on the ground that the party was in the service of the Crown, still continued.[4]

There being a great clamor in the time of Lord Keeper

[1] Cary, 46.
[2] In a MS. treatise on the Court of Chancery, written by the famous lawyer and antiquary, Sir Robert Cotton, which I have perused by the kindness of my friend, Mr. C. P. Cooper, to whom with many other valuable documents of the same description, it now belongs, I find the following passage, showing the recent origin of the practice of references to the Master:
"Forasmuch as the Masters of the Chancery at this day are grave and wise men, though many of them of another profession, and are not employed in framing of writs as at the first, yet they do sit upon the bench with the Chancellor; and he, taking advantage of their opportunities and leisure (many times of late) refers matters which have depended in that Court, and are ready for hearing, unto their examinations, which, upon their certificate, are decreed accordingly. But it is a true saying that *new meats and old laws are best for use.* And I know not how, but the people do much complain of the new employment of them." He then proceeds invidiously to praise the publicity, regularity and dispatch which characterize the proceedings in the courts of common law.
[3] Woodcock v. Woodcock, 19 Eliz.—Cary, 90.
[4] Reynzt v. Pelserbocio. Lib. Reg. B. 4 & 5 Eliz. f. 124.

Puckering against excessive fees, he undertook to reform them with the assistance of Egerton, then Master of the Rolls; and on his sudden decease, Egerton, become Lord Keeper, went on with the inquiry, and corrected some abuses; but he was effectually thwarted by a combination of the Masters;[1] and when he was extending his reform to the Star Chamber, he received a remonstrance from Francis Bacon, who had a grant in reversion of the registrarship of that Court.[2]

Although there was nothing approaching to an exclusive bar in Chancery, there were particular barristers who acquired reputation by their cunning in drawing bills. One of these being found *too subtle*, an order was made by Lord Keeper Egerton that no bills signed by him should be put upon the file.[3] Sometimes the whole bar refused to be employed against a great man; whereupon the Court assigned counsel to the other side, and compelled them to act.[4]

Towards the end of this reign the business of the Court of Chancery was increased by a decision of the Court of Queen's Bench, which virtually abolished the Court of Requests. This was an inferior Court of Equity, which had taken its origin in the reign of Edward III. or Richard II., and was held before the Lord Privy Seal for the suits of poor men, or of the King's servants ordinarily attendant on his person. The Lord Privy Seal sitting there was assisted by the Masters of the Requests, who acted like Masters in Chancery,—and it had attracted much practice when the Judges decided that it had no contentious jurisdiction.[5] An order was afterwards made, allowing plaintiffs and defendants to sue in the Court of Chancery *in formâ pauperis.*

[1] See a petition against altering fees, signed by nine Masters.—Egerton Papers, 214.
[2] Ib. 272, 426, 427.
[3] Cary, 38.
[4] "27 April, 1562. Brande *v.* Hyldrache. Forasmuch as it is informed that because the matter in question toucheth Mr. Wray, of Lincoln's Inn, the plaintiff cannot get any to be of counsel with him, therefore Mr. Bell and Mr. Manwood are appointed by this Court to be of counsel with the said plaintiff."—Lib. Reg. 3 & 4 Eliz. f. 302.
[5] 41 Eliz. Palgr. 79, 99. 3 Bl. Com. 5. It was finally abolished by 16 Car. 1, c. 10. The old "Court of Requests," which Hume refers to as a place of exercise while debates are going on in parliament, afterwards became the Chamber of the Peers, and is now that of the Commons.

By statute 43 Eliz. c. 4, facilities were given to the Court in investigating abuses in charities. The most important cases arose out of trusts and executory contracts respecting land. However, looking to the Chancery cases in print down to this time, it is wonderful how few and trifling and jejune they appear, when we consider that Plowden's Commentaries, Dyer's Reports, and Sir Edward Coke's Reports were already published, containing masterly judicial reasoning, and satisfactorily settling the most important questions which have ever arisen in the history of the common law of England.

CHAPTER XLIX.

CONTINUATION OF THE LIFE OF LORD ELLESMERE FROM THE ACCESSION OF JAMES I.

EGERTON having joined in proclaiming King James, waited anxiously to see whether he was to be continued in his office by the new Sovereign. Elizabeth died at Richmond on a Thursday morning, and, by what then seemed the miraculously swift journey of Sir Robert Carey, the news was brought to Holyrood House on the following Saturday night; but James waited for the arrival of the messengers dispatched by the Council before he made it public, or would begin to exercise the authority of King of England.

He soon declared his intention to continue in office the wise councillors of his predecessor; and by a warrant under his sign manual, dated the 5th of April, he directed that Elizabeth's Great Seal should be used as the Great Seal of England, and that it should remain in the custody of the former Lord Keeper.[1]

Egerton's joy was a little damped by hearing at the same time that he had been represented to the King by some enemy as "haughty, insolent, and proud;" and he immediately sent off his son with a letter to Sir T. Chaloner, who was acting under Cecil, and had gained the King's confidence, to justify himself. He there says—

"Yf I have bene taxed of hautenes, insolencye, or pryde

[1] Cl. R. 1 Jac. 1.

in my place (as I partly hear relations), I hope it is by theym that have not learned to speake well; and against this poyson I have two precious antidotes: 1. The religious wyssdome, royall justice, and princelye virtues of the King my soveraigne, which wyll soon disperse such foggye mystes. 2. The innocencye and cleerness of myne owne conscience, which is more than *mille testes*.

"I must confesse that in the place of justice which I have helde I was never so servile as to regarde parasites, calumniators, and sycophantes, but always contemned them, and therefore have often fealte the malice of theyr thoughtes, and the venym of their tonges. I have learned no waye but the King's highe waye, and travelling in that, the better to guyde me, I have fastened myne eyes on this marke, *Judicem nec de obtinendo jure orari oportet, nec de injuria exorari*. Yf this have offended any I will never excuse yt; for I take yt to be incident to the place by severe examynyng of manie men's actions to offende many, and so to be hatefull to many, but those always of the worst sorte, agaynst whom I will say no more, but, with Ecclesiasticus, *Beatus qui tutus est a lingua nequam.*"

He likewise wrote a letter to Lord Henry Howard, to be laid before the King, in which he makes an effort at flattery.

"I have readde of *Halcyonis dies*, and *Lætus Introitus*, and *Sol occubuit, nox nulla secuta*: we see and feele the effectes of that which they fayned and imagined. Wee had heavynes in the night, but joy in the mornying. Yt is the great work of God: to hym onlye is due the glorye and prayse for it: and we are all bounden to yelde to hym our contynuall prayers, prayse, and thankes."[1]

These letters being received when the King had reached York on his way to the south, Sir Thomas Chaloner wrote in answer, "As for the objection of haughtines, which, by mistakinge of the relator, hath been imputed unto your Lp., I must cleare the Kinge's Majesty of any such suspition in your honor. For the woords hee used weer only bare questions, as being rather desirous to bee informed of the quality and affections of his subjects and principal counseylores, than any note or prejudicate opinion against your Lp., or any others." But he was much more relieved by Lord Henry Howard. "Your Lo. letter was so

[1] Eg. Pap. 361.

judiciously and sweetley written, as although on two sundrie tymes befor, in private discourse, I had performed the parte of an honest man, yet I could not forbear to present it to the sacred hand of his Majesty, who not onely redde it over twice with exceeding delight, witnessed by his owne mouth to all in his chambers, but besid, commanded me to give you verie greate thankes for the strong conceit you holde of him, and to let you knowe that he did hope that longer acquaintance would not make you like him worse, for he was pleased with persones of your partes and quality."[1]

Thus reassured, the Lord Keeper calmly expected James's approach; and on the 3rd of May he met him at Broxbourne, in Hertfordshire. Having then surrendered the Great Seal into his Majesty's hands, it was forthwith restored to him, still with the rank of Lord Keeper. But, on 19th of July, at Hampton Court, the old Great Seal being broken, a new one, with the King's name and style engraved upon it, was delivered to him as Lord Chancellor of England;[2] and, at the same time, the King put into his hand a warrant for creating him a Peer, by the title of Baron Ellesmere, with many compliments to his merits and his services. In a few days after he was duly installed in his new dignities; and he officiated at the coronation of the King and Queen in Westminster Abbey.

He now gave up the office of Master of the Rolls, which he had held nine years since his appointment to it, and seven years while Keeper of the Great Seal.[3] Having, during this period, done nearly all the judicial business of the Court of Chancery, it was thought that the office of Master of the Rolls might be treated as a sinecure; and, to the great scandal of Westminster Hall, it was conferred on an alien, who must have been utterly unac-

[1] Eg. Pap. 365.
[2] Cl. R. 1 James I. Two years after, this Great Seal was altered under a warrant to the Lord Chancellor, beginning thus: "Forasmuch as in our Great Seal lately made for our realm of England, the canape over the picture of our face is so low imbossed, that thereby the same Seal in that place thereof doth easily bruise and take disgrace," &c.—Eg. Pap. 402.
[3] Under the power given to the Masters of the Rolls by the grant of the office to appoint a deputy, he did, in 1597, appoint Mr. Lambard, but the deputation is expressly confined to the custody of the Rolls House, and the safe keeping and ordering of the records. See discourse on Judicial Authority of M. R., p. 34, where the author, in combating the arguments against the ancient judicial authority of this officer, arising from his power to make a deputy, shows that this applies only to his administrative duties.

quainted with its duties, and incapable of learning them,—Edward Bruce, Lord Kinlosse, one of James's needy Scotch favorites, who had accompanied him to England, and most unconstitutionally had been sworn of the Englsh Privy Council. This and similar acts much checked the popularity of the new Sovereign, and naturally excited great jealousy of his countrymen; whereby all his attempts to bring about an incorporating union between the two countries were defeated.[1]

The new Master of the Rolls had the merit of not interfering farther than taking an account of the fees and emoluments of his office; and the Lord Chancellor was still the sole Judge of the Court, continuing to give the highest satisfaction to the profession and to the public.[2]

[1] The Lord Chancellor, in his judgment in Calvin's case, tried, though very lamely, to apologize for such appointments. In answer to the argument that if the Scottish Postnati were acknowledged for natural-born subjects they would overrun England, he says, "Nay, if you look upon the Antenati, you shall find no such confidence hither, but some few (and very few in respect of that great and populous kingdome) that hath done longe and worthie service to his Majestie, have and still do attend him, which I trust no man dislikes; for there can be none so simple or childish (if they have but common sense) as to thinke that his Majestie should have come hither alone amongst us, and have left behind him in Scotland, and as it were caste off, all his ould and worthie servants."—2 St. Tr. 694.

[2] In the Egerton MSS. there is a curicus account, in the handwriting of the Lord Chancellor, of the presentation of the Lord Mayor of London in the first year of King James, for the royal approbation. First come the heads of the Recorder's address, which he seems to have sent before hand to the Chancellor:

"Reception of Lord Mayor."

After the humbling of our selves unto the King is noted—

" *The Person.* What glory we take in yt: to count the now Lord Maior the King's owne Maior, because he was the first his Ma^{ty} made, and therefor wee present him *tanquam simbolum* of like succeeding happiness to who shall follow him in London, government under his Ma^{ty}.

" *The place.* And as an augur of more than ordinary felicyty to follow, though the present dayes were heavy, it is noted, where others were wont *in foro* he *in Capitolio:* at the Tower of London tooke his othe of office.

" *The Tyme.* When affliction had taken hold of us: at this tyme it was his lott to take the sword, yet within a few weeks after it pleased God we were recovered: after a few months wee had the honor of his Ma$^{ty s}$ triumphall entry, and ever sence have enjoyed happiness and helth. The tearmes and parliament kept with us, and contrary to what was feared. Theyre resydinge hath made us freer than at theyr comminge. Concluded that *A domino factum est istud.*

" *Of London*, this on thinge observed, that amyd the variable fortune of all places in all tymes, even from the cominge of the Romans untyll now, still London hath florished, emynent amongst all cyttyes, *Quantum inter viburna cupressus.* The reason [not legible] her fydelity and that she

In the end of this year, before any parliment had met, he acted as a Peer, being appointed Lord High Steward, to preside at the trial of Lord Cobham and Lord Grey de Wilton, implicated in the conspiracy along with Sir Walter Raleigh, to place upon the throne the Lady Arabella Stuart, or the Infanta of Spain. He had the rare felicity of escaping any reproach in obtaining the conviction of state criminals, as there was ample legitimate evidence against both prisoners, in their voluntary confession, of plotting with the Flemish ambassador for an invasion to change the order of succession to the Crown, although the ultimate objects of the plot have ever remained a mystery.[1] James boasted, as a proof of his *kingcraft*, that he contrived that they should lay their heads on the block before he pardoned them; but that their lives were spared we may fairly ascribe to the mild counsels of the Chancellor.

The parliament, which had been long deferred on account of the plague, was at last summoned. In the writs which were very carefully prepared by the Lord Chan-

---

alwayes went with right. For witness, instanced that ladyes ere our Lord King James his day, when in company of so many councelors and nobles, auspitiosly before all other cyttyes wee did him right. Concluded with this,—

"We sayde it then, wee vow it still, to his Ma^{ty} and his posteryty, to be the truest, surest, and loyalest that ever cytty or was or shalbe to a kinge."

[At the back Lord Ellesmere has made the following memoranda of topics he should advert to in his reply] :—

"Jesuites and Seminaryes.
"Conventicles and Secretaryes.
"Novellistes.
"New Donatistes.
"Factions, Seditions.
"Machiavellian Atheistes, not secrett but publike.
"Delite and desire of alteration and ruyne of all states.
"Contemners of Lawes.
"Discoursers and Censurers of Princes.
"Syckenesse.
"Noysances.
"Vitaylles.
"Buylders.
"Proclamations.
"Rogues and Vacaboundes."

[1] Chief Justice Popham and the other Judges who tried and convicted Raleigh were by no means so fortunate ; for there was not a particle of evidence against him, except a written declaration of Lord Cobham, which he afterwards retracted. But the answer they gave to the request that he should be called as a witness and examined in open court, was that this was by no means to be permitted in the case of an accomplice.—2 St. Tr. 1.

cellor,[1] the Sheriffs were charged not to direct any precept for electing any burgesses to any ancient borough-town within their counties "being soe utterly ruyned and decayed that there are not sufficient resyantes to make such choice, and of whom lawfull election may be made." Nevertheless, representatives were returned for Old Sarum, Gatton, and all the villages to which, for the sake of Court influence in the House of Commons, the elective franchise had been granted by the Tudors, and there was no real intention of bringing about a parliamentary reform by the prerogative of the Crown.[2]

On the first day of the session, the King going to Westminster in a chariot of state, the Lord Chancellor followed, on horseback, in his robes, being placed on the left hand of Prince Henry, who had the Archbishop of Canterbury on his right, the other Lords, spiritual and temporal, following in due order.

The King, on this occasion, introduced the present fashion of the Sovereign personally declaring the causes of the summoning of parliament, but he still adhered to the ancient custom of doing so before the choice of a Speaker. James's speech was exceedingly long and learned, and he would have been highly incensed if any one had treated it as the speech of the minister. When he had concluded, the Lord Chancellor desired the Commons to withdraw and choose a Speaker; and on a subsequent day, the King being present, he announced the royal assent to the choice they had made.[3]

The first measure of the session was a bill brought in by the Lord Chancellor, entitled "A most joyful and just Recognition of the immediate, lawful, and undoubted Succession, Descent, and Right of the Crown," which was forthwith unanimously passed by both Houses.

But he was soon involved in a very unpleasant dispute with the House of Commons, in which he was happily defeated. Sir Francis Goodwin had been chosen member for the county of Bucks, and his return, as usual, had been made in Chancery. Before parliament met, the

[1] Eg. Pap. 384, 387.
[2] Although the scandal of small constituencies had begun thus early, it is a well ascertained fact that the abuse was in first giving the power of sending representatives to what were called the "rotten boroughs"—as almost all of them were more populous in 1832 than they had been at any former era.
[3] Parl. Hist. 967.

Chancellor, assuming jurisdiction over the return, pronounced him ineligible, there being a judgment of outlawry against him, vacated his seat, and issued a writ for a new election. Sir John Fortescue was elected in his place, and claimed the seat; but the House reversed the sentence of the Chancellor, and declared Sir Francis entitled to sit. The King took part with the Chancellor, saying, that all the privileges of the Commons were derived from his royal grant, and the Judges being consulted, gave the same opinion.

The Commons remained firm, and would not even agree to a conference on the subject with the Lords. "A Chancellor," exclaimed a popular orator, "may by this course call a parliament of whatever persons he pleases. Any suggestion, by any person, may be the cause of sending a new writ. It is come to this plain question—Whether the Chancery or parliament ought to have authority?"[1]

A compromise was at last agreed to, whereby Goodwin and Fortescue were both set aside, and a new writ issued, under the Speaker's warrant, and the House has ever since enjoyed the right to judge of the elections and qualifications of its members.

The Lord Chancellor next brought forward the important measure of the union with Scotland, which the King had strongly recommended in his speech from the throne. It was very coldly received, from the apprehension that if carried, England would be overrun with Scotsmen. A bill was however passed for the appointment of English commissioners, to meet commissioners appointed by the parliament of Scotland to treat upon the subject. The Lord Chancellor was the first commissioner; and conducting the negotiation on the part of England, earnestly endeavored to comply with the wishes of his master, but he soon found the project impracticable; "for," says an English writer, "the Scotch, though we had taken their King, absolutely refused to be governed by any of our laws."[2] However, not only were the arms of both kingdoms quartered on all standards, military and civil, but, contrary to the opinion of the Judges, who thought that the name of England could not be sunk or altered in the royal style without the authority of parliament, James, by the advice of the Chancellor and his Council, was now proclaimed

[1] Journ. March 30, 1604. 1 Parl. Hist. 1014.   [2] 1 Parl. Hist. 1023.

afresh as King of Great Britain, France, and Ireland, "that the names of England and Scotland might from henceforth be extinct." [1]

On the 5th of November, 1605, was discovered the famous Gunpowder Plot. A few days after, the King and the Chancellor gave a full narration to the two Houses of all the particulars respecting it ; and there was ordered the form of thanksgiving "for our deliverance from the great and apparent danger which threatened us in this place, still repeated in the daily prayers of the House of Lords. The Chancellor, assuming a power not conceded to his successors, who are not allowed to have more authority than any other Peer, gave direction to the clerk of parliament to take special notice of the names of such Lords as should fail in their appearance next session, having no license from his Majesty for their absence ; and some of the absentees were imprisoned on suspicion that they were implicated in the plot. No other subject could command attention for the rest of the session.

The following year, the Chancellor had again upon his hands the difficult measure of the union with Scotland. He zealously supported it in the Lords ; and that House was inclined to yield to the King's wishes, but the Commons were refractory, several members throwing out the most biting sarcasms against his countrymen and himself.[2]

They agreed that all hostile laws between the two kingdoms should be repealed, and that the Border courts and

---

[1] 1 Parl. Hist. 1052.

[2] *Mr. Fuller:* "Suppose one man is owner of two pastures with one hedge to divide them—the one pasture bare, the other fertile and good. A wise owner will not quite pull down the hedge, but make gates to let the cattle in and out at pleasure ; otherwise they will rush in in multitudes, and much against their will, return." "There are tenants of two manors, whereof the one hath woods, fisheries, liberties : the other, a bare common, without profit, only a little turf, or the like. The owner maketh a grant that the tenants of this shall be participants of the profits of the former. This beareth some show of equity, but is plain wrong, and the grant void."—1 Parl. Hist. 1082.

Sir Christopher Pigott: "I will speak my conscience, without flattery of any creature whatever. The Scots have not suffered above two kings to die in their beds these 200 years. His Majesty hath said that through affection for the English, he dwells in England ; but I wish he would show his affection for the Scots by going to reside among them, for *procul a numine procul a fulmine.*"—1 Parl. Hist, 1097. Boderia, vol. ii. 223. But for this speech he was afterwards, on the King's complaint, sent to the Tower, the Commons excusing themselves for not sooner noticing it upon the maxim, "Leves curæ loquuntur, ingentes stupent."

customs should be abolished; but they would not even go so far as that the subjects of each kingdom should be naturalized in the other. To carry this point, the Chancellor called in the Judges, and obtained an opinion from eleven out of twelve of them, "that such of the Scotch as have been, or shall be born in Scotland since his Majesty's coming to the Crown, are not aliens, but are inheritable by the law, as it now stands, as native English."[1] But the Commons denied this opinion to be law, and refused to abide by it.

Thereupon to have a regular judical decision, the Chancellor directed a friendly suit to be instituted in his own Court; and hence arose CALVIN'S CASE, or the famous "*Case of the Postnati.*" A piece of land in the county of Middlesex, was purchased in the name of Robert Calvin, a minor, born in Scotland since the accession of James to the Crown of England, and a bill in Chancery was filed by his guardian, complaining that the deeds were improperly detained from him by one who held them as his trustee. The defendant pleaded that the plaintiff was an alien,—showing his birth in Scotland since the King's accession. There was a demurrer to the plea. At the same time, an action claiming the land was brought in the Court of King's Bench, to which a similar plea was pleaded. Both suits, on account of the importance and alleged difficulty of the question which they raised, were adjourned into the Exchequer Chamber before the Lord Chancellor and all the Judges. Two of them, Walmesley and Foster, Justices of the Common Pleas, had the firmness, at the risk of being dismissed from their offices, to hold that "if a King of England should hold foreign dominions not in right of the crown of England, those foreign dominions must ever form separate states, the subjects of each standing in the same relation to each other as if they had still separate sovereigns, without acquiring new rights, and without the rights they before enjoyed being prejudiced." Such, I apprehend, would be the opinion of all constitutional lawyers at the present day. The arguments on the other side rest chiefly on the notion of England being an absolute monarchy, so that when it was joined under one Prince to another such kingdom, the inhabitants of both owed him a common allegiance, and,

[1] 1 Parl. Hist. 1078.

for purposes of empire, formed one state, though the ancient municipal laws of each might remain. No attempt was made to show that Scotland was under feudal subjection to England, and the reasoning employed would have applied equally to the inhabitants of all the countries under the dominion of Philip II. if he had had a son by Queen Mary.

The Lord Chancellor delivered a very long and elaborate judgment, in which, it must be confessed, he shows much more anxiety to please the King than to cultivate his own reputation. As a fair specimen, I will transcribe his answer to the objection that this was a question which ought to be settled in parliament, as there was no known law to solve it.

"I would aske of the novelists what they would have done in Sibbel Belknappe's case if they had lived in Henry the Fourth's time? Sir Robert Belknappe, that revered and learned Judge, was banished out of the realm, *relegatus in Vasconiam*. The lady, his wife, continued in England; she was wronged; she brought a writ in her own name alone, not naming her husband. Exception was was taken against it, because her husband was living, and it was adjudged good, and she recovered; and the Judge Markham, said,

'Ecce modo mirum quod fœmina fert breve regis
Non nominando virum conjunctum robore legis.'

"Here was a rare and a new case; yet it was not deferred until a parliament; it was adjudged, and her wrong was righted by the common law of England; and that *ex arbitrio judicum et ex responsis prudentum*, and yet it was accounted *mirum* with an *ecce!* Now, to apply this to R. Calvine's case. His case is rare and new: so was that. There is no direct law for him in precise and expresse tearmes; there was never judgment before touching any born in Scotland since King James beganne his happie raigne in England; hee is the first that is brought in question; so there was no direct law for Sibbel Belknappe to sue in her owne name without her husband, who was then living; nay, rather, there was direct law against it. Yet by the lawe of England, shee had judgment to recover with an *ecce modo mirum;* so by the lawe of England judgment ought to be given for Robert Calvine, but not with an *ecce modo mirum*.

but upon strong arguments deduced *à similibus* and *ex dictamine rationis.*"

But the Chancellor, no doubt, chiefly piqued himself upon the passage where he combats the apprehension of a Scottish invasion :

"Another argument and reason against the Postnati hath been lately made out of diffidence and mistrust that they will come into England *sans* number, and so as it were to surcharge our common ; and that this may be in *secula seculorum.* I know not well what this means. The nation is ancient, noble, and famous ; they have many honourable and worthie noblemen and gentlemen, and many wise and worthie men of all degrees and qualities : they have lands and fair possessions in Scotland. Is it therefore to be supposed, or can it in reason be imagined, that such multitude *sans* number will leave their native soile, and all transport themselves hither? Hath the Irish done so or those of Wales, or of the Isles of Man, Guernsey, and Jersey? Whie should we then suspect it now more for Scotland?"

The dissentient Judges were treated with great scorn, the Lord Chancellor saying that "they did not amount to the plural number in Greek ;"—and what the legislature had refused was made by this judge-made law ;'—but the project of a legislative union was so much prejudiced by the partiality displayed for the Scots, that the King was obliged to drop it, and it was not revived till the reign of Queen Anne, the last of the Stuarts.

In 1612 Lord Ellesmere was employed in assisting the King to institute the new order of hereditary knighthood, whereby a sum of £200,000 was raised,—two hundred Baronets being made at the price of £1,000 a piece.²

The next measure of the Government was not contrary to law, but it was so conducted as to give rise to much

---

¹ A question arose while I was Attorney-General, whether a person born in Hanover during the reign of George III. was to be considered an alien? Happily no doubt can exist as to Hanoverian *Postnati* since the accession of Queen Victoria. See Moore's Rep. 790. Lord Coke's Rep. part vii. 2 St Tr. 559. The only color of argument in favor of the Postnati was that persons born at Calais, or Guernsey and Jersey, and even in Normandy and Aquitaine, were considered natural-born subjects ; but all these places were, however inaccurately, soon considered as belonging to the Crown of England, and so loose were the notions on such subjects prevailing in early times, that Norman barons will be found, as such, sitting in the English parliament.

² Egert. Pap. 449

petty vexation. By the feudal constitutions the King was entitled to an aid from his military tenants to knight his eldest son, to marry his eldest daughter, and to redeem his own person should he fall into captivity. This had not been put in force in England for many ages; but Prince Henry having reached his fifteenth year, and being about to be knighted, it was revived as an expedient to fill the Exchequer without calling a parliament. The mode of proceeding was so little known, that the Chancellor was obliged to have many consultations on the subject with the Judges and the officers of the Exchequer. At last, a writ of Privy Seal was directed to him, commanding him to issue commissions into all the counties of England for assessing the aid; and under these commissions, inquiries were made into the tenure of all lands, and their ancient and present value.[1] These led to a negotiation for giving up entirely "wardship" and the other burdensome incidents of tenure by "knights' service," which would have been more advantageous for all parties; but the Chancellor discouraged it, and this improvement was not accomplished till the reign of Charles II. Before any considerable sum had been collected on this occasion, Prince Henry died, to the unspeakable grief of the nation, for he had given more earnest of great qualities than any of his race; but the event was probably favorable to our liberties; for if he had survived, and shown the genius for war of which he had given manifestation, such battles as Edge Hill, Newbury, and Naseby, would probably have had a different result, and the Long Parliament would have been the last that would ever have assembled in England.

The King did not venture to resort again to an aid from his military tenants, when he married his daughter Elizabeth to the Elector Palatine, but was obliged to submit to the disagreeable necessity of calling a parliament,—a step never taken during the Stuart reigns, except for the purpose of obtaining money.[2]

[1] Egert. Pap. 435.
[2] In contemplation of the meeting of parliament, the Lord Chancellor wrote a paper respecting the various subjects to be discussed. I will give, as a specimen, what he proposes "to equal exportation and importation," and the friends of "Protection" must not be too severe upon his political economy.

"Another thinge of greatest importance ys the contynuall and excessive

On the first day of the session, the King himself delivered a long oration; and the Chancellor's functions, in declaring the causes of the summons, were entirely superseded,—he being merely allowed to go through the forms respecting the choice of a Speaker. The royal eloquence, however, produced very little impression on the Commons; and, instead of voting a supply, they complained to the Lords of a speech which (as reported by common fame) had been made by the Bishop of Lincoln, reflecting upon them, and questioning their right to withhold a supply.[1] Lord Ellesmere was the adviser of the Lords in this controversy with the other House, and certainly showed that he had very undefined notions on the subject of privilege. Having ascertained, by a question he put to the messengers of the Commons, that they merely made a verbal complaint against the Bishop of Lincoln without following it up with any written charge, instead of standing upon the freedom of debate claimed by each House, and the exclusive right of each House to judge of its own proceedings, he recommended a conciliatory answer to the Commons, "that although common fame was not a sufficient ground to proceed upon, nevertheless they would give to the Commons all good satisfaction in this business."

The Commons sent another verbal message, insisting that common fame was sufficient, and repeating the substance of the words which the Bishop was supposed to have spoken; "desiring the Lords, if these words were not spoken, so to signify it to the House, otherwise that

importation of foreyen superfluous and vayne wares and merchandizes, farre exceeding the exportation of the rych and royal commodities of this kyngedome, by which the realme ys daylye more and more impoverished and wasted, and yf it be not remedyed in tyme, the state can not longer subsyste. This requireth great consideration, care, and industrye of men skylfull in the trade of merchandize, but such as feare God and love the Kynge and common weale, and wylle not preferre theyre private gayne for the present before the Kinges welfare and the publicke state of the realme. Yf this pointe for equallinge the exportation and importation be not effectually and spedilye dealte in, whatsoever else shall be attempted for abatinge our supplye wyll be to no little purpose, for this is a consumynge canker."—*Egerton MSS.*

[1] This is the Bishop who, according to Waller's story, being asked by King James whether he could not take his subjects' money without all this formality of parliament, replied, "God forbid you should not, for you are the breath of our nostrils;" which led to Bishop Andrews' witty answer when the same question was put to him, "Why, then, I think your Majesty may lawfully take my brother Neale's money, for he offers it."

the Lords would do as they had promised." "The Bishop made a solemn protestation, on his salvation, that he did not speak anything with an evil intention to the House of Commons, which he did with all hearty duty and respect highly esteem; expressing, with many tears, his sorrow that his words were so misconceived and strained further than he ever intended them." On the motion of the Chancellor, a message was sent to the Commons to inform them of this apology; and that "if the Bishop's words had been spoken or meant to cast any aspersion on the Commons, their Lordships would forthwith have proceeded to the censuring and punishing thereof with all severity; but that hereafter no member of their House ought to be called in question, when there is no other ground for it but public and common fame."[1] Still the Commons were unappeased, and they would proceed with no other business till they had more satisfaction.

The Crown now interposed in a very irregular manner; and a commission was passed under the Great Seal (to be used as a threat), authorizing the Lord Chancellor and others to dissolve the parliament. The Lord Chancellor then, according to the entry in the Journals, "in a very grave and worthy speech, gave the Lords great thanks for having so nobly borne with the many motions he had so unreasonably made unto them." He concluded by moving that a message be sent to the Commons, to say, "that forasmuch as they thought to have heard something from that House this morning, they had hitherto stayed the publishing of the commission, which had passed the Great Seal, to dissolve the parliament." An equivocal answer being received, they adjourned till the following day; and then no concession being made, the Lord Chancellor directed the commission to be read, and in the King's name dissolved the parliament. No other parliament met till 1620,—when a Lord Chancellor was impeached, and convicted of bribery and corruption.

[1] Parl. Hist. 1159.

CHAPTER L.

CONCLUSION OF THE LIFE OF LORD ELLESMERE.

LORD ELLESMERE, for the rest of his time, had only to attend his duties in the Court of Chancery, in the Privy Council, in the Star Chamber, and in the Court of the Lord High Steward.

He had obtained the assistance of an able Master of the Rolls, Sir Julius Cæsar, who had been regularly bred to the profession of the law,—and a commission had issued in which several common-law Judges were included, to hear causes in his absence. From his age and infirmities, he could no longer master the whole business of the Court single-handed, as he had done in former times. He showed, however, that his mental vigor remained unbroken.

The youthful minion who was now grasping at all power and patronage, tried to get into his hands even the appointment of the officers of the Court of Chancery, but this attempt was manfully resisted by the Chancellor. The following is a copy of the letter which he wrote to the Earl of Somerset on that occasion:—

"My Lord,

"I woulde be gladde to gyve you a good accompt of the late projecte of Sir W. Uvedall's sute. I wysh well to the Gent. in regarde of hym selfe, but specially for your recommendation, being desirous to accommodate any thinge you shall commende unto me. But the more I haue labored to understand what is lykely to be the scope and end of this projecte, the more I am perplexed. I doubt that, by the successe, he shall fynde yt more in shewe than substance. I perceive yt maye concerne many, some in the very right of their places, as they pretende namely, the Clerke & Comptroller of the Hanaper, but specially the Clerke who is Ciericus & Custos Hanaperii, and so a receyvor & accomptant to his Ma^{tye} and conceyveth, as his Counsell advise hym, that yt wyll prejudice hym in his frehoulde, havinge his office for terme of his lyfe by his M^{tys} letters patent. The Controller hathe a kynde of relation to the same office, and can not well be be severed the one from the other. The poore Sealer and Chaffewaxe, and their dependantes, are afrayed of they know not what, suspecting that this innovation, which they understande not, can not be for ther good, but lykely to end to their harm, whatsoever is pretended. And these poore men, whose labour and paynes are greatest, deserue moost to be pytyed & relieved, and so yt is lykely that some upon pretence of right, and some from necessitye, wyll move more discontentment & clamour than they can stoppe.

"But leaving these to theym selues, I must lett your Lordship know playnelye that yf I be pressed to deliver myne opinion, I can not gyve any furtherance to the sute. For where the constitution & frame or Hanaper hath contynued setled as yt is, I know not how many hundred yeares, this newe projecte ywll make such a breach and rupture in yt as I can not forsee yt; and your Lp. in your wysedome can not but know that all innovations be dangerous, and yt was, upon great reason, observed and sayed longe agoe, that ipsa mutatio consuetudinis etiam quæ adjuvat utilitate novitate perturbat. Such perturbations, by a new projecte, after so many hundred yeares quyette, I woulde be sory to see in this place in my tyme which can not be, and I desire not to be, longe. So, recommending the further consideration thereof to your wysedom, I rest

"Your Lps very lovinge frende,
"assured and redy at your command,
"T. ELLESMERE, C."[1]

In the case of the Countess of Shrewsbury, brought before the Privy Council, for being concerned in the marriage of the King's cousin-german, the Lady Arabella Stuart, without the King's consent, the Lord Chancellor laid it down for law, that this was a great misdemeanor, and that the defendant, though a Peeress, by refusing to answer on oath the questions put to her respecting it, ought to be fined £20,000.[2] The right of the reigning Sovereign to regulate the marriages of all members of the royal family was then enforced by the power of arbitrary fine and imprisonment; and when this power was gone, the right was found to be without any remedy till

[1] Egerton MSS.   [2] 2 St. Tr. 770.

the passing of the royal marriage act, in the reign of George III.

As a specimen of the mode of proceeding in the Star Chamber, while Lord Ellesmere presided there, I will give a short abstract of the famous "Cases of Duels." Sir Francis Bacon, Attorney General, filed an information against William Priest for writing and sending a challenge, and against Richard Wright for carrying it, although it had been refused. The case was very clear, and not attended with any circumstances of aggravation; yet to check the practice of duelling, which had then increased in a most alarming manner, the trial occupied a tedious length of time, and was conducted with great solemnity. After a most elaborate opening from Mr. Attorney, he called his proofs, and the defendants confessed their guilt. Still Lord Coke was called upon by the Chancellor to lay down the law, that "to send or carry a challenge is a misdemeanor, though there be no duel." Then the Lord Chancellor pronouned sentence, " that both defendants be committed to Fleet; Priest to pay a fine of £500, and Wright of 500 marks; that at the next Surrey assizes they should publicly in the face of the Court, the Judges sitting, acknowledge their offense against God, the King, and the laws; that the sentence should be openly read and published before the Judges on all the circuits; and lastly, that the Lord Chief Justice Coke should report the case for public instruction."[1]

It was a sore disappointment to the Lord Chancellor that he was prevented by illness from being present at the hearing of the case of Oliver St. John, prosecuted by Mr. Attorney General Bacon in the Star Chamber, for denying the legality of "Benevolences." The hearing had been put off to accommodate him, and he had expressed a strong hope to be able to attend, "and it were to be his last work to conclude his services, and express his affection towards his Majesty." However, he took occasion to express his approbation of the sentence, "that the defendant should pay a fine of £5,000, and be imprisoned during the King's pleasure."[2]

Though not chargeable with counseling acts of wanton cruelty, he always supported the King in all his pretensions to arbitrary power, never in a single instance

[1] 2 St. Tr. 1034.   [2] Ibid. 899.

checking the excesses of prerogative;—unlike his great contemporary, Lord Coke, who was redeemed from many professional and political sins, not only by acting the part of a patriot when turned out of office and persecuted by the existing administration, but who, even when Chief Justice—holding at the pleasure of the Crown,—with the Great Seal within his reach,—stepped forward on various occasions as the champion of the laws and constitution of his country.

The High Commission Court, established in the reign of Henry VIII. on the separation from Rome as a substitute for the papal jurisdiction, had been an instrument of more odious vexation than the Star Chamber itself. The Lord Chancellor stood up for its legality, and its power to fine and imprison; but Coke refused to sit upon it, denying that it had any such authority, either by the common law or act of parliament, and the Chancellor was obliged to excuse his absence from its meetings.[1]

So James arrogated to himself the power of issuing proclamations, not merely to enforce, but to alter the law —not limiting this prerogative to any particular subject, and merely taking this distinction between a proclamation and an act of parliament,—that the former is in force only during the life of the Sovereign who issues it, whereas the latter is of perpetual obligation. He had accordingly issued (amongst others) proclamations against erecting any new buildings in or about London, and prohibiting the making of starch from wheat. The legality of these coming in question, the Judges were summoned before the Council with a view to obtain an opinion that they were binding on all the King's subjects. Coke at first evaded the question, expressing doubts, and wished to have farther time to consider. The Lord Chancellor said, "that every precedent must have a first commencement, and that he would advise the Judges to maintain the power and prerogative of the King; and in cases in which there is no authority and precedent, to leave it to the King to order it according to his wisdom and the good of his subjects, for otherwise the King would be no more than the Duke of Venice." Coke answered, " True it is

[1] 12 Rep. 87. In the next reign this Court became still more tyrannical when directed by Laud against the Puritans, but it was abolished by 16 Car. I, c. 11.

that every precedent hath a commencement; but where authority and precedent are wanting, there is need of great consideration before anything of novelty is established, and to provide that this is not against the law of the land; for the King can not change any part of the common law, nor create any offense by his proclamation, which was not an offense before, without parliament; but at this time I only desire to have a time for consideration and conference with my brothers, for *deliberandum est diu quod statuendum est semel.*" Being taunted with having himself decided cases in the Star Chamber upon the proclamation against building, he said, "*Melius est recurrere quam male currere*—it is better to recede than to persevere in evils. Indictments conclude *contra leges et statuta*, but I never heard an indictment conclude *contra regiam proclamationem.*"

Time was given, and an unfavorable answer returned, which saved us from the uncertainty which, to this day, prevails in France, even under the Orleans dynasty, as to what may be done by royal ordonnance, and what can be done only by an act of the legislature.[1]

Lord Coke acquired great popularity by these proofs of spirit and independence; and the Government not then thinking it prudent to cashier him, he fondly conceived the notion that, on account of his reputation for learning and integrity, he never could be in jeopardy. The insolence of his nature in consequence broke out against the Chancellor, who had suffered some humiliation from such controversies, and who was now supposed to be dying. The Chief Justice deemed this a fit opportunity to revive the dispute between the Courts of common law and equity, —denying that the Chancellor had any right to interfere by injunction with an action in its progress,—and insisting that the suing out of a subpœna in Chancery, to examine the final judgment of a court of common law, was an offense which subjected all concerned to the penalties of a *premunire.* He now boldly pronounced judgment in a case in which the Chancellor had granted an injunction to stay proceedings;[2] he bailed and afterwards discharged

---

[1] 12 Rep. 74.—Written in 1845.—While this sheet is passing through the press, the Orleans dynasty is swept away—and a Republic is substituted—which may perish before the printing of this volume is completed.—*March* 14, 1848.   [2] Heath *v.* Ridley.

a person who had been committed by the Lord Chancellor for breach of an injunction against suing out execution on a judgment;[1] and in another case,[2] he got Justice Dodderige, a puisne Judge of the King's Bench, to express a strong opinion, along with him, that the interposition of equity in actions at law was illegal.

Still the Chancellor continued to exercise his jurisdiction as before; and in a case where a judgment had been fraudulently obtained in the Court of King's Bench, he pronounced a decree to set it aside, and granted a perpetual injunction against execution. The verdict had been gained in this action by decoying away the defendant's witness, who could have proved payment of the alleged debt, and making the Judge believe that he was dying. During the trial, this witness was carried to an adjoining tavern, and a pottle of sack was ordered for him. When he had put this to his mouth, the fabricator of the trick returned to Court, and arrived there at the moment when the witness was called. The Judge was asked to wait for a few minutes, but the cunning knave swore "that delay would be vain, for that he had just left the witness in such a state, that *if he were to continue in it a quarter of an hour longer*, he would be a dead man." Coke (we must hope, unconscious of the deceit which had been practiced) sent for the attorney for the plaintiff at law, and recommended him to prefer an indictment for a premunire against the party who had filed the bill in Chancery, his counsel and solicitor. In another case of the same nature, he gave the like advice; with a recommendation that the Master in Chancery, who had been assessor to the Chancellor when the order was made, should be included in the indictment.

In charging the Grand Jury in Hilary term, 1616, Mr. Justice Crook, on the suggestion of the Chief Justice, for the first time that such a matter had been mentioned to any inquest, gave them in charge "to inquire of all such persons as questioned judgments at law, by bill or petition, in the Court of Chancery." I now copy a paper indorsed in the handwriting of Lord Ellesmere:—

"Prooffes of the proceedinges, the last day of Hillary Terme:

"Glanvill, informing the Lord Coke that the Jury wold

[1] Courtney *v.* Glanvil.   [2] The King *v.* Dr. Gouge.

not finde the bills of Premunire, the Lord Coke sent for the Jury, yet protested he knewe nothing of the matter.

"The Jury, for the waightines of the case, desired further tyme and counsill, though at theire owne charge; but both denied, by the Lord Coke affirming that the case was plaine.

"The Lord Coke, perceiving the Jury were inclined not to find the bills, they alleadging that they were promised better evidence than the oath of the parties, and that they were not satisfied that the judgement was dulye gotten, being obtained out of Terme, he stood upp and said to them, "Have you not seen copies of the proceedinges in Chancery? Have not Allen and Glanvil made oath for the King that the same are true? Is not a party robbed a good witnes for the King against a theefe, and is there not a judgement in the case?'

"At the Jurors' second comeing to the Barre, the Lord Coke said unto them, that yf they wold not find the bills, he wolde comitt them, and said that he wold sitt by it untill the busines were done, and willed them to goe together againe. After which, a Tipstaff attending that Court came into the private room where the Jury were conferring touching those indictments, and told them the Lord Coke was angrye they staid soe long, and bade them feare nothing, the Lord Chancellor was dead.

"At the Jurors' third comeing, the Lord Coke caused them to be called by the poll, and perceiving that 17 of the 19 were agreed to return *Ignoramus*, he seemed to be much offended, and then said they had been instructed and tampered withall, and asked Glanvill and Allen to prepare themselves against the next Terme, when he wold have a more sufficient Jury, and evidence given openly at the Barr.

"Note, that upon the Lord Coke's threatening wordes one of the Jury formerly agreed with the rest fell from them, saying he found the Bills, Lord Coke said, 'I think theis Bills wilbe found anon.'

"Upon a motion made there that day between Goodwin and Goldsmith concerning a judgment in that Court, the Lord Coke said openly to the lawyers, 'Take it for a warning, whosoever shall putt his hand to a bill in any English Court after a judgement at lawe, wee will foreclose hym for ever speaking more in this Court. I give you a faire warning to preserve you from a greater mischief. Some must be made example, and on whome it lighteth it will fall heavy. Wee must looke about us, or the common law of England wilbe overthrowne.' And said further, that the Judges shold have little to doe at the assizes by reason the light of the lawe was lyke to be obscured, and therefore, since the said case then moved was after judgment, he willed the party to preferr an indictment of præmunire.

"Note, the Lord Coke said the Judges of that Court were the superintendents of the realm."[1]

The Chancellor meanwhile was confined to his bed, and this proceeding of Coke was considered the more reprehensible as an attempt to crush a dying rival. But Sir Francis Bacon, the Attorney General, gave information of the collision to the King, " commending the wit of a mean man, who said the other day, '*Well, the next term you shall have an old man come with a beesom of wormwood in his hand that will sweep away all this*,' for it was Mylord's fashion, especially towards the summer, to carry a posy of wormwood."

Accordingly the Chancellor, having unexpectedly recovered, prepared a case, which he laid before the King, concluding with the question, " Whether, upon an apparent matter of Equity which the Judges of the law by their place and oath can not meddle with or relieve, if a judgment be once passed at common law, the subject shall perish, or that the Chancery shall relieve him? and, whether there be any statute of premunire, or other, to restrain this power in the Chancellor?"[2] The King referred it to the Attorney and Solicitor General, the King's Sergeants, and the Attorney General of the Prince of Wales, who made a report to him, "that the statutes of premunire did not apply to such a case, and that, according to reason and many precedents, the Chancellor had the jurisdiction which he had exercised, to examine the judgments of the Courts of common law, and to stay execution, if he should find that they had

---

[1] Unpublished MS. in possession of Lord Francis Egerton. In the margin there is a list of twelve witnesses by whom this statement is to be proved, with an intimation that " theise thinges can be further proved by sundry other witnesses not yet examined, yf it be required."

[2] 5 Bacon's Works, 416.

been obtained by fraud, for which the Courts of common law could not afford sufficient remedy."

James, however, in deciding for the Chancellor, thought fit to rest on the plenitude of his royal prerogative, assuming that " it appertained only to his princely office to judge over all Judges, and to discern and determine such differences as at any time might arise between his several Courts touching their jurisdictions, and the same to settle and determine as he in his princely wisdom should find to stand most with his honor."[1] To settle the question of jurisdiction in all time to come, the royal decree was ordered to be enrolled in the Court of Chancery. Coke made rather a humiliating submission, and during the short remainder of his judicial career offered no further resistance to injunctions; but, being convinced against his will, he retained his opinion, and in his " Third Institute" he stoutly denies the jurisdiction of the Chancellor on this subject, which he maintains is contrary to 27 Ed. 3; and after citing the pretended authorities in his favor, he says, " The Privy Seal of 1616 to the contrary was obtained by the importunity of the then Lord Chancellor, being vehemently afraid; *sed judicandum est legibus*, and no precedent can prevail against an act of parliament."[2]

Some thought that this would have been a good opportunity for getting rid of Coke as Chief Justice. But Bacon writes to the King: " My opinion is plainly that my Lord Coke at this time is not to be disgraced, both because he is so well habituate for that which remaineth of these capital causes,[3] and also for that which I find in his breast, touching your finances and matters of repair of your estate. On the other side this great and public affront, not only to the reverend and well deserving person of your Chancellor (and at a time when he was thought to lie on dying, which was barbarous), but to

---

[1] 1 Chanc. Rep. Append. 26. Council Book, July 26, 1616. 3 Bl. Com.

[2] 3 Inst. c. 54, p. 125. After Lord Coke's death the question of equitable jurisdiction was again mooted, and it was revived at intervals down to 1695, when an elaborate treatise in support of Lord Coke's doctrine was published by Lord Chief Baron Atkyns, but the jurisdiction of equity, as well after as before judgment, has been ever since exercised without controversy or interruption.—See all the authorities collected by Mr. Hargrave in a note to the Life of Lord Ellesmere, in the Biogr. Brit. vol. v. p. 574. 1 Hall. Const. Hist. 469. 2 Swanst. 24, n.

[3] The prosecutions arising out of the murder of Sir Thomas Overbury.

your high Court of Chancery, which is the Court of your absolute power, may not, in my opinion, pass lightly, or end only in some formal atonement; but use is to be made thereof for the settling of your authority and strengthening of your prerogative, according to the true rules of monarchy. If it be true, as is reported, that any of the puisne Judges did stir this business, or that they did openly revile or menace the jury for doing their conscience as they did, honesty and truly, I think that Judge is worthy to lose his place. And to be plain with your Majesty, I do not think there is any thing a greater *polychreston* or *ad multa utile* to your affairs, than upon a just and fit occasion to make some example against the presumption of a Judge in causes that concern your Majesty, whereby the whole body of those Magistrates may be contained the better in awe." He concludes, however, by giving the milder advice, which appears to have been followed, "that the Judges should answer it on their knees before your Majesty or your Council, and receive a sharp admonition."[1] The Attorney General was directed to prosecute in the Star Chamber the parties who had preferred the indictments; but the matter was allowed to drop without any farther judicial proceeding, the attention of the nation being now entirely absorbed in the prosecutions going forward for the murder of Sir Thomas Overbury.

The occurrences connected with this murder throw a deep stain on the reign of James; and Lord Ellesmere can not be entirely cleared of the disgrace in which all concerned in them were involved. He was not answerable for the King's fondness for Car, the handsome, unlettered youth, nor the favors bestowed upon this minion, nor the young Countess of Essex's preference of him to her wedded husband; but he was answerable, as Head of the Law, for countenancing the infamous process instituted to dissolve her marriage, and for putting the Great Seal to a commission for that purpose. Though Archbishop Abbot, to his honor, refused to concur in the divorce, which was pronounced on the fantastical plea of "*maleficium versus hanc,*" produced by witchcraft, which James himself wrote a treatise to support,—the Chancellor, several Bishops, and the most eminent statesmen, concurred in the judgment;

[1] Bacon's Works, vol. iv 606.

and Sir Thomas Overbury became the victim of the advice he honestly gave to his friend, not to unite himself in marriage with an abandoned woman.

The Earl and Countess of Somerset being now detected as the instigators of the murder, they were lodged in the Tower. It was indispensably necessary that they should be brought to trial, and the greatest consternation prevailed at Whitehall. Little sympathy was felt for the favorite whose fall had been foreseen, as he had been supplanted in the King's affections by the younger, the handsomer, and more sprightly Villiers; but he and his wife had some royal secrets in their keeping, which there was a dreadful apprehension that they might disclose when they stood at the bar, and had nothing more to hope or to fear on this side of the grave. The plan adopted, with the sanction of the Chancellor, was to hold out to them an assurance of mercy, if they demeaned themselves discreetly; but, by way of precaution,—along with some frivolous questions, such as "whether the axe was to be carried before the prisoners, this being a case of felony?" and "whether, if there should be twelve votes to condemn, and twelve or thirteen to acquit, it would not be a verdict for the King?"—the Judges were asked "whether, if my Lord of Somerset should break forth into any speech taxing the King, he be not presently by the Lord Steward to be interrupted and silenced?"

The inferior agents in the murder, having been convicted under a special commission sitting at the Guildhall, London, Lord Ellesmere, the Chancellor, was appointed Lord High Steward for the trial of the Earl and Countess of Somerset before their Peers. It was concerted that the Lady was to plead *guilty*, and her trial was appointed to come on the first. Lord Ellesmere, as Lord High Steward, rode on horseback in great state from York House to Westminster Hall, attended by the Peers who were summoned to sit on the trial. Then came the Judges and Sergeants at Law who were to act as assessors. The Court being constituted, the Countess was brought into the Hall; but the ceremony of carrying the axe before her was omitted. She stood pale and trembling at the bar, and when addressed by the Lord High Steward she covered her face with her fan; but I do not find any question made as to her having been personally present on this occasion, although in a prior judicial investigation she was supposed, concealing her face, to have been represented by a young virgin of her age and stature. Making a low courtesy to the Lord High Steward, she now confessed that the charge against her in the indictment was true, and she prayed for mercy.

The Lord High Steward, holding his white wand in his hand, thus addressed her:—" Francis, Countess of Somerset, whereas thou hast been indicted, arraigned, and pleaded guilty, it is now my part to pronounce judgment; only thus much before, since my Lords have heard with what humility and grief you have confessed the fact, I do not doubt they will signify as much to the King, and mediate for his grace towards you; but in the mean time, according to the law, the sentence must be this, that thou shalt be carried from hence to the Tower of London, and from thence to the place of execution, where you are to be hanged by the neck till you be dead; and the Lord have mercy upon your soul."

Ten days after, the Earl of Somerset was brought to his trial with the like solemnities; but as he refused to plead *guilty*, the Lieutenant of the Tower told him roundly that "if in his speeches he should tax the King, the justice of England was that he should be taken away, and the evidence should go on without him, and then all the people would cry *Away with him!* and then it should not be in the King's will to save his life, the people would be so set on fire."

When he had been arraigned, Ellesmere, as Lord High Steward, affected to desire him to make his defense boldly, "without fear," but evidently attempted to intimidate him by adding, "To deny that which is true increases the offense; take heed lest your wilfulness causes the gates of mercy to be shut against you." [1]

The prisoner abstained from any attack on the King, and the trial was conducted decorously to its close, the counsel for the Crown first reading the written depositions of the witnesses, and then presenting the witnesses themselves to be examined by the prisoner or the Peers. The

---

[1] Who would suppose that a poetical thought should be borrowed from a Lord High Steward on a trial for felony?—Yet the coincidence between Ellesmere and Gray could hardly be accidental:
"Forbad to wade through slaughter to a throne,
And shut the gates of mercy on mankind."

proofs were complete, the verdict of guilty unanimous, and sentence of death was pronounced in due form.

These two titled culprits were far more guilty than the inferior agents employed by them, on whom the rigor of the law had taken its course; yet, according to the understanding which had been entered into with them, they were respited from time to time, and at last a pardon was granted to them, reciting that Lord Ellesmere, and the other peers who had tried them, had undertaken to intercede in their favor.[1] In the annals of crime there is not a murder more atrocious for premeditation, treachery, ingratitude, and remorselessness, than the poisoning of Sir Thomas Overbury by the Somersets. The execution of Lord Sanquhar for killing the fencing-master, was the subject of much self-laudation to James; but the guilt of this nobleman was venial in comparison. Although it be possible that the remains of tenderness might alone have now actuated the royal mind, there must ever remain a suspicion that Ellesmere assisted him in screening from justice persons who, while convicted of a crime of the deepest malignity, were in possession of some secret which the monarch on the throne was desirous should be for ever buried in oblivion.

These prosecutions being over, the Lord Chancellor joined in a scheme, not much to his credit, to dismiss Sir Edward Coke from his office of Lord Chief Justice of the King's Bench. This is supposed to have originated with Buckingham, who then had a private quarrel with him about the appointment to a lucrative place in his Court; but the Chancellor, instead of standing up, as would have become him, for the independent administration of justice, rejoiced in the opportunity of being revenged upon a man who had injured him—little conscious that he was lowering his own character, and giving fresh luster to that of his hated rival.

A cause happened to be argued in the Court of King's Bench wherein the validity of the grant of a benefice to be held *in commendam*, or along with a bishopric, came into question, and counsel at the bar had denied the pre-

---

[1] "Cumque Tho. Dominus Ellesmere Cancellar nr' Angliæ et Magnus Senescallus nr' Angliæ ea vice existens necnon omnes pares ejus per quorum judicium convicta fuit ad humil. petitionem ejusdem Franciscæ publice fact. promisso suo ad intercedend. pro misericordia nostra regia erga eam solemniter se obstrinxerunt," &c.

rogative of the King to make such a grant. For the purpose of involving the Chief Justice in a quarrel that might give a pretense for cashiering him, the Chancellor and the Attorney General concocted a letter to him in the King's name, under the Privy Seal, forbidding the Court to proceed further in the cause, "*Rege inconsulto*,"—until the King's advice should be taken upon a matter touching his prerogative. At Coke's request, similar letters were written to all the other Judges, so that the obligation created by such a prohibition might be solemnly considered.

The twelve Judges having assembled,—by a writing which they all subscribed, they certified his Majesty that "they were bound by their oaths not to regard any letters contrary to law; and that the letters in question being contrary to law, they were bound to proceed to hear the cause argued, and to do justice between the parties." They were summoned, as criminals, before the Council, and the King, with the Chancellor on his right hand, inveighed against the manner in which popular lawyers were allowed to tread on his prerogative, and pronounced the remonstrance of the Judges highly indecent, as they ought at once to have submitted to his princely judgment. All the twelve dropped down on their knees, and acknowledged their error as to the form of their answer; but Coke manfully entered on a defense of the substance of it, maintaining that "the delay required was against law and their oaths."

James appealed to the Lord Chancellor, who, showing an utter want of dignity and courage, said he should first like to hear the opinion of the Attorney General. Bacon, without hesitation, asserted that " putting off the hearing of the cause, in obedience to his Majesty's command, till his Majesty might be consulted,—to his understanding, was, without all scruple, no delay of justice nor danger of the Judges' oaths, and begged the Judges to consider whether their conscience ought not to be more touched by their present refractory conduct, for it is part of their oath to counsel his Majesty when called; and if they will proceed first to give judgment in Court in a business whereon they are called to counsel, and will counsel him when the matter is past, it is more than a simple refusal to give him counsel."

The Chief Justice fired up at this impertinence, and took exception that the counsel, whose duty it was to plead before the Judges, should dispute with them. Mr. Attorney retorted, that "he found that exception strange, for that the King's learned counsel were, by oath and office, and much more where they had the King's express commandment, without fear of any man's face, to proceed or declare against any the greatest peer or subject of the kingdom, or against any body of subjects or persons, were they Judges or were they of the upper or lower House of Parliament in case they exceed the limits of their authority, or take anything from his Majesty's royal power or prerogative; and concluded that this challenge, in his Majesty's presence, was a wrong to their places, for which he and his fellows did appeal to his Majesty for reparation." James affirmed that "it was their duty to do so, and that he would maintain them therein."

The Lord Chancellor, now plucking up courage, declared his mind plainly and clearly that "the stay by his Majesty required was not against the law, nor a breach of the Judge's oath."

This question was then propounded to the Judges, "Whether if at any time, in a case depending before the Judges, his Majesty conceived it to concern him either in power or profit, and thereupon required to consult with them, and that they should stay proceedings in the mean time, they ought not to stay accordingly?" With the exception of Lord Chief Justice Coke, they all submissively said *they would*, and acknowledged it to be their duty so to do. "Having been induced," says Hallam, "by a sense of duty, or through the ascendency Coke had acquired over them, to make a show of withstanding the Court, they behaved like cowardly rebels, who surrender at the first discharge of cannon, and prostituted their integrity and fame through dread of losing their offices, or rather, perhaps, of incurring the unmerciful and ruinous penalties of the Star Chamber."[1] Not so the undaunted Chief Justice. He returned his memorable reply, which, for firmness, moderation, simplicity, and true grandeur, is not surpassed by any recorded saying of a constant man threatened by power in the discharge of a public **duty.**

---

[1] Const. Hist. vol. i. p. 476.

"When the case shall be, I will do that which shall be fit for a Judge to do."

The recreant *puisnes*, from whom nothing was to be feared, were pardoned, but the Chief had shown a spirit which might be troublesome in the execution of the plan now adopted of trying to govern without a parliament, and he was to be punished. First he was suspended from the public exercise of his office, being directed, instead of sitting in Court and going the circuit, to do business at chambers, and to employ himself in correcting his reports; and soon afterwards he was superseded, and a successor was appointed in his place.[1] Although he soon rallied from the blow, and had his revenge by becoming leader of the opposition when it was found necessary to call a parliament, his enemies had the gratification to hear that when the supersedas was put into his hand, he trembled and wept,—indicating that he would have been better pleased to involve himself in his robes than in his virtue.[2]

Although the aged Ellesmere, prompted by Bacon, took a very active and cordial part in the dismissal of Coke, he decently pretended to regret it. In a letter written by him to the King on that occasion, he says, " I know obedience is better than sacrifice ; for otherwise I would have been an humble suitor to your Majesty to have been spared in all service concerning the Lord Chief Justice. I thank God I forget not the fifth petition *dimitte nobis debita nostra sicut*, &c. But, withal I have learned this distinction : there is, 1. *Remissio vindictæ;* 2. *Remissio pœnæ;* 3. *Remissio judicii*. The two first I am past, and have freely and clearly remitted. But the last, which is of judgment and discretion, I trust I may, in Christianity and in good conscience, retain."[3]

His speech on swearing in Sir Henry Montagu, Coke's successor, however, shows that he had neither remitted his desire of vengeance nor of punishment. He ungenerously took the opportunity of insulting his fallen foe, by cautioning the new Chief against the supposed faults of the one dismissed, and by an affected contrast between the latter and Montagu's grandfather, who had been Chief Justice of the Common Pleas in the reign of Elizabeth.

---

[1] Bacon's Works, vi. 123, 125, 127, 130.   [2] Ibid. v. 433.   [3] Ibid. vi. 399

Lord Ellesmere.—"This is a rare case, for you are called to a place vacant not by death or cession, but by a motion and deposing of him that held the place before you. It is dangerous in a monarchy for a man holding a high and eminent place to be ambitiously popular; take heed of it. In hearing of causes, you are to hear with patience, for patience is a great part of a Judge; better hear with patience prolixity and impertinent discourse of lawyers and advocates than rashly, for default of the lawyer, to ruin the client's cause: in the one you lose but a little time, by the other the client loseth his right, which can hardly be repaired. Remember your worthy grandfather, Sir Edward Montagu, when he sat Chief Justice in the Common Pleas: You shall not find that *he* said, vauntingly, that he would make Latitats Latitare ; when *he* did sit Chief Justice in this place, he contained himself within the word of the writ to be Chief Justice as the King called him *ad placita coram nobis tenenda*, but did not arrogate or aspire to the high title of Capitalis Justitia Angliæ or Capitalis Justiciarius Angliæ—an office and title which Hugh de Burgh, and some few others, held in the times of the Barons' wars, and whilst the fury thereof was not well ceased.¹ He devised not any new construction of laws against Commissioners and Judges of sewers, nor to draw them into the danger of premunire. *He* never strained the statute of 27 Edward 3, c. 1, to reach the Chancery, and to bring that Court, and the ministers thereof, and the subjects that sought justice there, to be in danger of premunire, an absurd and inapt construction of that old statute. *He* never made 'Teste Edwardo Montagu' to jostle with *Teste meipso*, but knew that the King's writ *teste meipso* was his warrant to sit in this place. *He* doubted not but if the King, by his writ under his Great Seal, commanded the Judges that they should not proceed *Rege inconsulto*, then they were dutifully to obey. *He* challenged not powers from this Court to correct all

---

¹ There had been a keen controversy respecting Coke's right to call himself "Chief Justice of England." Ellesmere is quite wrong in supposing that this was a title only during the Barons' wars, as the office of Chief Justice of England, the highest both in the law and the state, certainly subsisted from the Conquest till the reign of Edward I. From the time when that monarch remodeled the judicial system, the head of the King's Bench was generally called "Chief Justice to hold pleas before the King himself," and he became subordinate to the Chancellor.

misdemeanors, as well extra-judicial as judicial, nor to
have power to judge statutes void if he considered them
to be against common right and reason, but left the
parliament and the King to judge what was common
right and reason.[1] Remember the removing and putting down your late predecessor, and by whom, which
I often remember unto you, that it is the great King
of Great Britain, whose great wisdom, and royal virtue,
and religious care for the weal of his subjects, and
for the due administration of justice, can never be forgotten."

This may be considered Ellesmere's dying effort. His
indisposition returned, and he seemed sincerely to have
wished to retire from public life. He thus wrote to the
King:—

"MOST GRACIOUS SOVEREIGN,

"I find through my great age, accompanied with griefs
and infirmities, my sense and conceipt is become dull and
heavy, my memory decayed, my judgment weak, my hearing imperfect, my voice and speech failing and faltering,
and in all the powers and faculties of my mind and body
great debility. Wherefore *conscientia imbecilitatis* my
humble suit to your most sacred Majesty is, to be discharged
of this great place, wherein I have long served, and to
have some comfortable testimony, under your royal hand,
that I leave it at this humble suit, with your gracious
favor; so shall I with comfort number and spend the days
I have to live in meditation and prayers to Almighty God
to preserve your Majesty, and all yours, in all heavenly
and earthly felicity and happiness. This suit I intended
some years past, ex dictamine rationis et conscientiæ;
love and fear staid it; now necessity constrains me to
it; I am utterly unable to sustain the burthen of this
great service, for I am now come to St. Paul's desire,

---

[1] This is Ellesmere's best hit, for Coke had written such nonsense (still quoted by silly people) as "that in many cases the common law shall control acts of parliament, and sometimes shall judge them to be merely void ; for where an act of parliament is against common right and reason, the law shall control it and judge it void."—Dr. Bonham's case, 8 Rep. When questioned for this doctrine before the Council, he was so absurd as to defend it, and give as an example, " that if an act of parliament were to give to the lord of a manor conusance of all plea arising within his manor, yet he shall hold no plea whereunto himself is a party, for *iniquum est aliquem suæ rei esse judicem*," thus proceeding on the *construction*, not the *repeal*, of the Act by the Court.—See Bacon's Works, vi. 397.

Cupio dissolvi et esse cum Christo: Wherefore I most humbly beseech your Majesty most favorably to grant it.
"Your Majesty's most humble and loyal
"poor subject and servant,
"THOMAS ELLESMERE, Canc."[1]

The King sent him a kind answer, saying, among other things, "When you shall remember how ill I may want you, and what miss your Master shall have of you, I hope the reason will be predominant to make you not strive with, but conquer, your disease, not for your own sake, but for his of whom you make promise yourself as much love and hearty affection as might be expected from so thankful and kind a Master to so honest and worthily deserving a servant." Prince Charles likewise wrote him a kind letter, concluding with a prayer "that God would give him health and strength of body and mind, so that the King, Queen, the Prince himself and whole kingdom, might long enjoy the fruit of his long, wise, and religious experience."

The Chancellor pressed his application in a second letter, very long, pedantic, and twaddling, which must have convinced the King that the interest of the suitors required that the resignation should not much longer be refused.[2] The King, however, wishing to treat him with all respect and delicacy, although he promised speedily to comply with his request, urged him to hold the office a short time longer, and meanwhile raised him to the rank of a Viscount, by the title of Viscount Brackley.[3]

[1] Down to the reign of Charles II., Peers, in signing, prefixed their Christian name to their title. All persons in office, in signing the most familiar letter, subjoined their official designation.

[2] After many quotations from the classics, he cites stat. 13, Ed. 1: "Homines excedentes 70 annorum non ponantur in assisis et juratis."

[3] He is always called, in law books and histories, Lord Ellesmere—and Lord Brackley would sound as strange in our ears as Lord Verulam or Lord St. Alban's. In the Egerton Papers there is a curious bill by Garter King at Arms, of "Fees due to the Kinge's Servants for the Creation of a Viscount:

To Mr. Garter himself	Imprimis to Mr. Garter for his Lp.'s garmentes . . . . x^{li}
To Mr. St. George.	To the officers of Armes . . . . . . x^{li}
To Hughes, their servant.	To the Gent. Ushers dayly Wayters. . . . . x^{li}
To Sir William Twisden.	To the Gent. Ushers of the Privy Chamber . . . . v^{li}
To Serjt. Benet et al.	To the Serjeants of Armes . .. . . , v^{li}

He was installed with great pomp before the King, although parliament was not sitting, and we have a programme of the ceremony from a letter addressed to him from Garter King at Arms:—

"To the Right Honorable my very good Lord Sir Thomas Egerton, Knight Baron of Ellesmere, &c. Lord Chancellor of England.

"Right Honorable and my very good Lord, my manyfold occasions of service at this tyme hath caused some neglect, wch I hope your Lp. will excuse.

"For your Lp.'s Creation theis thinges are necessarilye required to be in redynes,—your Letters Patentes, and your Creation robes of a Viscount, being crimson vellet, a Capp, and Circlett.

"Touching the manner of your Lp.'s introduction, you are to brought in to his Matie between a Viscount and an Earle, myself going formost bears your Lp.'s Letters Patents. A Baron followeth after with your upper robe crosse his armes; and a second Baron beareth your capp and circlett. All theis estates are invested in their robes, your Lp. onlye in your Kirtle or undergarment, with your whood.

"When wee approche the Kinges presence wee make three lowe reverences, wch my self, being first in the pro-

To M^r. Lovell.	To the Quarter Wayters . . . . . . v^{li}
To M^r. Roffingam.	To the Sewers . . . . v^{li}
To M^r. Armiger	To the Yeomen Ushers . . . iij^{li} vj^s viij^d
To Sir T. Cornwallis.	To the Groome Porter . . . . . . x^{li}
To M^r. Hoddesdon.	To the Groomes and Pages . iij^{li} vj^s viij^d
To the Serj^t. &c.	To the Trumpettes . . . . . . vj^{li}
To M^r. Gosson, Drum Major.	To the Drommes . . . . x^{ls}
To old M^r. Harden, et al.	To the Kinges Musicions, 4 companyes . . . . vj^{li}
To M^r. Huntley.	To the Buttry . . . . xx^s
To M^r. Serj^t. Blagrove.	To the Pantry . . . . xx^s
To M^r. Snowe.	To the Ewery . . . . xl^s
To M^r. Todd.	To the Sellor . . . . xx^s
To M^r. Daniel, clearke.	To the Cookes . . . . xl^s
To M^r. Fynch.	To the Porters . . . . iiij^{li}
Tc Rafe, &c.	To the Kinges footmen . . . iij^{li} vj^s viij^d

"Summa tot. lxxxvij^{li}

"WILLM. SEGAR, Garter."

ceeding, dothe direct. The Letters Patentes I deliver to the Lo. Chamberlen, and hee the same to his Matie. His Matie givith yt to one of the Secritarys to read.

"Your Lp. kneeling before the King, at the woords 'Creamus & investimus,' your robe is putt on, and your capp and circlett sett upon your head. And so the Patent beig redd throughe, your Lp. concludes with a speache of thankfullnes to his Ma^{ti} which you can best perform.

"Publique feast there needeth none, nor any divulgation of your Lps. stiles, thoughe antiently that hath byn used, for the three last Barons that were made, viz. Wing, Houghton, and Tenham, had not any which may searve for presidentes. And so I rest ever,

"At your Lp.'s service,

WILLIAM SEGAR, Garter."[1]

He had little enjoyment of his new dignity, and infirmities sorely oppressed him.

At last on the 3rd of March, 1617, when he had become bed-ridden, James kindly paid him a visit at York House, and in person consented to accept his resignation, with many acknowledgments of his past services.[2] Two days after, Buckingham and Secretary Winwood, by the King's command, came to York House to receive the Great Seal. The aged Chancellor, still in bed, ordered his son, Sir John Egerton, to produce it, and in its white leather bag, inclosed in the silk purse adorned with the royal arms, it was reverently delivered to them, and they, accompanied by Sir John Egerton, conveyed it to the palace at Whitehall, and placed it in the hands of King James, who ex-

[1] See F. Egerton MSS. The letter is indorsed in Lord Ellesmere's handwriting, "The manner of creation of a viscount, things necessary thereto. Rec^d 4° 9^{hris} 1616."

[2] Mendum qd die Lune, &c. Dns Rex accessit Yorkhouse in pochia Sci Martini in Campis London Dom. Mancional. Thome Vicecomitis Brackley Dni Cancell. Angl. ut ipsum ægrotantem visitaret et tunc dignatus est Dns Rex humili petitioni dci Dni Cancell. gratiose annuere qm pr duos annos integros a Majestate sua regia petebat videl. ut mgm sigill. Angl. in manus Dni Regis sursum redderet et toleret et ab ejusdem custodia libaret quia pro etate egritudine aliisque corporis infirmitatibus seipsum ad onera et servicia debita et assueta sustinenda inhabilem omnino se sentiret."—Cl. R. 16 Jac. 1. Camden says, "Rex invisit Cancellarium languentem et ex invalida senectute officio cedere volentem, Cancellarlus sigillum in manu Regis lachrymantis tradidit."—Camd. Ann. Jac. A great question has been raised as to the exact time when he actually delivered up the Seal, but all doubt is removed by a reference to the Close Roll.

ercised the unconstitutional privilege, prized by Elizabeth, of sealing a grant with it while there was no responsible Chancellor or Lord Keeper.

On the 7th of March it was in the hands of FRANCIS BACON, the greatest of the great men who ever held it.

Lord Ellesmere survived his resignation only a few days. While his indisposition was gaining ground Buckingham and the new Lord Keeper waited upon him with an offer from the King to create him Earl of Bridgewater, to make him President of the Council, and to grant him a pension of £3,000 a year. " He was so far past that no words or worldly compact could work with him, and thanking his Majesty for his gracious favors, he said, *that these things were all to him but vanities.*"[1]

He expired at York House on the 15th of March, 1617, in the seventy-seventh year of his age, having held the Great Seal for a longer period, continuously, than any of his predecessors or successors.[2] He met his end with such composure as to call forth the observation from Camden, " Fortè quando propius reipublicæ mala viderat, ut integer honestum finem voluit."

He was buried at Doddlestone, in the county of Chester. He lies in the chancel of the parish church, under a flagstone without any name upon it, but with these words on a white lozenge, in the center of the stone—

> " Anchora Animæ
> Fides et Spes:
> In Christo,
> Orimur, Morimur.
> Sequentur qui non
> Præcesserint."

In the year 1829 a handsome monument was erected to his memory by Francis, the last Earl of Bridgewater, which bears the following inscription from the classical pen of the late Archdeacon Wrangham, the rector of the parish:—

> " Majorum Gloria Posteris quasi Lumen est
> Subtus jacet
> Quicquid mortale fuit

[1] Carleton's Letters, Birch MS. 4175. In the month of January preceding he had resigned the Chancellorship of the University of Oxford, which had been conferred upon him in 1610.

[2] From May 6, 1596, to March 5, 1617. Lord Eldon was Chancellor longer, but with an interval of above a year, during the Fox and Grenville administration.

> Thomæ
> Baronis de Ellesmere
> Et Vice Comitis de Brackley
> Viri antiquâ virtute ac fide
> Per viginti plus annos
> Regni Angliæ
> Cancellarii
> Scientia Scriptis Facundia
> Spectatissimi
> Hominibus exemptus est
> IV ID April
> Anno sacro M DC XVII
> Æ circiter LXXVII
> Orimur Morimur
> Sequentur qui non præcesserint."[1]

Considering the times in which Lord Ellesmere lived, and comparing him with his contemporaries who reached high office, we are bound greatly to respect his memory. Neither he nor any other mortal man could deserve the panegyric upon him by a contemporary historian who knew him well. "Nihil in vitâ nisi laudandum aut fecit, aut dixit, aut sensit;"[2] but in thought, word, and deed, his errors were venial. We may pardon his enmity to Sir Edward Coke, who had tried to cover him with disgrace when he was supposed to be upon his death-bed. With all his other rivals and political opponents he seems to have lived on terms of courtesy, if not of kindness. He never betrayed a friend.

His great natural abilities had been assiduously cultivated, and he was one of the best public speakers who had yet appeared in England. His apprehension was keen and ready, his judgment deep and sound, and his elocution elegant and easy. "He was a grave and great orator, and best when he was provoked."[3]

As a politician he always stood up for the extension of the prerogative, and his doctrines were often inconsistent with our notions of a free constitution; but we must remember that precedents might then be cited for almost every exercise of arbitrary power; and that the great patriot, Sir Edward Coke, followed by other eminent men, laid it down for law, that an act of parliament to abolish

---

[1] This mark of respect to a great man was paid on the suggestion of my valued friend Mr. Sergeant Atcherley, to whose kindness I am indebted for the copy of the inscription, and several important particulars respecting the Egerton family.
[2] Hacket's Life of Bishop Williams.   [3] Ben Jonson.

the dispensing power would be inoperative, as the King would first dispense with the abolishing act, and then with the act to be dispensed with.

While Lord Ellesmere was Chancellor the few state prosecutions which were instituted took a milder and more regular form; and if the Somersets were improperly pardoned, he was not accessory, like many of his predecessors, to the unjust shedding of noble blood.

His severity in the Star Chamber has been censured, and it is humiliating to find that he concurred in the sentence that Mr. Pound, a Catholic gentleman nearly eighty years old, should be fined £1,000, lose his ears, stand on the pillory at Westminster and Lancaster, and suffer perpetual imprisonment, for merely presenting a respectful petition to the King, praying for inquiry into the conduct of one of the Judges of assize, who had condemned to death a neighbor for entertaining a Jesuit.[1]

Nor can it be denied that while Solicitor General, while Attorney General, and while Chancellor, he frequently attended when torture was adminstered to criminals. But for such matters he was not worse thought of by his contemporaries.

As an Equity Judge he gained more applause than any one who had sat before him in the marble chair. With a knowledge of law equal to Edward III.'s lay Chancellors, Parnynge and Knyvet, so highly eulogized by Lord Coke, —he was much more familiar with the principles of general jurisprudence. Not less noted for dispatch and purity than Sir Thomas More, he was much better acquainted with the law of real property as well as the practice of the Court in which he had long practiced as an advocate; and exhibiting all the patience and suavity of Sir Nicholas Bacon, he possessed more quickness of perception and a more vigorous grasp of intellect. Many ecclesiastical holders of the Great Seal were to be admired as statesmen and scholars, but none had been competent, without assistance, satisfactorily to preside in the judgment-seat.

Ellesmere, while in his vigor, had himself disposed of the whole business of the Court of Chancery. In his declining years he required assistance; but to the last, every case of magnitude he heard and decided in person. Dur-

[1] Jardine's Criminal Trials, ii. 38.

ing the whole of his time, there seems to have been an entire cessation of all impeachment of the Court of Chancery either for delay or corruption; and the only complaint against him that he exceeded his jurisdiction, was decided in his favor.

He was very solicitous for the honor of the bar, which then seems to have had members much given to lying, quarreling, making fraudulent bargains with their clients, and, when it suited their purpose, to insulting the Judge. During the hearing of the case of Ranolph Crew, 9 Jac. 1, according to an accurate reporter, "Le Seignior Chancellor dit, Benedictus Dominus Deus justitiæ! et il-exhort les Lawyers destre veriloqui, pacidici, et nemy de pticipater en le benefit dascun suit; ut gratiose se gerant et Judici id judicio ne prejudicent." [1]

The practice of the King interfering with suits by writs of Privy Seal, under pretense that one of the suitors was in the royal service, still continued; [2] but there is no reason to suppose that Ellesmere was influenced by these beyond granting delay,—and all members of parliament were considered entitled to the like privilege.

When any cause was depending before him in which a Peer was concerned, he gave him notice, by a missive under his hand, of the time appointed for hearing it; [3] but

[1] Moore, p. 819, 820.
[2] I subjoin a specimen:—
"To our right trustie and welbeloved Councellor Thomas Lord Ellesmere, our Chancellor of England.
"JAMES R.
"Right trusty and welbeloved councellor, wee greet you well. Wee have heretofore recommended to you the case of Robert Wulverstone depending before you in Chauncery, because he had in the Parliament house shewed himself forward in our service, and our desire was, that either so much favour might be shewed him as with equitie might stand, or that nothing were done against him till the next terme: since wee have been informed from him that his adversary presseth him now out of terme, whereupon wee have thought good to require you, that because he hath other busines to attend in the vacation, he may not be urged to any thing till the terme, and that then a day certaine be given for the hearing of his cause, which wee must leave to the equitie of the Court, not doubting but that you will regard one of whose service wee are pleased to take notice, so farre forth as in justice you may. Given under our signet, at Leicester, the eighteenth day of August, in the twelfth yeare of our raigne of England, France, and Ireland, and of Scotland the eight-and-fortieth."—*Eg. P.ip.* 464.
[3] Lord Ellesmere to the Earl of Shrewsbury:—
"After my verie hartie comendacions unto yor Lo^{pp}. Whereas the cause dependinge in the Chancerye wherein Humfrey Briggs, Esqr. is pl. and yor L^{pp} deft, is sett downe to be heard in Courte on Thusday, the 9th day of No-

he never was suspected of unduly leaning in favor of the aristocratic party any more than of seeking vulgar praise by becoming counsel for the poor; and he had the rare good fortune to be, at the same time, the favorite of the Court and of the people.

Ellesmere is particularly to be commended for the exercise of his patronage. Unlike Cecil the father, and Cecil the son, to whom it is imputed by Bacon, their kinsman, that out of jealousy they wished to depress all rising men of merit, he was eager to befriend and bring forward all who were likely to be able to serve their country with credit and advantage. He strongly supported Bacon's claim to the offices of Solicitor and Attorney General; and recommended him as his successor. As another example, I may mention that having heard Williams, afterwards Bishop of Lincoln and Lord Keeper, when a tutor at Cambridge, preach a sermon which displayed great talent,—although a stranger to him, he made him his chaplain, and advanced him in the King's service, so that he afterwards attained the highest honors in the church and state.

In making Judges (a most important part of the duty of a Lord Chancellor, for by a bad judicial appointment no one can calculate the aggregate amount of evil inflicted on the community) Ellesmere deserves particular credit. His anxiety on this subject appears from a letter he wrote on the accession of King James, recommending a new call of Sergeants, "consideringe that moost of the Judges are aged, and the Serjeantes at lawe now servinge at the barre not so sufficyent to supplye judiciall places as were to be wyshed (ne quid dicam durius)."[1]

Afterwards, two vacancies occurring, he applied for advice to the Lord Chief Justice, as better acquainted with the common-law bar,—and Popham's answer shows that

vember next, I am att the pl^{ts} instance to give yor L^{pp} notice thereof by this my l^{re}, according to the manner used toward suche persons of honor; praying and requyring yor Lo^p hereby to take knowledge thereof, and to give order unto those whom you employe in such yor causes to attende the hearing of judgement in the sayd cause accordingly; whereof hoping there shall be no default on your Lo$^{pp's}$ parte, I bidd yor Lo^{pp} verie hartely farewell.
"Y^r Lo$^{p's}$ assured friend,
"T. ELLESMERE, Canc.
"Att York House, July 16, 1609.
"To the right Ho   my good Lorde the Earle of Shrewsbury.
[1] Egerton Pap. 372.

wealth (probably on account of the low salaries) as well as skill in the law, was considered necessary for a Judge. " I have thought good to recommend these names to your L., to be preferred to hys Matie, to make his choyse of two, if it may so seeme good to your L., or to add or to alter the same as your L. shall think best : my brother Danyell, my brother Williams, my brother Tanfyld, and my brother Altham, all men learned *and of good estate.*"[1]

His great church patronage, likewise, he dispensed with a single view to the public weal. " Livings," said he, " rather want learned men than learned men livings, many in the Universities pining for want of places. I wish, therefore, some may have single coats before others have doublets; and this method I have observed in bestowing the King's benefices."[2]

Lord Ellesmere was too deeply engaged in professional and official pursuits himself to worship the Muses ; but he was the friend and patron of poets. He was particularly kind to Spenser, with whom he was connected by marriage, and assisted him in his suits both in Ireland and at the Court of Elizabeth. We have seen that he patronized the plays of Shakespeare ; and he is said to have been assisted by Ben Jonson in masques which he gave to Royalty. The name of Milton will be associated with the Egerton family while the English is known as a spoken or a dead language ; but the author of " Comus " was only nine years old at the death of the Chancellor ; and although he was, no doubt, carried from Horton to Harefield to see the old Peer, he could only have been patted by him on the head, and sent into the buttery to have the wing of a capon and a glass of sack.

Although Lord Ellesmere had so little leisure for polite literature, he is to be placed in the catalogue of noble and royal authors. He wrote four treatises: 1. On the Prerogative Royal ; 2. On the Privileges of Parliament ; 3. On Proceedings in Chancery ; 4. On the Power of the Star Chamber. These remaining in MS. at the time of his death, Williams, his chaplain, when offered any legacy he might choose, begged to have them, and afterwards presented them to King James. They have since been

[1] Egerton Pap. 389.
[2] Speech at the conference of Divines at Hampton Court, 1603-4.

printed, but they do not add much to the fame of the writer.

Lord Bacon has recorded two of his jests, which, although they appear among many of infinite value, in what Mr. Macaulay considers "the best jest-book in the world,"[1] make us rather rejoice that no more of them have been preserved.

"They were wont to call referring to the Master in Chancery *committing*. My Lord Keeper Egerton, when he was Master of the Rolls, was *wont*[2] to ask 'What the cause had done that it should be *committed?*'"

"My Lord Chancellor Ellesmere, when he had read a petition which he disliked, would say, 'What, would you have my hand to this now?' And the party answering 'Yes,' he would say farther, 'Well, you shall; nay, you shall have both my hands to it.' And so would, with both his hands, tear it in pieces."[3]

He was a remarkably handsome and athletic man, and in his youth was much addicted to the sports of the field.[4] He retained his personal beauty in his old age, insomuch that many went to the Court of Chancery to gaze at him;

---

[1] Macaulay's Essays, vol. ii. p. 372.

[2] This, it seems, was a standing equity jest, and threw the bar into an agony of laughter every term.

[3] Bacon's Apophthegms. Works, vol. ii. 426, 462.

[4] In the Egerton Papers is preserved a license to sport granted to him when Solicitor General. Indorsed "The L. Pagettes Warraunt.

"These are to will and commaunde youe, and every of youe, that whensoever my verie good frend Mr. Thomas Egerton, Esquier, hir Maties Sollycitour Generall, shall come into any my parkes in Staffordshier within your severall chardges, thatt youe attend uppon him and make him the best sporte that youe maie, geving him free libertie to hunt and kill within the same parkes att his pleasure. And likewise whensoever he shall dyrect his letters to youe, or anie of youe, for the having off anie somer or winter deare, that youe deliver the same unto such persons as he shall appointe, takinge care thatt he be verie well served thereoff, and these letters shalbe a suffycyent warrant from tyme to tyme, to youe and euerie of youe in this behalfe. Fare youe well. From Draiton, this xxiiij^th off Maie, 1583.

"Yo^r ma^r.
"J. PAGET.

"To Richard Sneade, keper of my parke at Beaudesert. Willm Crispe, keper of my parke att Seney. And to John Godwin, keper of my great parke att Bromley Pagett. And to every of them, and in ther absence, to the deputie and deputies, and to every of them."—*Egerton Pap.* 95.

There is likewise in the same collection the formal appointment of him while Solicitor General as "Master of the Game" to Henry, Earl of Derby, with the fee of a buck in summer and a doe in winter, with an annuity of five marks, and a power to distrain in case of arrears.—*Eg. Pap.* 96.

"and happy were they," says the facetious Fuller, "who had no other business there!!!"

Although he always lived in a style suitable to his station, he left entirely of his own conquest landed estates to the value of £8,000 a year—equal to the wealth of the high hereditary nobility of that time.[1]

His first wife was Elizabeth, daughter of Thomas Ravenscroft, of Bretton, in the county of Flint, by whom he had two sons,—Sir Thomas, whose death in Ireland we have mentioned, and Sir John, who succeeded to his honors. The Chancellor married, secondly, the widow of Sir John Walley, of Pittfield, sister of Sir George More; and, lastly, Alice, daughter of Sir John Spencer, of Althorp, in the county of Northampton, and widow of Ferdinando, Earl of Derby, by neither of whom he had any issue. The latter survived him many years, and fostered the opening genius of Milton.

"The Grandeur of the Law"[2] shows that many distin-

[1] In 1606 he proposed that, like other Chancellors, he should have a grant of lands from the Crown (Egerton Papers 408), but none appears to have been made to him. Among other reasons he urged the great expense to which he had been put in entertaining Queen Elizabeth at Harefield.

[2] The last edition of this book reckons 82 existing peerages sprung from the law:—

Dukes, 3.—
  Norfolk.
  Devonshire.
  Manchester.

Marquesses, 7.—
  Winchester.
  Townshend.
  Salisbury.
  Exeter.
  Camden.
  Aylesbury,
  Bristol.

Earls, 31.—
  Suffolk.
  Winchelsea.
  Sandwich
  Cardigan.
  Carlisle.
  Shaftesbury.
  Coventry.
  Tankerville.
  Aylesford.
  Cowper.
  Macclesfield.

  Buckinghamshire.
  Egremont.
  Guildford.
  Hardwicke.
  Bathurst.
  Clarendon.
  Mansfield.
  Talbot.
  Fortescue.
  Rosslyn.
  Harrowby.
  Verulam.
  Bradford.
  Eldon.
  Somers.
  Burlington.
  Effingham.
  Yarborough.
  Leicester.
  Lovelace.

Viscount, 1.—
  Sydney.

Barons, 40.—
  I e Despenser.

guished noble houses owe their origin to Westminster Hall; but I do not recollect any instance of the family of a lawyer who had raised himself from obscurity being so soon associated with the old aristocracy, or rising so rapidly to the highest rank in the peerage. John, the eldest surviving son, being created Earl of Bridgewater soon after his father's death, was married to a daughter of the Earl of Derby; and being Lord President of the Principality and Marches of Wales, and Lord Lieutenant of the counties of Salop, Hereford, Gloucester, Monmouth, Glamorgan, Caermarthen, Pembroke, Cardigan, Flint, Caernarvon, Anglesea, Merioneth, Radnor, Brecknock, Montgomery, and Denbigh, kept his Court at Ludlow Castle, where his children were going

"———to attend their father's state
And new entrusted sceptre—"

—when passing through Haywood Forest they were benighted, and Lady Alice was for a short time lost. This incident gave rise to COMUS, which was acted by her and her brothers, Lord Brackley and the Honorable Thomas Egerton.

After this illustration, the family derived little additional splendor from the Ducal Coronet, which, in another generation, was bestowed upon them.

The male line of Lord Chancellor Ellesmere, after pro-

De Clifford.	Lyndhurst.
Zouch of Harringworth.	Tenterden.
Howard de Walden.	Teynham.
Clifford of Chudleigh.	Grantley.
Middleton.	Redesdale.
Montfort.	Wallace.
Walsingham.	Wynford.
Montagu of Boughton.	Brougham.
Kenyon.	Chaworth.
Thurlow.	Denman.
Lyttleton	Abinger.
Bayning.	Hatherton.
Bolton.	Cottenham.
Lilford.	Stratheden.
Basset.	Langdale.
Alvanley.	Bruce.
St. Helens.	Campbell.
Ellenborough.	
Erskine.	To these are now to be added—
Crewe.	Cranworth.
Manners.	St. Leonards.
Gifford.	Wensleydale.

ducing many great and honorable characters, has failed. Several distinguished families are proud to trace their descent from him through females, and every one would rejoice to see his titles restored to the English peerage.[1]

CHAPTER LI.

LIFE OF LORD BACON FROM HIS BIRTH TILL HE BECAME A MEMBER OF THE HOUSE OF COMMONS.

IT will easily be believed that I enter with fear and trembling on the arduous undertaking of attempting to narrate the history, and to delineate the character, of

" The wisest, brightest, meanest of mankind."

I must say, that I consider a life of Lord Bacon still a desideratum in English literature. He has often been eulogized and vituperated; there have been admirable expositions of his philosophy and criticisms on his writings; we have very lively sketches of some of his more striking actions; and we are dazzled by brilliant contrasts between his good and bad qualities, and between the vicissitudes of prosperous and adverse fortune which he experienced. But no writer has yet presented him to us familiarly and naturally, from boyhood to old age—shown us how his character was formed and developed—or explained his motives and feelings at the different stages of his eventful career.

We desire to become acquainted with him as if we had lived with him, and had actually seen him taught his alphabet by his mother;—patted on the head by Queen Elizabeth; mocking the worshippers of Aristotle at Cambridge;—catching the first glimpses of his great discoveries, yet uncertain whether the light was from heaven; —associating with the learned and the gay at the Court of France;—devoting himself to Bracton and the Year Books in Gray's Inn;—throwing aside the musty folios of the law to write a moral essay, to make an experiment in

[1] The title of Earl of Ellesmere and Viscount Brackley have since been conferred on Lord Francis Egerton, a descendant of Lord Chancellor Ellesmere.—3*rd Edition.*

natural philosophy, or to detect the fallacies which had hitherto obstructed the progress of useful truth;—contended for a time with taking "all knowledge of his province;"—roused from these speculations by the stings of vulgar ambition;—plying all the arts of flattery to gain official advancement by royal and courtly favor;—entering the House of Commons, and displaying powers of oratory of which he had been unconscious;—seduced by the love of popular applause, for a brief space becoming a patriot;—making amends by defending all the worst excesses of prerogative;—publishing to the world lucubrations on morals which show the nicest perception of what is honorable and beautiful, as well as prudent, in the conduct of life:—yet the son of a Lord Keeper, the nephew of the prime minister, a Queen's counsel, with the first practice at the bar, arrested for debt, and languishing in a spunging-house;—tired with vain solicitations to his own kindred for promotion, joining the party of their opponent, and, after experiencing the most generous kindness from the young and chivalrous Essex, assisting to bring him to the scaffold, and to blacken his memory;—seeking, by a mercenary marriage, to repair his broken fortunes;—on the accession of a new Sovereign offering up the most servile adulation to a Pedant, whom he utterly despised;—infinitely gratified by being permitted to kneel down, with 300 others, to receive the honor of knighthood;—truckling to a worthless favorite with slavish subserviency that he might be appointed a law-officer of the Crown;—then giving the most admirable advice for the compilation and emendation of the laws of England;—next helping to inflict torture on a poor parson whom he wished to hang as a traitor for writing an unpublished and unpreached sermon;—attracting the notice of all Europe by his philosophical works, which established a new era in the mode of investigating the phenomena both of matter and mind;—basely intriguing in the mean while for further promotion, and writing secret letters to his Sovereign to disparage his rivals; riding proudly between the Lord High Treasurer and Lord Privy Seal, preceded by his mace-bearer and purse-bearer, and followed by a long line of nobles and Judges, to be installed in the office of Lord High Chancellor; by-and-by settling with his servants the account of the bribes they had received for him;—embarrassed by being obliged out of decency, the case being so clear, to decide against the party whose money he had pocketed, but stifling the misgivings of conscience by the splendor and flattery which he now commanded; when struck to the earth by the discovery of his corruption, taking to his bed, and refusing sustenance;—confessing the truth of the charges brought against him, and abjectly imploring mercy;—nobly rallying from his disgrace, and engaging in new literary undertakings, which have added to the splendor of his name;—still under the influence of his ancient vanity refusing to "be stripped of his feathers;"—inspired nevertheless, with all his youthful zeal for science, conducting his last experiment of "stuffing a fowl with snow to preserve it," which succeeded "excellently well," but brought him to his grave;—and, as the closing act of a life so checkered, making his will, whereby, conscious of the shame he had incurred among his contemporaries, but impressed with a swelling conviction of what he had achieved for mankind, he bequeathed his "name and memory to men's charitable speeches, to foreign nations, and the next ages."

I am very far from presuming to think that I am about to supply the deficiencies of his former biographers. My plan and my space are limited; and though it is not possible in writing the life of Bacon to forget that he was a philosopher and a fine writer, I must chiefly consider him as a lawyer and a statesman. But I am not without some advantages for the task—from my familiarity with the scenes through which he passed as an advocate, as a law officer of the Crown, as a Judge, as a member of either House of Parliament, and as a supporter of legal reform. Others from greater leisure are better acquainted with his philosophy; but I, too, have been a diligent student of all his works, and while in his Letters, his Speeches, his Essays, and his Histories, I have tried to gain a knowledge of human affairs and of man as he is,—from daily and nightly perusal of his "Advancement of Learning," his "De Augmentis Scientiarum," and his "Novum Organum," I have humbly striven to initiate myself in the methods of observation and induction by which he has opened to our species a career of boundless improvement.

Francis Bacon was the youngest son of Sir Nicholas

Bacon, Lord Keeper to Queen Elizabeth, by Anne Cooke, one of the daughters of Sir Anthony Cooke, tutor to King Edward IV. He was born at York House, in the Strand, on the 22nd of January, 1561.[1] Like several other extraordinary men, he is supposed to have inherited his genius from his mother,[2] and he certainly was indebted to her for the early culture of his mind, and the love of books for which during life he was distinguished. Young Francis was sickly, and unable to join in the rough sports suited for boys of robust constitution. The Lord Keeper was too much occupied with his official duties to be able to do more than kiss him, hear him occasionally recite a little piece he had learnt by heart, and give him his blessing. But Lady Bacon, who was not only a tender mother but a woman of highly cultivated mind after the manner of her age, devoted herself assiduously to her youngest child, who, along with bodily weakness, exhibited from early infancy the dawnings of extraordinary intellect. She and her sisters had received a regular classical education, and had kept up a familiarity with the poets, historians, and philosophers of antiquity. She was likewise well acquainted with modern languages, and with the theology and literature of her own times. She corresponded in Greek with Bishop Jewell respecting the then fashionable controversies, and she translated his *Apologia* from the Latin so correctly that neither he nor Archbishop Parker could suggest a single alteration. She also translated admirably a volume of sermons on "Fate and Free Will," from the Italian of Bernardo Ochino.

Under her care, assisted by a domestic tutor, Francis continued till he reached his thirteenth year. He took most kindly to his book, and made extraordinary proficiency in the studies prescribed to him. His inquisitiveness and original turn of thinking were at the same time displayed. While still a mere child, he stole away from his playmates to a vault in St. James's Fields, for

[1] Some modern writers, who generally reckon by the new style, erroneously place his birth in January, 1560. See Mont. L. of B., p. 1.

[2] Anthony, the elder brother, not being by any means a brilliant character the case of the Bacon family might be cited to illustrate the retort upon the late Earl of Buchan, who was eldest brother to Lord Chancellor Erskine and the famous Henry Erskine, Dean of Faculty, but very unequal to them in abilities, and who, observing boastfully, " We inherit all our genius from our mother," was answered, " Yes, and (as the mother's fortune) it seems to have been all settled on the *younger* children."

the purpose of investigating the cause of a singular echo, which he had discovered there; and, when a little older, he amused himself with very ingenious speculations on the art of legerdemain, at present flourishing under the title of Mesmerism. He enjoyed at the same time the great advantage, on account of his father's station, and his being the nephew of the Prime Minister, of being early introduced into the highest and most intellectual society, —in which he displayed most extraordinary gravity of deportment, as well as readiness of wit. So much was Queen Elizabeth struck with his manner and his precocity, that she used to amuse herself in conversation with him, and to call him her "young Lord Keeper." On one occasion he greatly pleased her by his answer to the common question put to children, *how old he was?*— "Exactly two years younger than your Majesty's happy reign."[1]

In his thirteenth year he was sent to Trinity College, Cambridge, and put under the care of Whitgift, then Master of the College, afterwards Archbishop of Canterbury, and famous for his bigotry and intolerance, as well as his love of learning. Here Bacon resided three years. We have rather vague accounts of his studies during this period, and we judge of his occupations chiefly from the result as testified in after life, and by his subsequent declarations respecting academical pursuits. It is said that he ran through the whole circle of the liberal arts as they were then taught, and planned that great intellectual revolution with which his name is inseparably connected. But all that is certain is, that at his departure he carried with him a profound contempt for the course of study pursued there. Had it been improved to its present pitch, and the tripos had been established, in all probability he would still have selected his own course of study. Academical honors are exceedingly to be valued as a proof of industry and ability; but the very first spirits have not affected them, and men of original genius, such as Swift, Adam Smith, and Gibbon, could hardly have submitted

---

[1] We owe this and the most authentic anecdotes respecting his early years to Rawley. "Ille autem tanta gravitate et judicii maturitate, supra ætatem se expedire valebat, ut Regina eum 'Dominum Custodem Sigilli minorem' appellare solita sit. Interroganti *Quot annos natus esset?* ingeniose etiam puer adhuc, respondit *Se regemini ejus felici duobus annis juniorem fuisse*" p. 2, Ed. 1819.

to the course of mechanical discipline which is indispensable to be thoroughly drilled in the knowledge of what others have done, written, and thought. If he had devoted his residence at the University to the drudgery necessary to take a high degree, and had actually been Senior Wrangler or Senior Medalist, or both, and a Fellow of Trinity to boot, he might afterwards have become Lord High Chancellor, but he never would have written his "Essays," or the "Novum Organum." He must be considered as expressing his opinion of the Cambridge residents of his day, when he speaks of "men of sharp and strong wits and small variety of reading, their wits being shut up in the cells of a few authors, chiefly Aristotle, their dictator, as their persons were shut up in the cells of monasteries and colleges, and who, knowing little history, either of nature or time, did spin cobwebs of learning admirable for the fineness of thread and work, but of no substance or profit."[1] He paid due homage to the gigantic intellect of the "Dictator;" but he ridiculed the unfruitfulness of his method, which he described as strong for disputations and contentions, but barren for the production of works for the benefit and use of man, the just object for acquiring knowledge, and the only value of knowledge when acquired.[2] He left Cambridge without taking a degree, and with the fixed conviction that the system of academical education in England (which has remained substantially the same since his time) was radically vicious.

We now come to a passage of his life which has hitherto received too little attention in tracing the formation of his mind and character. Allusion is made by his biographers to his residence in France, but generally in such terms as might be used in describing a trip to Paris by a modern student of law during the long vacation, with the advantage of an introduction to the English minister there from our Secretary of State for foreign affairs. In

[1] Advancement of Learning.
[2] Says Rawley, his chaplain and biographer, "Whilst he was commorant at the University, about sixteen years of age (as his Lordship hath been pleased to impart unto myself), he first fell into dislike of the philosophy of Aristotle. Not for the worthlessness of the author, to whom he would ever ascribe all high attributes, but for the unfruitfulness of the way—being a philosophy (as his Lordship used to say) only strong for disputations, but barren of the production of works for the life of man. In which mind he continued to his dying day."

reality, Bacon spent three whole years in France—the most valuable of his life—and his subsequent literary eminence may be traced to his long sojourn in a foreign country during the age of preparatory studies—almost as much as that of Hume or Gibbon. He first resided at Paris under the care of his father's friend, Sir Amyas Paulet, the English minister at the French Court, where "he sought that which is most of all profitable in travel,— acquaintance with the secretaries and employed men of ambassadors, and so in traveling in one country he sucked the experience of many."[1] It is said that the stripling so far won the confidence of the wary diplomatist, that he was employed on a secret mission to the Queen, which having performed with great approbation, he returned back into France; but the nature of his negotiation is not hinted at, and the probability is, that, going on a short visit to his family, he was merely employed to carry dispatches, for the purpose of facilitating his journey through the provinces, which were then rather in a disturbed state.[2]

After passing a few weeks more in the gay society of Paris, under the auspices of Sir Amyas Paulet, Bacon made a tour through the southern and western parts of France, and then fixed himself for steady application at Poictiers.[3]

---

[1] Essay of Travel.

[2] On his return, Sir Amyas thus writes to the Lord Keeper: "I rejoice much to see that your son, my companion, hath by the grace of God passed the brunt and peril of his journey; whereof I am the more glad, because in the beginning of these last troubles it pleased your Lordship to refer his continuance with me to my consideration. I thank God these dangers are past, and your son is safe, sound, and in good health, and worthy of your fatherly favor."—From Poictiers, Sept. 1577.

[3] His Essay of Travel shows him to have been most familiar with touring, and there the foreign traveler will find excellent advice, even to furnishing himself with a copy of "Murray's Handbook." "Let him carry with him also some card or book describing the country where he travelleth, which will be a good key to his inquiry."—1st Edition.

I have since discovered a very interesting letter written to him while on his travels by his cousin, Sir Thomas Bodley, founder of the Bodleian Library, at Oxford. This announces to him a present of thirty pounds, remitted by his "merchant" for "present supply," and conveys a world of good advice— particularly urging him to read books of "cosmography" of the countries through which he passed, and, keeping a journal, "to note their buildings, furnitures, their entertainments, all their husbandry and ingenious inventions, in whatsoever concerneth either pleasure or profit." "For the people," he adds, "your traffic among them, while you learn their language, will sufficiently instruct you in their habilities, dispositions, and humours, if you a little

His original plan had been to visit Italy, but, on inquiry, all accounts agreed that, from the rigors of the Inquisition an English Protestant would not then have been safe in that country. He now began his "Notes on the State of Europe," which display very minute accuracy of statement, without attempting any profundity of observation. Probably with a view of being engaged in diplomacy, he studied with great interest the art of writing in cipher, and he invented a method so ingenious, that many years after he thought it deserving of a place in the "De Augmentis." While thinking that he should spend his life in such speculations and pursuits, he heard of the sudden death of his father, and he was reserved for a very different destiny.

He instantly returned to England, and had the mortification to find that he was left with a patrimony so slender, that it was wholly insufficient for his support without a profession or an office. "He had to think how to live instead of living only to think." Sir Nicholas had amply provided for his other children, and had appropriated a sum of money to buy an estate for Francis, but had been suddenly carried off without accomplishing his purpose, and Francis had only a ratable proportion with his four brothers of the fund which was to have been applied to his exclusive benefit.

He made a strenuous effort to avoid the necessity of taking to the study of the law,—the only resource which remained to him if he could not procure some political appointment. He sued to Burghley directly, and indirectly through Lady Burghley, his aunt, in a strain almost servile, that some employment should be given to him. Considering his personal merit and qualifications, and, still more, considering his favor with the Queen and his connection with her chief minister, it seems wonderful that he should have failed,—if we did not remember that the Lord Treasurer then wished to introduce into public life his favorite son, Robert Cecil, a very promising youth, but inferior in talents and accomplishments to his cousin, Francis Bacon, and that, "in the time of the Cecils, father and son, able men were by design and of purpose sup-

enlarge the privacy of your own nature to such acquaintance with the best sort of strangers, *and restrain your affections and participation for your own countrymen of whatsoever condition."*—4th Edition.

pressed."[1] Reports were spread that he was a vain speculator, and totally unfit for real business.

He was thus driven most reluctantly to embrace the law as a means of livelihood, and in 1580, in his 20th year, he began to keep terms in Gray's Inn, of which Society his father had been long a member.[2] He lived in Chambers, in Gray's Inn Square, which are still visited by those who worship his memory. There can be no doubt that he now diligently and doggedly sat down to the study of his profession, and that he made very great progress in it,—although he labored under the effect of the envious disposition of mankind, who are inclined to believe that a man of general accomplishments can not possibly be a lawyer; and *è converso*, if a man has shown himself beyond all controversy to be deeply imbued with law, that he is a mere lawyer without any other accomplishment. A competent judge who peruses Francis Bacon's legal treatises, and studies his forensic speeches, must be convinced that these were not the mere result of laboriously getting up a title of law *pro re natâ*, but that his mind was thoroughly familiar with the principles of jurisprudence, and that he had made himself complete master of the common law of England,—while there might be sergeants and apprentices who had never strayed from Chancery Lane to "the Solar Walk or Milky Way," better versed in the technicalities of pleading and the practice of the Courts.[3] He must sedulously have attended the "readings" and "mootings" of his Inn, and abstracted many days and nights from his literary and philosophical pursuits to the perusal of Littleton and Plowden.

His industry is the more commendable, as he had other powerful temptations to withstand. From his lively wit, from his having been in the best society at home, and from his travels abroad, he was a most delightful companion, and his society was universally coveted; yet he

---

[1] Bacon's letter to Buckingham.
[2] The records of Gray's Inn represent him as having been entered on the 21st of November, 1576, which must have been upon leaving the University.
[3] "The Temple late two brother sergeants saw
    Who deem'd each other oracles of law;
    Each had a gravity would make you split,
    And shook his head at MURRAY as a wit."
Even when I entered the profession this disposition continued; but the world now places the friend of Pope high above such narrow-minded judges as Kenyon, who sneered at "the equitable doctrines of Lord Mansfield."

courteously resisted these allurements, and, without losing popularity, remained master of his time. On high-days and holidays he assisted with great glee in all the festivities of the Inn ; and at the request of the Benchers he laid out walks in the garden, and planted trees, some of which, on a spot which got the name of "Lord Bacon's mount," very recently remained. He likewise found it impossible entirely to abstract his mind from the philosophical speculations which so early occupied it, and he published a little sketch of his system under the somewhat pompous title of "The Greatest Birth of Time." But this, like Hume's "System of Human Nature," seems to have fallen *stillborn from the press;* no copy of it is preserved, and we should hardly know of its existence but from the notice of it in a letter which after his fall from power he wrote to Father Fulgentio : " Equidem memini me quadraginta adhuc annis juvenile opusculum circa has res confecisse, quod magnâ prorsus fiduciâ et magnifico titulo TEMPORIS PARTUM MAXIMUM inscripsi."

In 1586 he was called to the outer bar, but I apprehend, according to the rules then prevailing, was not entitled to practice till he had got another step, which was "coming within bars."[1] To this he was not entitled by his standing, but he might have obtained it by the recommendation of his uncle, the Lord Treasurer. To an application for his interference, the old Lord, now peevish from age and gout, seems to have returned a very churlish answer, taking the opportunity to read Francis a sharp lecture on his "arrogancy and overweening." These bad qualities the young man earnestly disclaimed, but he submissively promised to profit by such good advice, "and so, wishing unto his Lordship all honor, and to himself continuance of his Lordship's good opinion, with mind and means to deserve it, he humbly took his leave."[2]

In a short time, however, he was admitted an inner barrister, and immediately after he was elected a Bencher of the Society. So great a favorite was he with his house

---

[1] See Or. Jur. 159.
[2] Letter of F. Bacon to Burghley, May 6, 1586. Some writers not unnaturally suppose that this was an application for *a silk gown*, and that Bacon, having got into great practice *in stuff*, now wished to be " called within the bar," in the modern sense of the phrase,—whereas, in reality, his ambition then was only to become "an inner barrister" before his time, that he might be entitled to begin practice in Court.—See Macaulay's *Essays*, ii. 300

that in two years more he was made Lent Reader, an office of much dignity, which gave him an opportunity of publicly exhibiting his learning, acuteness, and eloquence. He now acquired such reputation in his profession that the Queen, for the benefit of his assistance in her state prosecutions and revenue cases, appointed him her "Counsel Extraordinary." This was the first appointment of the sort, the counsel for the Crown hitherto having been only the royal Sergeants, who had the highest rank, and the Attorney and Solicitor General, with the Attorney of the Duchy of Lancaster, and the Attorney of the Court of Augmentations. The body of Sergeants came next in point of precedence,[1] and then inner and outer barristers or apprentices according to their "ancienty" or standing. Bacon was exceedingly delighted with this glimpse of Court favor, but he derived little solid advantage from it; for he was allowed no salary, and he had only a few stray briefs, with small fees, on occasions when it was thought that he might be of service to the Crown. The Queen frequently admitted him to her presence, and conversed with him not only about matters of law, but points of general learning and affairs of state, finding much satisfaction from the information and illustrations he communicated to her. Nevertheless, he could not remove from her mind the impression made upon her by the representation of his cousin, Sir Robert Cecil, that he was "a speculative man, indulging himself in philosophical reveries."

Bacon's higher aspirations prevented him from taking cordially to the profession of the law, and he still longed for leisure to be devoted to literature and science. With this view he continued to solicit for some place which would enable him to retire from the bar. A few extracts from his letters will best show the state of his feelings at this period of his life. "I wax now somewhat ancient; one-and-thirty years is a great deal of sand in the hourglass. My health, I thank God, I find confirmed, and I do not fear that action shall impair it; because I account my ordinary course of study and meditation to be more

[1] They long contended for precedence over the Attorney and Solicitor General, except in Crown cases, and this was sometimes adjudged to them (3 Bulstrode, 32); but now they do not sit within the bar in term time—an honor accorded to all King's Counsel, and to the Attorney and Solicitor General of the Queen-consort.

painful than most parts of action are. . . . Again, the meanness of my estate doth somewhat move me; for though I can not accuse myself that I am either prodigal or slothful, yet my health is not to spend nor my course to get. Lastly, I confess that I have as vast contemplative ends as I have moderate civil ends, for I have taken all knowledge to be my province; and if I could purge it of two sorts of rovers, whereof the one with frivolous disputations, confutations, and verbosities; the other with blind experiments and auricular traditions and impostures, hath committed so many spoils,—I hope I should bring in industrious observations, grounded conclusions, and profitable inventions and discoveries. . . . If your Lordship will not carry me on, I will not do as Anaxagoras did, who reduced himself with contemplation unto voluntary poverty; but this I will do,—I will sell the inheritance that I have, and purchase some lease of quick revenue, or some office of gain that shall be executed by deputy, and so give over all care of service, and become some sorry book-maker, or a true pioneer in that mine of truth which lies so deep."[1] "This last request I find it more necessary for me to make, because, though I am glad of her Majesty's favor that I may with more ease practice the law, which percase I may use now and then for my countenance, yet to speak plainly, though perhaps vainly, I do not think that the ordinary practice of the law, not serving the Queen in place, will be admitted for a good account of the poor talent that God hath given me, so as I make reckoning I shall reap no great benefit to myself in that course."[2] Such sentiments must have appeared very foolish to the crusty Lord Treasurer, who thought all qualities and occupations were vain and idle which did not lead directly to power and riches, and pronounced £100 too extravagant a gratuity to be given to the author of the FAERY QUEEN, which he derisively termed "an old song." To stop the mouth of his importunate nephew, the Lord Treasurer procured for him the reversion of the registrarship of the Star Chamber, worth about £1,600 a year; but the place not falling into possession till after the lapse of twenty years, the impatient Francis said "it was like another man's fair ground bat-

[1] Bacon to Burghley, 1591.   [2] Same to same, 1594.

tening upon his house, which might mend his prospect, but did not fill his barns."

Although he accomplished infinitely higher objects, he never appears to have had much practice at the bar. The profession of the law in England seems at all times to have required the undivided affections of those who would have the greatest success in it, and has not, as in France and in Scotland, easily admitted a rivalry with more liberal pursuits. When engaged in a *cause célèbre*, —the Queen and the Court coming to hear the arguments, or taking a lively interest in the result,—Bacon no doubt exerted himself to the utmost, and excited applause by his display of learning and eloquence; but on ordinary occasions, when he found himself in an empty Court, and before an irritable or drowsy Judge, he must have been unable to conceal his disgust,—and eager to get home that he might finish an essay or expose some fallacy by which past ages had been misled,—if he stood up for his client as long as he felt there was a fair chance of success,—we may well believe that he showed little energy in a hopeless defense, and that he was careless about softening defeat by any display of zeal or sympathy. Accordingly, that he was no favorite with the attorneys is clear from his own statements of his progress, from the abundant leisure which he still enjoyed, and from the poverty in which (without any extravagance) he continued to be involved.[1]

In the parliaments which met in 1586 and 1588, he had been returned to the House of Commons, but he does not seem to have made himself prominent by taking any decided part for or against the Court. The proceedings which then took place were not of a very stirring nature; and neither he himself nor others seem then to have been aware of the power of public speaking with which he was endowed.

Four years rolled on before another parliament was summoned, the government of the country being carried on solely by the prerogative of the Crown, unchecked by the interference of deliberative assemblies, and it seemed doubtful whether a much longer period might not elapse (as in former reigns) without any opportunity arising for a lawyer to raise himself by his talents for debate.

[1] See his Letters. Works, vol. v.

CHAPTER LII.

CONTINUATION OF THE LIFE OF LORD BACON TILL THE FALL OF THE EARL OF ESSEX.

AT last the quarrel with Spain rendered a vote of fresh subsidies indispensable. A parliament met on the 19th of February, 1593, and Francis Bacon took his seat as representative for the county of Middlesex.

In a discussion which arose a few days after upon the topics dwelt upon by the Lord Keeper, in explaining the causes of summoning the parliament (which we may consider "the debate on the address"), he made a great speech on "Law Reform." We have only scanty remains of his oratory in the House of Commons, but enough to account for the admiration he now excited, and the influence he acquired. On this occasion he observed, "The cause of assembling all parliaments hath been hitherto for laws or moneys; the one being the sinews of peace, the other of war: to one I am not privy, but the other I should know. I did take great contentment in her Majesty's speech, delivered by the Lord Keeper, how that it was a thing not to be done suddenly, nor scarce a year would suffice to purge the statute book, the volumes of law being so many in number that neither common people can half practice them, nor lawyers sufficiently understand them. The Romans appointed ten men who were to collect or recall all former laws, and to set forth those twelve tables so much of all men commended. The Athenians likewise appointed six for that purpose. And Louis IX., King of France, did the 'ike in reforming his laws."—We must try to conceive to ourselves the instances he gave of absurd penal laws remaining unrepealed, and the advantages he pointed out from digesting and codifying.

We know that he was ever after the most favored speaker in that assembly; and, for this reason, although when he was made Attorney General, and, according to all precedent, he was disqualified to act as a representative of the people, being summoned to the House of Lords,—it was unanimously resolved that he should retain his seat in the Lower House. " There happened in my time," says Ben Jonson, " one noble speaker who was full of gravity in his speaking. His language, where he could spare or pass by a jest, was nobly censorious. No man ever spoke more neatly, more pressly, more weightily, or suffered less emptiness, less idleness, in what he uttered. No member of his speech but consisted of his own graces. His hearers could not cough or look aside from him without loss. He commanded where he spoke, and had his Judges angry and pleased at his devotion. No man had their affections more in his power. The fear of every man who heard him was lest he should make an end."[1]

So intoxicated was Bacon with the success of his first great effort, that in the debate on the 7th of March, on the subsidy, he delivered a flaming oration against the Court, running a serious risk of being sent to the Tower, and punished by the Star Chamber for his presumption. The Queen demanded six subsidies, to be paid in three years. The grant of supply to resist foreign invasion he could not oppose, but the amount and mode of payment he denounced as extravagant and oppressive. "He propounded three questions, which he desired might be answered: the first, impossibility or difficulty; the second, danger and discontentment; and, thirdly, a better manner of supply. For impossibility, the poor men's rent is such as they are not able to yield it. The gentlemen must sell their plate, and farmers their brass pots, ere this will be paid; and as for us, we are here to search the wounds of the realm, and not to skin them over. We shall breed discontentment in paying these subsidies, and endanger her Majesty's safety, which consists more in the love of the people than in their wealth. This being granted, other princes hereafter will look for the like, so that we shall put an evil precedent on ourselves and our posterity."[2]

The courtiers were thrown into a state of horror and

---

[1] It has been supposed, from the use of the word "Judges," that Ben Jonson had never heard Bacon speak in parliament; but I apprehend that he refers to those who heard and formed a judgment of Bacon's eloquence without wearing black coifs and scarlet robes.

"A perfect JUDGE will read each piece of wit
With the same spirit that its author writ." *Pope.*

—See Macaulay's *Essays*, vol. ii. 302.

[2] D'Ewes's Journal, 1593.

amazement. The Queen, in the present temper of the House, and with news of the approach of a Spanish armament, deemed it prudent to take no public notice of this outrage; but she was deeply incensed, and desired it to be intimated to the delinquent, by the Lord Treasurer and the Lord Keeper, that he must never more look to her for favor or promotion. An eloquent eulogist says, " he heard them with the calmness of a philosopher;"[1] but his answers show that he was struck with repentance and remorse, and that, in the hope of obtaining pardon, he plainly intimated that he should never repeat the offense.[2] In all time coming, he never sought popularity more than might well stand with his interest at Court.

Ere long his compunction for his opposition to the subsidy was aggravated by the opportunity which occurred of obtaining professional honors. Egerton, the Attorney General, was to be made Master of the Rolls. Some of Bacon's friends were sanguine enough to think that *per saltum* he ought to have been appointed to succeed him ;[3]

[1] Montagu, who in his valuable edition of Bacon uniformly idolizes his hero.

[2] In his letter to Burghley he tries to explain away what he had said, as if only actuated by good wishes for the Queen's service; and thus concludes: " I must humbly pray your Lordship first to continue me in your own good opinion, and then to perform the part of an honorable and good friend towards your poor servant and ally, in drawing her Majesty to accept of the sincerity and simplicity of my zeal, and to hold me in her Majesty's favor, which is to me dearer than my life."

He must be supposed to have been sobbing when he thus addresses the flinty-hearted Puckering :—" Yet notwithstanding (to speak vainly as in grief) it may be her Majesty has discouraged as good a heart as ever looked towards her service, and as void of self-love. And so, in more grief than I can well express, and much more than I can well dissemble, I leave your Lordship, being as ever your Lordship's entirely devoted, &c."

[3] The following dialogue is said to have passed between the Earl of Essex and Sir Robert Cecil, as they were about this time traveling together, in the same coach:—*Cecil.* " My Lord, the Queen has determined to appoint an Attorney General without more delay. I pray, my Lord, let me know whom you will favor?"—*Essex.* "I wonder at your question. You can not but know that resolutely against all the world, I stand for your cousin, Francis Bacon."—*Cecil.* " I wonder your Lordship should spend your strength on ɪ unlikely a matter. Can you name one precedent of so raw a youth promoted to so great a place?"—*Essex.* "I have made no search for precedents of young men who have filled the office of Attorney General ; but I could name to you, Sir Robert, a man, younger than Francis, less learned, and equally inexperienced, who is suing and striving with all his might for an office of far greater weight."—*Cecil.* " I hope my abilities, such as they are, may be equal to the place of Secretary, and my father's long services may deserve such a mark of gratitude from the Queen. But although her Majesty can hardly stomach one so inexperienced being made her Attorney, if he would be con-

but Sir Edward Coke, who had served as Solicitor General for two years, was sure to be promoted almost as a matter of course,—and the great struggle arose respecting the office of Solicitor. To this Bacon. had the strongest claim, from the respect entertained for his father's memory,—from his relationship to the Prime Minister,—from his high accomplishments,—from his eminence at the bar,—from his success in parliament,—and from the services he had rendered as Queen's Counsel Extraordinary. He had two obstacles to surmount—his unlucky speech, and the jealousy of the Cecils. In more recent times his chance of promotion would have been increased by an occasional display of independence, showing how formidable he might be in regular opposition; but in Elizabeth's reign the system of retaining a wavering adherent or gaining over a formidable antagonist by appointment to office had not commenced, and constant subserviency to the Court was considered indispensable in all aspirants to Court favor. Burghley, and his hopeful son, Robert, now coming forward as Secretary of State, pretended to support their kinsman, but in reality were afraid that, with favorable opportunities, he would disconcert their deep-laid scheme of making the premiership hereditary in the house of Cecil.

Francis himself considered this the crisis of his fate, and resorted to means of gaining his object which would be spurned at by a modern expectant of the office, who does not interfere in any way regarding the appointment, till he receives a letter from the Lord Chancellor or the First Lord of the Treasury asking him to accept it.

His applications to the Lord Treasurer might be excusable, although couched in language which would now be considered very formal between a nephew and an uncle, and very abject even between a dependant and his patron.

tented with the Solicitor's place, it might be of easier digestion to her."—*Essex.* " Digest me no digestions. The Attorneyship for Francis is that I must have, and in that I will spend all my power, might, authority, and amity, and with tooth and nail procure the same for him against whomsoever." See Nares' *Life of Burghley*, vol. iii. p. 436. But although there may be some foundation for this conversation, it can not be accurately reported; as the office of Attorney General at this time was not vacant for a single day—Egerton having been appointed Master of the Rolls, and Coke appointed to succeed him as Attorney General, on the 10th of April, 1594 (Dugd. Chr. See Pat. 36 Eliz.)—and there is an extreme improbability in supposing that any of the Cecils would speak so openly against Francis Bacon, whom they were pretending to support, although they secretly sought to depress him.

The following is one of the answers which he received:—

"Nephew,—I have no leisure to write much; but, for answer, I have attempted to place you; but her Majesty hath required the Lord Keeper to give to her the names of divers lawyers to be preferred, wherewith he made me acquainted, and I did name you as a meet man, whom his Lordship allowed in way of friendship for your father's sake; but he made scruple to equal you with certain whom he named—as Brograve and Branthwayt, whom he specially commendeth. But I will continue the remembrance of you to her Majesty, and implore my Lord of Essex's help.

"Your loving uncle,
"W. BURGHLEY,"[1]

The office of Solicitor General continuing long vacant after the promotion of Coke to be Attorney General, in April, 1594, Bacon again went down on the knees of his heart to his obdurate uncle:

"I have ever had your Lordship in singular admiration; whose happy ability her Majesty hath so long used to her great honor and yours. Besides, that amendment of state or countenance which I have received hath been from your Lordship. And, therefore, if your Lordship shall stand a good friend to your poor ally, you shall but *tueri opus* which you have begun. And your Lordship shall bestow your benefit upon one that hath more sense of obligation than of self-love. . . . If her Majesty thinketh that she shall make an adventure in using one that is rather a man of study than of practice and experience, surely I may remember to have heard that my father was made Solicitor of the Augmentations, a Court of much business, when he had never practiced, and was but twenty-seven years old.

"Your Lordship's in all humbleness to be commanded,
"FRANCIS BACON."[2]

There can be no doubt that, on such an appointment, the Queen would have been guided by the sincere advice of him who had induced her to make Sir Nicholas Lord Keeper at the commencement of her reign; Puckering, on whom he threw the blame, had likewise been promoted by him, and was entirely under his control.

The anxious aspirant wrote repeatedly to the Lord Keeper, remonstrating with him, and trying to soften

[1] Sept. 27, 1593.   [2] June 7, 1594.

him. "If your Lordship consider my nature, my course, my friends, my opinion with her Majesty if this eclipse of her favor were past,[1] I hope you will think I am no unlikely piece of wood to shape you a true servant of."[2]
"I understand of some business like enough to detain the Queen to-morrow, which maketh me earnestly to pray your good Lordship, as one that I have found to take my fortune to heart, to take some time to remember her Majesty of a solicitor.[3] If it please your Lordship but to call to mind from whom I am descended, and by whom, next to God, her Majesty, and your own virtue, your Lordship is ascended, I know you will have a compunction of mind to do me any wrong; and therefore good my Lord, where your Lordship favoreth others before me, do not lay the separation of your love and favor upon myself."

In the reign of Elizabeth there was always a sort of "Opposition," which did not seek to form a party against Burghley in parliament or in the country,—which did not differ from him in religion,—had not any adverse system of policy to pursue, either at home or abroad,—but which engrossed the greatest share of the Queen's personal favor, and struggled for an equal share of the royal patronage.

The reigning favorite now was the youthful Earl of Essex, whose bad qualities were redeemed by chivalrous bravery, romantic generosity, and singular warmth in his friendships. Mistrusting the kindness and good faith of his natural allies, Francis Bacon cultivated him with great assiduity; and the soldier, disposed to admiration of all that is great and beautiful, was fascinated by the genius and accomplishments of the orator and philosopher. A close intimacy was formed between them, which, on the patron's side, amounted to pure and fervent friendship, but which ended most mournfully and discreditably for the party patronized.

The letters written by Essex about this time demonstrate the intense zeal with which he tried to use his influence with the Queen for the promotion of his friend; and are curious, as showing the terms on which he lived with his royal mistress, who, as tender as ever in her affections, had become more chary of her reputation, and did not continue to raise such suspicions in her Court as in the times of Leicester and Hatton:

[1] The subsidy speech.   [2] April 5, 1594.   [3] Aug. 19, 1594.

"I found the Queen so wayward, as I thought it not fit time to deal with her in any sort, especially since her choler grew toward myself, which I have well satisfied this day, and will take the first opportunity I can to move your suit."—" I have now spoken with the Queen, and I see no stay from obtaining a full resolution of what we desire."—" I went yesterday to the Queen, through the galleries, in the morning, afternoon, and at night. I had long speech to her of you, wherein I urged both the point of your extraordinary sufficiency, proved to me, not only by your last argument, but by the opinions of all men I spake withal, and the point of mine own satisfaction, which I protested should be exceeding great if for all her unkindness and discomforts passed, she should do this one thing for my sake. She did acknowledge you had a good wit and excellent gift of speech, and much other good learning. *But in the law, she rather thought you could make show to the uttermost of your knowledge, than that you were deep.* I added, her Majesty had made me suffer and give way in many things else, which all I should bear, not only with patience, but with great contentment, if she would but grant my humble suit in this one; and for the pretense of the approbation given you upon partiality that all the world, lawyers, Judges, and all, could not be partial to you; for somewhat you were crossed for their own interest, and some for their friends; but yet all did yield to your merit."—" I have received your letter, and since I have had opportunity to deal freely with the Queen. I have dealt confidently with her, as a matter wherein I did more labor to overcome her delays than I did fear her denial. I told her how much you were thrown down with the correction she had already given you, that she might in that point hold herself already satisfied. And because I found that Tanfield had been most propounded to her, I did most disable him. I find the Queen very reserved, staying herself upon giving any kind of hope, yet not passionate against you till I grew passionate for you. I urged her, that though she could not signify her mind to others, I might have a secret promise, wherein I should receive great comfort, as in the contrary great unkindness. She said she was neither persuaded nor would hear of it till Easter, when she might advise with her counsel, who were now all absent; and, therefore, in passion, bid me go to bed if I would talk of nothing else. Wherefore, in passion, I went away, saying, while I was with her I could not but solicit for the cause and the man I so much affected ; and, therefore, I would retire myself till I might be more graciously heard ; and so we parted. To-morrow I will go hence of purpose; and on Thursday I will write an expostulating letter to her. That night, or upon Friday morning, I will be here again, and follow on the same course."

Bacon, feeling "the misery 'tis in suing long to bide," took a bold step, and wrote a letter to the Queen herself, which is most highly creditable to her character,—at least as estimated by him,—for, from his language to the Lord Treasurer and the Lord Keeper, we need not doubt that he would have addressed her in the most fulsome and slave-like strain, if he had not thought that he was likely to succeed better by pretending independence, and avowing a consciousness of his own worth:

" Madam,—Remembering that your Majesty has been gracious to me, both in countenancing me and conferring upon me the reversion of a good place, and perceiving that your Majesty had taken some displeasure towards me, both these were arguments to move me to offer unto your Majesty my service, to the end to have means to deserve your favor, and to repair my error. Upon this ground I affected myself to no great matter, but only a place of my profession, such as I do see divers younger in proceeding to myself and men of no great note do without blame aspire unto. But if any of my friends do press this matter, I do assure your Majesty my spirit is not with them.[1] It sufficeth me that I have let your Majesty know that I am ready to do that for the service which I never would do for mine own gain. And if your Majesty like others better, I shall, with the Lacedemonian, be glad that there is such choice of abler men than myself. Your Majesty's favor, indeed, and access to your royal person, I did ever, encouraged by your own speeches, seek and desire, and I would be very glad to be reintegrate in that. But I will not wrong mine own good mind so much as to stand upon that now, when your Majesty may conceive

[1] This pretended indifference in our friend Francis is not a little amusing considering that he had been compassing heaven and earth—not altogether abstaining from the *black art*—to effect his object.

I do it but to make my profit of it. But my mind turneth upon other wheels than those of profit. The conclusion shall be, that I wish your Majesty served answerable to yourself. *Principis est virtus maxima nosse suos.* Thus I most humbly crave pardon of my boldness and plainness. God preserve your Majesty!"

According to the fashion of the times, he accompanied this letter with the present of a jewel.[1] His hopes were excited by a note he received a few days after from his friend, Foulke Greville, who was at Court when the offering arrived, and talked to her Majesty on the subject. "It pleased her withal to tell of the jewel you offered her by Mr. Vice Chamberlain, which she had refused, yet with exceeding praise. But either I deceive myself, or she was resolved to take it; and the conclusion was very kind and gracious. One hundred pounds to fifty you shall be her Solicitor."

The Queen could not forget the "*subsidy speech*," or was secretly influenced by Burghley, or was resolved to show that Essex was not her master,—and still no appointment took place. Bacon's patience had been entirely exhausted. He thus writes to Foulke Greville:—

"What though the Master of the Rolls, and my Lord of Essex, and yourself, and others, think my case without doubt, yet in the mean time I have a hard condition to stand, so that, whatever service I do to her Majesty, it shall be thought but to be *servitium viscatum*, lime twigs

---

[1] This was an extraordinary gratuity. Bacon had long been in the habit like other courtiers, of presenting a yearly present to Elizabeth at new-year's tide. Several of his letters accompanying them are preserved. I will give a specimen:

"Most Excellent Sovereign Mistress,

"The only new-year's gift which I can give your Majesty is that which God hath given to me,—a mind in all humbleness to wait upon your commandments and business; wherein I would to God that I were hooded, that I saw less, or that I could perform more: for now I am like a hawk that bates when I see occasion of service, but can not fly because I am tied to another's fist. But meanwhile I continue my presumption of making to your Majesty my poor oblation of a garment—as unworthy the wearing as his service that sends it, but the approach to your excellent person may give worth to both, which is all the happiness I aspire unto." This garment was "one pettycoat of white sattin embroidered all over like feathers and billets, with three broad borders fair embroidered with snakes and fruitage, *emblems of Wisdom and Beauty.*" In each year an exact inventory of new-year's gifts was taken and signed by the Queen, and attested by the proper officers. The donors vary in rank from the Lord Keeper Egerton to Charles Smith dustman, who presents "two bottes of cambric."

and fetches to place myself; and so I shall have envy, not thanks. This is a course to quench all good spirits, and to corrupt every man's nature, which will, I fear, much hurt her Majesty's service in the end. I have been like a piece of stuff bespoken in the shop; and if her Majesty will not take me, it may be the selling by parcels will be more gainful. For to be, as I told you, like a child following a bird, which, when he is nearest, flieth away, and lighteth a little before, and then the child after it again, and so *in infinitum*,—I am weary of it, as also of wearying my good friends."

He was last thrown in a state of mind still more painful than suspense, by the overwhelming intelligence that a patent was certainly to pass the Great Seal, appointing Mr. Sergeant Fleming Solicitor General to her Majesty. He was at first wholly overpowered by the blow, and then he resolved for ever to retire from public life, and travel in foreign countries,—a step which he thus defended: "Upon her Majesty's rejecting me, with such circumstances, though my heart might be good, yet mine eyes would be sore, that I should take no pleasure to look on my friends; for that I was not an impudent man that could face out a disgrace, and I hoped her Majesty would not be offended that, not able to endure the sun, I fled into the shade."[1]

He next softened his purpose to exile for the rest of his days in the University of Cambridge, where the degree of A.M. had been recently conferred upon him.[2] Writing to Essex, after stating that his health was almost overthrown by what he had suffered, he says, "When I revolved the good memory of my father, the near degree of alliance I stand in to my Lord Treasurer, your Lordship's so signalled and declared favor, the honorable testimony of so many councillors, the commendations unlabored and in sort offered by my Lords the Judges, and the Master of the Rolls;—that I was voiced with great expectation, and, though I say it myself, with the wishes of most men

---

[1] Letter to Sir Robert Cecil, January, 1595.
[2] Grace, July 27, 1594. "Placet vobis ut Mr. Franciscus Bacon armiger honorabilis et nobilis viri domini Nicholai Bacon militis, &c., filius post studium decem annorum, partim in hac academia nostra, partim in transmarinis regionibus in dialecticis, philosophicis, Græcis, Latinisque literis ac cæteris humanioribus disciplinis sufficiat ei ut cooptetur in ordinem magistrorum in artibus," &c.

to the higher place;[1] that I am a man that the Queen hath already done for,—and that Princes, especially her Majesty, love to make an end where they begin,—and then add hereunto the obscureness and many exceptions to my competitors,—I can not but conclude with myself that no man ever read a more exquisite disgrace; and therefore truly, my Lord, I was determined, if her Majesty reject me, this to do. My nature can take no evil ply; but I will, by God's assistance, with this disgrace of my fortune, and yet with that comfort of the good opinion of so many honorable and worthy persons, retire myself with a couple of men to Cambridge, and there spend my life in my studies and contemplations without looking back."[2]

He indulged in a short retreat to Essex villa, Twickenham Park, "where he once again enjoyed the blessings of contemplation in that sweet solitariness which collecteth the mind as shutting the eyes does the sight." While there he writes to the Lord Keeper, "I thought it right to step aside for nine days, which is the durance of a wonder, and not for any dislike of the world; for I think her Majesty hath done me as great a favor in making an end of this matter as if she had enlarged me from some restraint. I will take it upon me that which her Majesty hath often said, that she doth reserve me and not reject me."[3] To Burghley he says, "My hope is that, whereas your Lordship told me her Majesty was somewhat gravelled upon the offense she took at my speech in parliament, your Lordships's favorable and good word that I spake to the best will be as good a tide to remove her from that shelf."[4] He soon returned to business and ambition.

His submission gave great satisfaction to the Queen, and an attempt was made to bring about a vacancy in the office of Solicitor General for him; but Fleming could not be conveniently got rid of—and there was no other move among the law officers of the crown during the remainder of this reign.

Immediately upon his disappointment, Essex sought most munificently to console him. "After the Queen," he writes, "had denied me the Solicitor's place, for which his Lordship had been a long and earnest suitor on my

---

[1] The Attorney Generalship—a little outbreak against Coke.
[2] 30 March, 1595.   [3] 20 May, 1595.   [4] 7 June, 1595.

behalf, it pleased him to come to me from Richmond to Twickenham Park, and brake with me, and said, *Mr. Bacon, the Queen hath denied me the place for you, and hath placed another; I know you are the least part of your own matter; but you fare ill because you have chosen me for your mean and dependence; you have spent your time and thoughts in my matters: I die* (these were his very words) *if I do not somewhat towards your fortune; you shall not deny to accept a piece of land which I will bestow upon you.*" Francis, having made a decent show of resistance, yielded, and was enfeoffed of land at Twickenham, which he afterwards sold at an underprice for £1,800. He could not cancel all the past obligations of affectionate friendship, but he might at any rate have reconveyed this estate before he appeared as counsel against his benefactor, and before he entered on the task of writing " A Declaration of the Practices and Treasons attempted and committed by Robert, Earl of Essex."

To prove that he was not deficient in legal acquirements, as his detractors had represented, he wrote a treatise " Upon the Elements and Use of the Common Law," giving a specimen of the application of his favorite mode of reasoning to jurisprudence by the enunciation of general truths or " maxims," established by an extensive collection of particulars. In his preface he inculcated the doctrine which he often repeated, and which he acted upon notwithstanding his preference of other pursuits,—that there is a debt of obligation on every member of a profession to assist in improving the science in which he has successfully practiced. He dedicated this work to the Queen, " as a sheaf and cluster of fruit of the favorable season enjoyed by the nation from the influence of her happy government, by which the people were taught that part of the study of a good prince was to adorn and honor times of peace by the improvement of the laws!"[1]

To indemnify himself for this effort, in the early part of the year 1597 he gave to the world his " Essays," which we may fairly ascribe to his residence in France when Montaigne's Essays were first published and were read with rapture by all classes in that country, although it

[1] It was only then handed about in MS., but it has passed through several editions as a separate treatise, and containing much recondite and accurate learning, it is still cited as authority under the title of " Lord Bacon's Maxims of the Law."

was not till long after that, by means of a bad translation, they became popular in England. If not equal in lightness and grace to his original, he greatly exceeded him in depth of observation and aphoristic sententiousness; he did not succeed so much as a delineator of manners, but he laid open the springs of human action, and he clothed his thoughts in diction which, for the first time, showed the richness and melody of English prose. The Essays were not only very favorably received in England, but, being immediately translated into Latin and most of the Continental languages, they spread the fame of Bacon, as an elegant writer, all over Europe.[1] But this luster of reputation did not seduce him from his greater purposes. "As for my Essays, and some other particulars of that nature," said he, "I count them but as the recreations of my other studies, and in that manner purpose to continue them; though I am not ignorant that these kind of writings, would, with less pains and assiduity, perhaps yield more luster and reputation to my name than the others I have in hand."[2]

He was again returned to the parliament which met in October, 1597, and early in the session introduced two Bills against "Enclosures and the depopulation of towns." The practice of "*clearing estates*" was then going on in some parts of England, and we can easily forgive some bad political economy brought forward in attempts to prevent or mitigate the suffering which this system causes when recklessly pursued without regard to the maxim that "property has its duties as well as its rights. In his speech introducing his Bills he said, "I should be sorry to see within this kingdom that piece of Ovid's verse prove true, *Jam seges ubi Troja fuit*,—in England nought but green fields, a shepherd, and a dog. *Nemo putat illud videri turpe quod sibi sit quæstuosum*, and therefore there is almost no conscience made in destroying the savor of life; *panis*

---

[1] In the first edition there were only ten, but he afterwards expanded some of these and added considerably to their number. In his dedication to his brother he says, he published it to check the circulation of spurious copies, like some owners of orchards, who gather the fruit before it is ripe to prevent stealing; but this was only a pretense of authorship, and there can be no doubt that, by infinite pains, he had brought his compositions to his own standard of excellence before he committed them to the press. The 2nd edition was published in 1598, the 3rd in 1612, when he was Solicitor General, and the 4th in 1626, after his fall and the year before his death.

[2] Letter to the Bishop of Winchester.

sapor vitæ." The Bills were referred to a committee, but did not pass.[1]

He was successful, however, in that which probably interested him a good deal more,—in for ever effacing the impression of his unlucky patriotic speech. The Chancellor of the Exchequer having moved for a supply, and been seconded by Mr. Secretary Cecil, Mr. Francis Bacon rose, not to say anything of "gentlemen selling their silver plate and yeomen their brass pots," but "to make it appear by demonstration, *what opinion so ever he pretended by others*,[2] that, in point of payments to the Crown, never subjects were partakers of greater freedom and ease. Whether you look abroad into other countries, or look back to former times in this our own country, we shall find an exceeding difference in matter of taxes;—which now I reserve to mention—neither will I make any observation upon her Majesty's manner of expending and issuing treasure,—being not upon excessive and exorbitant donations, nor upon sumptuous and unnecessary triumphs, buildings, or like magnificence, but upon the preservation, protection, and honor of the realm. I dare not scan her Majesty's actions, which it becometh me rather to admire in silence. Sure I am that the treasure which cometh from you to her Majesty is but a vapor which riseth from the earth, and, gathering into a cloud, stayeth not there long, but, on the same earth, falleth again."[3] Accordingly a bill for a larger supply than was asked last parliament passed without opposition.

Bacon was now in high favor at Court, as well as still popular in the House by his eloquence,[4] and in the country by his writings. But he was desperately poor, for authorship, as yet, brought no profit, and his general practice at the bar was very inconsiderable. In spite of his economical habits, he had contracted some debts which were troublesome to him; and it was uncertain whether there might be an opening for him in the office of Solicitor General during the life of the Queen, who was now laboring under the infirmities of age. He there-

---

[1] 1 Parl. Hist. 890.
[2] Thus he already has learned to sneer at the liberal party.
[3] 1 Parl. Hist. 905.
[4] "Comitiis parliamentariis inferioris concessus, dum in ea domo sedit, pergratus semper fuit; in qua sæpe peroravit non sine magno applausu."—*Rawley*

fore made a bold attempt to restore his position by matrimony. He was ever cold-blooded and calculating, not even affecting anything romantic or tender. "You may observe," says he, " that amongst all the great and worthy persons whereof the memory remaineth, either ancient or recent, there is not one that hath been transported to the mad degree of love,—which shows that great spirits and great business do keep out this weak passion. There was never proud man thought so absurdly well of himself as the lover doth of the person loved ; and therefore it is well said that it is impossible to love and to be wise."[1] He did not, on this occasion, at all depart from his notions of what was becoming in "a great and worthy person ;" for instead of offering incense to Venus, he was only considering of a scheme to make his pot boil. A daughter of Sir Thomas Cecil, the eldest son of Lord Burghley, had married Sir William Hatton, the nephew and heir of Lord Chancellor Hatton, and was soon after left a widow with a very large fortune at her own disposal. She was likewise noted for her wit, spirit, and turn for fashionable amusements. What was worse, she was said to be of a capricious and violent temper. Upon the whole, Bacon thought that the advantages of the connection predominated, and after a proper course of attention, in which he met with little encouragement, he proposed to her. It was a curious circumstance that she was at the same time addressed by his successful rival for the offices of Attorney and Solicitor General, Sir Edward Coke, who was then a widower with a large family and an immense fortune. If she had not read Francis Bacon's Essay on Love, and so suspected him to be of a cold contitution, one would have thought that she could not have hesitated for a moment between her accomplished cousin, —a bachelor between thirty and forty,—although then a briefless barrister, yet destined to high office,—and the crabbed Attorney General, with all his practice and large estates, who was well stricken in years, and to whom there were " seven objections—his six children and himself." Bacon met with a flat refusal, and she evidently favored his rival. He thought, however, that he might succeed through the recommendation of Essex, who was then embarking on his famous expedition to Cadiz, and whom he

[1] Essay on Love.

thus addressed:—"My suit to your Lordship is for your several letters to be left with me dormant to the gentlewoman and either of her parents. Wherein I do not doubt but, as the beams of your favor have often dissolved the coldness of my fortune, so in this argument your Lordship will do the like with your pen."

Essex's letter to the cruel young widow would have been a great curiosity, but it is lost. To Sir Thomas Cecil he writes, "My dear and worthy friend Mr. Francis Bacon is a suitor to my Lady Hatton, your daughter. What his virtues and excellent parts are, you are not ignorant. What advantages you may give, both to yourself and to your house, by having a son-in-law so qualified, and so likely to rise in his profession, you may easily judge. Therefore, to warrant my moving of you to incline favorably to his suit, I will only add this, that, if she were my sister or daughter, I protest I would as confidently resolve to farther it as I now persuade you." He wrote a similar letter to Lady Cecil, who was one of the co-heirs of Neville, Lord Latimer, assuring her that she would happily bestow her daughter on Francis Bacon, "and if," says he, "my faith be anything, I protest, if I had one as near to me as she is to you, I had rather match her with him than with men of far greater titles." Nevertheless, the wayward Lady Hatton thought fit to run off with the future Chief Justice, and to enter into a clandestine and irregular marriage with him, for which they were both prosecuted in the Ecclesiastical Court. Bacon, in the result, had great reason to rejoice at this escape; for the lady, from the honeymoon onwards, led Coke a most wretched life—refusing even to take his name, separating from him, doing everything to vex and annoy him, and teaching his child to rebel against him.

However, the first effect of this discomfiture of Bacon, which, as we may suppose, was much talked of at Court and in the City, was to bring down upon him a relentless creditor; and, instead of entertaining Elizabeth as he had expected at Harefield—part of Lady Hatton's possessions which had belonged to Sir Christopher,—he soon found himself confined in a spunging-house. He had borrowed the sum of £300 from a usurer in Lombard Street of the name of Sympson, for which he had given a bond. An action having been brought against him on the bond,—as he had no defense, he gave a *cognovit*, with a stay of execution. The time of forbearance expired, and he was still unprepared to pay. He denounces "the Lombard"¹ as very hard-hearted, seemingly without much reason; for when there was a writ out against him in the city, and he came to dine with Sheriff More, orders were given to the officer not to disturb the festivity of the day by arresting him. But a few days after, information being given that he had been seen to enter the Tower, he was "trained" as he returned through the city, and a "b—— bailiff" sacrilegiously placed his hand on the shoulder of the future Lord Chancellor, and author of the *Novum Organum*. They wished to carry him immediately to gaol: but his friend Sheriff More "recommended him to an handsome house in Coleman Street." The "Lombard," who lived close by, was sent for divers times, but would not so much as vouchsafe to come and speak with the poor prisoner, or take any order in the affair, but would leave him to his fate: "although," says Bacon, "a man I never provoked with a cross word—no, nor with many delays."

In this extremity he wrote a letter to Lord Keeper Egerton, suggesting that, as he had gone to the Tower on "a service of the Queen of no mean importance," he was privileged from arrest even in execution, "*eundo manendo et redeundo;*" but without insisting on his privilege, requesting the Lord Keeper to send for Sympson, and to bring him to some reason.² He wrote a similar letter from his place of captivity to Mr. Secretary Cecil, in which he says,—"To belay me while he knew I came from the Tower about her Majesty's special service was, to my understanding, very bold."³ A satisfactory arrangement was made for the payment of the debt, and in a few days he was set at liberty.

To this *disgrazia* Coke ungenerously alluded in the famous altercation he afterwards had with Bacon at the bar of the Court of Exchequer. Mr. Attorney seems to have taken great offense because, without his sanction, and without his having a brief and a fee, the Queen's

---

¹ This seems then to have been used as a term of reproach, as Jew now is with us.
² Letters to the Lord Keeper and Sir R. Cecil, September, 1598. Works, vol. vi. 42.   ³ Ibid.

Counsel had presumed to make a motion about re-seizing the lands of a relapsed recusant in which the Crown was concerned. Bacon, in his own defense, having used as gentle and reasonable terms as might be, Mr. Attorney kindled and said, "Mr. Bacon, if you have any tooth against me, pluck it out, for it will do you more hurt than all the teeth in your head will do you good."

Bacon (coldly).—" Mr. Attorney, I respect you; I fear you not: and the less you speak of your own greatness, the more I will think of it."

Mr. Attorney.—" I think scorn to stand upon terms of greatness towards you, who are less than little,—less than the least (adding other such strange light terms, with that insolence which can not be expressed)."

Bacon (stirred, yet self-possessed).—" Mr. Attorney, do not depress me so far; for I have been your better, and may be again when it please the Queen."

"With this," says Bacon, "he spake neither I nor himself could tell what, *as if he had been born Attorney General*, and in the end bade me not meddle with the Queen's business but with mine own, and that I was unsworn."¹

Bacon.—" Sworn or not sworn is all one to an honest man; I have ever set my service first, and myself second; and I wish to God you would do the like."

Mr. Attorney.—" It were good to clap a *capias utlegatum* upon your back."

Bacon.—" I thank God you can not,—but you are at fault and hunt upon an old scent." ²

An account of this scene was immediately sent by Bacon to Secretary Cecil, "as one careful of his advancement and jealous of his wrongs;" and it must be taken with some grains of allowance,—though he says, "he dared trust rumor in it, unless it were malicious or extreme partial," but on both sides it greatly exceeded the license of the forensic logomachy in our times, and with us much less must have led to a hostile meeting on Wimbledon Common or at Calais. But the law of the *duello*, which was studied so sedulously in the reigns of Elizabeth and James I. by all other classes of gentlemen, seems to have been entirely neglected by those

---

¹ *I.e.* not sworn as Attorney or Solicitor General; yet he must have taken the oaths to serve her Majesty as Queen's Counsel.
² Bacon's Works, vol. vi. 46.

who addicted themselves to the common law of this realm.

Coke, conscious of his own inferiority in all liberal acquirements, continued to take every opportunity to "disgrace and disable" Bacon's law, and his experience, and his discretion as an advocate. Yet this year the Essayist and leader of the House of Commons gave proofs of professional learning and skill, which ought for ever to have saved him from such taunts. He wrote " The History of the Alienation Office," a treatise worthy of Hale, —showing a most copious and accurate acquaintance with existing law, and with our legal antiquities.

He likewise published his celebrated argument in the Exchequer Chamber in Chudleigh's Case, or "the Case of Perpetuities."[1] About this time occurred a very important crisis in the history of the Law of Real Property in England. An attempt, which in the following century succeeded in Scotland, was making to introduce, by the artifices of conveyancing, a system of unlimited substitutions, or strict entails, which should effectually bar every species of alienation. The great question in this particular case was, "whether, there being a remainder limited by way of use upon a contingency, the destruction of the contingent estate by feoffment before the contingent remainder came *in esse* destroyed the contingent remainder?"—it being denied that, where the contingent remainder was limited by way of use, there was any necessity that it should vest, as at common law, at or before the determination of the preceding estate. Bacon's argument against this subtle device to create a perpetuity,—one of the most masterly ever heard in Westminster Hall,—he afterwards shaped into a " Reading on the Statute of Uses," which he delivered when Double Reader of Gray's Inn, a tract which we now possess, and which shows the legal acuteness of a Fearne or a Sugden. He did not himself undervalue his exertion in placing the law on the satisfactory footing on which it has remained in England ever since,—striking the happy medium between mere life interests and perpetuities,— and providing at once for the stability of families, necessary in a mixed monarchy, and freedom of commerce in land, necessary for wealth, under every form of govern-

[1] 1 Rep. 120, *a*.

ment whatever. "I have chosen," says he, "to read upon the Statute of Uses, a law whereupon the inheritances of this realm are tossed at this day like a ship upon the sea, in such sort, that it is hard to say which bark will sink and which will get to the haven; that is to say, what assurances will stand good, and what will not. Neither is this any lack or default in the pilots, the grave and learned Judges, but the tides and currents of received error, and unwarranted and abusive experience, have been so strong as they were not able to keep a right course according to the law. Herein, though I could not be ignorant either of the difficulty of the matter which he that taketh in hand shall soon find, or much less of my own unableness which I have continual sense and feeling of, yet, because I had more means of absolution than the younger sort, and more leisure than the greater sort, I did think it not impossible to work some profitable effect; the rather where an inferior wit is bent and constant upon one subject, he shall many times, with patience and meditation, dissolve and undo many of the knots which a greater wit, distracted with many matters, would rather cut in two than unknit; and, at the least, if my invention or judgment be too barren or too weak, yet by the benefit of other arts I did hope to dispose and digest the authorities and opinions which are in cases of uses in such order and method as they should take light one from another, though they took no light from me."

This, I think, may be considered the most auspicious period of Bacon's career. By increased practice at the bar he had overcome his pecuniary difficulties. He was sure of professional advancement upon the next vacancy. He had been slighted by Lady Hatton, but the Queen showed much more personal favor to him than to his rival, Coke, the Attorney General, and consulted him about the progress and conduct of all her law and revenue causes. She not only gave him frequent audiences at her palace, but visited him and dined with him in a quiet way in his lodge at Twickenham.[1] His literary eminence was very great both

---

[1] Bacon has himself given us a very amusing specimen of the royal talk on such occasions. It seems her Majesty was mightily incensed against a book lately published, which she denounced as "a seditious prelude to put into the people's head boldness and faction," and, having an opinion that there was treason in it, asked him, "if he could not find any places in it that might be drawn within case of treason?"—*Bacon.* "For *treason*, Madam, I surely find

in England and on the Continent,—not only from what he had already published, but from the great works he was known to have in hand, an outline of which he was at all times willing to communicate to such as were capable of appreciating his plans and discoveries. Above all, his reputation was as yet untarnished. His sudden wheel from the liberal to the conservative side—an occurrence which, even in our days, society easily pardons from its frequency—was then considered merely as the judicious correction of a youthful indiscretion. All was now bright hope with him for the future—without self-reproach when he reflected on the past.

none; but for *felony* very many."—*Elizabeth* (*very eagerly*). "Wherein?"— *Bacon.* "Madam, the author hath committed very apparent theft, for he hath taken most of the sentences of Cornelius Tacitus, and translated them into English, and put them into his text."—*Apology.* Works, vol. vi. 221.

www.ingramcontent.com/pod-product-compliance
Lightning Source LLC
Chambersburg PA
CBHW032029150426
43194CB00006B/200